Animated Landscapes

Animated Landscapes

History, Form and Function

Edited by
Chris Pallant

Bloomsbury Academic
An imprint of Bloomsbury Publishing Inc

B L O O M S B U R Y
NEW YORK · LONDON · OXFORD · NEW DELHI · SYDNEY

Bloomsbury Academic
An imprint of Bloomsbury Publishing Inc

1385 Broadway
New York
NY 10018
USA

50 Bedford Square
London
WC1B 3DP
UK

www.bloomsbury.com

BLOOMSBURY and the Diana logo are trademarks of Bloomsbury Publishing Plc

First published 2015
Paperback edition first published 2017

© Chris Pallant and Contributors, 2015

Library of Congress Cataloging-in-Publication Data
Animated landscapes : history, form, and function / edited by Chris Pallant.
pages cm
Includes bibliographical references and index.
ISBN 978-1-62892-351-3 (hardback)
1. Animated films–History and criticism. 2. Landscapes in art. 3. Landscapes in motion
pictures. 4. Animation (Cinematography) I. Pallant, Chris.
NC1765.A525 2014
791.43'34--dc23
2015006537

ISBN: HB: 978-1-6289-2351-3
PB: 978-1-5013-2011-8
ePub: 978-1-6289-2350-6
ePDF: 978-1-6289-2349-0

Typeset by Integra Software Services Pvt. Ltd.

791.
433
4
ANI

'It is the soul that sees; the outward eyes
Present the object, but the Mind descries.'
We see nothing till we truly understand it.

—John Constable, quoting George Crabbe

Contents

List of Illustrations

Acknowledgements

Editors owe an enormous debt to the enthusiasm, intelligence and rigour of their contributing authors – this project is no different and would not have been possible without the support of the people collected within the pages of this volume. It is a certainty that every contributor included here will also have cause to extend thanks to an even wider supporting network of family members (I, for one, would like to thank my wife for her support over the course of editing this book), friends, colleagues and perhaps even professional practitioners for sharing invaluable insights regarding their working practice. I would like to thank Katie Gallof, for backing this project and who has provided excellent editorial support, Mary Al-Sayed, for helping to make the cover design process a smooth one, and the rest of the team at Bloomsbury who worked on this project alongside me. Lastly, thanks must go to those responsible for crafting the imaginative and immersive landscapes that provide the focus of this collection.

Introduction

Chris Pallant

At the 2013 Society for Animation Studies International Conference, hosted by the School of Cinematic Arts, at the University of Southern California, only a few miles from the famous sign that once read Hollywoodland, I presented a paper boldly entitled 'Redefining the Animated Landscape'. Those in attendance will testify that the ambition signalled by the title was hardly matched by the twenty minutes of conference paper delivered; however, in the discussion that followed my plea for greater attention to be directed towards the study of animated landscapes, there was a sense that I had touched a nerve. Like the Hollywoodland sign, which originally drew attention to the then newly developed and cheaply available real estate situated in the Hollywood Hills, but which now serves, in its cropped nine-letter form, as a symbolic backdrop, the animated landscape has come to be viewed (in a cinematic context at least) in a similar way – evolving over the past hundred or so years, moving from being an active, focalizing force, to a site that is often fixed and static and which serves as a background *upon* which animation is staged.

Clearly, this is a provocative statement, and it is one that I will unpack in greater detail below and – more importantly – a proposition that is challenged in the chapters included in this collection; yet, it serves as a useful starting point. It immediately serves to bring the domination of character as an object of study (and production) into sharp relief. Character has become the conceptual core around which the production and interpretation of animation frequently gravitates. This collection seeks to address this imbalance.

When I posted the call for contributions to this collection, I hoped a wide range of topics would be suggested. These expectations were quickly surpassed and the work collected here captures the rich and varied histories, ontologies, forms, practices and functions of animating landscape. For the general or speculative reader, however, it is worth pausing for a moment to consider what is meant here by the multivalent phrase: 'animated landscape'.

I

Given the focus of this collection, it is worth revisiting the popular cliché that animation can trace its origins back to the real-world cave paintings of the Palaeolithic period. Although criticized in scholarly circles for obvious reasons – cave people were not seeking to make animated images of the type we recognise today – this analogy continues to enjoy popular purchase. This is perhaps a consequence of Richard Williams's passing comment in his influential book, *The Animator's Survival Kit*, that: 'We've always been trying to make the pictures move, the idea of animation is aeons older than the movies or television. Here's a quick history: Over 35,000 years ago, we were painting animals on cave walls, sometimes drawing four pairs of legs to show motion.'[1] This pseudo-mythical origin story gained further momentum in recent years when Werner Herzog returned to this refrain in his captivating documentary *Cave of Forgotten Dreams* (2010).

To this speculative origin story could also be added the Mesolithic petroglyphs, such as those found at Val Camonica in Northern Italy, which go further than the Palaeolithic paintings to draw connections between the landscape and its inhabitants. In the case of the petroglyphs at Val Camonica, rather than 'provide a balanced commentary on the events of daily life… they stress certain aspects at the expense of others. In particular, they emphasize the importance of crop production'.[2] What is evident, beyond the speculative myth-making, is that the landscape becomes a selective record, a site of inscribed information that might serve to guide, if not animate, agricultural behaviour across generations. While the animated landscape may or may not have originated in the real world, through new digital projection technologies it has, in recent years, returned in spectacular ways to inhabit the lived environment once more through projection-mapped animation. The instrumental dynamic – if not dialectic – here, between artist and real-world environment, remains central to these forms of animated landscape, whereby the physical landscape can both become *animated* and itself be an *animating* space – forcing the animator to respond in unique, site-specific ways.

Given the cinematic *lingua franca* that binds many of us today, the phrase 'animated landscape' is perhaps more likely to prompt thoughts of the fantastical, imagined and perhaps even shape-shifting worlds that proliferate in animated film. In a more orthodox sense, referring to the long-established traditions of hand-drawn and stop-motion animation, readers might think of the verisimilar animated landscapes of the Disney-Formalist mode,[3] the provocatively limited landscapes of United Productions of America (UPA)'s short-form animation, the obsessively detailed landscapes of Aardman's stop-motion oeuvre, the frequently metamorphic landscapes designed by animator Steve Cutts or the often unpredictable and antagonistic landscapes found in early Fleischer and Disney short-form animation, and more recently in Cartoon Network's *Adventure Time* (2010–present). Animated landscapes have become truly pervasive in recent years as a consequence of the fully and partially computer-generated environments that have become a common feature of the Pixar and DreamWorks studios' house styles, or as seen in films such as *Avatar* (2009), *The Avengers* (2012) and *Gravity* (2013).

Over the past decade, digital animation – whether visibly rendered or otherwise – has become *the* core ingredient of contemporary moving-image production, prompting much to be written on the perceived passing of a cinematic epoch: from the photochemical filmstrip to digital image processing and consumption.[4] Suzanne Buchan's edited collection, *Pervasive Animation* (2012), has recently tackled this subject head-on, and Buchan writes in the introduction to her volume:

> In the past 30 years, digital technologies have increasingly encroached upon traditional forms of non-representational moving image-making and the introduction of (animated) digital cinema has engendered significant debates, some about the potential of this technology, others raising concerns about the dissolution of celluloid. Because much of digital cinema's technology and styles originates in animation practice, in my view, animation belongs at the heart of these debates.[5]

While few would argue with this proposition, the ability to make popular – and critical – distinctions between 'animated' and 'live action' 'film' remains useful. Much like we continue to use 'silent cinema' as a descriptor to refer to a period of cinema exhibition that was anything but silent (while sound was not synchronized with image via the celluloid strip, this did not stop exhibitors making their 'silent' films noisy spectacles with frequent piano-based accompaniment), it is unlikely that shorthand distinctions between animated and live-action film will cease to make sense any time soon.

Clearly, though, as the animated and live-action traditions are folding in on each other, we need to be able to make critical distinctions that cut across these moving image production modes. Here, the continuum of photo-reality provides a good option. By considering the photo-reality of an image, its believability, rather than questioning any implied or simulated connection to the real, pro-filmic world, we might elide the Schrödinger-like thought experiment that is conjured with the mention of indexicality within the digital domain. The animated landscapes of Pandora – and the aptly named reserves of unobtanium – offer no indexical link to the real world, they are pure fantasy, yet their photo-real representation in *Avatar* offers the viewer a believable entry point into this alien landscape.

Photo-real animated landscapes have become increasingly commonplace in recent years – so much so that the green screen technique, which was originally a trick up cinema's sleeve, has become a feature frequently commented on in popular discourse, much in the same way that non-specialist discussions of cinematic practice might include a comment on the 'quick cutting' of the shower scene in *Psycho* (1960), the 'hand-held camerawork' of *Green Zone* (2010), or the 'black and white aesthetic' of *The Artist* (2011). Furthermore, thanks to the technological advances prompted by James Cameron, computer-generated animated landscapes have also recently become an instrumental part of the pro-filmic event. During the production of *Avatar*, Cameron's production team perfected a system that would generate rough, real-time pre-visualizations of *the animated landscape to be* – therefore affording the production team greater scope to respond in the moment to potential compositional opportunities that might otherwise have been missed if the landscape were to be animated in post-production.

Despite the pervasion of animated landscapes throughout the seemingly live-action cinema of the present, the mainstream cinematic tradition frequently imposes a photo-real logic upon the creation of these landscapes. The release of *The Hunger Games: Mockingjay – Part 1* (2014), shortly before the publication of this collection, serves as a timely indication of the standing of animated landscapes within so-called live-action cinema. Approximately halfway through the film, Katniss Everdeen (Jennifer Lawrence) is tasked with the delivery of a call to arms, which is to be staged in front of a rousing, flag-waving, computer-generated backdrop. The dislocating artificiality of this environment, which is exaggerated through the isolated positioning of Katniss on the holodeck's podium, separated by a wall of glass from Plutrach Heavensbee (Philip Seymour Hoffman), who offers direction, results in an unconvincing performance. Shortly after, Katniss is taken to visit the burnt ruins of her home District (twelve) in a bid to prompt in her the emotion required to deliver the call to arms. During this excursion, Capitol military aircraft attack the rebel party and the makeshift hospital that they had visited. Seeing this massacre, Katniss makes use of her new explosive arrows to bring down the two aircraft, resulting in a spectacular, explosive crash-landing. Instinctively, the documentary crew that are accompanying Katniss quickly act to channel her obviously emotional state, directing her to deliver the call to arms, while tracking around her so as to fill the shot's background with burning wreckage. In this instance, the landscape works *with* Katniss, providing the basis of a powerful call to arms.

Some viewers may find comfort in the film's return to a photo-real world, where the *real* landscape provides Katniss with all the emotional motivation needed to deliver her call to arms; yet, other viewers may delight in the irony that this seemingly photo-real environment remains one dependent on animation – from the digitally enhanced flames that engulf the partially computer-generated destroyed architecture, to the digitally composited reflections in Kitniss's pupils and the cameraman's visor. With the release of *The Hunger Games: Mockingjay – Part 1*, it is tempting to see the culmination of a computer-generated (CG) cinematic trajectory, where the discourse of landscape animation has moved from a backstage trick to a centre stage attraction.

Inhabiting a periphery domain between the classically cinematic, animated modes discussed above and the computer-based, interactive animated landscapes discussed below are the abstract works of animators such as Oskar Fischinger, Norman McLaren, Len Lye, and John and James Whitney. Working across a range of animation process, including hand-drawn, stop-motion, computer-based and many hybrid variations in between, and often in an abstract mode, these animators produced works that effectively call into question – if not problematize entirely – the basis upon which distinctions such as landscape and character might be made in the animated form. Fischinger's *Kreise/Circles* (1933), for example, produced to match the advertising agency Tolirag's slogan 'Tolirag reaches all circles of society', synchronizes the movement and metamorphosis of multi-coloured circles with musical excerpts from Richard Wagner and Edvard Grieg.[6] By refusing to reduce the hermeneutic potential of *Circles* through the imposition of recognizable characters and landscapes, Fischinger creates a universal space within which each viewer can read their own meaning, while extending a powerful, and unmistakable, visual metaphor that sees the circle become the unifying force throughout the abstract animation. McLaren's direct 'cameraless' animation also offers an interesting redefinition of how we might interpret the animated landscape. Working in this manner, McLaren took to 'scratching the film emulsion or painting directly onto the film to generate his images'; furthermore, 'his synchronized soundtracks, which accompanied his animation were scratched, painted or printed onto the film stock creating a new form of animated music'.[7] By working directly on the celluloid without the intermediary camera processes, McLaren's 'cameraless' work extends the animated landscape *beyond* the image frame, effectively enveloping the soundscape within the same abstract space, in both a figurative and a material sense.

To complete this brief survey, we must also consider the rise of the video game and the animated landscapes contained therein. Just as in the more passive domain of cinema, there are a great variety of animated landscapes found across the more interactive realm of the video game. There are games that are *only* animated landscapes, resembling in some ways the abstract works just discussed, including the likes of *Pong* (1972), *Candy Crush* (2012) and the best-selling game of all time, *Tetris* (1984). Games such as *Flower* (2009), *PixelJunk Eden* (2008) and *Minecraft* (2011) are also directly dependent on their animated landscapes for meaning, and are equally concerned with the (re)animation of this landscape itself, but share a more stylized graphical approach. By virtue of the processing powers of modern games consoles and personal computers, many of the animated landscapes now found in fantasy games actively encourage the same kind of spectatorial wonderment offered by the likes of *Avatar*, with the digital environment constructed in such a way as to channel players through the open world so that they reach a certain location in a visually spectacular fashion. Examples of this manipulation occur throughout games such as *Shadow of the Colossus* (2005), *Journey* (2012), *The Elder Scrolls V: Skyrim* (2011), *Dragon Age: Inquisition* (2014) and *Destiny* (2014). Then there are games with animated landscapes that ape our real, lived world (both past and present), and therefore serve to present some form of social critique or comment through the medium of play. In this regard, Rockstar Games have led the way with their *Grand Theft Auto* games (1997–present), *Red Dead Redemption* (2010) and *LA Noire* (2011), but game series such as *Far Cry* (2004–present) and *Call of Duty* (2003–present), and the recent, post-apocalyptic masterpiece *The Last of Us* (2013), also encourage moments of self-reflection. Finally, it is also important to note that the player's ability to create his or her own animated landscape within a given game has become an increasingly popular design feature, with games such as *SimCity* (1989–2013), *Theme Park* (1994), *Tony Hawks* (1999–present), *Little Big Planet* (2008–present) and *Minecraft* providing the player with considerable scope to create imaginative environments of their own.

Having mapped these competing interpretations of the phrase 'animated landscape', it strikes me that rather than trying to develop a multitude of parallel taxonomies to account for this textual variety, it might well be possible to situate all of the aforementioned, in relation to the intersecting axes of interactivity and mimesis (Figure 1). Here we are building upon an earlier continuum proposed by Maureen Furniss to address the difficulties of photo-realism when thinking about animation in relation to live action, with the extremes of 'mimesis' and 'abstraction' serving to suggest 'opposing tendencies under which live action and animation imagery can be juxtaposed'.[8]

Such an all-encompassing mapping, as presented in Figure 1, reveals how it is the common characteristic of being animated that unifies all of the many varied landscapes discussed earlier. It is this quality that our collection seeks to directly address, and, in the process, offer analyses that have remained beyond the remit of previous, cinematic and conventionally live-action-minded collections that have engaged with the subject of moving-image landscapes, such as Deborah A. Carmichael's *The Landscape of Hollywood Westerns* (2006), Martin Lefebvre's *Landscape and Film* (2006) and the two collections edited by Graeme Harper and Jonathan Rayner, *Cinema and Landscape* (2010) and *Film Landscapes: Cinema, Environment, and Visual Culture* (2013). These collections provide an

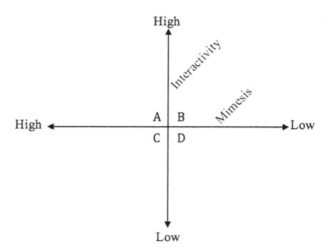

Figure 1 Animated landscapes – axes of experience and perception

excellent entry point vis-à-vis contemporary debates concerning the cinematic landscape; yet, their attention is understandably focused upon questions related to the politics, the psychology and the ecocritical significance of place – questions which are framed in relation to debates surrounding the perceived photo indexicality of the cinematic landscape. For the animated landscape, such concerns represent only part of the equation.

Moving beyond the live-action cinematic tradition, and by adopting a more inclusive approach to animated landscapes, paves the way for previously unconsidered readings and relationships. For example, adopting the framework proposed in Figure 1, the aforementioned Palaeolithic cave paintings could be seen to occupy the same quadrant (along the axes of high interactivity and low mimesis) as the cubic juggernaut that is *Minecraft*. Not only does such a coupling suggest an interest in the animated landscape as a malleable space that cuts across millennia, but also that the manipulation of light – firelight (either kindled upon the floor or conveyed by wooden torches) – has been a central feature of our (re)construction of both the painted cave and the pixelated mine. Once the focus is re-framed in this way, patterns emerge more readily: the colossi of *Shadow of the Colossus* and the mountainous protagonist from LAIKA's short *A Tale of Momentum & Inertia* (2014), a pairing that bridges the axis of interactivity; between *Trolley Troubles* (1927) and *Get a Horse* (2013), two shorts separated by more than eighty years of animation history and differing aesthetic procedures, but which display an interest in the mechanical navigation of an unruly animated landscape; or via the animated map, which provides the overarching game mechanic of the *Total War* series (2000–present), viewed from a bird's-eye and allowing the player to reshape the landscape through geographical domination, and which provides the platform for a non-interactive short animation that went viral in spring 2014, depicting the evolution – and devolution – of nation states across 1,000 years of European history,[9] coinciding with Russia's annexation of Crimea in March of that year.

From this brief survey, it is hopefully apparent that the phrase 'animated landscape' can conjure any one of a multitude of meanings and interpretations. The animated landscape can be simultaneously everything and yet virtually nothing, visible and yet invisible. As Paul Wells notes in Chapter 12 of this collection, our understanding of what might constitute the animated landscape should not be conceptually straightjacketed, and simply 'be understood as something that apes the landscape in the traditional filmic or painterly sense – a "background", for example, or the consequence of layout, or even an obvious depiction of the countryside or a city skyline', rather it is: '*ultimately a specifically imagined and constructed environment dramatized through its plasmatic motion in the moment, and revealed by the cognate disciplines it relates to or represents*'.[10] Ultimately, our active cognitive negotiation and visual exploration of the animated landscape – whether literal or figurative – foregrounds it as an object of meaning within the realm of moving images. In response, the chapters collected here seek to advance our understanding of the animated landscape through discussions of history, form and function.

II

This collection, therefore, seeks to consider the animated landscape from a number of perspectives ranging across the historical, formal and functional. In the first section, chapters from Bryan Hawkins, myself, and Malcolm Cook seek to sketch out formal histories relating to the creation of animated landscapes in the hand-drawn, stop-motion and computer-generated traditions, respectively.

This historical agenda is developed further in the second section, which shifts the focus to national cinemas. While not intended to offer an exhaustive survey of every national cinema, this second section seeks to contribute to the de-Westernizing initiative that has had success of late in the fields of film and media studies, and thereby serve as a partial corrective to the predominantly Western focus of this collection as a whole. This section comprises four chapters: Steven Allen's discussion of the communication of 'Australian-ness' through landscape animation; Melanie Chan's consideration of a particularly Japanese environmentalist dynamic in selected Studio Ghibli works; Kiu-wai Chu's interrogation of the concept of 'shanshui' in relation to Chinese landscape animation; and Mihaela Mihailova's mapping of aesthetic resistance, against computer-generated imagery and the often connected obsession with photorealism, in Latvian animation.

A more formal focus is adopted in the chapters constituting sections three and four. In section three, María Lorenzo Hernández, Birgitta Hosea and Fran Pheasant-Kelly offer chapters that consider the significance of animated space as site through which we might travel and as a site carrying newfound digital agency. Hernández draws attention to the developing animated travelogue genre, in which the landscape becomes central to the revival of the animator's experiences of a now distant country. Hernández focuses on three films: Bastien

Dubois's *Madagascar, carnet de voyage* (2009), Isabel Herguera's *Ámár* (2010) and José Miguel Ribeiro's *Viagem a Cabo Verde* (2010). Hosea's chapter considers animations that move between locations and are concerned with trajectory and locomotion rather than landscape as a static entity. Establishing the train journey as her critical framework, Hosea covers substantial ground, bringing together analyses of *Ivor the Engine*, *Thomas the Tank Engine*, *Madame Tutli-Putli*, transport information films, post-filmic subway zoetropes and railway simulation games. Pheasant-Kelly's chapter builds upon Aylish Wood's notion of 'timespaces' – convergences between time and space – to argue that settings have become credible sentient entities, with digital technologies prompting a diminishing/absent margin between character and setting.[11]

Section four brings together three chapters that share an interest in subjects relating to animated landscapes that have remained relatively peripheral to date. Dan Torre's chapter focuses on the growing trend for large-scale, projection-mapped animation, paying particular attention to the precise production processes required in terms of both construction and presentation. To illustrate the significance of the real-world landscape to such projects, which plays an integral role in both of these phases (construction and presentation), Torre offers a range of international case studies, including the projection-mapping of Rio de Janeiro's Christ the Redeemer statue, the Prague Clock Tower and Hamburg's Galerie Der Gegenwart. Paul Wells tackles another under-developed subject within animation studies: sport. Highlighting the fact that both sport and animation are defined by their material codes and their conventions of practice, relating to complex and highly specific preparatory and developmental processes that give rise to pre-choreographed movements that support pre-determined outcomes, Wells observes how such choreography, 'also functions as the visualization of temporal and spatial flow within the formal parameters yet fluid landscapes of the places in which sport is played'.[12] In James Newton's chapter, while the subject matter may appear familiar, being concerned with the socio-politically charged quality of zombie cinema, the reader's attention is drawn to the symbolic shift that has occurred in recent years as a consequence of how computer animation has radically altered the formal characteristics of this genre of filmmaking, and thereby blurring the distinction between character and landscape – the binary on which much of the earlier socio-political commentary was predicated.

Interactivity provides the focus in the final section, with chapters from Tom Klein and Alan Meades exploring ways that animated landscapes might be understood differently through a consideration of the video game form. Klein makes a convincing case for a reconsideration of the perceived hierarchies of influence that exist between cinema and the video game, proposing that the mechanics of an invented space are most apparent in games because rules exist for players to interact meaningfully with this animated landscape. Klein, therefore, takes the visual logic of gamespaces found in games such as *Portal* (2007) and *Monument Valley* (2014) as the foundation upon which to base a larger discussion of the role-animated space in cinema. Meades draws the collection to a fitting close, reflecting on our attitudes more broadly to the concept of landscape/nature as one half of a culturally constructed equation, and highlighting how the animated landscape of the video game can provide a useful vehicle through which to problematize this understanding. Meades does not approach animated landscape from a passive stance, exploring landscapes simply as designed, but focuses on the complexities of player action, specifically the exotic mode of play termed glitching – where players seek to subvert and exploit the game code. Meades argues that glitching presents an interesting context against which to reconsider the animated landscape, as players, who explore these subverted, remediated animated landscapes, begin to interrogate their own constructed understanding of landscape – prompting the question: what might exist *beyond* the animated landscape?

Notes

1   Richard Williams, *The Animator's Survival Kit: A Manual of Methods, Principles and Formulas for Classical, Computer, Games, Stop Motion and Internet Animators* (London: Faber and Faber, 2001), 11.

2   Richard Bradley, *Ritual and Domestic Life in Prehistoric Europe* (London: Routledge, 2005), 98.

3   For a speculative discussion of the Disney-Formalist tradition, which refers to a historically specific model of animation practice that results in a particular aesthetic quality, see: Chris Pallant, 'Disney-Formalism – Beyond Classic Disney', *Animation: An Interdisciplinary Journal* 4.4 (2011): *passim*.

4   This subject provides key discussion point in the following: Thomas Elsaesser's and Kay Hoffman's edited collections *Cinema Futures: Cain, Abel or Cable? The Screen in the Digital Age* (1998), Lev Manovich's *The Language of New Media* (2001), Laura Mulvey's *Death 24× a Second: Stillness and the Moving Image* (2006), Dudley Andrew's *What Cinema Is!* (2010) and J. P. Telotte's *Animating Space: From Mickey to WALL-E* (2010).

5   Suzanne Buchan, 'Introduction', in *Pervasive Animation*, ed. Suzanne Buchan (New York: Routledge, 2013), 6–7.

6   William Moritz, *Optical Poetry: The Life and Work of Oskar Fischinger* (Bloomington: Indiana University Press, 2004), 220.

7   Nichola Dobson, 'Innovation and Limitation', *AnimationStudies 2.0*, 28 May 2013, accessed 15 December 2014, http://blog.animationstudies.org/?p=266.

8   Marueen Furniss, *Art in Motion: Animation Aesthetics* (Eastleigh: John Libbey, 2007), 5.

9   Cf. Adam Withnall, 'Crimea Just a Blip? Time Lapse Map Video Shows 1000 Years of Europe's History in Three Minutes', *The Independent*, 19 March 2014, accessed 16 December 2014, http://www.independent.co.uk/news/world/europe/crimea-just-a-blip-time-lapse-map-video-shows-1000-years-of-europes-history-in-three-minutes-9201414.html.

10 Paul Wells, 'Plasmatic Pitches, Temporal Tracks and Conceptual Courts: The Landscapes of Animated Sport', in *Animated Landscapes: History, Form and Function*, ed. Chris Pallant (New York: Bloomsbury, 2015), 218.

11 Aylish Wood, 'Timespaces in Spectacular Cinema: Crossing the Great Divide of Spectacle versus Narrative', *Screen* 43.4 (2002): 374.

12 Wells, 'Plasmatic Pitches, Temporal Tracks and Conceptual Courts', 219.

Part One

History: Formal Traditions

1

Seeing in Dreams – The Shifting Landscapes of Drawn Animation

Bryan Hawkins

Every epoch sees in dreams the epoch which is to succeed it.

Walter Benjamin[1]

… Nature has no Outline,
But Imagination has. Nature has no Tune, but Imagination has.
Nature has no Supernatural, and dissolves: Imagination is Eternity.

William Blake (1822)[2]

Introduction

The visionary artist and poet William Blake's recognition of the significance of 'outline' (he always drew with an emphasis on and commitment to outline as a clarity of imagining and vision and rejected drawing directly from nature) suggests drawings' importance as a technology of the imagination. The distinction Blake makes between the products of the imagination and 'nature' marks drawing as an intellectual and cultural achievement as it marks our separation, as humans, from the simplicity and otherness of nature. It can be argued that for Blake this separation parallels the significance of the Biblical exclusion of Adam and Eve from a pre-lapsarian, Edenic paradise that Blake himself imagined through the visionary and imaginative technology of drawing and outline allied to the emergent technologies of mass printmaking.

The Greek myth of the Corinthian Maid as the birth of painting is linked to an opposition of drawn outline and a physically present, tangible and sensual world. The myth marks drawing as a vital energy and form and as a substitute or alternative to the world as much as it is a representation of the world. In the myth, Dibutades (the maid) seeks to possess and preserve her, soon to be departed, lover by drawing around his shadow an outline and thus capturing his likeness. In this way the lover's shadow projected onto a wall by what often appears, in illustrations, as the light of a lamp, or of the moon as spectral projector, becomes fixed and held by drawing as a stand-in for both Dibutades's lover and their love. Drawing here is the fixing of this fleeting transient shadow through outline. Indeed, in certain images of the myth, the focus of the intensity of the love, desire and sensuality that is Dibutades's motivation is shifted from lover to shadow and from relationship to art. The act and action of drawing as love and sensuality and memory becomes independent of the male lover as subject. The sensuality of the act of drawing is in some illustrations of the myth underlined by the presence of Cupid whose piercing arrow and its associations become the chosen drawing implement of Dibutades. The illustrated neglect of the lover in favour of the image suggests a dawning scoptophilia.

Drawing enacts love and the drawing replaces the lover. Drawing and outline are born, in this myth, from a heady mix of desire, fear of loss, sensuality and artifice. The act of drawing for Dibutades creates an alternative sensuous world. Through the outline as drawing, the world is given a new form and new animation. The image dreams its future.

Outline, as the basis of picture making, may also be understood in relation to the drawn marks that emerge from the pre-historic fecundity of our ancient landscapes, from nature and from the rich supply of surfaces and media nature has provided for human exploitation. These early images as artefacts and sites preserved in our museums and as tourist venues and in the preserved natural landscape provide evidence for the later archaeological myths of beginning, not only of the image but of culture/s as well. Simply the caves provide the material images and myths of our shared beginnings. The pre-historic 'painted' cave, engraved stones and inscribed artefacts of pre-history amaze and enthral and animate us as we animate them with what Gombrich has called 'the beholder's share',[3] that element of meaning and significance, and even unknowing, which the viewer must bring to the image and that the curator, critic and pre-historian must engineer.

We see clearly the caves, we think, and identify the horses, handprints and other images of the Altamira, Chauvet, Cueva de las Manos, Lascaux, Peche Merle and Sulawesi caves and yet we are divided from them by thousands of years and by an all but unimaginable cultural distance. We touch the visual language of horse and creature and movement and we see and almost touch our own hands in those hands. Yet, so much of the complex cultures that generated these animated and enchanted images eludes us and drops away as a void as dark and impenetrable as the caves from which the images came. Not only do these ancient drawings, however, mark the origins of our human history and culture but they also mark the beginnings of our narrative, our visual story of ourselves within the world. The ancient inscribed stained and marked surfaces are the surfaces from which our visual histories emerge. Through them we see first see ourselves as image and from them our visual self-consciousnesses emerges.

These images are also the surfaces upon which human history is extinguished. Before these images the pre-human is unknown to us, a part, not apart from nature. The landscape and our place in it as 'natural' retreats from us. We may see, through artist's eyes, an Eden, an innocent harmony, a fantastic planet to be yearned for and imagined as other, but this innocent landscape is never again to be lived in. From the time of the first-drawn images the human landscape is changed forever as it is animated by the visual languages and images and the individual, collective and cultural and social imaginings of the human. As the drawings of the caves mark the emergence of the human we may reflect also on the extent to which drawing, animated by the filmic and the wonderful traditions of Japan and manga, for example, have contributed to our recognition of the cyborg and the 'post-human'.

For Ruskin, the influential Victorian art critic and philosopher, drawings' significance was intellectual, mysterious and spiritual. In the act of drawing the landscape, Ruskin encouraged artists, his disciples and his classes of students and workers to draw the 'awful lines'. By this Ruskin suggested not bad drawing but rather the exhortation to draw those lines that might reveal the awe Ruskin saw and felt and discovered in nature and the landscape:

'Try always, whenever you look at form, to see the lines in it which have had power over its fate and will have power over its futurity. Those are its *awful lines*; see that you seize on these...'[4] For Ruskin, drawing could, and should, be a tool for the exploration of the deep structures of plant and geology, sky and mountain, the landscape and nature itself. Such lines discovered in the landscape and nature and plants and moss and the tiniest elements of our world meant that drawing existed at the edge of the invisible. This invisible was in part the recognition of the limitations of the eye and the technologies of the lense and it was also the realization, facilitated by scientific technologies, apparatus and method, that nature and landscape conformed to patterns and laws such as the 'law of radiation' applied to leaves, foliage and trees and which formed part of a greater 'organic law'. Such laws, argued Ruskin, for the artist who studied, worked and looked with vision, pointed to a revelation of the nature of the world and beyond that to god. In this, Ruskin's attitude to drawing reflected the great intellectual trajectories and dynamics, discoveries and motivations of the Victorian period and emergent modernity.

In the painted cave

Drawing marks our beginning as it hints at our ending. It delineates the proto-human as it has suggested the post-human. The ancient drawings of the caves more recently defined as art and as emergent language, mark our emergence from the natural landscape into the landscapes of human culture as they delineate and announce the moment of the surfacing of human consciousness itself. The lion, bear, buffalo and elephant mark man from human and re-invent the embodied connections they characterize. Disney, Halas and Batchelor, and 20th Century Fox's *Avatar* (2009) are evoked and may be seen to emulate and re-think the connections between man and creature. The hand-prints and representations of the human form and body mark the emergence of our self-consciousness in their proto-photographic qualities and the shapes, patterns and hybrid creatures of the caves hold as fossils of the psyche the energy of the human imagination and its creative potential to pattern, order and understand the world. This pre-historic intellectual exploration touched many areas of human life. The clearly different and differentiated handprints arranged in neat order on the caves surface order the social. These pre-photographic images, in a sense, dream the family photograph into being.

The surface of the cave parallels and becomes simultaneous with the animated screen we know from our contemporary culture. Images come alive for us through their description of the world beyond them and as a structured separate world of images. The caves structure a landscape of dream. This creative potential resonates through the ever-imminent potential newness and exhilaration of the connection of drawing's ability to re-materialize and re-cognize itself in our lived presents and on our multiple screens. Through animated pornography, computer modelling, self-constructed drones, avatars and Google Glass, the potential is renewed in new and in re-constructed ancient forms.

The understanding of drawing as a tool for thought links with an understanding of drawing itself as a sign and rule-based system linked to, yet vitally different from, understandings of written language and other sign systems. Charles Sanders Peirce's[5] reflection on the sign was deeply influential in relation to the significance and growth of semiotics and casts a significant light on drawing as a system of signs. Peirce's marvellously adaptable trichotomy of signs identifies a way of understanding drawing's potential and versatility, then and now. This structure marks a progression and connection between characteristics of the sign that can be identified in the earliest drawn images of the caves. This progression moves for Peirce from the indexical (the sign, connected to its referent by contact) through the iconic (the connection of the sign to meaning through likeness) and to the symbolic (the connection of the sign to the constructed meanings and associations of culture and the accretions and accumulations of social conventions of meaning). Through Peirce's valuable looking glass we can see the implied developmental trajectory of the sign (from simple mark to complex language) and the suggestion that the images of the caves aspire to and pre-figure to the complexities of future meanings. Indeed, Werner Herzog suggests in the *Cave of Forgotten Dreams* (2010) that it may even be that the genesis of the earliest human drawing emerges from the indexical marks (scratches) of animal marks connected and over-written by human marks much as the image of the Peche-Merle horse seems to have pre-existed in the shape of the rock on which it is painted. Such a trajectory moves from the naïve 'natural' indexical and iconic mark, through the recognition and enhancement of its iconic significance as 'horse', to the mysterious and complex symbolic resonances of 'horse' that echo through the arts, myth and culture. However, this progression is not exhausted by the caves – it remains with us.

The significance of the (indexical) mark, (iconic) likeness and (symbolic) cultural association of Peirce's trichotomy of the sign is a definition and identification of the re-cognizable potential of the drawn. These elements remain fundamental to the image and its animation. As just one example, Phil Mulloy's animated parody of human evolution 'Intolerance' is played out through the mystery of the direct, powerful and expressive indexical mark, the iconicity of drawn forms that echo through the history of visual representation and the powerful associations of the symbolic as the image leaves the anchorage of iconicity to expand into the relay of the symbolic. Mulloy's film, which combines cultural, sexual, parodic, carnivalesque and undeniably funny imagery, provides a masterful and powerful articulation of the potential of drawn animation.

Reading the painted cave

From the natural landscapes that fostered the development of *Homo sapiens* and the emergence of the human come the human landscapes, communities, technologies, systems and artefacts of the contemporary world. The extraordinarily imaginative and intellectual technology we may call drawing has stayed with us. The history of drawn animation, as normally defined, is a fragment of this history of the image, but the roots of drawn imagination lie in the ancient pre-historic landscapes and the myths of the beginning of imagery as much as in the technologies of projection, the multi-platforms and the unique pervasiveness of drawing's contemporary forms. Drawing defines and reflects our pre-historic past as its technologies contribute to the post-modern, hyper-accelerated, post-human world.

In his astounding film *Cave of Forgotten Dreams*, filmed using drone technology, 3D digital wizardy and using the state-of-the-art stereoscopic cameras, Herzog weaves around his filming of the ancient Chauvet caves in France and the 30,000-year-old drawings. They contain a complex parable of human imagery and film as palimpsest (a connected deep layering and archaeology of images) and polyphony (the sense in which to imagine the visual experiences of the ancient caves is to simultaneously rehearse and experience the technologies of imagery from cave to fantasmagoria, cinema to video game and the virtual). In short, as Walter Benjamin has suggested, Herzog argues in relation to the image, that each epoch dreams the next as the contemporary dreams the past.

In Herzog's and Benjamin's analysis the past's images pre-figure the contemporary image and the contemporary image post-figures the past image. Images also contain simultaneous current and historical meanings, significances and significations. Thus, two significant dimensions, the dimension of palimpsest as a historical, layering, defacement and re-emergence of the various technologies of drawing and drawings' production and reception, in connection with polyphony, as the simultaneous experience of drawings pasts and presents and futures in the specificities of particular drawn images, are identified. These two dimensions – palimpsest and polyphony – mark two of the significant axes through which we can define, navigate and locate the landscape of drawn animation.

These two axes, polyphony and palimpsest, manifest the axes of an imagined and permanently contingent map, which can orient and re-orient us in relationship to the landscape of drawn animation. These axes also form the map of drawn animation – each finely calibrated by the history and details and artefacts of both drawing and drawn animation's technological and filmic achievements and explorations. The map is a contribution to the ever-changing map of the human landscape.

The polyphonic and palimpsestic cave

In a particularly significant sequence of *Cave of Forgotten Dreams* we move, or are moved by the camera from the flickering shadows of the pre-historic cave to the dark commonwealth of the cinema in a sequence that unites the two in a seamless flow, Herzog simulates with LEDs and 3D cameras the vital and animating light of the torches and fires of the ancient caves evidenced by their archaeology, which provided the charcoal for their magical imagery. From this enchanting sequence in which the drawn creatures of the cave come alive and flicker, twisting and moving, through the embodiment and simulation of the human eye by the camera, we move to a clip of Fred Astaire dancing in front of what appears as three super-large shadows (as simulacra) of Astaire's actual and filmic presence. In a moment of visual drama and revelation, the Astaire/ shadows separate from Astaire as the filmic index and dance to and for themselves and ourselves as audience – the moment is, in the context of Herzog's film, an epiphanaic visual allegory of film and animation as the liberation of the shadow and outline as independent forms, born in the ancient caves and pre-figuring cinema and animation, as cinema post-figures the drawings in the cave. Such a progression from shadow to magical dance is enacted in *The Skeleton Dance* (1929) of Disney's Silly Symphonies series, which moves from the depiction of light and the shadow and the nocturnal to a fantastic and impossible animation of the dead.

And of course we are reminded of the primacy and procession of the drawn image so that the ancient fantastic drawn images manipulated by the catoptrics of lenses, pierced lanterns, the fantasmagorias, the magic lanterns and the painted and slipping slides that long preceded the projection of the photographic moving image, dance and enthral us as the Cabaret de Neantes of Paris enthralled and as the animated painted glass, projected images and visual spectacles of Paris preceded the verite cinematic moving photographs of the Lumières.

Through this pan-historical journey and polyphony of images that dance on the screen in front of us, a palimpsest of drawn animation's texts is also revealed in Herzog's film. The shadows and their flickering animate the creatures of the cave perceived in close-ups, as fragments and as sequences, mimicking the conventions of painting, drawn animation and film as they mimic the conventions of the repetitions of limbs employed in comics to suggest movement. Their forms seem amazingly and at times even comically familiar as we recognize in them images that evoke, for example, Disney's *The Lion King* (1994) and the muscular outlines of Picasso's art, the flickering outline and invention of Émile Cohl's *Fantasmagorie* (1908), the multiple limbs of Billy Whizz and the forms that twist and stretch in a Loony Tunes fashion. The images of the caves resonate and connect. In the hybridity and transmutations of forms and the magic of the primal and archaic given life by the relationship of image to both real and pictorial space we might even recognize the spacial simulations, hybridities and monstrosities of our high technology of the twenty-first century: dark spaces of spectacle, which contain such hybrid visions as James Cameron's *Avatar* (the film and the video game). Herzog connects the ancient drawings of the female human form in the caves with the visual and cultural conventions of *Baywatch* (1989–2001) and to that we might add the eponymous Betty Boop, Lara Croft from the *Tomb Raider* franchise (1996–present), and Jade (aka Shauni) from the video game *Beyond Good & Evil* (2003).

The animated images of the caves may be seen to announce an epochal shift in human consciousness and society. The term epochal is here used as in Arthur Danto's recognition of the artistic and epochal shifts in the visual that are marked by the shifts from pre-modern to modern and post-modern worlds. In this, Danto articulates his argument through the assertion that the difference between the art of Giotto, Picasso and Warhol is more than a matter of style but is a matter of essential and significant shifts in the nature of art, culture and even being.[6] In this sense, whilst there is much in common between the images of the caves, especially as interpreted by Herzog's camera, and, for example, Cohl's *Fantasmagorie*, the contrast between the two visual artefacts is also of immense significance.

This significance of Cohl's extraordinary film *Fantasmagorie* and the emergent language of filmic drawn animation it reflects is as much to be identified in the epochal shift of the emergence of cultural modernism as it is in a response to the social conditions of emerging modernity as it is in the palimpsestic and polyphonic resonances and connections and contrasts between the two animated forms: that of cave and that of film. We cannot in other words locate 'Fantasmagorie' or for that matter any other drawn animation other than in a multidimensional and complex landscape.

The very title of the film recalls the tradition of the visual entertainments and technologies of spectacle of the nineteenth century, and even the cave. However, the film, through its extraordinary and dynamic use of metamorphosis (Wells)[7] and qualities of plasticmacness (Eisenstein),[8] surpasses these effects. Indeed, more than this, the film connects with the emerging recognition of the characteristics of modernity as defined by the now conventional linking of Albert Einstein and Sigmund Freud with the modern period and as interpreters of modernity. Cohl, we can argue, finds equivalents for Einstein's connection, disintegration and re-invention of time, space, light and movement in the high speed, mutations, metamorphoses, links and disjunctures of this film. Similarly, Cohl reflects in *Fantasmagorie* the action of desire, dream and conflict in the structure of a newly anxious, insecure, multiple and ever-shifting reality as defined by Freud.

All this alongside the film's fantastic pre-figuration of the strategies of modernism. Surrealism as the dream and nightmare vision suggesting the *sur-above-the-real* of new possibilities and anxieties. Abstraction as the expressive potential of liberated, cleansed and purified form. Cubo-Futurism as the hybrid innovative and profoundly new potential of the visual to destroy, defile, rethink and re-imagine itself as a new language for a new era: the era of the Modern.

Disney's modern landscape

The Silly Symphonies provide us with complex allegories of modernity as they invent and establish the new and adored filmic language that the modernist avant-garde and most notably Eisenstein celebrated. Disney's *Lullaby Land* (1933), for example, extends and popularizes the strategies of the American modernist visual avant-garde (abstraction, surrealism, cubo-futurism) popularizing and domesticating them within the solipsistic form of the child's lullaby. This modernist lullaby, however, occurs in a surreal and fantastic landscape that (extending Cohl) hybridizes, mutates and makes monsters from the everyday, the banal, mass products of modernity, and innocent childhood itself.

In The Forbidden Garden of the film's landscape, the soft-quilted innocence of our initial encounter with the film's surrealism is threatened and challenged by a world of Freudian and deeply uncanny spectacles in which domestic objects become animated and electrified and in which threatening mechanical automatons assemble themselves. The garden landscape of Disney's dream here clearly draws on Modernist art as Miró, Arp and Dali are clearly quoted. Additionally, The Forbidden Garden announced in the film is the modernized Boschian Garden of Earthly Delights. A hell and heaven extended and darkened by Freud and Disney. Indeed, the film leads us from the innocent heaven of urban idealized childhood through the monstrous hell of the forbidden realm of Freudian anxiety and nightmare, just as Bosch's extraordinary painting takes us from The Garden of Eden to hell. In Disney's fantastic garden of visual, modernist delights, however, the redemption of domestic, Middle-American landscape and family as safety is added and held out as a resolution and a happy ending.

In Disney's *The Band Concert* (1935) a ramshackle artifice of a Bandstand situated in 'nature' or a 'park', or even theme-park, which resembles an idealized rural America, is visually allegorized as a focus and embodiment of the theatre of American identity. European cultural heritage and archaic establishment are juxtaposed with a version of the American Dreamer. A red-coated Mickey battles to maintain the discipline of an assorted but conventional orchestra in a rendition of a classical European favourite – The William Tell Overture. Into this landscape – and representing an individualized, feisty, independent rebellious and entrepreneurially aware counterpart to the conservative order and conservatoire of Mickey's European orchestra – comes a duck.

The connection with the 'coonskinism' (echoes of the American War of Independence) that Harold Rosenberg associated with Abstract Expressionism's (which Rosenberg termed 'Action Painting') battle to achieve recognition within an art world dominated by Europe is significant.[9] Donald, who appears undisciplined, subversive and republican, plays his own tune and battles to play his tune against the serried ranks of the outnumbering, well-equipped and voluble redcoat orchestra. He is Jackson Pollock's pre-cursor as a duck and with flute rather than brush. He stands against the dominance and weight of European culture as Pollock challenged Picasso and the weight of European art. Donald's endurance and pugnacious independence speak of American identities' difficult and combative emergence from the European order and from the American landscape.

However, the real threat and energy of the film is a dark and powerful storm that overtakes all in its path, raging through the idealized rural landscape, demolishing the fragile Euro-Bandstand, overturning Donald's emergent business hopes and turning the fragile order of the orchestra and rural to a comic surrealist nightmare and whirlwind of monstrous hybrid forms as it turns the landscape to a devastated wasteland. The tensions of old and emergent modern America are all but engulfed by the dark storm of modernity and disaster. The storm, dark and terrifying, gives form to modernist anxiety and predicts disasters, crashes and whirlwinds to come.

In *Music Land* (1935), the metaphor of music, which is so important to American culture and identity and to avant-garde artists for whom music represented an abstract art form and object of paintings aspiration, is extended within the curious structure of a modernized and instrumentalized version of Romeo and Juliet. Two landscapes, binarily opposed, the Land of Symphony and the Land of Jazz, stand separate, each powerful and each independent across an ocean as divide. Extending the allegory of *The Band Concert*, Land of Symphony is classical, European, rigid, ordered, whilst the Land of Jazz, despite its erasure of an Afro-American identity, is characterized by energy, vitality and by Jazz. In an extraordinary visual metaphor, the Lands of Symphony and Jazz become vast battleship-like war machine-juke-boxes that fire salvoes of music and notes as explosive pyrotechnic visual spectacles of a simulated total war and conflict to come.

These examples and their interpretation here rehearse, in part, the great schism in interpretation of Disney evident in the contrasting writings of Benjamin and Theodor Adorno.[10] For Adorno, Disney represented a fundamentally reactionary force, yet for Benjamin, Disney suggested 'emancipatory potential'. In this the opposed landscapes of Land of Symphony and Land Of Jazz reflect a tension that Adorno and Benjamin externalize in relation to Disney's landscape.[11] Whilst Adorno's and Benjamin's analyses have been, and remain of, great value, an alternative interpretation might suggest that these tensions reflect the opposed visions of modernity, as utopic or dystopic trajectories, and as such are not so much mutually exclusive externalized positions but rather are characteristic of modernism's internal dynamism, ambivalence and complexity.

Paul Ricouer in his essay 'Ideology and Utopia' (1991) suggests that the contradictory and opposed dynamics of *utopia* as the possibilities of the new and previously unimagined are in constant dynamic relation with *ideology* as the tendency to order, structure, stabilize and repeat.[12] In this way the arts' general tendency to 're-make reality' suggested by Ricouer represent a constantly shifting dynamic tension in which utopia and ideology avoid the pathology of their extremes through their mutual and unresolved reframing of their dynamics. Ricouer suggests:

> This interplay of ideology and utopia appears as interplay of the two fundamental directions of the social imagination. The first tends towards integration, repetition and the mirroring of the given order. The second tends to disintegration because it is eccentric. But the one cannot work without the other… This is why the tension between ideology and utopia is unsurpassable.[13]

The early twentieth century, the age of the excitement, the innovation and the traumas of the modern and modernity and the vast changes they brought about, demanded and achieved a new language and new forms to reflect and give form to its tensions, anxieties and ambivalences. Cohl and Disney are examples. The new language and new form was animation.

Animating the hybrid landscape

Władysław Starewicz's amazing animation *The Cameraman's Revenge* (1912), it can be argued, is to early twentieth-century animation as Dziga Vertov's *Man with a Movie Camera* (1929) is to early twentieth-century film. Starewicz's innovations can stand as an introduction to and example of animations' innovatory forms as it draws upon and invents its emergent practices. In *The Cameraman's Revenge*, animated cadaverous insects and wire replace humans as protagonists and an insect camera-man usurps and overpowers the adulterous and wayward artist bohemian. In the process of this storytelling, amazing feats of visual spectacle are achieved as dead insects as performers ride bicycles and an insect-artist paints within the animation a painting.

This simple moment of hybridity of film and of drawn and model animation is hugely prescient, suggesting even at the birth of drawn and model animation's conventions that new and yet-to-be-imagined potentials for monstrosity and hybridity were forming. The animation connects with visual artefacts as yet unmade but dreamed possible by Starewicz's innovations. For the slightly outdated bohemian painter-insect in *The Cameraman's Revenge* the painting remains a tool of seduction and power, but the real power in the film is held by the cameraman-insect as it is by the cameraman in Vertov's *Man with a Movie Camera*. The central power and engine of both films is the camera itself. In *The Cameraman's Revenge* it is the camera and cameraman-insect that ultimately exposes both the adulterous couples of the plot and the more significant ultimate power of the camera itself via a public screening of an illicitly filmed sexual dalliance. Not only does this animation reflect a potential conflict between avant-garde and anti-garde within the modernist environment of motorcars, cinema and the urban, but it also reflects conflicts and uncertainties of morality and judgement policed, somewhat prophetically and ultimately by the camera and the law.

A further amazing feat of animation in *The Cameraman's Revenge* introduces us not only to the surface of the canvas as image screen but also to the screen of the cinema and the technologies of projection, which become the focus of the drama and action of the film. An insect-projectionist provides a simulacrum of the animation's projection. All screens in *The Cameraman's Revenge* become broken, pierced and obliterated within the film, except of course for the screen on which we perceive the film's drama. The painter's canvas screen is pierced not by Cupid's arrow but by a disaffected lover. The cinema screen, in the animation, is destroyed, allowing the artifice of a further level of false nature behind it to be revealed, by a vengeful victim of camera's power. The film suggests an allegory of art, artist film, camera, screen, and their influence on a newly urbanized and commodified society. However, allegory and meaning itself are ultimately overwhelmed by the complexities of mediation of the camera, the lens and the repeated prophetic pre-figuring of the pervasiveness of multiple screens in modern urban life. The film ends with a scene from a prison cell.

Starewicz's great early animation sacrifices simple allegory and clarity to the ambivalence of the modern and the complexity of the technologies of the visual such as painting, spatial, illusion, camera, cinema, surveillance and image screen as elements of modernity are engaged. Pre-figuring Hal Foster's writings on 'traumatic realism',[14] it is the violation of the image screen within the animation that returns us to the now fragile and complex possibility of a real beyond the increasingly pervasive screen. The possibilities of desire, anarchy invention, subversion and excitement and pure modernist spectacle of Starewicz's film end with the triumph of law and punishment and harsh judgement and control made possible by the new technologies of surveillance and the pervasiveness of screens. This is the landscape of the failed desire of the modern for freedom and individual liberty merging with and collapsing into the post-modern landscapes of control and surveillance.

The twenty-first century and labyrinthine space caves

The many tensions, contradictions and complexities of the late twentieth century and early twenty-first century life are explored in animations with a clearly post-modern aesthetic such as *Serial Experiments Lain* (1998) and Ryan Trecartin's *Tommy Chat Chat Just E-Mailed Me* (2006). These two films are two examples, among many possibilities, of animations which expose the post-modern landscape as the 'landscape of the sign' and landscape of contemporary life. In *Serial Experiments Lain*, the long tradition of manga and Japanese drawing hybridizes with Western animation and culture so that a dense and multi-layered sense of the 'weird' emerges as the dissonance between the spiritual real, the real as lived adolescent experience, and the real as the emerging hyper-accelerated digital world of e-mail, computers and video games. This drama is played out within the traditions of Japanese storytelling; the pilgrimage of individuals towards enlightenment, folklore and myth; and the generational conflicts the animation recognizes and identifies.

Through this, Ryūtarō Nakamura's *Serial Experiments Lain* links with hugely popular feature animations such as Hayao Miyazaki's *Spirited Away* (2004). In *Spirited Away*, as in *Serial Experiments Lain*, the parental generation is denounced for its superficiality, greed and lack of thought and the sense of hopelessness and empty materialism it has generated. Nature is seen as complex, fugitive and threatened. The virtual, as theme park, in *Spirited Away* mimics and displaces the landscapes of tradition and nature. The landscape as nature and its animal, human and spiritual ecologies are identified as threatened and hope is placed in the hands of youth rather than the commodified stupidity of age.

In *Tommy Chat Chat Just E-Mailed Me*, drawing as mark making, aggressive defilement, diagram and bodily adornment, theatrical make-up and computer screen diagram is hybridized with film and the pervasive screens of social media and search engines to suggest a terrifying, mindless and infantilized nightmare carnival of multi-, trans- and pan-media systems of communication; yet, these are communication systems without communication and signification or meaning – systems that act to mask their uselessness through empty simulation of that which is absent. The film's infantilized puerile, violent, population mirrors the anxieties and criticisms of the post-modern landscape suggested by the work of Japan's Superflat artists. Adulthood and power act negatively in *Serial Experiments Lain* and *Spirited Away* and reproduce a new, plagued generation and an emergent sense of a newly anxious and dis-integrated contemporary life.

Trecartin's film ends with an abject re-encounter with the real. The natural world becomes the 'Oh My God' of a de-sensitized, numbed humanity. The actions of the dysfunctional, media-social, non-family change through their experiences in nature from haptic dysfunctionality to a pronounced terror at the unknown (Oh my god what's out there!), and this is only assuaged by their parodied, deeply pathetic and inept attempts to mould materials into meaning, as an attempt to make art. Their empty actions are a parody of art itself and of modern and romantic sensibilities.

This dysfunctionality contrasts deeply with the dignity and respect afforded the early human by Herzog's readings of the animated art of the cave. In Richard Linklater's *Waking Life* (2001), the post-modern is imagined in various rich and complex, poetic and lyrical manifestations. In this rotoscopic animation, the world is drawn and re-structured as a series of post-modern landscapes. Furthermore, through the technique of rotoscoping, the animation encourages an expanded and nuanced awareness of the relationships between photorealism, pop art and the team of skilful artists Linklater employed to create the multiple, hugely unstable, deeply subjective and complex series of animated worlds that are characteristic of his film. However, in contrast to Trecartin's film, Linklater's suggests it is the power of the imagination and of philosophy that provides the dominant themes of the film and which offer the only real hope of meaningful orientation in the post-modern landscape.

The film begins with a moment of animated epiphany similar in some ways to the 'Astaire moment' in Herzog's *Cave of Forgotten Dreams*. The drawn world of the opening sequence of *Waking Life* mirrors the ideologies and conventions of mainstream cinema, which was the common ideology of the animated feature film of the twentieth century. Dreamy and languid, the animation asserts a generally familiar emotional and geographical landscape of American film. However, slight shifts in scale of drawing and mildly erratic animated movement in the film begins to unhinge and unravel the easy familiarity of the narrative. Drawing starts to invade and disrupt its own illusion. Yet, overall, the generally hegemonic surface of the film's reality, the child-like voices, Middle-American urban landscape and seductive replication of cinematic normality, brilliantly (and yet so mildly perversely) structured in the medium of drawn animation, lulls us as the audience. The moment of epiphany is the moment a child holding onto a car (as though to anchor themselves in a newly made false reality) levitates, floats, inverts and seems to fall or rise into the world of planets, stars and galaxies. The shadow and the outline liberated in Herzog's film from the material and the human is in this moment re-liberated by Linklater from the world itself, as it is from cinematic and animated 'ideology' as conceived by Ricouer. It is a moment of sublime Utopian possibility – the announcement of the possibility not just of a new world and a new reality to be made – but also of the infinite and magical possibilities of that re-making.

This moment announces the world turned upside down by animation, by drawing and within the fabricated worlds of *Waking Life*: dream and philosophy. Throughout the film, drawing re-makes the multiple realities and landscapes of contemporary lived life. Not so much just turned upside down by the inversion of dream and waking and of reality and idea this world whirls rotates and folds around itself as a visual and philosophical carnival of utopias and ideologies, shadows and outlines.

Life is visualized as dream. Linklater's animation defines, structures and dominates the real as the philosophical world manifests itself not just through the discussions of the post-modern pilgrim protagonist with the thinkers, teachers and street characters he meets, but through the visual, the repetitions of the worlds turned upside down, the dominance of seeing and vision, as a vital and necessary dream of the world emerges. This world – this waking life – is constructed by the dream, the shadow and outline. Linklater's drawn animation is that dream that sees. It is a dream that has eyes and it has vision.

Tim Travers Hawkins's 2012 multi-platform, interactive, drawn animation *Invisible Picture Show* employs drawing to visualize both the invisible detainee and the invisible suffering of those without images and made un-visible in (and by) a contemporary media soaked world. The film in its interactive form creates an un-natural yet illusionistic hybrid space between the architecture and illusions of surveillance and imprisonment and the virtual spaces of computer game and social media. The film locates the viewer in an engaging and disturbing labyrinth of virtual, psychological and moral and political spaces through which the viewer passes and within which actions and choices count. The film's trajectory from animation to screen actions *Continue Exploring* and *Take Action* seek to involve the viewer in political action beyond the screen and give a positive form to the link between animated simulation and power identified in Harun Farocki's film *Serious Games* (2014) as it subverts the connection Anselm Franke[15] identifies between computer animation and reality in which 'living beings' increasingly 'supplement the machine' and reflect a world in which 'ideal-typical' forms of the animated human as 'augmented realities, intelligent environments and self-learning systems' provide constructions of a commodified and industrialized drone post-humanity as 'the measure of an always imperfect reality' and an un-ruly and feral outsider humanity.

Conclusion

The future of drawn animation to judge by its past is change and continuity. As animation technologies and the medium of drawing expand, develop and realize drawn animation's potential, we can look to new, inventive, creative possibilities that will echo the past. In 1972, artist Rebecca Horn made and performed a piece titled 'Pencil Mask'. The pencil mask was a lattice attached to and covering Horn's head holding sharpened pencils placed at close intervals and projecting away from her. Horn made a number of drawings with her mask by bringing her head and the sharpened pencils on her mask into contact with paper. The mask allowed Horn's body movements to find their equivalent in drawing through the 'technology' of her invented mask.

The motion capture suit provides a contemporary extension of Horn's mask and the connection between the human body and image. Through the motion capture suit, the indexical mark as stencilled from the real of the body links with the iconicity of its programming to the likeness of human form – as avatar. The symbolic resonances of the image extend this potential as the image resonates through the multi-platforms of its performance and the labyrinthine cultural networks of communication and signification. So the motion capture suits alongside the images of the painted caves provide an extended polyphony and palimpsest of drawing – as the embodied medium of the new drawn landscapes of the human.

Drawing is a pervasive and persistent technology that has always been animated. This animation occurs through the action of individual and social imaginations and the technologies of production and reception. Drawing in its manifestation as drawn animation has been of enormous significance to the twentieth century and its significance as a technology and dream that sees and shapes our understandings of the landscapes we inhabit whether internal or external virtual or real remains with us into an uncertain and accelerated twenty-first century.

We walk the line.

Notes

1   Walter Benjamin, *Charles Baudelaire a Lyric Poet in the Era of High Capitalism*, trans. Harry Zohn (London: Verso, 1997), 159.

2   William Blake, *1759–1827: The Poetic Works of William Blake* (Oxford: Oxford University Press, 1908), 584.

3   Ernst Gombrich, *Art and Illusion a Study in the Psychology of Pictorial Representation* (Oxford: Oxford University Press, 2000), 181–242.

4   John Ruskin, *The Elements of Drawing Three Letters to Beginners* (London: George Allen, 1904), 119.

5   Charles S. Peirce, 'Logic as Semiotic The Theory of Signs', in *Semiotics an Introductory Anthology*, ed. Robert. E. Innis (Bloomington: Indiana University Press, 1985), 1–24.

6   Arthur C. Danto, *The Madonna of the Future Essays on a Pluralistic Art World* (London: University California Press, 2001), 416–427.

7   Paul Wells, *Understanding Animation* (Oxford: Routledge, 1998), 69–76.

8   Sergei Eisenstein, *Eisenstein on Disney*, ed. Jay Leyda, trans. Alan Upchurch (Calcutta: Seagull, 1986).

9   Harold Rosenberg, *The Tradition of the New* (New York: Da Capo Press, 1965), 13–23.

10 Andy Birtwistle, *Cinesonica, Sounding Film and Video* (Manchester: Manchester University Press, 2010), 232–233.

11 Birtwistle, *Cinesonica*, 232–233.

12 Paul Ricouer, *From Text to Action: Essays in Hermeneutics II*, trans. Kathleen Blamey and John B. Thompson (Evanston, IL: Northwestern University Press, 1991), 323.

13 Ricouer, *From Text to Action*, 323.

14 Hal Foster, *The Return of the Real, The Avant-Garde at the End of the Century* (New York: MIT Press, 1996), 127–171.

15 Anselm Franke, 'A Critique of Animation', *e-flux Journal*, 2014, accessed 15 December 2014, http://www.e-flux.com/journal/a-critique-of-animation/.

2

The Stop-Motion Landscape

Chris Pallant

Stop-motion animation, also described as object animation and three-dimensional animation, can be traced back to the trick cinema of Georges Méliès – with the Frenchman's 'one turn one picture' method constituting something of a shared Big Bang for both the animated and live-action traditions of filmmaking. As legend goes – one actively perpetuated by Méliès himself – while testing his Kinétographe camera in 1896 (developed and patented with Lucien Korsten and Lucien Reulos),[1] his filming of a horse-drawn carriage was interrupted by the device jamming, allowing enough time for a horse-drawn hearse to replace the carriage in exactly the same position just in time for the camera to resume recording, so that when played back the carriage appeared to magically transform into a hearse.[2] Beyond the immediate exploitation of this tactic within the trick film genre, this ability to reshape the viewer's experience of time and continuity through the physical manipulation of the film stock encouraged filmmakers to consider the potential of montage and for animators to begin exploring the possibilities of stop-motion animation.

In this root commonality, between the differently coded worlds of live-action and stop-motion moving imagery, is contained much of the appeal of stop motion: that being the tension between familiarity and difference that results from the overtly fabricated, yet recognizably material, quality of the form. Expanding on this, Paul Wells writes:

> Three-dimensional animation is directly concerned with the expression of materiality, and, as such, the creation of a certain *meta*-reality which has the same physical property as the real world. This *fabrication* essentially plays out an alternative version of material existence, recalling narrative out of the constructed objects and environments, natural forms and substances, and the taken-for-granted constituent elements of the everyday world. In a certain sense, this is the *re-animation* of materiality for narrative purposes.[3]

Wells's discussion of the stop-motion form is unusual, in that, from the outset, he places equal significance on both the objects *and* environments of the animated world. This is unusual because in much of the extant literature that discusses the stop-motion form, considerations of the environment are, at worst, absent or marginal and, at best, decidedly secondary to the considerations of character.[4]

Typically, it is imperative to provide a multi-purpose point of entry to the stop-motion form, where practical considerations must be balanced alongside theoretical insight, which has led to the marginalization of landscape as a prominent object of study. Barry Purves's thoughtful studies, *Stop Motion: Passion, Process and Performance* (2008) and *Stop Motion* (2010), capture this dialectic well. While Purves engages with the subject of the animated landscape throughout both books, this is almost always framed in such a way as to consider how the animated landscape might influence the creation and consequent reception of character. Where landscape is discussed on its own terms, it is in the manner of setting and set design. Rather than considering the metamorphic potential of the animated landscape, a key concern when designing sets, as noted by Purves, 'is not what they look like to the passer-by in the studio, but what they look like through the lens, and whether they compliment or distract from the characters'.[5] While Purves leads with this practical consideration, he later argues strongly for a more considered approach:

> An architecturally solid set, with no stylistic tweaking, on stage or in animation makes my heart sink, as the enormous potential is not realised. In all I do, I make sure every colour, every prop, every item of the set has a reason to be there or makes a comment. If that reason is just to be pretty, that's not enough. It has to add to the story or atmosphere or go.[6]

As the work discussed in this chapter will demonstrate, the stop-motion animated landscape need not simply be just the sum of its parts.

An important characteristic of the stop-motion animated landscape that distinguishes it from the animated landscapes of the hand-drawn and computer-generated (CG) variety is its frequent construction from recognizable materials. While the viewer may well be familiar with techniques such as Multiplane depth or vector-based three-dimensional texture mapping, the material immediacy of the stop-motion landscape, where the viewer is presented with recognizable objects and materials, can endow the form with a *knowable* quality. It is this sense of tangible space, established through material familiarity, which endows the stop-motion landscape with the potential for great symbolic significance. Depending on how the landscape is framed, either in a narrative or in a non-narrative sense, it can be made to serve as more than just a surface, more than just a set, more than just a location. Therefore, this chapter considers the active status of the animated landscapes of the stop-motion form in several ways, which, if categorized, might be defined tentatively as instrumental landscapes, symbolic landscapes and narrative landscapes.

The instrumental landscape

Given the fundamental *raison d'être* of this collection to challenge the historical privileging of character over landscape as the favoured object of study, it is difficult to imagine a more fitting place to begin than by considering animation that operates through landscape alone. In many ways, the instrumental landscape, as I have termed it here, describes a type of animated landscape that becomes most potent in the stop-motion form. Animation that might be defined in this sense operates in such a way that the story world develops from, yet remains contained within, the symbolic framework of landscape. In fact, the instrumentality of landscape does not preclude the development of character; rather it encourages the viewer to continually re-evaluate the relationship that exists between character and landscape within the medium of animation.

The utilization of landscape in this manner is not unique to the stop-motion form, with Pixar's short *Day and Night* (2010) providing an excellent example of a stereoscopic landscape that brings both definition and meaning to the two-dimensional cut-out characters whose bodily outlines, in turn, serve as windows through which the three-dimensional diurnal and nocturnal landscapes are viewed. In what is essentially a morality tale about prejudice and tolerance, with the characters shaping the landscape in a literal sense with the movements of their bodies, it is the transformative power of the landscape that ultimately proves most significant at the short's conclusion. While *Day and Night* succeeds in highlighting the ability of landscape to re-shape our conception of character not only through story, but also through the aesthetic decision to impose a seemingly hand-drawn two-dimensional layer over the CG stereoscopic landscape, this approach is far from typical. If *Day and Night* had been constructed in a more conventional way, wholly reliant on either hand-drawn or CG animation styles, the power of the landscape to shape character would have been reduced as a consequence of both character and landscape appearing to be aesthetically similar. It is in this regard that the fragmentary landscape of stop-motion animation can become instrumental for the animator seeking to interrogate the relationship between character and landscape.

Perhaps the most prolific animator in this regard is the street artist Blu. Having worked anonymously under this tag since 1999, Blu has revealed a consistent desire to animate the environments within which he works. Across animations such as *Fantoche* (2007), *Letter A* (2007), *Walking* (2007), *Muto* (2008), *Combo* (2009), *Morphing* (2009) and *Big Bang Big Boom* (2010), Blu adopts a wall-painting method to bring the landscapes in which he and his team of street artists work to life. The most ambitious of these projects is without doubt *Big Bang Big Boom*, which depicts the evolution of life through a wall-painted animation that sprawls across a decaying urban landscape (recalling, particularly in the short's conclusion, Blu's 2007 non-animated wall painting, *Evolution*).

Big Bang Big Boom brings together a range of stop-motion techniques, including pixilation, hand-drawn imagery and the spatial manipulation of objects. This hybridity is neatly captured in the short's opening sequence. In classic lightning sketch fashion, the viewer is visually confronted with the pixilated presence of the animators on screen, overtly connected to the imagery that they are animating (Figure 2.1).

While pixilation is an important feature at the start of the short, serving to establish the street art production context, it is quickly reduced to only an intermittent ingredient, with the focus shifting towards the hand-drawn subject matter on which the animators can be seen to be working. Throughout

Figure 2.1 Blu at work on *Big Bang Big Boom* (Blu, 2010)

Big Bang Big Boom (and much of Blu's earlier wall-painted animation) the environment proves instrumental in shaping the animation. For example, the implied limitations of the real-world environment help communicate the non-sentient nature of the atomic structure that develops at the start of the short: first, bouncing off a fixed staircase, before being channelled via some discarded mesh fencing into a drainage pipe. Crucially, not only does the real-world environment literally contain the animation, as is the case here, but it also shapes Blu's approach to the project, presenting real-world opportunities and obstacles to be creatively negotiated.

At one extreme, Blu and his team playfully exploit these affordances by having a large dinosaur interact with a passer-by, roaring with such ferocity so as to blow the pedestrian into the air, causing them to cling desperately to a nearby telegraph cable. Although at first glance this sequence might simply appear to serve as a moment of artistic showmanship, it actually captures in microcosm the tension that informs the creation and curation of street art in the broadest sense. Just as metamorphosis is a core element of animation, animated street art is also fundamentally reliant on the metamorphic act. Beyond the fact that street artists transform the landscapes in which they work from the outset, the works that they leave behind are subject to further metamorphosis. Complete removal is one such potential metamorphosis, reworking of the image or the surrounding area by another street artist is another. Clearly, the fact that *Big Bang Big Boom* is animated further exaggerates the metamorphic quality of the work – in order to create the illusion of movement, the images created by Blu are subject to immediate removal and renewal – as evidenced through the white-washed walls that conceal the dinosaur's path. In a blog entry posted after concluding work on the dinosaur sequence in Buenos Aires, Blu reflects on this impermanence, noting that 'it is a pity to leave just blurry animation tracks on that wall much better to erase everything and start a proper piece'.[7]

The instrumentality of the landscape to be animated means the stop-motion animator is presented with a unique opportunity, to make use of something material, something solid and recognizable, and to refashion it on a frame-by-frame basis to serve the narrative agenda, or to refashion the narrative in order to take advantage of the physical affordances of the surrounding environment. This instrumental position of the animated landscape in relation to the construction of visual form and narrative, which is evident in the work discussed above, arguably represents the animated landscape in its purest form, both the subject of animation and serving as an animating force in its own right.

The symbolic landscape

Although now a lost film, surviving accounts of Quirino Cristiani's *El Apóstol* (1917) suggest that the film served as a political satire that made use of the animated landscape to emphasize its satirical critique. Centred on the character of Hipólito Irigoyen, who in real life had just led the Radical Party to majority victory in Argentina's 1916 presidential elections, Cristiani sought to poke fun at the new leader and his party, who could be long-winded, and, as Giannalberto Bendazzi writes, also had 'a certain tendency toward demagoguery'.[8] At the film's conclusion, attempting 'to bring morality to public life and eliminate corruption in Buenos Aires', Irigoyen 'ascends to heaven where Jupiter lends the new president his thunderbolts. Irigoyen then hurled the redemptive fire at the city, which made for a most impressive blaze'.[9]

Similar in practical execution to Lotte Reiniger's surviving *The Adventures of Price Achmed* (1926), Cristiani made use of cut-out figures animated through stop motion. Again, while it is impossible to write with certainty about this long-lost work, from contemporary accounts, audiences described the film as a 'graphic work that reveals enormous labor, patience and even genius'.[10] This appraisal, coupled with Bendazzi's revelation that the audience 'particularly enjoyed the final sequence, which combined models built by the French architect Andrés Ducaud and special effects', hints that Cristiani made use of a three-dimensional background in at least part of *El Apóstol*.[11] While Reiniger suggested three-dimensional space throughout her *One Thousand and One Nights*-inspired feature, building her background up with multiple layers, it is unlikely that we will ever never know for certain whether Cristiani made use of similar strategies throughout his feature.

That Cristiani went to the trouble of developing a three-dimensional diegetic landscape for at least the conclusion of his film hints a possible satirical edge. Given the visual contrast that would have been explicitly apparent to viewers, between the two-dimensional cut-out characters and the three-dimensional landscape, it is tempting to see symbolic value in this creative choice. Cristiani's hyperbolic depiction of Irigoyen (ascending to Jupiter and raining down redemptive fire) would surely have been viewed with an added satirical edge, given Irigoyen's depiction in two dimensions compared to more rounded three dimensions of the landscape that he is attempting to save.

Animation is undoubtedly a symbolically rich medium by the very virtue of its method of creation, with every detail being carefully crafted. However, as

Wells rightly cautions, 'symbols may be unconsciously deployed, and, therefore, may be recognised as a bearer of meaning over and beyond the artist's overt intention.... This can, of course, radically alter the understanding of a film arguably making it infinitely richer in its implications, or misrepresenting its dominant project altogether'.[12] It is therefore possible to find symbolic value, on some level, in all moving image works. Nonetheless, as the discussion of Cristiani illustrates, certain filmmakers do work harder than others to establish animated landscapes that challenge our perceived – and received – understanding of the symbolic order, whether politically or otherwise. While filmmakers such as Oscar Fischingaer, Norman McLaren, Jan Švankmajer and Jiří Trnka have all done this in both abstract and narrative forms, the focus here will rest on the latter two animators, as we reflect on the ways that symbolic landscapes have been used in their animated works to offer political comment.

Trnka's 1965 masterpiece, *Ruka/The Hand*, makes use of several techniques, including pixilation, live-action, and stop-motion animation, throughout the eighteen-minute short, in which he offers a powerful symbolic critique of state oppression. Responding to a political system that had relied on Stalinist perversions of governance, such as intellectually motivated purges of oppositional individuals, secret policing and totalitarian central planning, the critical potency of the film's political symbolism resulted in Trnka's bleak short being banned in 1970, shortly after the artist's death in 1969, but not before garnering 'international recognition (not only the Jury Prize at the 1965 Annecy, but also the prizes at non-animation festivals in Oberhausen, Melbourne and Bergamo) as a denunciation of Societ control over the arts and media'.[13]

Central to Trnka's symbolic commentary is the contested figuration of the private, interior landscape that is inhabited by, and restricts, the harlequin character. The opening title sequence effectively frames the harlequin's world, first establishing the limits of the interior space both through the construction of a black rectangle – which later reveals the harlequin's room – adrift in the centre of the screen, followed by the title, first in Czechoslovakian as 'Ruka', and then appearing in a number of translations, which appears arranged squarely against the sides of the black rectangle, providing an additional layer of visual containment. The arrangement of the title translations in this fashion suggests a connection between the titular hand character, and the dark space that surrounds the harlequin's interior landscape. This association of the hand with the tight framing of the harlequin's world is further extended halfway through the film when the hand delivers a propagandistic message via television – appearing on the rectangular screen of the television set. Additionally, at the film's conclusion, after the dead harlequin is placed by the hand into a coffin (another rectangular compartment of confinement) the frame collapses inward, once again revealing the emptiness surrounding the interior landscape.

However, this is a contested space, and Trnka offers the viewer a vision of artistic resistance. At the centre of this resistance is the harlequin's determined attempt to remain the master of its own interior landscape, a narrative that is symbolically played out through the repeated refashioning of the harlequin's clay. Every time the harlequin attempts to work the clay into a plant pot, of which we see numerous examples around apartment, the hand seeks to interrupt and alter the harlequin's work. Rather than plant pots, the hand tries to encourage the harlequin to sculpt miniature hands resembling the hand's own image. Initially, this takes the form of *gentle* coercion, but this quickly escalates as the hand forces the harlequin to watch the aforementioned propaganda film – the blunt, rhetorical force of which prompts the harlequin to resist the hand's indoctrination. Going on the attack, the harlequin quickly incurs the wrath of the hand, which, after turning black and forming a fist, smashes violently through on the interior landscape before eventually grasping the harlequin and placing it at forcefully at the potter's wheel. Too dazed to follow the hand's instructions, the harlequin is ultimately seduced by an erotic dance – signified by a hand in a lace glove, which, accompanied by rhythmic music, gyrates slowly under the glow of orange and blue light. In this apparently hypnotic state, and now attached to strings in the fashion of a puppet, the harlequin is placed within a birdcage where it begins to sculpt a giant pointing hand from a large block of stone. In recognition of this compliant reconfiguration of the symbolic landscape (the stone), the harlequin 'is awarded medals and honours as if he was, indeed, an artist willingly in the service of the state propaganda, as all notions of his resistance, and ideological difference, are ignored'.[14] Ultimately, the harlequin regains his spirit, after burning through his strings with candle flame he topples the giant hand statue, breaking the bars of the cage. As he falls through the surrounding void, he intermittently breaks through images of the hand as they had appeared in the early propaganda, before climbing back into his room. After boarding up all possible entry points, the harlequin places his remaining plant pot on top of a cupboard for protection. However, the hand's forceful attempts to enter cause the plant pot to fall, hitting and mortally wounding the harlequin in the process. While the hand and harlequin characters take centre stage, it is the contested landscape of the film, the repeated symbolic reconfiguration of a malleable animated landscape, which lays the foundation upon which Trnka is able to construct his political critique.

While the work of surrealist filmmaker Švankmajer, perhaps the most symbolic of all animators, arguably deserves a section – if not a chapter – dedicated solely to the exploration of what could be justifiably termed the Švankmajerian landscape, the desire to cover as much ground as possible in this chapter dictates that our discussion of Švankmajer be limited to a few brief observations. Throughout his work, Švankmajer consistently challenges the implied binary between character and landscape, whether with a surrealist intent to fashion double images, or as means to draw repeated attention to the materiality of his animated worlds – and, by extension, our lived world – in order to defamiliarize the once familiar.

Švankmajer's 1971 short *Jabberwocky*, which offers a visual counterpoint to the Lewis Carroll poem that is read in voice over during the film's opening sequence, provides a good example of his symbolic use of landscape. Given the care taken by Carroll to achieve a similar effect in his poem, it is fitting that Švankmajer invests such effort to defamiliarize the landscape in *Jabberwocky*: from the cupboard, a familiar symbol of the interior, domestic landscape, which roams through a wintery woodland in the film's opening; the invasion of the external landscape, in the shape of creeping vines that overgrow the interior space; to the jigsaw-like pastoral scene that refuses to fall into a settled shape, remaining in a constant state of re-animation, and thereby establishing the repeated visual refrain throughout the film. Then there is the doll, which is literally deconstructed, becoming a surface, an unfamiliar landscape, when several smaller dolls emerge from its body. After passing through the floor of a doll's house by means of a hole in the floor, the dolls are unpicked and transformed by other – more commonly inanimate – animated objects (including a metal bean grinder and a pair of irons) within the room, effectively destabilizing any remaining sense of a stable character–landscape binary. Švankmajer continued to explore this dynamic in many of this following works, with the 1982 *Dimensions of Dialogue* showing Acrimboldo-esque heads evolve into more human-like forms, but only via a regurgitatory dialectic in which each head in turn swallows the other and its constituent parts, which are initially coded in a binary fashion: as natural versus man-made.

Perhaps the most explicit example of this comes in the feature-length *Otesánek/Little Otik* (2000). Here, an element of the exterior landscape, a tree stump, is brought into the interior, domestic realm, at which point it metamorphosizes into an all-consuming creature of destruction – transgressing, in the process, the perceived binaries of natural versus man-made and that of landscape and character. The genius of Švankmajer's animated filmmaking is its ability to highlight the constructedness our world – whether natural or man-made – and the oscillation that occurs in our perception of this space: between seeing the landscape as a whole and the almost simultaneous recognition of its many discrete constituent ingredients. Švankmajer notes:

> For me objects always were more alive than people. More permanent and also more expressive. They are more exciting for their latent content and for their memories, which far exceed the memories of men. Objects conceal within themselves the events they have witnessed... I have always tried in my films to 'excavate' this content from objects, to listen to them and then illustrate their story... This creates a meaningful relationship between man and things, founded on a dialogue, not on consumer principles.[15]

Yet, ultimately, as Švankmajer himself urges in the preface to the publication of his *Faust* script, it is important to recognize that the symbolism of his work – and of any artist, he would argue – must remain open to 'the viewer's own interpretations, which are so necessary for communication to take place with any imaginative work, whether it is painting, poem, or film'.[16] By virtue of its foregrounded materiality, stop motion therefore represents an ideal medium for animators seeking to work on a more symbolic level.

The narrative landscape

In recent years, stop motion has enjoyed something of a mainstream renaissance, with the likes of *A Grand Day Out* (1989), *The Nightmare Before Christmas* (1993), *The Wrong Trousers* (1993), *A Close Shave* (1995), *James and the Giant Peach* (1996), *Chicken Run* (2000), *Wallace & Gromit: The Curse of the Were-Rabbit* (2005), *Corpse Bride* (2005), *A Matter of Loaf and Death* (2008), *Coraline* (2009), *Mary and Max* (2009), *A Town Called Panic* (2009), *Fantastic Mr. Fox* (2009), *The Pirates! In an Adventure with Scientists!* (2012), *ParaNorman* (2012), *Frankenweenie* (2012) and most recently *The Boxtrolls* (2014) and the simulated stop motion of *the Lego Movie* (2014) finding a popular audience as well as, in some cases, critical recognition and Academy Award success. Compared to the works previously discussed in this chapter, it is clear that the animated landscapes present in these films operate in a much more conservative fashion. Whereas Blu, Kirsten Lepore, McLaren, Švankmajer and Trnka, to name but a few, have exploited the metamorphic potential of their chosen medium, the teams responsible for the films listed above typically limit metamorphosis almost exclusively to their characters. However, this is not to say that the filmmakers in question do not make use of the landscapes of their films in important ways.

Perhaps the most obvious role that non-metamorphic landscapes play is to invest the fictional space with a sense of stability, coherence and predictability. It is through characteristics such as these that filmmakers hope to establish believable story worlds, which can in turn add value to the narrative through the details introduced via the *mise-en-scène*. Consider, for example, the landscape that we associate with the *Wallace and Gromit* franchise, films that draw heavily on the North of England for inspiration. This environment does just as much, if not more, to establish the story world than the Yorkshire accent that Peter Sallis affects when voicing Wallace. Then there is the stark contrast between the worlds inhabited by Mary Daisy Dinkle and Max Jerry Horowitz in Adam Elliot's *Mary and Max*, where the detailed *mise-en-scène* frequently provides the basis for the observational exchanges shared between the two pen pals. Non-metamorphic animated landscapes can also provide the stable platform upon which fictional worlds can be built across multiple episodes, as demonstrated by Cosgrove Hall and their serial adaptation of *The Wind in the Willows* (1983–1989), and also in the children's television shows *Postman Pat* (1981–present) and *Thomas the Friends* (1984–present), which, while now reliant on CG animation, originated in stop motion.

For Suzie Templeton, writer and director of the Oscar-winning short *Peter and the Wolf* (2006), creating the right environment in which to stage her film was a critical consideration. Taking advantage of computer modelling software during the film's pre-production, Templeton notes, 'we started right from the beginning designing it in Maya with the set designer, and making the spaces. We knew where we were going to put the camera for each shot, so we could make sure it made sense and it gave the feeling of space'.[17]

Templeton continues, while highlighting the level of work required to create a materially convincing landscape:

> Another thing is that the Polish model makers we were working with were amazing, like really incredible, and they didn't just sort of make us something, they actually made the real objects. The grandfather's house, for example, they

built a *real* house, they really started from scratch and worked out how to do it, so that it was architecturally correct.[18]

As Figure 2.2 illustrates, the time invested in creating the film's three-dimensional set and populating it with convincing, patinated structures, all serves to ensure that the animated landscape of *Peter and the Wolf* feels less like a surface upon which action happens to take place, and more like a believably lived-in space.

While the examples discussed above share a common trait in their construction of depth through three-dimensional sets, director Henry Selick and LAIKA animation studios turned to stereoscopic cinematography for *Coraline* to further enhance the film's three-dimensionality. While stereoscopic, three-dimensional cinema was far from a new concept in 2009, *Coraline* was released on the cusp of a new wave of enthusiasm for the technology as a product of its digital rebirth – a resurgence intensified by the huge international success enjoyed by the stereoscopic spectacular *Avatar* (2009). Looking back through the history of cinema for a similar instance where emerging technology provided a way for filmmakers to extend the narrative impact of the story world, Selick reflects:

> One of the most amazing things in *The Wizard of Oz*, especially when it first came out, was that this fantasy world Dorothy wakes up in is in color. She comes from a black-and-white world on the farm to this world full of magic. I needed an equivalent of that for Coraline. Well, *The Wizard of Oz* did it with color and, in its day, that was a relatively new thing. We are using 3-D technology and the advent of digital projection in this new theatre format to bring 3-D to our

Figure 2.2 A still from *Peter and the Wolf* (Breakthru Films, Se-ma-for Studios, Channel 4 Television Corporation, Storm Studio, Archangel, TV UNAM, Polish Film Institute, Storm Films, 2006)

04/06

film. So, when Coraline leaves her compacted, claustrophobic, colorless life and goes through the secret door in the Other World, each of those places she thinks she knows is expanded and dimensional and rich and gives you a sense of breathing room.[19]

It is a little surprising, given the depth effect achieved by adopting stereoscopic cinematography, that Selick chose not to offer the multiplane camera rigs that were being developed in the 1930s – most expensively at Disney – as his earlier point of technological revolution. Like the three-dimensional effect in *Coraline*, which serves to enhance character and, to a certain extent, anthropomorphosize the animated landscape, the use of the multiplane camera Disney feature films such as *Bambi* (1942) and *The Jungle Book* (1967) makes the animated landscape a key storytelling component; as I have proposed elsewhere, 'the shifting animated landscape of the Indian Jungle becomes an antagonistic presence itself, with its depth providing a seductive framework for potential adventure amidst the omnipresent threat of concealed danger'.[20]

On a practical level, shooting *Coraline* in stereoscope presented the team at LAIKA with a number of challenges during production. Selick recalls how it took 'months to learn that something was going to look awful in 3-D. A lot of our theories proved wrong'.[21] On a stereoscopic production, Selick's remark about the quality of the image could apply just as much to the aesthetic composition as it could to the physical act of viewing the image. With reference to the latter, *Coraline* cinematographer Pete Kozachik notes:

> After constantly looking at 3-D for a year and a half, we expected to develop immunity to extreme stereo. We definitely pumped up our eye muscles, but we also learned to be more eloquent in the new language. We gained an eye for subtle differences in 3-D, even a memory for depth, which helped us set up shots for emotional effect as well as audience comfort.[22]

Kozachik also lobbied for a more conservative use of extreme moments of stereoscopic depth:

> Besides getting more intuitive about setting up, we learned to make the most of a big 3-D moment – it takes planning, not overdoing IO [Interocular] distance [IOD]. That includes using modest settings for several shots leading up to the big moment.
>
> We learned that a quick cut doesn't register 3-D in the eyes of the viewer. The shot has to be onscreen long enough to fuse, and only then can you concentrate on the subject. Increasing IO[D] is futile on a short shot; it exacerbates viewer difficulty and does not make the shot feel deeper.

Although we strove to avoid 'coming out' shots for pure gimmickry, Coraline includes a few legitimate uses of the effect. In every case, we made the emergence as slow as the tempo allowed so viewers could follow. We also did our best to connect emerging objects to the background – an outthrust hand was much more effective when the arm and shoulder were also visible.[23]

Additionally, more traditional practical strategies were also employed, such as creating props 'using forced perspective to achieve a desired 3-D optical effect'.[24]

Recognizing the aesthetic parallels with German Expression, Scott Higgins notes how the distorted sets of *Coraline*'s Other World locations recall the raked interiors in F.W. Murnau's *Sunrise* (1927), but take on added power by virtue of their stop-motion construction: 'While the effect in 2-D is unsettling, 3-D amplifies the contradictory cues because cinematographers narrowed the IOD in these shots to reduce stereo depth. The dimensional space behind the screen is shallower than that suggested by the sets' forced perspective'.[25] Here, the fact that the *Coraline* crew were capturing each ocular perspective independently by moving the digital stills camera fractionally side to side means that the film's 'visual design effectively isolates two and three-dimensional cues as independent variables; an experiment made possible by the use of miniatures and the obsessive frame-by-frame control of stop motion'.[26]

Ultimately, the capacity of stereography to give a sense of miniaturization (due to the fact that objects at a distance from the implied plane of the screen retain a greater sense of volume than would otherwise be the case with conventional two-dimensional cinematography, and also because objects subjected to negative parallax are forced to occupy the same perceived space as the audience and the arena (cinema or living room) in which the three-dimensional film is being viewed, and therefore appear smaller by comparison) arguably enhances the aesthetic appeal of *Coraline* as a stop-motion film. While this sensation of miniaturization would be an unwanted side effect of the stereoscopic process when watching films such as *Avatar*, *Life of Pi* (2012), *Gravity* (2013) or *Interstellar* (2014) for the explicitly and self-reflexively hand-crafted story world presented in *Coraline*, this brings added value – giving the viewer the sensation of looking at a 'diorama-like space behind the screen'.[27] As Selick notes, 'it's easy to punch people in the eyes with 3-D, and that's appropriate for *My Bloody Valentine* [2009], but for this film, it was more about bringing people into the space as Coraline is seduced by this Other World'.[28]

Conclusion

Michael Fink, a veteran visual effects supervisor who has helped create dozens of animated worlds in the digital domain over the past thirty years, discusses the process of creating cinematic stories in a compellingly poetic fashion:

> I often see the telling of cinematic stories as very similar to jazz music. In all jazz that has staying power, that moves and is emotional and compelling, there is a core structure around which the music is woven. Jazz artists can improvise broadly on that core structure and create beautiful music. But, if they should improvise the structure itself, the music loses its way, and the arc of the piece doesn't form. So the best narrative media creators learn to develop a strong structure around which he or she can improvise. He or she creates a core theme that is the solid spine of the piece. Then, as the film takes shape, decisions can be made that are improvisations around the structure, but the film retains the clear sense of that spine.[29]

It is tempting to read the words of 'structure' and 'spine' as related to – if not interchangeable with – 'landscape', thereby capturing the centrality of this element to the production of stop-motion animation. This is unlike traditional mainstream hand-drawn animation, where the animated landscape is constructed with the character action in mind, but is physically created in a separate space to those other planes of animation, thus rendering improvization largely undesirable. In CG animation, while all of the animated elements can co-exist within the same digital space during the creative process, the software structure that underpins the process as a whole, which might be generating in-betweens or automatically re-drawing elements of the virtual set, again limits the ability of the animator to easily assess all of the freeform opportunities available at any given moment.

Contrastingly, the stop-motion landscape, whether instrumental, symbolic or narrative, is all encompassing: it provides structure and is the practical backbone of production; it is the original frame, which the animator must physically navigate in order to construct the imagined cinematic frame. Hopefully the argument offered in this chapter will find a sympathetic reader, one who is able to recognize that the animated landscapes of stop-motion cinema represent richly visual texts in their own right, and one who will in the future consider these landscapes on an equal footing with the often more prominent animated characters that inhabit them.

Notes

1   Elizabeth Ezra, *Georges Méliès: The Birth of the Auteur* (Manchester: Manchester University Press, 2000), 13.

2   This version of events corresponds with the details described by Ezra in *Méliès: The Birth of the Auteur*, 28, by David A. Cook in *A History of Film Narrative* (New York: Norton, 1996), 14, and by Paul Hammond in *Marvelous Méliès* (London: Gordon Fraser, 1974), 34; however, as is often the case with such apocryphal stories, the exact details of this incident vary, with Mark Cousins, in *The Study of Film* (London: Pavilion, 2011), 27, simplifying the plot to include streetcars that jump forward and people that disappear.

3   Paul Wells, *Understanding Animation* (Oxford: Routledge, 1998), 90.

4   Ken A. Priebe's, *The Art of Stop Motion Animation* (Boston, MA: Cengage, 2009) is the most generous text currently available in terms of word count dedicated to the animation of stop-motion landscapes, but the focus remains squarely on how to construct such landscapes in the most efficient manner. The 'how-to' manuals that discuss stop-motion animation production all fall into a predictable pattern, and typically offer some cursory discussion of landscape in terms of set and prop design, as is the case in the Susannah Shaw's *Stop Motion: Craft Skills for Model Animation* (Oxford: Focal Press, 2008), and Tom Brierton's *Stop Motion Armature Machining* (Jefferson, NC: McFarland, 2002) and *Stop Motion Filming and Performance* (Jefferson, NC: McFarland, 2006). The 'Art of' companion books that are released alongside modern animated feature films may also serve as useful entry points, but here discussion is typically limited in favour of numerous reproductions of pre-production illustration.

5   Barry Purves, *Stop Motion: Passion, Process and Performance* (Oxford: Focal Press, 2008), 158.

6   Purves, *Stop Motion*, 163.

7   Blu, 1 January 2010, comment on 'Buenos Aires 06', BluBlu.org, 3 December 2014, http://blublu.org/sito/blog/?paged=101.

8   Giannalberto Bendazzi, 'Quirino Cristiani, The Untold Story of Argentina's Pioneer Animator', trans. Charles Solomon, *Animation World Network*, December 1984 (originally published in Graffiti by ASIFA-Hollywood), accessed 3 December 2014, http://www.awn.com/mag/issue1.4/articles/bendazzi1.4.html.

9   Bendazzi, 'Quirino Cristiani'.

10 Ibid.

11 Ibid.

12 Wells, *Understanding Animation*, 83.

13 William Moritz, 'Narrative Strategies for Resistance and Protest in Eastern European Animation', in *A Reader in Animation Studies*, ed. Jayne Pilling (Sydney: John Libbey, 1997), 40.

14 Wells, *Understanding Animation*, 87.

15 František Dryje, 'The Force of Imagination', trans. Valerie Mason, in *Dark Alchemy: The Films of Jan Švankmajer*, ed. Peter Hames (Trowbridge: Flicks Books, 1995), 128.

16 Jan Švankmajer, *Faust: The Script* (Trowbridge: Flicks Books: 1996), v.

17 Suzie Templeton, conversation with author, 28 April 2014.

18 Ibid.

19 Stephen Jones, *Coraline: A Visual Companion* (London: Titan, 2009), 115.

20 Chris Pallant, 'Animated Landscapes', in *Film Landscapes: Cinema, Environment and Visual Culture*, eds. Graeme Harper and Jonathan Rayner (Newcastle: Cambridge Scholars Publishing, 2013), 191.

21 Thomas J. McLean, 'Mr. Selick's Other-Worldly Magic', *Animation Magazine*, 10 March 2009, accessed 9 December 2014, http://www.animationmagazine.net/ features/mr-selicks-other-worldly-magic/.

22 Pete Kozachik, '2 Worlds in 3 Dimensions', *American Cinematographer*, February 2009, accessed 3 December 2014, https://www.theasc.com/ac_magazine/ February2009/Coraline/page4.php.

23 Kozachik, '2 Worlds in 3 Dimensions'.

24 Jones, *Coraline*, 92.

25 Scott Higgins, '3D in Depth: Coraline, Hugo, and a Sustainable Aesthetic', *Film History* 24.2 (2012): 202–203.

26 Higgins, '3D in Depth', 203.

27 Ibid., 202.

28 Bill Desowitz, 'Selick Talks 'Coraline': The Electricity of Life', *Animation World Network*, 6 February 2009, accessed 3 December 2014, http://www.awn.com/articles/ stop-motion/selick-talks-icoralinei-electricity-life.

29 Michael Fink, interview with author, 21 August 2014.

3

Pixar, 'The Road to Point Reyes', and the Long History of Landscapes in New Visual Technologies

Malcolm Cook

Figure 3.1 *The Road to Point Reyes*, USA, 1983, courtesy of Pixar

Introduction: 'The hunger has begun'[1]

In March 1983 the Computer Graphics project of the Lucasfilm Computer Division, destined to become better known as Pixar following its separation in 1986, embarked on a project to demonstrate their new rendering algorithm.

Having already created the groundbreaking 'Genesis Effect' sequence for *Star Trek II: The Wrath of Khan* (1982) they were experienced in creating computer-generated landscapes and chose as their subject a view of the local vicinity, Marin County's Point Reyes, which also lent its name to their renderer: REYES ('Renders Everything You Ever Saw'). The subsequent landscape image 'The Road to Point Reyes' (Figure 3.1; hereafter 'Pt. Reyes') marks a critical moment in digital imaging.[2]

Prior work from the team, such as the Genesis sequence, had been created at video resolution due to the limits of computer hardware, especially the dedicated memory used to store images, called frame buffers, and the computational capacity of existing hardware for the detailed mathematics involved.[3] Computer graphics had already appeared in other mainstream films but, as with *Star Trek II*, these were always placed within a narrative context that explained their lower resolution, such as appearing on video monitors within the *mise-en-scène* (*Futureworld* [1976], *Star Wars* [1977], *Alien* [1979], *Looker* [1981]) or representing the internal world of the computer (*Tron* [1982]). In other words, they were computer graphics representing computer graphics. The Lucasfilm culture was one where technical excellence was a primary objective, as demonstrated by the Theater Alignment Program (TAP) and subsequent development of the THX standards to improve sound and image in exhibition venues.[4] To meet these standards and have their work incorporated into Lucasfilm productions, or to create a fully computer-generated theatrically released film, it would be necessary to meet or exceed the image quality of the long-established industry standard 35 mm film.

There was no accepted correlation between 35 mm photochemical film and the number of pixels that determined picture resolution for computer graphics. Calculations by Alvy Ray Smith estimated that a resolution 3,000 pixels wide and 1,500 pixels tall would approximate Panavision or Cinemascope widescreen images, but the calculation of a feature film at that resolution would require massive computing power unavailable in 1983. Despite these constraints, the group wanted to demonstrate the theoretical possibility of this goal and signal their intent or 'hunger' to achieve it.[5] By limiting themselves to a single frame, the group could produce their first film-resolution image.[6] Even with this restricted ambition the production of 'Pt. Reyes' took several months of preparation and approximately a month to compute. Lucasfilm's 'one-frame movie' demonstrated the possibility of creating full-length sequences, or even a feature film, composed of computer-generated images that matched the quality of 35 mm film and might represent something other than the output from a computer display.[7]

The technological importance of 'Pt. Reyes' was recognized immediately. The lessons learnt and demonstrated by it were presented as papers at SIGGRAPH, the conference of the Special Interest Group on Graphics of the Association for Computing Machinery (ACM), which, by 1983, had become the most important forum for computer graphics research. Those papers subsequently appeared in the organization's publication *Computer Graphics*, including items by Computer Graphics Project team members Smith, Loren Carpenter, Rob Cook, Tom Duff and Tom Porter who all directly referenced 'Pt. Reyes', while Bill Reeves's work on particle systems used in the image had been published just before work on the image commenced.[8] These papers have since been cited hundreds of times in later research. The landscape was also prominently featured on the title page of *Computer Graphics* and has been used in later historical retrospectives of SIGGRAPH, indicating its status within the industry as a milestone.[9] Its importance to Pixar as a company was acknowledged by a five-feet square print of it being hung in the lobby of their second headquarters in Point Richmond, to which they moved in 1990, seven years after the image's production, suggesting it remained emblematic of the company's goal to create cinema quality movies.[10] It was also used in 2011 as a backdrop to the company's SIGGRAPH promotion of their Renderman software, whose origins lay in the REYES renderer that shares the landscape image's name.[11]

Despite this recognition, 'Pt. Reyes' has been little considered in terms of its aesthetic content and context. It is not simply a technical demonstration, nor is it a teleological marker for the later commercial success of Pixar. While technologically this image marked a further step towards digital cinema, away from the photochemical, its choice of landscape as a subject places it in a historical lineage in which landscapes were repeatedly used as a proving ground for new visual technologies. Landscapes were central to the development of photography, with 'proto-photographers' seeing the fixing of views from nature as a central purpose and test for their experiments.[12] Similarly, in the 1890s, landscapes were among the most celebrated subjects of the earliest moving image presentations. By examining these parallel moments and understanding the genealogy of the landscape iconography deployed in 'Pt. Reyes' we can better understand the implications this image has for computer-generated images more generally.

'The Road to Point Reyes' and the photographic

Photography in general was clearly an important reference point for the Lucasfilm team, with their research papers indicating a clear aspiration to the condition of photography. Cook, Carpenter and Ed Catmull's 1987 paper describing the 'Reyes Image Rendering Architecture' that was being developed and tested during the production of 'Pt. Reyes' clearly states 'high-quality means virtually indistinguishable from live action motion picture photography', while a presentation by Smith in 1982 stated '[the Computer Graphics Project] goal is to bring the digital world... in close communion with the world of real photography'.[13] Photography was also incorporated directly into computer images during this period in the form of textures, which were used to provide visual complexity where the underlying modelling primitives (polygons, quadrics and patches) were too simplistic due to the need to minimize computation.[14] Moreover, 'Pt. Reyes' shares with early photography the desire to establish and define a new technology for visual representation, and uses the depiction of a landscape to achieve this. The tension between nature and culture that Geoffrey Batchen identifies as central to photography's ontology is derived from its use of landscape as subject and aspiration. Early photography's ambiguous position challenges attempts to define its medium specificity, as Batchen argues 'where photography's contemporary commentators want to identify it with *either* nature *or* culture, the medium's earliest proponents offer a far more equivocal articulation that incorporates but declines to rest at either pole'.[15] 'Pt. Reyes' use of the same subject similarly raises the same conflict, seen immediately when viewing the actual image, with the constructed road dominating the foreground, contrasted with the natural scene ahead, a theme explored in further detail later in this chapter.

A more direct and revealing connection between the issues Batchen raises in photography and 'Pt. Reyes' may be found in the work of M. G. J. Minnaert, a scientist specializing in solar research, and in particular his book *The Nature of Light and Colour in the Open Air*.[16] Smith and Cook both acknowledge this work as an important source for 'Pt. Reyes', particularly the double rainbow that provides one of its key natural components.[17] The first edition of Minnaert's book was published in the Netherlands in 1937; it was subsequently translated and published in England in 1940 and reprinted in the United States in 1954. As might be expected from Minnaert's biography, the book is an account of the physics of nature. It contains many explanations of visual phenomena seen in the open air, including mathematical accounts of the principles of reflection and refraction that produce them, formula that would clearly prove invaluable for modelling the same phenomena in a computing machine. Yet Minnaert's book is also punctuated with quotations from literature and references to painters, linking the natural phenomena described to their artistic representation.

Most pertinent for the present context, the chapter that addresses rainbows and related phenomena includes quotations from the Romantic poets William Wordsworth and Samuel Taylor Coleridge. The Coleridge quotation appears as part of the description of 'the glory' the phenomenon in which observers on a raised position with the mist below them and the sun behind them will see not only their shadow outlined on the mist, but also a multicoloured halo centred on their shadow's head. Significantly, as Minnaert states, 'the glory can be seen by each person around his or her own head only', it is an example of the role the observer plays in constructing nature as seen.[18] The quotation from Coleridge's *Constancy to an Ideal Object* reinforces precisely this point. It describes a 'woodman' walking in nature who observes

> An image with a glory round its head.
> The enamoured rustic worships its fair hues.
> Nor knows he makes the shadow, he pursues![19]

While the naive woodman inhabits the eighteenth-century understanding of the observed phenomenon being independent of him, Coleridge and his reader have become aware of the role of the observer in producing that which is observed, exhibiting the nineteenth-century discourses that Coleridge was a key figure in circulating, and, in doing so, shaped early photography.

A photograph of an example of the glory is used as the frontispiece of the 1954 edition of Minnaert's book, indicating its emblematic role, and the importance of the observer is evident throughout Minnaert's book.[20] He eschews the study of any phenomena not visible to the human eye unaided, for example, rejecting the use of microscope or telescope, and equally excludes anything requiring long series of statistical observation or theoretical speculation.[21] His descriptions regularly return to the importance of the position of the observer and its effects upon what is observed, most clearly expressed in the sixth chapter, which is simply titled 'The Eye' and argues forcefully 'the study of nature must necessarily involve the study of the human senses as well'.[22] In its incorporation of artistic references in general, and its adherence to the active observer, Minnaert's book may be seen as a continuation of the complex relationships between nature/culture and subject/

object seen in the development of photography and consequently introduces them as an influence on 'Pt. Reyes'.

While rainbows may not be as noticeably specific to the observer as the glory, they nevertheless have no fixed location and are only visible with the correct alignment of spectator, sun and water droplets, as Minnaert makes clear. Likewise, the quotation Minnaert reproduces from Wordsworth's *The Rainbow* ('My heart leaps up when I behold/A rainbow in the sky') emphasizes the sublime, embodied response of the spectator in relation to their observation of nature. The double rainbow in 'Pt. Reyes' was constructed with reference to this section: Cook confirms great care was taken to ensure the configuration of sun, camera/observer and rainbow adhered to Minnaert's mathematical account. This is evident in 'Pt. Reyes' with the shadows on other objects being consistent with the sun's position behind and to the right of the viewpoint, with the rainbow's curve centred on the antisolar point off the left side of the image.[23]

'Pt. Reyes' may thus be understood as being closely linked with photography as both a direct source and influence, and in its equivocal expression of nature and culture expressed through landscape. Yet it must also be seen as a historically specific extension of those concerns raised by photography, with its use of fractal algorithms being a crucial example.

'The Road to Point Reyes' and the fractal dimension

Fractals were central to the creation of the mountain ranges in the background of 'Pt. Reyes' as well as the rock formations in the foreground. These elements were the work of Carpenter who had been asked to join Lucasfilm on the basis of his fractal work, which he had previously presented at the SIGGRAPH conference in 1980 and subsequently published in *Computer Graphics*.[24] Before joining Lucasfilm, Carpenter was working at Boeing, conducting computer image synthesis research and wanted to be able to create backgrounds for the aeroplane images he created.[25] Exposure to mathematician Benoit Mandelbrot's work on fractals led him to develop an implementation of them for the creation of computer-generated landscapes and develop a showcase for that work, the animated film *Vol Libre* (1980) which he premiered as part of his SIGGRAPH presentation. Fractals also provided inspiration for Smith's work on plant forms, although in giving them a new name 'graftals' he acknowledged they did not follow Mandelbrot in a strict mathematical sense.[26]

The term fractal was coined by Mandelbrot in the 1970s to describe a range of objects and mathematical formulae that share several key characteristics, bringing together under a single name research he had published previously, as well as the work of earlier mathematicians dating back to the nineteenth century. The name fractal is in part derived from their defining characteristic of fractional dimension. Dimension describes the number of co-ordinates required to identify a unique point on a form within mathematics. On a line only one value is needed (x: one dimension), on a surface two values (x,y: two dimensions), and on an object three values (x,y,z: three dimensions). Fractional dimensionality thus describes mathematically a shape between these familiar categories. As Freeman Dyson recounts in his review of Mandelbrot's first book in the journal *Science*, the consideration of such shapes and patterns had been developed in the late nineteenth and early twentieth centuries by figures such as Jean Perrin and Henri Poincaré, but

> these new structures were regarded by contemporary mathematicians as 'pathological.' They were described as a 'gallery of monsters', kin to the cubist painting and atonal music that were upsetting established standards of taste in the arts at about the same time. The mathematicians who created the monsters regarded them as important in showing that the world of pure mathematics contains a richness of possibilities going far beyond the simple structures that they saw in nature. Twentieth-century mathematics flowered in the belief that it had transcended completely the limitations imposed by its natural origins.[27]

Mandelbrot's singular contribution to this area of mathematics, an area that for most of the twentieth century had been considered a form of abstraction removed from nature, was to identify that it closely modelled patterns and shapes seen in nature. Mandelbrot had put forward such observations in earlier work, such as his paper 'How Long Is the Coast of Britain? Statistical Self-Similarity and Fractional Dimension.'[28] In that paper Mandelbrot showed how the measurement of the length of the coast of Britain was dependent upon the scale at which it was measured, that as one measured at an ever closer level so the measurement increased and approached infinity, and that fractional dimensionality offered a way to model this situation. It was the publication in English of his 1977 book *Fractals: Form, Chance and Dimension*, along with its 1982 revised edition titled *The Fractal Geometry of Nature* that brought his ideas to a wider audience and popularized the term fractal.[29] As the title of the revised edition makes clear, these works identified the same characteristics in a range of natural phenomenon, including mountains, rivers, island groupings, diamonds, as well as the human body's vascular, respiratory and nervous systems.

In this respect Mandelbrot's work may be seen as further extending the convergence between observer and observed discussed previously. Mandelbrot's example of the length of Britain's coastline being dependent upon the scale at which it is measured points towards the role the position of the observer plays in determining the measurement of what is observed. Furthermore, fractals describe not only nature 'out there' but also are fundamental to the embodied observer 'in here', in our corporeal existence. Yet, as a model for aesthetic practice, as they are adopted in 'Pt. Reyes', fractals constitute a significant break from the implications of that same history.

Jonathan Crary indicates that one aesthetic result of the 'transformation in the makeup of vision [that] occurred in the early nineteenth century' was the seed of the shift to abstraction: 'modernist painting in the 1870s and 1880s... can be seen as later symptoms or consequences of this crucial systemic shift'.[30] As we have seen in Freeman Dyson's account, for much of the twentieth century the mathematics underlying fractals were likewise seen as abstract, pure mathematics, unconcerned with nature as a model. Mandelbrot's intervention reversed this: in identifying these patterns in nature and naming them fractals he realigned them as an index of nature. Crucially, Mandelbrot acknowledged the role computer graphics played in supporting his arguments. Hand drawing of fractals was 'prohibitive', whereas computers could calculate and visualize these forms with ease, making their connection with nature palpable.[31] The mutually responsive relationship between fractals and computer graphics thus marks a historically specific moment that 'Pt. Reyes' is a beneficiary and exemplar of, signally a new aesthetic paradigm in computer imaging. From the 1950s to the 1970s John Whitney had used the capacity of computers, analogue and digital, to calculate complex pure mathematics and paired it with the creation of abstract, non-figurative images that extended modernist painting into cinema.[32] 'Pt. Reyes' adoption of fractals to create a figurative landscape is not an aesthetic corruption of an essential quality of computer technology, rather it is an expression of the new understanding of pure mathematics as constitutive of nature. The natural landscapes in 'Pt. Reyes' are not synthetically created by hand but are a single expression of a natural algorithm. Fractals serve as a way for nature to self-inscribe itself through the technology of computers, refiguring, but not resolving, the nature/culture dichotomy in new ways.

Landscapes and cinema: Technology and sensation

As we have noted briefly, landscapes played a central role as a proving ground for early photography, offering a site for the interaction of discourses of nature and culture. 'Pt. Reyes' photographic aspirations, the use of landscape as a subject and the methods used to depict it can be seen to engage those same concerns. Of course, it was not simply photography that provided the context for the work at Lucasfilm, but also motion photography or cinema. Landscapes played a similarly central role in early cinema, but inflected with the new technology's ability to depict movement, as well as wider social issues, particularly those in the United States, including the expansion of railroads, the closing of the frontier and the formation of the National Parks in the late nineteenth century.

The depiction of landscapes is evident in some of the earliest moving images produced, including Robert Paul and Birt Acres's *Rough Sea at Dover* (UK, 1895), the Lumière's *Barque Sortant du Port/Boat Leaving the Port* (France, 1895) and Edison's *Surf at Monterey* (US, 1897), all of which use the moving sea as their subject. Both the Paul/Acres and Lumière films overtly engage with the nature/culture dichotomy seen in photography. In *Rough Sea at Dover* the landscape has been framed so as to depict the waves crashing against a harbour wall, while in the *Barque Sortant du Port* we see three men in a rowboat battling the rough waves, while several ladies and a child watch from the relative safety of an artificial harbour wall. In each case there is a thematic contrast between the surging sea and the technologies attempting to contain it. While the Edison film features only natural subjects visibly, it may nevertheless be considered to point towards the moving image camera's ability to frame, capture and contain nature.

Early cinema did not simply replicate modes of representing landscapes from earlier forms, however, and as Tom Gunning has argued it may be seen as a significant break from them. In his 2010 essay 'Landscape and the Fantasy of Moving Pictures: Early Cinema's Phantom Rides' Gunning places early cinema's depictions of landscape within the context of two predecessors, landscape painting and the panorama.[33] Gunning shows how the tradition of Ideal Landscapes, from Claude Lorrain through to the American 'Great Picture' movement, offered the promise of expansion and immersion into the landscape they depicted, suggesting a depth to the landscape that might be entered into. This was achieved through a variety of techniques including linear perspective, the placement of figures within the image, and paths or streams that offer a route into the landscape. Within American traditions these aesthetic concerns can be linked to a wider social one, the desire to depict not only the scale of the landscape but also the manifest destiny of the nation to expand into it. Of course, static landscape paintings could only offer the potential for this expansion, not its realization. In contrast, early cinema fulfils a technological expansion into the landscape, a representational extension equivalent to the physical expansion offered by the railroads, upon which these early films were dependent for their mobile viewpoint. As Gunning states, 'as opposed to the carefully framed, distanced and *static* picture offered by Claudean Ideal Landscape, early landscape films actually moved into the landscape via technology'.[34]

As this quotation suggests, Gunning also sees landscape painting as contemplative, contrasting it with the experiential mode of viewing early landscape films. Following Iris Cahn, he traces this shift in the spectatorial mode of landscapes, showing how the expansion of the frame and changes in exhibition practices in both the Great Picture tradition and the panorama, that other important nineteenth-century venue for the depiction of landscapes, inaugurated an increased attention to the experience of landscape over its rational appreciation.[35] This would be fully realized in early cinema where the phantom train ride may be seen an exemplar of Gunning's influential 'cinema of attractions', in which the sensation of the embodied spectator is aroused.

'The Road to Point Reyes' and the cinematic

Early moving image depictions of landscapes are an important reference point for the production of 'Pt. Reyes'. In his seminal essay on the cinema of attractions, Gunning directly links the spectacle of early cinema with what he calls 'the Spielberg-Lucas-Coppola cinema of effects', and the Lucasfilm Computer Graphics project might be expected to exemplify this connection, given their primary objective was to incorporate digital technology into Lucas's filmmaking activities.[36] It is tempting to adhere to this line of argument: the Genesis sequence in *Star Trek II* offers a moment of technological spectacle in that narrative film and presents a penetrating journey into the landscape it depicts, the latter quality shared with Carpenter's *Vol Libre*. By depicting landscapes through these soaring, unbounded camera movements, these films anticipate the unbridled exploration of computer-generated worlds that have become commonplace in later films utilizing this technology.[37] Yet 'Pt. Reyes' cannot be straightforwardly accounted for in these terms, and despite being underwritten by Lucasfilm and being described as a 'one-frame movie' by its makers, in many respects may be seen as a return to the painterly depiction of landscape.

As with the traditions of painting that Gunning and Cahn discuss, 'Pt. Reyes' offers the promise of expansion, both of and into the frame. As recounted earlier, one of the primary aims of 'Pt. Reyes' was to demonstrate the ability to produce images on a large scale that could be projected to be indistinguishable in quality from photochemical 35 mm film images requiring considerable effort to move beyond the 512 × 512 pixel resolution of existing frame buffers. Computer-generated images had rarely, if ever, been produced on such scale before, and in this regard 'Pt. Reyes' may be considered an inheritor of the 'Great Picture' tradition, expanding the scale of the representation to match the grandeur of the landscape depicted. Yet, in another sense, 'Pt. Reyes' has an indeterminate scale, and may thus be considered akin to cinema, in which scale is determined at the point of exhibition by the *dispositif* of screen, spectator and machinery, not at the point of production. During production it would have been viewed on a small scale on the raster monitors available at the time, and then mostly in a fragmented state until final rendering could be complete. As suggested earlier the image appeared in print in SIGGRAPH's *Computer Graphics* journal, projected as a 35 mm slide during presentations, and later printed at large scale for Pixar's Point Richmond headquarters. Like the fractals that were used to make up the image, 'Pt. Reyes' has no inherent scale, dependent upon the contingency of the observer's position in relation to the image.

As a static image 'Pt. Reyes' cannot offer the movement into the landscape that Gunning identifies as crucial to early cinema's depiction of landscapes.[38] Using the iconography of earlier landscape depictions, 'Pt. Reyes' expresses the historical moment it represents through potential, rather than actual, movement into the image. Both the image and its title are centred on a road as a subject, a thoroughfare offering passage to another place, but, as implied already, the destination is not only, or not simply, a geographical one, but also a historical and technological one.

Point Reyes is a geographically specific area, located within Marin County in California. As such the title 'The Road to Point Reyes' offers a negotiation of nature and culture, the constructed road offering to transport the viewer into nature. More specifically, as a part of the Pacific coastline, Point Reyes represents the geographical extent of the West, the absolute limit of westwards expansion and America's manifest destiny. The area has also been designated part of the

National Park System (since 1963), the need to preserve the space indicative of a growing awareness of the limited, not limitless, bounds of American natural resources. Thus, in contrast to the American 'Great Picture' whose 'imagined trajectories into the distance increasingly manifested a national sense of destiny in the westward course of the empire', the imagined journey of this picture marks the end of the frontier.[39] Nevertheless, 'Pt. Reyes' does not express a sense of melancholic lament that might be expected of such a location. Cook suggests the original subject for the image was an overlook, a point on the coast with a car park where sightseers could stop to admire the coast, which would carry a much greater sense of the finality of the position.[40] In shifting the subject to a road, especially with the end of the rainbow at its vanishing point and its curve leading off towards the rainbow's centre, 'Pt. Reyes' offers the viewer a sense of optimism and purpose that would seem to derive from more than the landscape's geographical implications.

Marin County, within which Point Reyes National Seashore is set, is not only an area of outstanding beauty but was also the location for Lucasfilm at the time, and its title may be understood as offering an account of the Computer Graphics team's journey to Lucasfilm, widely considered one of the centres of excellence for graphics research at that time. 'Pt. Reyes' is a catalogue of the techniques that brought the team together: Carpenter's work on fractals, Reeves's work on particle systems, Cook's work on textures and shading, Porter's work on compositing and Smith's work on 'graftals'. Likewise, the team came to Lucasfilm in Marin County from a wide area: Carpenter from Boeing in Seattle, Reeves from the University of Toronto, Cook from Cornell University, Porter from Ampex in California (a major producer of tape recording equipment and consumables who were expanding into video paint systems), and Smith from Stanford University via the New York Institute of Technology, Xerox Parc and the Jet Propulsion Laboratory (JPL).[41] Thus, this still image may be considered to incorporate a historical account of the development of the computer technology used to create it and the geographical journey the team had taken to arrive at Lucasfilm.

At the end of that historical journey is not only a geographical location (Point Reyes) but also a technology (REYES), the name given to the group's renderer, the name reverse engineered from the acronym: 'Renders Everything You Ever Saw' or 'Renders Everything You'll Ever See'.[42] The destination of 'Pt. Reyes' is both a natural, geographical location and a technological development. As a consequence, the national destiny this road offers is less the expansion into limitless geographical space: as described above, Point Reyes the place marks the end, the limit of that expansion. Rather it offers a new frontier, an expansion into a technological space, the limitless potential of representation through technology.[43]

The dialectic between nature and culture is again clearly in evidence here, yet never stable and resisting binary opposites. As 'Pt. Reyes' makes clear, the area of Point Reyes is most easily accessible through the manufactured road, a visitor's entry into the natural space is mediated by a manufactured route, although here the motorcar and the road become a twentieth-century analogue to the nineteenth-century railroad and train. Likewise, conceptually, the idea of Point Reyes as a natural space is based on cultural constructions. We have already seen how Point Reyes as a geographical location may be framed through the discourses of the American West, as the physical limit of the frontier. More specifically, the region in which Point Reyes sits had been portrayed on numerous occasions, establishing an iconography of its representation. In the nineteenth century, American painters, including Albert Bierstadt and William Keith, had depicted Mount Tamalpais, a peak in the same region, now covered by the Mount Tamalpais State Park, linked to the Point Reyes National Seashore via a third park: the Golden Gate National Recreation Area. Mount Tamalpais was also featured in the Edison film *Panoramic View of the Golden Gate* (1902) an example of the phantom train rides Tom Gunning discusses, a significant departure from the earlier representations, indicating the diachronic nature of the image of the area. Given this history of its representation, Point Reyes cannot be considered an unmediated natural feature. This is institutionally acknowledged in the designation of the area as a part of the National Parks, an act that Richard Grusin has argued is in itself technological: 'to establish a national park is to construct a complex technology, an "organic machine" that operates according to and within discursive formation, a set or network of discursive practices'.[44] This is by no means to deny the area's beauty or importance to ecological diversity, merely to acknowledge that such designations are culturally and historically specific. Point Reyes cannot be considered unmediated nature; rather, it is a landscape, framed by access methods, prior representation and its designation as national park, even before its representation in 'Pt. Reyes'.

Similarly, we have seen that 'REYES' as a technological destination, encompassing the renderer as well as the broader computer technology it presents to the world, remains intimately bound up with nature. The textures of the road and fenceposts, the visible signs of human intervention in the landscape, are perversely the only elements that offer a direct trace of the world, dependent as they are on photographic images. Equally, we have seen already how fractals, born from pure mathematics, seemingly the invention of the human mind, have come to be understood as having strong affinities with natural phenomena, including the topography of the brains that observed them.

Even the name of the technology 'REYES' expresses an equivocal perspective on the fundamental balance between nature and culture. On the one hand, 'renders everything' is suggestive of an objective, totalizing intention, yet the role of the observer in constructing the observed is acknowledged by the suffix 'You Ever Saw'. This uncertainty is evident in wider attempts to name the activity the group was undertaking. 'Computer Graphics' was the dominant term used, exemplified by its use as the title of the SIGGRAPH publication and the Lucasfilm team being called the Computer Graphics Project.[45] In his 1984 paper describing his 'graftal' plant algorithms, Smith suggests the term 'Computer Imagery' to differentiate new procedural methods from work built only from Euclidean geometric primitives. Smith also uses the non-capitalized 'computed pictures' to describe the work the Lucasfilm group undertook.[46] A 1983 article by Smith broadens the scope of what is being attempted in 'Pt. Reyes' even further by labelling it simply 'Digital Filmmaking'.[47] As with the struggle proto-photographers and early moving picture pioneers had in settling on a common name for their activities, this hesitancy in naming is indicative of an uncertainty as to where 'The Road to Point Reyes' would lead in both practical and philosophical terms.

'The Road to Point Reyes' and the computer graphic

The tension over the terms to use in describing 'Pt. Reyes' and the techniques underlying it is indicative of its status as a liminal work and raises the question of the relationship between this image and its wider historical implications. As the first film resolution image produced by the unit that would form the basis of Pixar, whose *Toy Story* (1995) is commonly considered 'the world's first computer animated feature film',[48] 'Pt. Reyes' might be understood primarily in these terms. Such a position, evident in most accounts of this image, is teleological, simply projecting later developments back to this early period, and as such is historiographically problematic and cannot fully account for this image. Despite the clear causal links between 'Pt. Reyes' and the later founding and development of Pixar, it does not unequivocally point to that end.

Most obviously, as a still image with no human or anthropomorphized characters visible, 'Pt. Reyes' challenges any definition of it as 'animated' and certainly does not evoke the Disney character animation tradition with which Pixar is now closely associated. John Lasseter only joined the Lucasfilm group from Disney after 'Pt. Reyes' was complete, and even following his arrival the idea that the organization was inevitably destined to its eventual shape is problematic. After all, this was a company divested by Lucasfilm because it did not fit George Lucas's vision for content creation, and its spin-off financed by Steve Jobs who was closely associated with Apple, primarily a computer hardware manufacturer.[49] Certainly, individuals at the company aspired to the production of computer-animated films, with Smith's description of the 'hunger' for the computer power to achieve this in his presentation to the United States Congress being the best contemporaneous evidence.[50] Yet, at the time of its separation, Pixar was presented as a computer hardware and software manufacturer, encapsulated in the adoption of the name of their only commercial product, the Pixar Image Computer, as the company name. Furthermore, this hardware was not exclusively aimed at filmmaking, and was being touted for medical, geographic and other scientific imaging purposes.[51]

In addition to the ambiguous relationship 'Pt. Reyes' has with animation, it also points to two other fields of artistic and entertainment activity. In the same period that Carpenter was contributing his work on fractals to create the mountains in 'Pt. Reyes', he was also using the same principles to create interactive mountain ranges for the Lucasfilm computer game *Rescue on Fractalus!* (1984), working within the technical constraints of the Atari 8-bit series of home computers.[52] This game offered the player an unprecedented opportunity to explore the computer-generated landscape interactively. Thus, 'Pt. Reyes' points to the potential for the interactivity seen in videogames and virtual reality. Simultaneously, 'Pt. Reyes' offered a demonstration of the high-end techniques for image compositing that would be an important component in allowing computer-generated imagery to be incorporated into live-action footage for the purposes of special effects, an aim achieved in the Computer Graphics project's contribution to ILM's work on *Young Sherlock Holmes* (1985).[53]

'The Road to Point Reyes' offers to lead to not only computer animation, but also medical and scientific imaging, interactive video and computer games, and photorealistic special effects, all of which remain important venues for computer animated landscapes. In each case, the association not only disavows a teleological reading of 'Pt. Reyes' that has it only and directly leading to *Toy Story* and Pixar's subsequent films, but they point again to an inherent dialectic between nature and culture in computer animation. Medical and scientific imaging and photorealistic manipulation of images have a commitment or aspiration to objective nature, at least at the level of the visual, while feature-length computer animation and videogames are oriented to culturally determined meaning, to the artificial construction of worlds and interactive control that sees the observer become a participant or protagonist.

The liminality of 'Pt. Reyes' may thus be seen as a challenge to the institutional history of Pixar and, given that company's centrality to it, the history of computer animation more generally. Furthermore, 'Pt. Reyes' not only brings into question linear histories, but also as a formative example of computer animation provokes questions of attempts to provide a definition or medium specificity for digital cinema, not least whether those two terms are synonymous. This is not the place to rehearse the many, multifaceted discussions of this topic, given its intersection with central concerns of film theory, including indexicality and the implications of digital technology for cinema. Limiting ourselves to the observation that such theories have a tendency towards either cultural[54] or natural[55] explanations and definitions, we can see that 'Pt. Reyes' equivocal expression of the dichotomy between nature and culture challenges the ability of essentialist theories to fully account for it.

Landscape as a subject is central to this paradox. Tom Gunning observes that 'placing a view of nature within a frame, fixing that view within a geometrical frame of reference, defined landscape as an art form.'[56] Landscape is, by definition, caught in a tension between nature observed and the means by which it is framed, be it the subjectivity of the observer or a mediating technology. The earlier visual technologies of photography and cinema used the depiction of landscapes to explore the implications of their technological, indexical reproduction of nature, reflecting wider social and cultural developments but never fully resolving the nature/culture dichotomy. The creation of images using computer technology might be expected to reject such conflicts, to embrace artifice or even abstraction, to become painterly in outlook. 'Pt. Reyes' and, it may be argued, the computer animation that preceded and followed it, did not do this. Continuing the complex, contradictory position between nature and culture seen in cinema and photography, while manifesting historically specific cultural shifts, 'Pt. Reyes' offers a snapshot of the conflicts involved in its destination and goal, to 'render everything you ever saw'.

Epilogue

Disney's most recent blockbuster film *Frozen* (2013) provides one supporting case for the continuation of the concerns seen in 'Pt. Reyes' in recent computer animation. Landscapes play a central role in the film, serving an expressionistic purpose in reflecting the lead character Elsa's feelings, as she constructs an ice palace for herself and inadvertently turns the whole of her kingdom, Arendelle, to an eternal winter. Elsa's control over the landscape is not simply a metaphor for a mastery over nature, be it rooted in computer animation (it is no simple return to painterly control) or wider cultural discourses of national identity. Rather the landscape is an expression of Elsa's *natural* self, derived from a magical force she has from birth that is never rationalized or explained in the film. Importantly, her mastery is expressed in natural terms, as snow and ice, and built upon patterns inherent in nature including snowflake fractals and fibonacci sequences.

Equally in production terms the film might be understood as the latest demonstration of completely digitally created images rejecting any trace of the natural world or the photographic basis of cinema. Yet, it is also the latest showcase of the simulation of natural phenomenon, with the film's snow and ice effects heavily emphasized both in publicity and in promotional material and SIGGRAPH papers.[57] Thus, *Frozen*'s landscapes are tightly bound up with the same concerns evident in the first one-frame computer animated film: nature/culture, technology/art, photorealism/painterly fabrication. CGI's conflicted personality is (virtually) embodied in Elsa, as demonstrated in her show-stopping song *Let It Go* with its line 'my soul is spiralling in frozen fractals all around'. Not only have fractals become a popular cultural reference point by 2013, but also the lyric erases clear boundaries between nature and culture: nature expressed as the personal, subjectivity expressed as natural 'I am one with the wind and sky'.

Acknowledgements

The author wishes to express his gratitude to Loren Carpenter, Rob Cook and Alvy Ray Smith for generously sharing their time and thoughts during the writing of this chapter.

Notes

1   Alvy Ray Smith used this term in his presentation to the United States Congress on 21 October 1983 as part of its investigation into Supercomputers: Committee on Science and Technology, Computer Power for Film and Flight: Technical Memo No. 95 First Session, 1983, 72.

2   The basic history of the development of the Computer Graphics Project, including its origins at the New York Institute of Technology (NYIT) and its future as Pixar, is recounted in many sources, which present to a large extent the same narrative. Examples include Karen Paik and Leslie Iwerks, *To Infinity and Beyond!: The Story of Pixar Animation Studios* (London: Virgin, 2007); David A. Price, *The Pixar Touch: The Making of a Company* (New York: Alfred A. Knopf, 2008); Michael Rubin, *Droidmaker: George Lucas and the Digital Revolution* (Gainesville, FL: Triad Publishing Company, 2006); and Tom Sito, *Moving Innovation: A History of Computer Animation* (Cambridge: MIT Press, 2013).

3   Alain Fournier and Donald Fussell, 'On the Power of the Frame Buffer', *ACM Transactions on Graphics* 7.2 (1988).

4   Rubin, *Droidmaker*, 231–233, 80–82.

5   Computer Power for Film and Flight: Technical Memo No. 95.

6   The exact original resolution of 'Pt. Reyes' remains unverified. Alvy Ray Smith and Rob Cook recall the image was 4,096 × 4,096 pixels (4k) requiring the stitching together of 8 × 8 frame buffer images, as they held only 512 × 512 resolution images. Loren Carpenter recalls the image being 2,048 × 2,048 pixels (2k) requiring 4 × 4 frame buffer images. Carpenter's 1984 SIGGRAPH paper suggests 'The background of the picture was computed at 1,024 lines and the foreground at 2,048 lines resolution' implying the lower 2k resolution. In either case the scale of the endeavour was unprecedented for computer-generated images. Alvy Ray Smith, Rob Cook and Loren Carpenter e-mails to the author 18 July–3 August 2014, Loren Carpenter, 'The A-Buffer, an Antialiased Hidden Surface Method', *SIGGRAPH Computer Graphics* 18.3 (1984): 107.

7   Alvy Ray Smith, 'Pt.Reyes', accessed 14 August 2014, http://alvyray.com/Art/ PtReyes.htm.

8   Carpenter, 'The A-Buffer, an Antialiased Hidden Surface Method'; William T. Reeves, 'Particle Systems—A Technique for Modeling a Class of Fuzzy Objects', *SIGGRAPH Computer Graphics* 17.3 (1983): 359–376; Robert L. Cook, 'Shade Trees', *SIGGRAPH Computer Graphics* 18.3 (1984): 223–231; Thomas Porter and Tom Duff, 'Compositing Digital Images', *SIGGRAPH Computer Graphics* 18.3 (1984): 253–259; and Alvy Ray Smith, 'Plants, Fractals, and Formal Languages', *SIGGRAPH Computer Graphics* 18.3 (1984): 1–10.

9   Alvy Ray Smith, 'The Road to Point Reyes', *SIGGRAPH Computer Graphics* 17.3 (1983); and Judy Brown and Steve Cunningham, 'A History of ACM Siggraph', *Communications of the ACM* 50.5 (2007): 56.

10 Alvy Ray Smith email to the author, 18 July 2014.

11 Samad Rizvi, 'Silhouette Clues Us into 2011 Renderman Walking Teapot Design (Update: Design Revealed)', accessed 12 December 2014, http://pixartimes .com/2011/08/02/silhouette-clues-us-into-2011-renderman-walking-teapot-design/.

12 Geoffrey Batchen, *Burning with Desire: The Conception of Photography* (Cambridge: MIT Press, 1999), ix.

13 Robert L. Cook, Loren Carpenter, and Edwin Catmull, 'The Reyes Image Rendering Architecture', *SIGGRAPH Computer Graphics* 21.4 (1987): 95; and Tom DeFanti, 'Nicograph '82 Symposium', *SIGGRAPH Computer Graphics* 17.2 (1983): 92.

14 This topic is discussed by William (Bill) Reeves, one of the Lucasfilm team in a SIGGRAPH panel at the 1983 conference when 'The Road to Point Reyes' was first shown: James Blinn et al., 'The Simulation of Natural Phenomena (Panel Session)', *SIGGRAPH Computer Graphics* 17.3 (1983): 139. Rob Cook confirmed that within 'Pt. Reyes' 'the textures of the asphalt and wood grain patterns were taken from scanned photographs'. Rob Cook email to the author 23 July 2014.

15 Batchen, *Burning with Desire*, x.

16 M. G. J. Minnaert, *The Nature of Light and Colour in the Open Air*, trans. H. M. Kremer-Priest and K. E. Brian Jay (New York: Dover Publications, 1954).

17 Alvy Ray Smith email to the author 18 July 2014; Rob Cook email to the author 19 July 2014.

18 M. G. J. Minnaert, *Light and Color in the Outdoors*, trans. Len Seymour (Berlin and New York: Springer-Verlag, 1992), 248.

19 Samuel Taylor Coleridge, *Constancy to an Ideal Object* (1826) quoted in Minnaert, *The Nature of Light and Colour in the Open Air*, 226.

20 Minnaert, *The Nature of Light and Colour in the Open Air*, ii (frontispiece).

21 Ibid., vi.

22 Ibid., 90.

23 Rob Cook email to the author 19 July 2014.

24 Loren C. Carpenter, 'Computer Rendering of Fractal Curves and Surfaces', *SIGGRAPH Computer Graphics* 14.3 (1980): 9–15.

25 Loren Carpenter email to the author 3 August 2014.

26 Smith, 'Plants, Fractals, and Formal Languages.'

27 Freeman Dyson, 'Characterizing Irregularity', *Science* 200.4342 (1978): 678.

28 Benoit B. Mandelbrot, 'How Long Is the Coast of Britain? Statistical Self-Similarity and Fractional Dimension', *Science* 156.3775 (1967).

29 Benoit B. Mandelbrot, *Fractals: Form, Chance and Dimension* (San Francisco, CA: Freeman, 1977); and Benoit B. Mandelbrot, *The Fractal Geometry of Nature* (Oxford: Freeman, 1982).

30 Jonathan Crary, *Techniques of the Observer: On Vision and Modernity in the Nineteenth Century* (Cambridge and London: MIT Press, 1990), 5.

31 Mandelbrot, *The Fractal Geometry of Nature*, 22.

32 R. Russett and C. Starr, *Experimental Animation: An Illustrated Anthology* (New York: Da Capo, 1988), 180.

33 Tom Gunning, 'Landscape and the Fantasy of Moving Pictures: Early Cinema's Phantom Rides', in *Cinema and Landscape*, eds. Graeme Harper and Jonathan Rayner (Bristol: Intellect, 2010).

34 Gunning, 'Landscape and the Fantasy of Moving Pictures', 37.

35 Iris Cahn, 'The Changing Landscape of Modernity: Early Film and America's "Great Picture" Tradition', *Wide Angle* 18.3 (1996); and Gunning, 'Landscape and the Fantasy of Moving Pictures.'

36 Tom Gunning, 'The Cinema of Attractions: Early Film, Its Spectator and the Avant-Garde', in *Early Cinema: Space – Frame – Narrative*, ed. Thomas Elsaesser (London: BFI, 1990).

37 See for instance *Aladdin* (1992), *WALL-E* (2008) and *Avatar* (2009). This trope is ubiquitous, but these three examples begin to indicate the breadth of its usage.

38 The full temporal implications of 'Pt. Reyes' must remain for future discussion: there is clearly a case for arguing that 'still' images, whether paintings or photographs, are nevertheless dynamic in varied ways, something Alan Cholodenko and Anne Hollander observe in very different ways in their writing. Likewise, given 'Pt. Reyes' aspiration towards movement, as well as the relationship between the still image and the extended time necessary to 'render' it, it might productively be related to Tom Gunning's discussion of animation and the instant. Alan Cholodenko, 'Still Photography?', *International Journal of Baudrillard Studies* 5.1 (2008); Anne Hollander, *Moving Pictures* (New York: Alfred A. Knopf, 1989); Tom Gunning, 'Animating the Instant: The Secret Symmetry between Animation and Photography', in *Animating Film Theory*, ed. Karen Beckman (Durham, NC and London: Duke University Press, 2014).

39 Gunning, 'Landscape and the Fantasy of Moving Pictures', 38.

40 Rob Cook email to the author 19–20 July 2014.

41 Rubin, *Droidmaker*, 173, 71, 234, 133, 19.

42 Carpenter, 'The A-Buffer, an Antialiased Hidden Surface Method.'; Alvy Ray Smith email to the author 18 July 2014.

43 In this context it is apposite that the group's previous work on *Star Trek II*, with its focus on 'the final frontier', was inspired by Jim Blinn's work at JPL. Blinn's innovative computer graphic work producing mission visualizations for NASA is the apotheosis of the alignment between geographical expansion through technology and the imagining of that expansion through technologically aided visualization. In this respect Blinn's position is a striking parallel with those painters in the nineteenth century who were commissioned by the railway companies to depict their technological expansion into the frontier. Gunning, 'Landscape and the Fantasy of Moving Pictures', 40; Sito, *Moving Innovation*, 48–52.

44 R. Grusin, *Culture, Technology, and the Creation of America's National Parks* (Cambridge: Cambridge University Press, 2004), 3.

45 Loren Carpenters 1984 paper serves as a source for both usages: Carpenter, 'The A-Buffer, an Antialiased Hidden Surface Method.'

46 Smith, 'Plants, Fractals, and Formal Languages', 1.

47 Alvy Ray Smith, 'Digital Filmmaking', *Abacus* 1.1 (1983).

48 Pixar, 'The Pixar Timeline: 1979 to Present', accessed 6 March 2015, http://www .pixar.com/about/Our-Story.

49 Rubin, *Droidmaker*, 411–414; and Barbara Robertson, 'Pixar Goes Commercial in a New Market', *Computer Graphics World*, June 1986.

50 Computer Power for Film and Flight: Technical Memo No. 95.

51 This positioning of the company is evident in numerous press reports: 'Steven Jobs Buys Lucasfilm Unit', *The Associated Press*, 8 February 1986; 'Steven Jobs's Stake in Pixar', *The New York Times*, 8 February 1986, 35; 'Jobs Buys Lucasfilm Graphics Division', *The Washington Post*, 11 February 1986, E1. Alvy Ray Smith indicates that the perception that Jobs 'bought' the Graphics Division is erroneous. Alvy Ray Smith email to the author, 6 December 2014; http://alvyray.com/Pixar/ PixarHistoryRevisited.htm.

52 Rubin, *Droidmaker*, 302–303.

53 Porter and Duff, 'Compositing Digital Images'; Cook, Carpenter, and Catmull, 'The Reyes Image Rendering Architecture.'

54 Lev Manovich, *The Language of New Media* (Cambridge: MIT Press, 2001); Julie Turnock, 'The ILM Version: Recent Digital Effects and the Aesthetics of 1970s Cinematography', *Film History* 24.2 (2012).

55 Stephen Prince, 'True Lies: Perceptual Realism, Digital Images, and Film Theory', *Film Quarterly* 49.3 (1996).

56 Gunning, 'Landscape and the Fantasy of Moving Pictures: Early Cinema's Phantom Rides', 33.

57 Lewis N. Siegel, 'Frozen on Ice: Rendering Frost and Ice on Frozen', in *ACM SIGGRAPH 2014 Talks* (Vancouver: ACM, 2014); Keith Wilson et al., 'Simulating Wind Effects on Cloth and Hair in Disney's Frozen', in *ACM SIGGRAPH 2014 Talks* (Vancouver: ACM, 2014); and Alexey Stomakhin et al., 'A Material Point Method for Snow Simulation', *ACM Transactions on Graphics* 32.4 (2013).

Part Two

History: National Perspectives

4

Australian Animation – Landscape, Isolation and Connections

Steven Allen

The Australian government's animation webpage states that the key features of the indigenous product are 'animators musing on personal relationships, the environment and the place of the individual in a world of thought and dreams'.[1] All three are prominent in the four films discussed here, *Dot and the Kangaroo* (1977), *FernGully: The Last Rainforest* (1992), *Mary and Max* (2008) and *$9.99* (2008), with particular emphasis on the function of place and the need to belong. Australia's live-action cinema, especially in the wake of the flourishing of cinematic production in the late 1970s and early 1980s (the 'revival'), has been characterized as depicting an innate Australianness through its distinct landscape. Such a tradition does emerge in animation, but its manifestation is modulated by the ontological status of animated images, which I set out in the next section, as well as by its place within the cinematic institution, explored in the section that follows that. Subsequently, I examine animation from a thirty-year period to suggest that the landscapes depicted can be mapped onto a reconfiguration of Australian identity, which shifts from an interiorized, isolationist stance to an outward focus that seeks to connect with the world. Running through all, however, is a sense of disquiet regarding one's place within the landscape.

Australian cinema and landscape

Ross Gibson asserts that 'the land looms large in white Australian culture' embodying 'one of the society's governing obsessions'.[2] Charting, containing, occupying and mastering the land was central to settler society. Falsely ascribing the landscape the status of *terra nullius*, that is, belonging to no one, white settlers laid claim to the continent. Bringing a European eye, the landscape did not contain the familiar markers of 'civilizations', such as cathedrals and palaces, nor did the land give up its meanings: there were no great parklands to suggest human shaping, and yet the low fertility of the soil was in part a consequence of centuries of burning by the Indigenous people. What the settlers saw was in fact an overlaying of their beliefs on the visible. Thus George Seddon concludes, ' "landscape" is a cultural construct' informed by context, and fabricated to serve societal demands.[3] For early settlers, Australia became an environment of enchantment yet also dangers. Peter Pierce has explored the prevalence of Australian narratives featuring lost children, which, through synthesizing the allure of the beautiful land with its threat, deliver cautionary tales for offspring; simultaneously, 'The figure of the child stands in part for the apprehensions of adults about having sought to settle in a place where they might never be at peace.'[4] For both Gibson and Pierce, the landscape functions in relation to belonging, and cinematic representations of Australia reveal much about that relationship.

During the 'revival', Australian filmmakers, prompted by sympathetic funding policies and propelled by a groundswell of nationalist sentiment (governed by economic, cultural and political rationales), produced a series of films that reinvigorated the local film industry and contributed to a conscious act of national identity formation. A primary means for achieving this was through the display of the landscape. Writing in 1987, Brian McFarlane stated that, 'No account of Australian films of the past fifteen years could fail to consider how landscape has been used in fiction films.'[5] Its sustained representation reasserts the cultural significance of place within the post-settler society, for the landscape served 'as a short cut to establishing a distinctively Australian look and feel for their films',[6] whilst renegotiating its post-colonial (cultural) identity, especially in relation to Britain and the United States.

Animation's ability to construct worlds raises fundamental issues in respect of Australian animation defining itself via the country's distinctive landscape. When all is created, how does animation assert such idiosyncrasy of setting, and so stand out on the world stage? A heightened mimetic response can only go so far if the referent has limited recognizability. Australia's live-action cinema could sell itself on its uniqueness of setting during the 'revival', but its animation could not, and it goes some way to explaining the limited number of animated feature films produced in the country at that time.

As the Australian film industry matured, live-action cinema began to look elsewhere for its settings. At the end of the 1980s, McFarlane describes it thus:

> Just as Australian poetry came to terms with a strange and often hostile landscape before addressing itself to the issue of man in society (that is to say, largely, man in urban life), so there seems to have been a need felt on the part of many of the major directors of the new Australian cinema to respond to the physical facts of the country.[7]

Nick Prescott argues changes in the representation of landscape in Australian cinema are tied to such shifts in cultural identity, but are also 'linked with changes and developments in the Australian film industry itself'.[8] Whereas location shooting had been desirable during the years of the 'revival' because it reduced costs of building sets and lighting setups, later increases in funding and the expansion of studio facilities vastly altered the economics. Such rationales, of course, do not underpin animation, and so with no immediate advantage to utilizing the nation's locales, we need to look elsewhere for explanations for landscapes chosen and the depiction of place and belonging.

Australian animation

Harry Julius is regarded as Australia's first animator, making the topical series 'Cartoons of the Moment' in the 1910s, but it would not be until 1972 that the country produced its first feature-length animation: *Marco Polo Junior Versus the Red Dragon*. The intervening years, especially the sound era, were dominated by imported Disney and Warner Bros. films, although alongside these were indigenous short films and adverts, notably those produced by Eric Porter during the 1930s, 1940s and 1950s. Animator and writer Alexander Stitt has argued that *Marco Polo* betrays an 'Americanisation'[9] of the output of Porter's studio (the film features the mythical land of Xanadu and contains only one Australian voice actor[10] in spite of being partially funded by the Australian Film Development Corporation). The uncertain commitment to expressing an Australian identity at a time of active nation formation via film was in part due to the Eric Porter Studios being contracted to produce episodes of American cartoon series. Thus, as Keith Bradbury describes, the United States was 'the primary inspiration for, but also the primary menace to, an indigenous film and animation industry'.[11] As is so often the case with English-speaking nations, its commercial cinema is in a Janus position of trying to emulate the successful Hollywood product, whilst also desiring a distinctive film output for the domestic (and sometimes international) audience. The battle so often rages over representing the local, and as we have seen, in Australia the landscape was key to this.

That US companies were looking to subcontract work to Australia was a testament to the strength of animation in the country. The introduction of television in the 1950s 'led to a boom in animation, one that was assisted by sympathetic government legislation';[12] these included a requirement of broadcasters to employ Australians (1956) and a quota in respect of Australian content (1961). Consequently, television companies began establishing in-house animation studios. The flourishing brought negatives too, namely, limiting the number of film productions and encouraging US studios to set up operations in Australia, with Bradbury declaring 'Hanna-Barbera Productions in the 1970s turned the Australian animation industry into a virtual subsidiary of the American'.[13] The studio would become DisneyToon Studios Australia (1988–2006), which would mostly produce direct-to-video sequels, and so attracted talent away from local productions. Even the in-house studios were not immune, with Artransa (set up by ATN 7, Sydney) 'sub-contracted by Paramount Studios in America' to produce various television cartoon series, including *The Lone Ranger*.[14] Although economically such collaborations were welcomed, there was much debate regarding the content of animated television series, with the criticism that they were American-centric and so did not inform the next generation about Australian culture. The feature-length animations discussed below fit into such debates, with their sense of place key to the construction of a distinctive cultural product.

In 2008, Terri Dentry commented that only 'Three Australian animated features have been produced in the last twenty years, *Blinky Bill* (Yoram Gross, 1992), *The Magic Pudding* (Karl Zwicky, 2000), and *Happy Feet* (George Miller, Warren Coleman and Judy Morris, 2006)' and yet 'Australians punch well above their weight on the world animation circuit'.[15] Rather than features, short films have largely been the success story – a legacy of the earlier television series and funding strategies – but these are increasingly regarded as a foundation for longer works. The Australian government animation webpage states that, 'Today Screen Australia supports the production of short animation as a means of career progression for leading emerging animation talent'.[16] Similarly, the Special Broadcasting Service (SBS) has played a major role in promoting animation, including supporting Adam Elliot's successful short films such as the Academy Award-winning *Harvie Krumpet* (2003), as well as his feature *Mary and Max*. These institutions shape the emerging animations. Alison Sharman, the Head of Commissioning at SBS, declares that the role of the SBS is to encourage the Australian public 'to explore, appreciate and celebrate contemporary Australia'.[17] Similarly, Melbourne International Animation Festival director, Malcolm Turner, states they select films based on a number of criteria but 'believe that films that tell Australian stories, use Australian images – films that sound and look distinctively Australian – should be seen by Australian audiences who don't get enough chances to see their own culture on the movie screen'.[18] Paralleling the SBS sentiments, it shows the ethos of the 'revival' persists, with animation a favoured means by which to explore Australianness. The remainder of the chapter explores how the landscape has informed four animated films and what the relationship with the environment, both 'natural' and man-made, tells us about Australia's changing sense of identity.

Isolation, nature and the lost home

Dot and the Kangaroo along with *FernGully* form what I consider to be a first phase in the representation of landscapes in Australian animation. Undoubtedly different, the two nonetheless share a focus on exploring belonging. The commonalities can be categorized as follows: a distinctiveness of the Australian environment, an isolationist approach to social interactions across borders, a world where communication is transparent, and the home-grown theme of lost 'children' is reworked in relation to what is home.

Dot and the Kangaroo begins with live-action panning shots of the misty, morning bush landscape before cutting to an animated, pale mauve morepork owl emerging from the mountain haze, before the image reveals the photographed crags below. The combination of live and drawn elements would become a defining feature of Gross's studio; used here for the first time, it suggests the film fits into the 'revival' trend of using the Australian landscape to elevate the locally particular, and utilizing location shooting to reduce expenses (in this case, labour and time as opposed to studio sets).[19] Creating a niche to differentiate his animation from those of Hollywood, the duality seems to have impacted on Australian filmmaking, with the combination appearing in the recent live-action film *Look Both Ways* (2005) and television series such as *Noah and Saskia* (2004).

The defining aesthetic of *Dot and the Kangaroo*, its two modes of filming, has implications for our understanding of the bush landscape. Referencing the pictorial qualities of the Heidelberg School of artists, who worked *plein-air* and have been called the Australian Impressionists, the film draws attention to its artifice with its painterly, yet filmed, backgrounds mismatching the animated characters set against it. Working with a (mostly) realistic aesthetic, we are drawn into comparing the two forms of image. The counterpointing is at its most apparent when the real and the cel elide. This occurs repeatedly around water so that when the drawn spoonbill dives into the waterhole it coincides with a real splash, and the platypus emerge from the water with a photographed splosh but land on the bank with illustrated water droplets. Such techniques serve to integrate the two components yet simultaneously expose their different ontological status. The bush backgrounds are given a greater sense of permanence. The imagery works against Gibson's view that the 'very notion of nature is a cultural construct';[20] here it is given the sense of timeless beauty, a magical, unique landscape, full of strange animals (kangaroos, lyrebirds, wombats, platypus) and so falls into the familiar dialectic of nature and culture, or more precisely, nature and humans. The Indigenous people are contradictorily positioned as both part of the bush, and therefore nature and as disrupting the harmony: their dingoes (operating as surrogates) chase Kangaroo and Dot, and Kangaroo states, 'Humans are no good in our bush' because they are 'not fit for this country at all'. In conjunction with the discontinuity of style that elevates the 'natural' bush to a heightened state of reverence, we witness a denial of belonging, a sense of being out of place. The Australian landscape needs to be left alone, to remain as it ever was.

Interestingly, *Dot and the Kangaroo* does not fully adopt the 'revival' cinema trope of representing the landscape in Australian cinema via an 'awareness of menace as well as spectacular beauty';[21] although Dot is lost, scared by a snake and her parents distraught at her disappearance, the bush does not take on the primeval terror of the forest in *Snow White and the Seven Dwarfs* (1937). The footage instead celebrates the landscape as a place to respect not fear, taking advantage of picturesque locations in the Blue Mountains National Park. Furthermore, it sets out to make the bush a parallel world to that of (white) humans. Just as Dot is lost, so too has Kangaroo lost her joey (as a result of human hunters). What enables Dot to bridge the two worlds is that Kangaroo gives her 'the food of understanding'; once eaten, the two are able to communicate. The theme of understanding across different groups is repeatedly mapped onto the landscapes of Australian animation, and in the earlier films tends towards dialogue being easily achieved, albeit temporarily, and only to reveal the incompatibility of parties and an assertion of isolationism. In the case of *Dot and the Kangaroo*, we might take Richard Dyer's designation of 'transparency', which he uses as one of five terms to express how utopian solutions are coded in Hollywood musicals (but also applicable to other forms). For Dyer, transparency refers to 'open, spontaneous, honest communications and relationships'.[22] My point is not to assert that Kangaroo's world is utopian, although it contains some elements that overlap with Dyer's other categories, such as abundance and community; rather it is that the issues of the landscape are made communicable to outsiders. Dot is able to explain she is lost, and Kangaroo can empathize ('I feel just the same myself'). However, there remains an incompatibility in relation to the approach to the land.

When Dot states, 'I have lost my way', Kangaroo believes there is a physical entity that needs to be found. When it becomes apparent that Dot has actually lost her bearings in terms of her house, Kangaroo haughtily replies, 'if you only have one home in one place you must lose it'. It establishes a different conceptualization of the relationship between home and the land. As Gibson notes in a different context, 'homelessness can mean destitution, but it can also mean freedom'.[23] Kangaroo cannot conceive of Dot's predicament for she does not have the mindset of someone from a settler culture, who requires the landscape to be dominated, to become a subject of knowledge. It is in this context we might recall Pierce's comment that the lost child anxiety relates to the colonists' position, there is a longing to return home, with the term acting as an over-determined place of control as much as comfort. The notion of domination comes through clearly in the film, with the platypus providing a natural history lesson (in part via song) that rejects his persistent investigation by biologists ('I can't stand any more books being written about me') whilst emphasizing the mammal's classification as *Ornithorhynchus paradoxus* through the nomenclature forming much of the chorus. Such language correlates to how explorers of Australia's interior documented their searches: 'along with the comprehensive list of the Latin names of all flora and fauna observed en route', it was 'only when land was satisfactorily mapped was it brought into conformity with the Enlightenment ideal of order'.[24] Thus, through inspection and naming the landscape was mastered.

Platypus also stresses that his ancestors had been on earth millions of years before humans, even correcting Dot when she says a million years. Tying the fauna to the land makes them a (relative) constant in comparison with the human interlopers. The difference in attitude to the land is therefore accounted for by the notion of belonging. Dot is eventually returned home, and although she pleads with Kangaroo to stay, the creature is adamant 'my home is out there'. A tracking shot shows the animated kangaroo dissolve into a live-action one hopping at speed across the bush, emphasizing a permanent disconnect from the animated, stationary Dot of the surrounding shots. The film suggests a knowable but separate world that humans do not belong in, and much the same can be said of *FernGully*.

Screened at the United Nations Earth Summit in Rio in 1992, *FernGully* has a more explicit conservation theme, reconfiguring the notion of being lost to encapsulate both a human out of place and the destruction of an environment. Like *Dot and the Kangaroo* it proclaims the need to save the landscape for future generations: where the earlier film is dedicated to 'the children of Australia', *FernGully* is for 'our children and our children's children'. The narrative tells of a young fairy, Crysta, living in FernGully, a pristine rainforest threatened with destruction (humans left so long ago they are seen as mythological). Magi, the maternal overseer of the rainforest, had vanquished the evil spirit Hexxus who had threatened the habitat in the past, but humans clearing the forest destroy the tree he had been ensnared in, releasing the spectre to assault the land via human tools of logging. Through Magi's self-sacrifice, Crysta's planting of a seed to tap into the magical powers of the Web of Life, and a human logger called Zak (who sees the error of his ways), the 'natural order' is restored.

We can interpret *FernGully* as a lost child narrative, with Zak (lost both physically and ideologically through being a logger) rescued by the charming Crysta and benevolent wildlife in the form of Batty Koda after she accidentally shrinks him to fairy size. Just as Pierce argues the small race of moths in Atha Westbury's tale 'Mothland' (1897) function as 'alternative indigenes',[25] so do the fairies in *FernGully*; in both instances it is at the expense of depicting the Indigenous people of Australia. As Smith and Parsons argue, this is done so that only the fairies can personify a harmonious relationship between land and anthropomorphic beings: any sense of Indigenous people living in concert with the land is erased through relegation to the past.[26] It is the fairies not 'nature' that house the regenerative properties, prompting Zak to stop the destruction of the rainforest. Humans are also partly exonerated for the devastation through the presence of the fantastical Hexxus. Nonetheless, it conforms to the pattern of *Dot and the Kangaroo*, whereby a human is made aware of the fragility of the landscape, of the role mankind plays in destroying it, and the assertion that humans do not belong there as it is a distinct yet parallel world. The latter is apparent through Zak, who although now in love with Crysta, must return to the human world to warn them not to destroy the forest. The closing song may state 'Live in our world, not some other world. You don't live in some other world', but evidently we do.

The need to not interfere with the landscape is central to an Australian post-settler society questioning its belonging. The country has some of the toughest quarantine regulations around the globe, shaped by white settlement having resulted in 'some of the highest extinction rates in the world'.[27] That FernGully is special is evidently defined by the magical fairies living there, but the animation supports the tone of the landscape's uniqueness. Combining hand-drawn and computer-generated (CG) animation, the backgrounds are incredibly detailed, with much emphasis on shading to create naturalistic lighting effects of the forest. Leslie Sharman notes that significant care was 'taken to recreate the rainforest's hues', but ultimately sees these lost amidst the 'supersaturated colours of the characters'.[28] However, I tend to support Roper's view, that along with the sense of movement through the forest (via CG animation), the effect is 'entrancing' in terms of creating a spectacular world.[29] More significantly, it again positions the background as different from the foreground, giving the landscape a distinction that we can associate with its permanency (and threat to that). The detail-rich settings may not always come to the fore, but the setting is repeatedly referred to, with Zak exclaiming 'Wow' at a number of vistas he comes across, and proclaiming 'this is so incredible' when he stands on a bracket fungus while surveying the forest, before contrasting it with the 'Traffic. Roads. Lights' of the city. The sense of different worlds is again underlined, with a privileging of an organic landscape that is defined as unadulterated. But we should ask how specific to Australia this is.

Sharman is correct to say the filmmakers are 'tuned to a wider market',[30] and that it is displayed by the film largely avoiding the sustained representation of indigenous species we saw in *Dot and the Kangaroo*. However, there is more than the pair of cassowaries and a kangaroo Sharman notes, with shots of native plants such as *Xanthorrhoea australis*, and the key character for comic relief, Batty Koda, being an Australian fruit bat, although by being voiced by Robin Williams, he loses any regional specificity (it is almost an all-American voice cast). The film reveals a continued introspection by Australia of its landscape and human's place within it. Nonetheless, there is a dual stress, that of a global sense of belonging to the planet, which is not found in *Dot and the Kangaroo*, but will become the focus in the subsequent films. That noted, what ties the film to *Dot and the Kangaroo* is that its 'underlying message is an isolationist one',[31] which suggests an incompatibility of the landscape and humans, for they do not belong there. The familiar Australian anxiety of possession and destruction of the environment remains. As with *Dot and the Kangaroo*, there are initial obstacles to understanding those from another world that might explain the discordancy. Zak uses slang, and has to enlighten Crysta that 'cool' means 'hot', but these misunderstandings are overcome to suggest transparency once more. When Crysta employs the term correctly, his response is 'Yeah, we're communicating now'. Moreover, music via Zak's (now) giant (no longer) personal stereo brings everyone together, and it is via such unity the fairies stave off Hexxus. Zak can aid that community, but he can never be a part of it for he does not belong, just as Dot did not belong in the bush. Ultimately, the visual presence of the landscape, a uniqueness of place, even if not as nationally specific as that portrayed in *Dot and the Kangaroo*, is in attendance, indicating how both films question the contact with humans.

Lost at home

Both *Mary and Max* and *$9.99* are fundamentally different from the earlier films: they are predominantly stop motion as opposed to cel and computer-based animation; they contain adult themes that takes them away from the family audience; and although still raising questions of identity and belonging to your surroundings, are no longer concerned with the 'natural' environment but instead explore the social landscape of the town and city. Indeed, we can characterize the films by their aversion to depicting the bush iconography that had served as a template for national identity. Nick Prescott contends that by the twenty-first century, investment to entice overseas productions meant large-scale studio-based productions could be accommodated in Australia, making city-based films, and therefore city settings, more attractive for home-grown live-action cinema.[32] That animation again follows suit, yet its landscapes are not dependent upon where the film is made, suggests there are cultural reasons alongside institutional factors.

The move towards cityscapes means the loss of the expressly Australian, 'natural' landscape; instead of evoking difference, the familiar location connotes commonalities, the breaking down of borders and the creation of connections.

The tone aligns with the more conciliatory approach to internal divides between the wider Australian community and Aboriginal and Torres Strait Islander peoples, with the National Reconciliation Week now firmly established after being founded in 1996 and Prime Minister Kevin Rudd's parliamentary 'Apology to Australia's Indigenous peoples' in 2008. However, with Indigenous peoples notable by their absence in these mainstream films, it is connections to other nations that seem key. In essence, we might define the sense of identity being formed from looking outwards rather than inwards.

What unites the Australian feature animations discussed in this chapter is their depiction of characters 'lost' in their landscape. Yoram Gross's films have been described thus: 'each story revolves around displaced figures, i.e., characters that are forced from their homeland, or animals whose natural habitat is under threat'.[33] The sentiment can be extended to all films so far discussed. In the later city films, characters are not physically displaced, thus avoiding the explicit colonial disquiet of being lost in another land, rather they are isolated and disconnected from their everyday world: lost souls as opposed to lost children. In other words, we see the continuation of a mediation on the inability to find peace in, and with, the environment, but where the earlier films espoused segregation, these characters are currently isolated and seek out connections.

Although alienation in the city is a 'universal' theme, it takes on a specific nationalist resonance when set against Australia's repeated representation of loss in the landscape. *Mary and Max* and *$9.99* seem to comment on, even redress, what has served as the defining feature of Australian identity. The 'natural' landscape no longer appears to hold its currency. It is perhaps unsurprising; in 2011, 69 per cent of Australians lived in 'major cities' with another 20 per cent in 'inner regional areas', and only 2.3 per cent living in 'remote' or 'very remote' areas.[34] Additionally, over a quarter of the population (29 per cent) were born overseas.[35] Moreover, Australia has experienced a shift in its pattern of immigration, for example, 'the proportion of migrants born in Asia increased from 24% of the overseas-born population in 2001 to 33% in 2011', whilst in the same period those born in Europe decreased from 52 per cent to 40 per cent.[36] The part the land, especially the bush, had played for settler identity is therefore not only greatly reduced in its relevance, but also connotes an anachronistic understanding of multicultural Australia. To reject the landscape is a cultural act.

$9.99, an Australian-Israeli co-production, is so called because it features a book that promises the meaning of life for that sum. The episodic narrative

depicts the lives of neighbours in an apartment block, all of whom are struggling to find meaning and connections: there is the repo man (Lenny) who falls for the model (Tanita) who has a fetish for completely smooth men, his unemployed brother (Dave) who buys the titular book, and their father (Jim), who witnesses the suicidal shooting of the man he refuses to give change to for a coffee. That the beggar becomes a curmudgeon angel who visits the lonely widower Albert gives a sense of the film's black humour, but there is also the lightness of the boy (Zak) who becomes so captivated by his piggybank's smile he sets it free in the park. With the script adapted by Israeli writer Etgar Keret from his short stories, and the voice cast mostly Australian, yet the location never directly named, it is the ubiquitous city. If the setting is vague, the landscape is nonetheless detailed and textured, as well as being of prime concern: the opening shot has the apartment building and its environs emerging from a black background as various interior and exterior lights come on, before the sun, only slightly distinguished from the very pale sky, rises to cast strong shadows. The palette is dominated by browns, sandy beiges and muted primary colours. Throughout there is a sense of sunlight, but contradictorily the sky appears as if it is etiolated, lacking the expected blues so that it merges with the concrete edifices. The sky only becomes truly pronounced at two junctures: a cobalt blue when Albert looks back up to the building after confessing to pushing the angel to his death from the rooftop, and subsequently, a sunset scene of Albert at the Sunshine Coast (said to be what heaven is like).[37] Apart from these rare moments of release, the landscape is at once infinite and claustrophobic as there is only a void beyond the city. Inside the apartment, the tone of confinement continues, with limited windows, and when present, masked by net curtains or oblique angles, and shots of characters in corridors and elevators. The world is robbed of the 'natural' landscape that had dominated the previous animation.

The only expansive outside location is the man-made park. It is here that Dave reconnects with his father, getting him to swim like a dolphin in the lake – the objective of another self-help book he has received. Ironically, the tome is a substitute for the out-of-print text he had sent for: *How to Make People Listen*, which itself appears to be different from the book the film implies he planned to order, which was *Being Heard*. That the latter promised 'No more miscommunication with those that matter' reveals where the film's emphasis lies; rather than transparent communication, all is confused but needs to be resolved. Belonging is no longer perceived in respect of the right to be in a space, but thought about in terms of connections and communications; consequently, some characters, such as the dope-smoking Ron, remain lost, his addiction isolating him in an imaginary world, far removed from his girlfriend. With the land rejected as the defining feature of the nation, and through no longer being deemed special, there is nothing to preserve. The film reconfigures Australia in global terms, via some kind of placelessness where identity comes via exchange not isolation, but with a recognition that communication is not easy. *Mary and Max* similarly points towards the need to connect spaces, but reinstates the national.

Mary and Max unashamedly foregrounds its Australian origins and setting: it begins with a fade-in crane shot that moves down from bush-land hills to suburban homes located via a sign that reads 'Welcome to Mount Waverley'. The shot acts as a metaphor for the rejection of the 'natural' landscape as the defining feature of Australian identity, instead referencing a Melbourne suburb and a series of cultural touchstones: the traditional Australian cake forms the street location of 'Lamington Drive', a Sherrin Australian Rules football sits on a roof, a sprinkler lies on a parched lawn, a mailbox is fashioned in the shape of infamous bushranger Ned Kelly, and there is the ubiquitous barbecue. This is familiar territory for Australians; the voiceover by Barry Humphries helps confirm it for those overseas. It is a different form of distinctiveness, but it exudes Australianness nonetheless. But in many respects it is the antithesis of Australia's appellation of the 'lucky country'.[38] Its envisioning in lumpy Claymation is a world of pale chocolate, sepia and beige that complements the lonely world of Mary (favourite colour brown), daughter of an alcoholic mother and a father who attaches strings to teabags for a living. In a quest to avoid her isolation she writes to a name she picks from a New York telephone book, and so begins a pen pal relationship with Max, who transpires to be a middle-aged, overweight man who has Asperger syndrome. His world is demonstrably black and white, giving Mary's realm a comparative golden hue that suggests its location whilst remaining equally uninviting. Both are effectively alienated from their homes: bullied, shunned, made outcasts, they do not fit the landscapes they find themselves in. They are lost without even leaving home.

The two characters connect via a shared love of chocolate and an animated television show. That the film cuts between these two characters and their visually distinct locations draws attention to space, whilst the reliance upon letters for communication (it begins in the 1970s) stresses time and disjunction ('Nine days, six hours and forty-seven minutes later'). In the gaps, there is speculation and concern regarding meaning, motive and understanding of messages received. For both Mary and Max the world is confusing, based on misrecognitions and false perceptions. For Max, it results from Asperger's, which manifests in a problem understanding non-verbal symbols and anxiety attacks upon receiving the letters, whilst Mary has (in the most part) a child's perception, so that she believes babies come from beer glasses and takes her mother's word that her sherry addiction is merely tea for grown-ups that requires constant testing. But there are also moments of clarity and elation amidst confusion and disappointment, and the aesthetic illustrates these instances of connection – the parcel Max receives from Mary into his black and white home is decidedly brown, whilst the pompom she has knitted for him is a contrasting red. These visualize his number one life-time goal of having a friend ('not invisible') and represents Australian identity in relation to other nations rather than through the introspective depiction of the unique Australian landscape.

Mary and Max is an almost perfect encapsulation of what McFarlane witnessed happening in Australian live-action cinema over twenty years earlier. He notes the best films that dealt with urban living 'show a striking awareness of both city man's lack of solitude *and* of his increased difficulty in forming and sustaining relationships'.[39] The small number of Australian animation features perhaps accounts for its late flourishing in the medium, but we might also consider animation's formal qualities, which enable successful anthropomorphism of indigenous creatures and so supports a greater tendency to situate stories in the wilderness. McFarlane's description suggests an exploration of a universal condition, within which any distinctiveness of the Australian city is not apparent. However, he speculates it might exist in 'a quality of light, a monotonous sprawl',[40] and it is noteworthy that both *Mary and Max* and *$9.99* invest heavily in the tonal qualities of luminosity to depict their cityscapes. It is more productive though to regard the two films as reformulations of the long-standing trend to work through a sense of troubling disconnectedness and being out of place in the landscape. Across the four case study films, *$9.99* contains a mixture of reconciliations, new relationships and breakdowns in partnerships, amidst an entangled, claustrophobic landscape, whilst *Dot and the Kangaroo*, *FernGully* and *Mary and Max* all feature separations tied to the landscape: Dot is left by Kangaroo returning to the bush, Zak returns to the human world leaving Crysta, and Mary discovers Max dead in his apartment when she finally visits the United States. Whether looking inwards or outwards, Australian animation seems adept at exploring a sense of needing to belong.

Conclusion

To attempt a singular classification of feature animation of any nation, however small the number produced, is evidently foolhardy. However, what I have endeavoured to trace is the dominant themes of landscape in Australia's animated films. Of specific concern is the negotiation of a fretfulness regarding dislocation, whether that be in an unfamiliar location or not being secure in your home environment. The theme is underpinned by a long-standing cultural anxiety in settler and post-settler society regarding the landscape and loss. All the case study films seek to reconcile the need to belong within a landscape, whether natural or social. Where once difference was sought, now connections are found, and what formerly required isolation now necessitates continued communication, however faltering. The land still looms large in the Australian psyche, after all, it remains a place defined by vast distances and a diverse, but at times harsh, environment; but its feature-length animation reveals that its Janus position of looking both outwards and inwards is going through a realignment, as increasingly it depicts the country in a global, not merely a national, landscape.

Notes

1   Shevaun O'Neill and Kathryn Wells, 'Animation in Australia', last modified 15 June 2012, http://australia.gov.au/about-australia/australian-story/animation-in-australia.

2   Ross Gibson, *South of the West: Postcolonialism and the Narrative Construction of Australia* (Bloomington: Indiana University Press, 1992), 1.

3   George Seddon, 'The Landscapes of Australia', *Studies in the History of Gardens & Designed Landscapes: An International Quarterly* 21.1 (2001): 1.

4   Peter Pierce, *The Country of Lost Children: An Australian Anxiety* (Cambridge: Cambridge University Press, 1999), xii.

5   Brian McFarlane, *Australian Cinema* (New York: Columbia University Press, 1988), 42.

6   McFarlane, *Australian Cinema*, 72.

7   Ibid., 42.

8   Nick Prescott, ' "All We See and All We Seem…" – Australian Cinema and National Landscape' (abstract for Understanding Cultural Landscapes Symposium, Flinders University, 11–15 July 2005), accessed 30 July 2014, http://dspace.flinders.edu.au/xmlui/bitstream/handle/2328/1565/N_Prescott.pdf?sequence=1.

9   Alex Stitt, 'Animation', in *The Oxford Companion to Australian Film*, eds. Brian
    McFarlane, Geoff Mayer and Ina Bertrand (Oxford: Oxford University Press, 1999), 13.

10 Valerie Carr, 'An "Anonymous Actor"', *The Australian Women's Weekly*, 17 January,
    1973, 7.

11 Keith Bradbury, 'Australian and New Zealand Animation', in *Animation in Asia and
    the Pacific*, ed. John A. Lent (Eastleigh: John Libbey, 2001), 207–208.

12 Bradbury, 'Australian and New Zealand', 208.

13 Ibid.

14 Ibid., 213.

15 Terri Dentry, 'From Good Devils to Supermarket Musical Massacres: An Overview
    of Australian Animation', *Metro Magazine* 157 (2008): 86.

16 O'Neill and Wells, 'Animation in Australia.'

17 Alison Sharman, 'Commissioned Content', accessed 30 July 2014, http://www.sbs
    .com.au/shows/commissionedcontent.

18 Quoted in Dentry, 'From Good Devils', 86–87.

19 An additional cost was synchronizing the animated and the live.

20 Gibson, *South of the West*, 75.

21 McFarlane, *Australian Cinema*, 70.

22 Richard Dyer, 'Entertainment and Utopia', in *Only Entertainment*, 2nd edn (London:
    Routledge, 2002), 26.

23 Gibson, *South of the West*, 65.

24 Roslynn D. Haynes, *Seeking the Centre: The Australian Desert in Literature, Art and
    Film* (Cambridge: Cambridge University Press, 1998), 61.

25 Pierce, *Lost Children*, 60.

26 Michelle J. Smith and Elizabeth Parsons, 'Animating Child Activism:
    Environmentalism and Class Politics in Ghibli's Princess Mononoke (1997) and Fox's
    FernGully (1992)', *Continuum: Journal of Media & Cultural Studies* 26.1 (2012): 30.

27 Seddon, 'Landscapes of Australia', 2.

28 Leslie Sharman, 'FernGully: The Last Rainforest – Review', *Sight and Sound* 2.4
    (1992): 54.

29 Jonathan Roper, 'FernGully: The Last Rainforest – Review', in *Australian Film
    1978–1992*, ed. Scott Murray (Melbourne: Oxford University Press, 1993), 339.

30 Sharman, 'FernGully', 54.

31 Nicole Starosielski, ' "Movements That Are Drawn": A History of Environmental
    Animation from *The Lorax to FernGully to Avatar'*, *International Communication
    Gazette* 73.1–2 (2011): 154.

32 Prescott, 'All We See'.

33 Raffaele Caputo, 'The Animated Features of Yoram Gross', in *Australian Film
    1978–1992*, ed. Scott Murray (Melbourne: Oxford University Press, 1993), 354.

34 Jennifer Baxter, Matthew Gray, and Alan Hayes, *Families in Regional, Rural and*

Remote Australia (Melbourne: Australian Institute for Family Studies, 2011), 2.

35 Baxter, Gray, and Hayes, *Families*, 2.

36 Australian Bureau of Statistics, '2071.0 – Reflecting a Nation: Stories from the 2011 Census, 2012–2013', last modified 16 April 2013, http://www.abs.gov.au/ausstats/ abs@.nsf/Lookup/2071.0main+features902012-2013#Endnote3.

37 A rare reference that explicitly locates us in Australia (see also Zak mentioning the Socceroos).

38 Donald Horne's application of the phrase 'the lucky country' in the book of the same name was originally negative, but has subsequently been used favourably.

39 McFarlane, *Australian Cinema*, 96.

40 Ibid., 109.

5

Environmentalism and the Animated Landscape in *Nausicaä of the Valley of the Wind* (1984) and *Princess Mononoke* (1997)

Melanie Chan

This chapter will explore the animated landscape in relation to *Nausicaä of the Valley of the Wind* (*Kaze no Tani no Naushika*) (1984) and *Princess Mononoke* (*Mononoke-hime*) (1997), which were written and directed by Hayao Miyazaki. These films will be shown to be significant because they provide a mechanism for provoking and contributing to debates concerning environmentalism.[1] At present, environmental debates, especially those concerning climate change, have become a contentious and politically charged realm.[2] Moreover, in the second decade of the twenty-first century, advanced technological and industrial societies are subject to environmental risks that have global consequences.[3] For instance, the earthquake, tsunami and nuclear reactor accident that occurred in Fukushima, Japan in, March 2011 had far-reaching impact in terms of environmental pollution.[4] Documentary films such as *An Inconvenient Truth* (2006), *The Polar Explorer* (2011) and *Trashed* (2013) tend to highlight environmental issues through the use of detailed investigation and presentation of rational arguments. In contrast, *Nausicaä of the Valley of the Wind* and *Princess Mononoke* attempt to enlarge our perspective of environmental issues on an emotional level through representing the beauty and majesty of the landscape and by illuminating the interconnections between the human and non-human realm. Indeed, this chapter will suggest that these films may leave audiences with memorable experiences through the representation of the beauty, fragility and powerful aspects of nature. Nonetheless, these films do not simply call for an outright rejection of science, technology and industrialization. Furthermore, they do not uncritically idealize or offer sentimental representations of the landscape. Instead, this chapter proposes that these films can be interpreted as an attempt to find ways of using technology wisely and establishing communal concern for environmental issues.

The existing scholarly literature surrounding the anime films of Hayao Miyazaki has focused on themes such as mythology, history and the representation of gender. For instance, John A. Tucker and Susan J. Bigelow provide in-depth studies of the mythological dimensions to *Princess Mononoke* as a historical drama.[5] Meanwhile, Susan J. Napier provides an overview of a range of anime films, paying particular attention to the representation of female characters in Miyazaki films.[6] In *The Anime Art of Hayao Miyazaki*, Dani Cavallaro also provides insight into the production processes involved in anime filmmaking and provides a thematic overview of Miyazaki's oeuvre.[7] Building on this existing scholarship, this chapter aims to provide a detailed account of *Nausicaä of the Valley of the Wind* and *Princess Mononoke* in relation to representations of the landscape through the particular qualities of anime as a medium.

To make the discussion manageable, this chapter will focus on three specific areas in relation to the animated landscape. First, we will explore the ways in which these films draw upon a range sources including Shinto, Buddhism, Taoism, Greek mythology and folk tales. Secondly, we will highlight how these films do not simply dismiss technology on the basis of the impact it has upon the landscape, in terms of the depletion and degradation of natural resources, but rather offer more nuanced and complex representations of technology and landscape that centre around the forces of emergence, growth, decay and renewal that can be found in nature. Thirdly, the chapter explores the ways in which these films represent the landscape as the site of awe and wonder through imagery of majestic forests and mountains that are lush and teaming with diverse life forms. By rendering the landscape as majestic and a site of biological diversity and ecological importance, *Nausicaä of the Valley of the Wind* and *Princess Mononoke* encourage audiences to care about environmental concerns.[8]

Before proceeding further, it will be useful to briefly outline the two films in question. Initially, *Nausicaä of the Valley of the Wind* was an epic manga production that spanned seven volumes produced between 1982 and 1994. The film version *Nausicaä of the Valley of the Wind* was produced by Top Craft Studios and released in 1984. However, as Jonathan Clements explains, when the story was transposed for the global market in 1986, it was made into a 'shorter, bowlderised video release called *Warriors of the Wind*.[9] Of note is that the shorter version of *Nausicaä* provides an optimistic resolution to the narrative in comparison to the darker apocalyptic vision of the manga. One explanation for the changes that were made to the film version is that they aimed to maximize the appeal of the film to global audiences and maximize revenues from box office and subsequent video and DVD releases.[10]

Nausicaä of the Valley of the Wind opens *in medias res*, prompting the audience to figure out how the situation that is represented has occurred. The opening sequence is set 1,000 years into the future, at a time when industrialized civilization has been destroyed by a cataclysmic war. Toxins have been released into the environment, and this has enraged a species of giant insects known as the Ohmu. After rampaging through the environment, the Ohmu and humans now live in a state of conflict. This back-story is told through the reading of a tapestry featuring mythological images of fearsome monsters, great battles and the use of voice-over.[11] During the opening sequence, a series of tracking shots of the tapestry are intersected by flashbacks that portray giant demon-like figures (known as God Warriors in the film), which tower over a fiery apocalyptic landscape of burning skyscrapers and ruined buildings. In this post-apocalyptic world there are a series of small nations, including the Valley of the Wind, which are surrounded by huge areas of toxic, un-inhabitable land.

Princess Mononoke, which was released over a decade later in Japan by Dentsu Inc. and in the United States by Miramax films (1999), presents a similar vision of environmental degradation. The film is set in a period of Japanese history known as the Muromachi era (1392–1573), when Japan made contact with the Portuguese and firearms were imported into the country. The narrative of the film concerns the tensions between iron production (for items such as firearms) and how this impacts upon natural resources, the habitat of different species and the landscape. The main setting of the film is the Tatara Iron Works, which has been built on land that was formerly a forest, and the subsequent iron production is shown to impact upon the environment through the usage of raw materials such as sand and wood. Tensions arise between human civilization and the environment when Lady Eboshi, leader of the Iron Works, shoots a wild boar (Nago) – who we discover was the guardian of the forest.

This causes Nago to become an enraged demon (Tatari kami) who rampages through the forest.[12] Notably, Nago has become a vengeful spirit after coming into conflict with human society and industrial production processes. Eventually Nago reaches the land of the Emishi people where Prince Ashitaka fatally wounds him. As Nago is dying, the wise woman of the village reverentially bows to Nago and explains that he will receive funeral rites and a proper burial ground. Despite the wise woman's reverence, Nago continues to be spiteful towards human beings and curses them due to the suffering he has experienced. Later at a village gathering to discuss Ashitaka's fate, the wise woman explains that an iron ball was found in Nago's body and this is what caused him to suffer and become enraged. Ashitaka who has since become infected with this hate, following his skirmish with Nago, must now go on a journey to find out the source of Nago's suffering in order to find a possible cure. Kozo Mayumi, Barry D. Soloman and Jason Chang explain that 'a curse by the Tatari represents a mythical belief of the Japanese that the forest is full of gods who occupy a superior position to humans, and that when humans are aggressive against the forest the forest god tortures humans in return'.[13]

It is also important to consider different definitions of the terms 'animation' and 'anime', because prior to the twentieth century other terms such as 'senga' (line art), 'kuga' (flip pictures) and 'manga-eiga' (cartoon film) were used to refer to Japanese animated films. However, during the twentieth century, 'anime' became the most commonly used term to denote animated films that were mainly produced in Japan. More recently, the term 'anime' refers to Japanese animation in the contemporary era of global media consumption – at this time anime is not simply a genre, but rather the term refers to a specific medium.[14] Shinobu Price also contends that Westerners often conflate Japanese animation with children's cartoons that are pejoratively associated with simplified storylines and formulaic happy endings.[15] On this basis, cartoons are perceived as an inferior art form in comparison to other forms of visual culture. Countering these assumptions, Price states that when: 'The term cartoon is applied to the world of Japanese animation, a great injustice is made. Partaking in this mind-set is just another form of ethnocentrism, looking at a different culture through your own culturally specific set of values and definitions.'[16]

There are also important differences in terms of the aesthetic qualities of contemporary Hollywood animation and the oeuvre of Miyazaki. At present, the overwhelming majority of animated films made by Disney, DreamWorks Animation SKG and Pixar are predominantly made using computer-generated imagery, which features strong outlines and flat blocks of bright colour. In contrast, Miyazaki's anime films seem to be aligned more with the codes and conventions of painted and hand-drawn images. Furthermore, commenting on the detailed hand-drawn qualities of Princess Mononoke, John Grant notes that Miyazaki altered or 'touched up' numerous film cels.[17] Additionally, images of the landscape in *Nausicaä of the Valley of the Wind* and *Princess Mononoke* are rendered through the use of perspective and subtle use of light and shade, evoking the qualities of eighteenth- and nineteenth-century European landscape painting. The association of Miyazaki's films with visual arts is further reinforced by the lavish book publications that detail the preparatory sketches and watercolour paintings he produces for his anime films, of which *Nausicaä of the Valley of the Wind* is an excellent example.[18]

Clearly, *Nausicaä of the Valley of the Wind* and *Princess Mononoke* are part of a much larger animated filmmaking tradition, but as films that directly address the subject of environmentalism, they do not simply represent the landscape through a series of still images that are animated, they also represent the landscape in a way that suggests that it is animated in an ontological sense. Indeed, the representation of humans, animals, other life forms and the landscape in these films operates via sequences and movements between still images, which create the illusion of a dynamic environment infused with life. Discussing definitions of environmental animation in film, Nicole Starosielski observes that what is significant about environmental animation is that it can create 'imperceptible and imagined worlds'.[19] Going further, Starosielksi remarks that 'with its ability to contort the space and time of representation, animation can more easily visualize imagined environmental change'.[20] It is this final point that we will focus on in this chapter, with the ambition of revealing the myriad ways that these films invite us to consider the landscape as animated, as alive and as part of an interdependent web of life.

Shinto, animism and kami

Nausicaä of the Valley of the Wind and *Princess Mononoke* both feature Shinto symbolism and mythology. In Japan, Shinto has a long history and relates to matters of daily life such as social welfare, the importance of community and purification rituals. A major aspect of Shinto is animism, whereby natural phenomena are regarded as life forms or expressions of divinity. Discussing the importance of animism in Japanese culture, C. Scott Littleton states that 'the reverence shown by the Japanese toward nature stems from Shinto's most ancient and fundamental belief that spirit-beings govern the natural world'.[21] The meanings associated with spirit-beings and animism carry implications in terms of how the non-human realm is perceived and valued. According to Shinto cosmology, throughout the universe there are various kami or spirits that can take numerous forms such as animals, humans and even natural phenomena such as mountains or forests. The Shinto approach to kami is evident in rituals and in ecological views towards the natural world. Discussing the role of kami in Shinto, Littleton states that they 'are believed to animate every object in the universe – from prominent geographical sites, such as Mount Fuji to the souls of deceased children'.[22] In Shinto mythology, kami is an animating force that permeates everything in the human and the non-human realm. From this perspective the landscape can be perceived as the site of wonder, awe and enchantment. However, film scholar Susan Bigelow points out that 'Miyazaki invokes Shinto myth, not as literal belief but as a metaphoric opening to the dimension of mystery and wonder that may offer clues on how to live a human life'.[23]

Animism continues to play an important part in contemporary Japanese culture, particularly in terms of conceptualizing the relationships between technology and living beings. For instance, scientists in Japan offer services to animals used in research, a practice known as kuyou and in some rural communities there are also memorial services to venerate the insects that have died during the farming season. Even inanimate objects have memorial services, for instance, there is the practice of Hari-Kuyo, an annual memorial for needles.[24] A further point to consider is that nature is a socially and culturally constructed concept that changes over time. In Western culture nature may be thought of as a pure, wild or untainted realm. However, Casper Bruun Jensen and Anders Blok remark that Japanese conceptions of nature are pragmatic and are based on the inter-relationships between life and death.[25]

The work of German philosopher Martin Heidegger (1889–1976) also provides useful insight into the rapacious impulses of capitalist production and consumption. These issues are particularly pertinent to the representations of the landscape in *Nausicaä of the Valley of the Wind* and *Princess Mononoke*. In particular, Heidegger's work can be used to provide a powerful critique of a controlling technological mind-set and the impact this has upon the environment. In *The Question Concerning Technology* (1993), Heidegger discusses human nature and our relationship to 'Being' (the grounds of existence). Heidegger notes that technology has a long historical trajectory in terms of finding ways to manipulate and master the world around us. Yet, Heidegger does not offer an outright rejection of technology. Instead, Heidegger argues that technology becomes problematic when it is used as a mechanism to dominate and master 'Being'.

In *Nausicaä of the Valley of the Wind*, the villagers are represented as living a medieval lifestyle as agricultural workers with their power provided by windmills. The Daoist (Taoist) concepts of wu-wei and you-wei are particularly insightful in relation to the medieval lifestyle represented in Nausicaä. Wu-wei is a concept that refers to non-action, yielding or flowing with natural forces. Therefore, wu-wei refers to technologically related activities that are aligned with natural processes such as windmills. Conversely, you-wei refers to those technologically related activities that disrupt natural forces such as using petroleum for fuel, which has environmental implications in terms of its extraction and usage since it releases carbon dioxide into the atmosphere.[26] In *Nausicaä*, the images that represent the destruction of a former technologically advanced era could be interpreted as an environmental warning of the dangers of you-wei, whereas the Valley of the Wind is represented as a place where humans utilize technology in a way that does not unduly disrupt natural processes. The representation of the demise of advanced industrial civilization, environmental pollution and toxicity in *Nausicaä of the Valley of the Wind* has particular resonance in the light of the Fukushima nuclear disaster of 2011. Indeed, the Fukushima disaster highlighted the risks involved in the production of nuclear energy and the vulnerability of advanced technological processes, in relation to powerful natural forces such as earthquakes and tsunamis. The tensions between industrial production and the landscape are also explored in *Princess Mononoke* through the representation of the depletion of natural resources during the production of iron.

The forest

Given the importance of the forest in *Princess Mononoke*, it is worthwhile briefly exploring the meanings and practices surrounding the forest in Japanese culture and society more generally. Environmental scholars, Hiromi Kobori and Richard B Primarck, outline the ways Japan can boast an incredible diversity of species and ecological systems, with the Satoyama – Japan's forests, rice paddies, fields and streams – being central to this.[27] In the past the Satoyama environment was closely intertwined with the social and cultural practices of Japanese life, as those who lived in the villages used the area to grow food and obtain clean water. Kobori and Primarck explain that during the Edo period

(1603–1867) the Satoyama was managed through human intervention through the cultivation of the environment. For instance, 'the constant collection of leaves and wood kept the forest open and prevented succession to large trees and dense shade'.[28] This openness of the environment was important because dense shade from overgrown trees prevented sunlight from reaching ground level and this impacted upon plant and animal life. So when villagers cultivated the area sunlight could reach ground level and this encouraged a diverse range of plant and animal life to thrive. As Kobori and Primarck contend 'though not "natural" in the usual sense… the Satoyama helped to maintain a rich biodiversity in the Japanese countryside'.[29] Cycles of renewal were also taken into account as trees were harvested in fifteen- to twenty-year periods.

Yet, forest environments in Japan changed as new modes of farming came into use such as the use of commercially produced fertilizers. Kobori and Primarck claim that when farmers started to use chemical fertilizers, this killed 'many insect and aquatic species'.[30] Village farmers were also unable to make a living selling timber because their production processes were labour intensive and expensive. Furthermore, wood was no longer the primary energy source and was replaced by coal, oil and electricity. Over time the Satoyama environment changed, trees were not cut down and the forests became overgrown. In addition, many of the Satoyama environments were transformed into industrial and residential areas. Ecologically, forests remain an important and contested terrain in Japan. Jensen and Blok also explain that 'the environmentalism manifested in attempts to preserve scenic and communal shrine landscapes does not oppose human activities against some pristine "wild nature". Rather, human intervention is valued here as a source of ecological cultivation'.[31] Similarly, *Nausicaä of the Valley of the Wind* and *Princess Mononoke* do not overly sentimentalize or simply glorify the natural environment; instead, they address the tensions arising from human intervention and ecological concerns.

The forest is a major location in *Princess Mononoke*, since this is where the main sites of conflict occur between humans, other species and nature. Through the use of voice-over, the opening sequence outlines the ways in which the forest was once the realm of the gods; however, as the narrative explains, over time things changed and most of the great forests have been destroyed by human intervention. The tension between other life forms and humans is highlighted in a scene in which Lady Eboshi and a group of workers are attacked by wolves whilst transporting food supplies back to Iron Town. The scene takes place during dark stormy weather and in an environment where the trees are blackened stumps, both of which serve to visually underscore the tensions between iron production and the impact this has upon the landscape. Whilst on his journey to find the source of Nago's rage, Ashitaka comes across some of the workers carrying injuries following the wolf attack, and proceeds to lead the men to safety. Upon encountering small white creatures called kodama (Figure 5.1) the workers display fear, but Ashitaka reassures the men that the kodama are tree-dwelling spirits that bring good luck and symbolize the health and vitality of the forest.

Ashitaka considers the forest as a magical environment and this is emphasized by horizontal panning shots of verdant green land, clean water and butterflies. However, the men from Iron Town tell Ashitaka that the forest is not safe because gods and demons haunt it. As the narrative unfolds, Ashitaka continues to be represented as a character that is attuned to Shinto beliefs about kami and the spiritual dimension of the landscape. In contrast, Lady Eboshi and the workers from Iron Town can be interpreted as representing a belief in technological progress rather than ancient cosmologies such as Shinto.

Figure 5.1 The tree-dwelling kadama (*Princess Mononoke*, Studio Ghibli 1999)

Toxicity, purification and renewal

The differences between natural cycles of purification and renewal and human existence were presciently highlighted by Rachel Carson in her 1962 book *Silent Spring*. Carson, discussing the temporal cycles of the physical environment and life on earth, states that, 'it has been a history of interaction between living things and their surroundings. To a large extent, the physical form and the habits of the earth's vegetation and its animal life have been moulded by the environment'.[32] Carson goes on to compare the long history of the cycles of evolution and the ways in which different forms of life impact upon their environment: 'Considering the whole span of earthly time, the opposite effect, in which life actually modifies its surroundings, has been relatively slight'.[33] However, writing in 1960s, Carson warned that 'only within the moment of time represented by the present century has one species – man – acquired significant power to alter the nature of his world'.[34]

The representation of toxicity in Nausicaä of the Valley of the Wind may also relate to catastrophic environmental events that occurred in Japan during the 1950s, namely, in the Minamata Bay area where the Chisso Corporation, a chemical company, dumped methyl mercury into the water over many years.[35] Consequently, many life forms became contaminated with toxins and when humans ate polluted fish they also became sick. Former fisherman and environmentalist Ogata Masato has written about the pollution of Minamata Bay, with a key theme in his writing being that it envisions 'people as being part of a complex and mutually supporting web of life'.[36] More recently Masato has raised concerns about the risks of nuclear power in Japan in the aftermath of the earthquake, tsunami and nuclear accident that occurred in Fukushima in 2011. Through its focus on such salient subject matter, *Nausicaä of the Valley of the Wind* opens up a space in which the issues and debates surrounding toxicity in relation to environmental risks throughout the world might be considered – a space that feels necessary today as it did in 1984.

In Homer's epic of Greek mythology, *The Odyssey*, Nausicaä features as a character who heals Odysseus after he was shipwrecked.[37] However, in *Nausicaä of the Valley of the Wind*, the character Nausicaä discovers the healing and restorative processes of nature. The toxins that were produced when industrialized civilization was destroyed take the form of airborne spores and if humans are exposed to them they become sick and die. Even Nausicaä's father King Jihl becomes infected by these environmental toxins and becomes weak and bedridden. When her father becomes ill, Nausicaä begins to carefully collect and study the flora and fauna of the Valley of the Wind and the surrounding lands, to understand how the toxins function in the hope of finding a cure for them.[38] Nausicaä's study of nature is reminiscent of the Japanese microbiologist, Minakata Kumagusu (1867–1941) who was a prolific and renowned writer who published numerous essays in the journal *Nature*. Kumagusu raised concerns about the preservation of the ecological system within forests that were threatened when the Japanese government instigated a Shrine Merger programme (1906–1910). He also argued for the importance of fungi to the forest eco-system.

Themes of purification and renewal are underscored further when Nausicaä attempts to rescue Asbel, the pilot of an aircraft from the toxic jungle.[39] During the rescue attempt, Nausicaä falls from her mehve glider and descends into the jungle. After falling through quicksand she lands in a pale blue landscape of underground caverns that represent a state of cleanliness and purification. After inspecting the caverns, she realizes that the cycles of nature are purifying the environment. During a dialogue with Asbel she says: 'The trees of the toxic jungle must have evolved to purify the earth of all the pollution that we humans have made. The trees absorb the pollution so it becomes inert then they die and petrify and crumble into purified sand. That's how these underground caverns must have formed and the insects evolved to guard this place.' Asbel considers the implications of Nausicaä's finding saying: 'If that is true, then mankind is destined to go extinct. It will take centuries for these trees to cleanse the earth. We can't survive with insects that long'. Yet Asbel swiftly moves towards a pragmatic and problem-solving approach stating that 'somehow we are going to have to find a way to stop this toxic jungle from spreading', serving to establish the tensions that drive the ecocritical narrative forward.

The landscape as the site of conflict

A key point identified by French sociologist Bruno Latour is that while environmental experts have already produced data that verify the human role in climate change, these data have not really resulted in fundamental changes in terms of environmental policies or behavioural practices.[40] Instead of urgent calls to do something about climate change, we appear to be in a quagmire of different ideological conflicts, scepticism, inertia and even denial. Although *Nausicaä of the Valley of the Wind* and *Princess Mononoke* do not provide factual, rational or logically consistent arguments about environmental concerns they do attempt to engage audiences at an emotional level. Indeed, these films invite audiences to identify with different locations and characters, and more significantly tensions between animism, technology and political power, in order to develop an emotional connection to the environmental concerns they represent.

In *Nausicaä*, for example, the character Kushana from the kingdom of Torumekia represents the priority given to economics and wealth creation at the expense of the environment. After the Torumekians invade the Valley of the Wind, Kushana addresses the villagers and claims that she has come to the valley to unify their different kingdoms and create prosperity. In addition, Kushana's approach to the environmental pollution, which threatens their kingdoms, is to 'put the toxic jungle to the torch'. Therefore, Kushana is represented as a powerful political leader, who offers promises of future prosperity and, at the same time, attempts to quell the fears of the villagers regarding the threat of pollution. However, Kushana's solution to pollution is to exercise power and control *over* the environment. Kushana's dominating approach to environmental concerns is contrasted with the character Obaba who is an old wise woman. After listening to Kushana's speech, Obaba warns them that they must not 'touch the toxic jungle'. Instead, Obaba issues a warning to the villagers stating that: 'Since the origin of the toxic jungle 1,000 years ago people tried time and time again to burn it. But time and again, their attempts did nothing but enrage the Ohmu and swarms of them emerged from the jungle and stampeded across the lands.' From Obaba's perspective, burning the toxic jungle is an act of aggression that will enrage the Ohmu and result in further destruction. However, Obaba's wisdom is undercut by Kushana's aide Kurotowa who dismisses her warning shouting 'silence you old hag. We will have none of your raving'. Through Kurotowa's statement we learn that Obaba's insights are dismissed and devalued.

In his study of fairy tales, Rudolf Meyer discusses the ways in which knowledge and the construction of meaning changes over time. For instance, Meyer notes that the emphasis placed on rational thought from the eighteenth century onwards shifted the value accorded to other forms of knowledge that were then devalued as mere superstition. Meyer states: 'Of course animals could not speak or princes become bears of lions, and there were no dragons laying the country to waste and devouring maidens. Life had been placed on a reliable bourgeois footing where the world moved strictly in accordance with the laws of nature; this was the victory of modernity.'[41] There are similarities to this changing view of knowledge and the character of Obaba. For as Meyer contends, 'the deeper intuition, the ancient original heritage of spirit is mocked and dethroned where its inner nature is no longer understood'.[42]

In *Princess Mononoke*, Lady Eboshi also represents the dethronement of ancient belief systems such as animism. From Lady Eboshi's perspective, Nago is considered 'a brainless pig'. Furthermore, Lady Eboshi tells Ashitaka that she wants to kill the spirit of the forest so that animals can be what she calls 'dumb again'. Once the animals are 'dumb again', Lady Eboshi intends to clear them from the surrounding landscape in order to produce more iron, and thereby increase the economic wealth of the population of Iron Town. By contrast, in *Nausicaä of the Valley of the Wind* the tensions between human activities and the landscape are resolved through an emphasis on the purification processes of nature and personal sacrifice. Finally, Nausicaä dies and is reborn, which resonates with the idea that elements of the landscape operate in an on-going cycle of creation, decay and renewal. Similarly, when Lady Eboshi shoots and decapitates the forest spirit, it emits black ooze that encompasses and destroys the landscape. When Ashitaka hands the severed head back to the forest spirit it falls on Iron Town totally destroying the forge, reducing it to rubble. However, the narrative ending in *Princess Mononoke* suggests that it is necessary to find ways of fostering economic wealth alongside the cultivation and preservation of the landscape. The forest spirit lifts Ashitaka's curse in recognition of his help in returning the severed head. Yet, Ashitaka does not return to the Emishi people, rather he remains in Iron Town to work alongside the existing inhabitants to rebuild their future.

Conclusion

This chapter has explored the anime films *Nausicaä of the Valley of the Wind* and *Princess Mononoke* in order to highlight debates around the relationships between the landscape, industrialization and environmentalism. In doing so, the chapter has emphasized the ways in which these films draw upon a range of mythological sources, which offer audiences a way of finding meaning about human life and our place in a wider interconnected web of ontological existence as conveyed through a cinematic – and animated – landscape. Miyazaki's films do not present rational arguments about the management of the landscape nor do they engage in didactic political environmental messages. Instead, *Nausicaä of the Valley of the Wind* and *Princess Mononoke* invite audiences to become enchanted with the natural world through the representation of the beauty and majesty of the landscape. Additionally, through identification and emotional involvement with the characters in these films, the audience is able to consider a range of different viewpoints that illustrate the challenges and tensions between industrialization, technological development and the environment. Indeed, these films do not offer easy solutions to these tensions, nor do they simply sentimentalize nature or provide a nostalgic vision of pre-industrial society. Ultimately, these films attempt to establish a shared sense of concern for environmental issues, which are especially acute in the context of growing levels of production and consumption in contemporary capitalist culture.

Notes

1 Other anime films such as *My Neighbour Totoro* (1988) and *Pom Poko* (1994), which was co-written and directed by Miyazaki and Isao Takahata, also offer intriguing representations of the landscape whilst engaging with environmental themes.

2 Bruno Latour, 'War and Peace in an Age of Ecological Conflicts.' (paper presented at the Peter Wall Institute, Vancouver, 23 September 2013).

3 Ulrich Beck, *Risk Society: Towards a New Modernity* (London: Sage, 1992).

4 Shoko Yoneyama, ' "Life-World": Beyond Fukushima and Minimate', *Asian Perspective* 4 (2013): 567–592.

5 John A Tucker, 'Anime and Historical Inversion in Miyazaki Hayao's Princess Mononoke', *Japan Studies Review* 7 (2003): 65–102. Susan J. Bigelow, 'Technologies of Perception: Miyazaki in Theory and Practice', *Animation* 4 (2009): 55–74.

6 Susan Napier, *Anime from Akira to Howl's Moving Castle* (New York: Palgrave Macmillan, 2005).

7 Dani Cavallaro, *The Anime Art of Hayao Miyazaki* (Jefferson, NC: McFarland, 2006).

8 This chapter is underpinned by an acknowledgement that film audiences are not passive recipients of ideological messages and may interpret these films in a variety of ways. Stuart Hall, 'Encoding/Decoding', in *Culture, Media, Language*, ed. Stuart Hall et al. (London: Hutchinson, 1980).

9 Jonathan Clements, *Anime – A History* (London: Palgrave Macmillan and BFI, 2013), 180.

10 In the Nausicaä' manga the Ohmu are referred to as Aums. In his study of the Nausicaä manga, Japanese scholar Inaga Shigami points out that it has a much darker and disturbing ending than the film. 'In the comic version, not only Aums but all kinds of insects continue their massive suicidal march of migration, presaging

the total environmental disaster called Daikaishō'. Inaga Shigemi, 'Miyazaki Hayao's Epic Comic Series: Nausicaä in the Valley of the Wind: An Interpretation', *Japan Review* 11 (1999): 117.

11 What is interesting is that in this opening sequence similarities can be drawn from tapestry (as a series of images and text that construct a narrative in an orderly sequence) and the medium of animation.

12 John A. Tucker explains that the word Mononoke in the title of the film 'refers to wrathful, vengeful spirits, either of the living or the dead'. John A. Tucker, 'Anime and Historical Inversion', 73.

13 Kozo Mayumi, Barry D. Soloman, and Jason Chang, 'The Ecological and Consumption Themes of the Films of Hayao Miyazaki', *Ecological Economics* 54 (2005): 4.

14 Clements, *Anime – A History*.

15 Shinobu Price, 'Cartoons from another Planet: Japanese Animation as Cross-Cultural Communication', *The Journal of American Culture* 24 (2001): 153–169.

16 Price, 'Cartoons from Another Planet', 154.

17 John Grant, *Masters of Animation* (London: B.T. Batsford, 2001), 161.

18 Hayao Miyazaki, *The Art of Nausicaä of the Valley of the Wind – Watercolour Impressions* (San Francisco, CA: Viz Media, 2011).

19 Nicole Starosielksi, 'Movements that Are Drawn: A History of Environmental Animation from Lorax to FernGully to Avatar', *International Communication Gazette* 73 (2011): 148.

20 Starosielski, 'Movements that Are Drawn', 150.

21 Scott C. Littleton, *Understanding Shinto* (London: Duncan Baird Publishers, 2002), 6.

22 Littleton, *Understanding Shinto*, 23.

23 Susan J. Bigelow, 'Technologies of Perception: Miyazaki in Theory and Practice', *Animation* 4 (2009): 61.

24 David Boyd, 'Hari-Kuyo', *The Japan Foundation* (2014), accessed 11 June 2014, http://www.jpf.org.au/onlinearticles/hitokuchimemo/issue7.html.

25 Casper Bruun Jensen and Anders Blok, 'Techno-Animism in Japan: Shinto Cosmograms, Actor-Network Theory, and the Enabling Powers of Non-Human Agencies', *Theory, Culture, Society* 30 (2013): 84–115.

26 The concepts of wu-wei and you-wei are outlined in Graham Parkes, 'Lao-Zhuang and Heidegger on Nature and Technology', *Journal of Chinese Philosophy* 30 (2003): 19–38 and John Lash, *The Yin of Tai Chi* (London: Vega Books, 2002).

27 Hiromi Kobori and Richard B. Primarck, 'Conservation for Satoyama The Traditional Landscape of Japan', *Arnoldia* 62 (2003): 4.

28 Kobori and Primarck, 'Conservation for Satoyama', 4.

29 Ibid.

30 Kobori and Primarck, 'Conservation for Satoyama', 6.

31 Jensen and Blok, 'Techno-Animism in Japan', 100.

32 Rachel Carson, *Silent Spring* (Harmondsworth: Penguin, 1962), 23.

33 Carson, *Silent Spring*, 23.

34 Ibid.

35 Justin McCurry, 'Japan Remembers Minamata', *The Lancet* 367 (2006): 99–100.

36 Shoko Yoneyama, ' "Life-World": Beyond Fukushima and Minamata', 579.

37 Homer's epic poem is thought to have been written circa 800 BCE, a revised and reprinted version translated by Robert Fagles was published by Penguin (London and New York) 1997.

38 These aspects to Nausicaä's character resonate with the Japanese text Mushi Mezuru Himegimi (which was written circa 1055–1185) The Young Lady Who Loves Insects. Michelle Osterfeld Li states that Mushi Mezuru Himegimi refers to '… the daughter of the Major Counselor and Inspector of The Provincial Administrations (Azechi no dainagon) who defies social convention by collecting insects'. Michelle Osterfeld Li, *Ambiguous Bodies: Reading the Grotesque in Japanese Setsuwa Tales* (Redwood City, CA: Stanford University Press, 2009), 156.

39 Asbel is from a neighbouring country Pejite and his plane has been attacked by forces from the kingdom of Torumekia, which illustrates the tensions between different human communities in the film and not just the relationships between humans, other species and the natural environment.

40 Latour, 'War and Peace in an Age of Ecological Conflicts'.

41 Rudolf Meyer, *The Wisdom of Fairy Tales* (Edinburgh: Floris, 1997), 10.

42 Meyer, *The Wisdom of Fairy Tales*, 21.

6

Animating *Shanshui*: Chinese Landscapes in Animated Film, Art and Performance

Kiu-wai Chu

The Master said, The wise delight in water; the humane delight in mountains
The Analects of Confucius: Book Six.[1]

Shanshui (山水), literally 'mountains and water' in Chinese language, refers to both landscape in general, and the philosophical concept that embodies a specific vision of Chinese people towards the physical (mainly natural) environment since ancient time. In this chapter, we will focus on the ideas of *shanshui* to examine the complex relationships between human beings and the environment, as depicted in a range of animated texts such as film, art and live performance.

Shanshui tells stories. Through works of poets and painters of the past thousands of years, one sees how thoughts and knowledge, emotions and affections, achievements and hardships, as well as dreams and disillusionments of Chinese people, are all projected in *shanshui*, in the representations of landscapes and the environment. *Shanshui* is never a static concept. Everywhere in China today, *shanshui* is undergoing transformation, construction and destruction, as well as commodification that aims to strengthen China's image as an ecological civilization. As the relationships between human beings and the environment continue to change over time, the understanding of *shanshui* evolves in tandem. In this age of prosperity, how has *shanshui*, and people's perceptions of it, changed? How has it been represented in animated media in China?

For decades, Chinese artists have been making painstaking efforts at turning animation, a modern media, into a culturally specific form of art in China. Through its visual representations of Chinese philosophical thoughts and aesthetics, animation was seen as a possible artistic medium for expressions of Chinese views on human values and the world.

'Unity of Human and Nature' (*tianren heyi* 天人合一), an important concept in Chinese philosophy, has over the course of history been the essence of classical landscape paintings. Since the mid-twentieth century, with periods of political turmoil followed by successive reforms, modernization and development, the idea of harmony between human and nature has increasingly been marginalized, as classical landscape aesthetics take on new meanings. By providing an overview of Chinese animations produced since the 1960s, and proceeding to focus on post-2000s' media art and performance, this chapter examines representations of a range of animated versions of landscapes, to reveal people's ambivalent perceptions towards the changing environmental conditions in China today.

Shanshui: Classical Chinese landscape aesthetics

One aspect that distinguishes Chinese landscape painting from Western scenic painting is the permeation of strong Chinese philosophical ideals in the former. In classical Chinese landscape aesthetics, the unity of nature and humans (*tianren heyi*), has often been stressed, which fundamentally implies an attainment of a harmonious relationship and holistic unity between human beings and the external environment. In China's predominant agricultural societies, the individual's dependence on natural environment and expectation of favourable weather for crops, make people particularly sensitive to seasonal climate changes. Over time, an 'anthropocosmic' mentality, which combines the cosmic (natural/*tian*) and the anthropocentric (human/*ren*), as Confucian scholar Tu Weiming coins it, is developed, which stresses a mutual dependence between the natural environment and all living matters in the universe, reflecting human beings' perennial pursuit of a harmonious relationship with nature.[2]

To better understand how classical landscape aesthetics defines people's perception and imagination of the harmonious relationship between human beings and the physical environment, and how it is reflected in animated films and art in the past few decades, it is important to focus our attention on three significant features in traditional Chinese aesthetics in classical paintings, namely, the motif of blandness (*dan* 淡); the composition of contrast (of substance and void); and the movement (the longscroll and the roaming lens).

Philosophy of blandness

When looking at a classical Chinese landscape painting, a contemporary viewer who is not acquainted with knowledge of Chinese aesthetics may feel alienated, and find himself 'wondering why the same subjects occur over and over again – the same misty mountains, the same scholars gazing at waterfalls or pretending to fish.'[3] Classical Chinese landscape painting uses mainly diluted ink and water, and is characterized by an absence of bright colours, or depiction of action and event in the content of a painting. Discussing a masterpiece by Yuan painter Ni Zan, French Sinologist Francois Jullien remarks that '[n]othing [in the painting] strives to incite or seduce; nothing aims to fix the gaze or compel the attention. Yet this landscape exists fully as a landscape. The Chinese critics traditionally characterize this in one word: *dan*, the "bland".'[4] Jullien sees *blandness* as a major characteristic that defines, since ancient times, 'all currents of Chinese thought – Confucianism, Daoism, Buddhism', a value that 'culminates in a sensibility common to all the arts (music, painting, calligraphy, poetry, and the martial arts)'.[5] Although Western tradition has often viewed blandness as a negative expression, *dan* in Chinese thoughts is rich in philosophical meanings and from which has evolved a unique idea of beauty and aesthetics. Such a pursuit of the aesthetics of blandness precludes attempts at thematic portrayals of uncommon scenes of nature such as thunderstorms, landslides or tsunamis.

In considering the motif of blandness and simplicity, the first chapter of *The Doctrine of Mean* claims that:

> When there is no stirring of pleasure, anger, sorrow, or joy, the state of equilibrium/centrality (*zhong*) is achieved. When those feelings have been stirred, and they act in their due course, they are in the state of harmony (*he*). Equilibrium/centrality is the great root of all human actings in the world, and harmony is the ultimate path of the world. Let the states of equilibrium and harmony (*zhong he*) exist in perfection, order will prevail throughout heaven and earth, and all things will be nourished and flourish.[6]

To Confucians, the feature of blandness reflects the state of equilibrium and harmony (*zhong he*), which avoids excessive or deficient human emotions, behaviours and actions. *Dan*, blandness, is thus the means by which the unity and oneness of Heaven, Earth, humans and everything else are expressed. At the same time, it defines the aesthetics that fundamentally adheres to the principles of nature being crucial in Chinese philosophical teaching.

Composition of contrast: Substance and void

In classical landscape aesthetics, the symphony of mountain (*shan*) and water (*shui*), the contrast of darkness and light, and the balance between substance (*shi* 實) and void/emptiness (*xu* 虛) are crucial to establishing the compositional design of a painting. *Shi* – which stands for concrete substance, solidity and reality – refers generally to 'the totality of information perceived through the human eyes'.[7] *Xu*, on the other hand, stands for void, emptiness and absence. Jerome Silbergeld calls voids 'the ultimate in visual abstraction, and they contribute immeasurably to the suggestive quality of Chinese painting'.[8] Spatial composition and scale in classical landscape paintings often violate perspectives of the real physical environment, as a painting does not aim to represent physical environments realistically. Instead, the landscape is being internalized, and the painter's emotion is projected into the painting to re-create the landscape out of his own contemplation, imagination and reflection of the physical environment, turning it into a landscape of void. Unlike filled surfaces in Western oil painting, Chinese painters would often leave a vast area of a painting blank to represent a wide range of landscapes ranging from the sea, the sky, a fish pond, a blurred misty background, depending on situations, to facilitate the expression of abstract spatial environments that produce 'more of an "idea" than an illusion of material reality', leaving it to the viewer's own imagination.[9] As Jullien suggests, 'blandness in painting bathes the landscape in absence: the various forms appear only to be withdrawn, opening upon distances that transcend them'.[10] Such void as an absence of form is thus also seen as a basis of the aesthetics of blandness.

Northern Song painter Guo Xi's (郭熙 c.1020–1090) masterpiece *Early Spring* (早春圖) presents a good example that, through its harmonizing of elements of substance and void, exposes the thematic intention of the painting to the full. With huge mountain peaks as its main body, the painting depicts natural scenery of the end of winter and an early arrival of spring. The foreground shows, in meticulous details, the gradual melting of mountain snow and the gentle flow of water, from the melting snow, through the gorge into a river at the foot of the mountain. High up in the distance, mountain peaks are seen encircled by hazy clouds with no specific indication of time and place but care in the painter's brush work. Viewing from the foot of the mountain close to the bottom of the painting and following one's vision up towards the peak, one sees along the way gorges large and small, little cascading waterfalls in between nature's display of a variety of meticulously designed trees and hidden pavilions along a plank-paved foot path. Thus, one travels, gradually, from an area of *shi*, an image of substance and form, through areas of *xu*, the valleys of void and emptiness without details of human and worldly dimensions. *Early Spring* portrays a realm of *shi* with *xu*, encouraging viewers to move slowly from images and sceneries of proximity and substance, gradually to a space of openness and infinity unbounded by geographical and temporal specificity – a space of *xu* – to achieve an expression of spiritual union between human and all things in the world, an expression of the abstract Dao itself.

Zong Baihua describes the void in Chinese paintings forms as 'a physical spatial structure that is never lifeless. It allows materials to move within it, which makes it the most vibrant space where life can be created'.[11] Though painted over six hundred years later, and with significant differences to Guo Xi's painting style and technique, Qing painter Bada Shanren's (八大山人c.1626–1705) *Fish and Rocks* continues to be characterized by the motif of blandness. His brush strokes are sketchy and light with simple compositions, leaving many areas of the painting white and blank. At the foot of mountain cliffs, he paints a number of fish swimming leisurely in abundant water. In so doing, real-life objects (*shi*) are expressively portrayed in between spaces of emptiness and void (*xu*), encouraging viewers to engage imaginatively with the objects' motions in the painting.

Movement within the image: The roaming lens

It is generally accepted opinion that in landscapes there are those through which you may travel, those in which you may sightsee, those through which you may wander, and those in which you may live. Any paintings attaining these effects are to be considered excellent, but those suitable for travelling and sightseeing are not as successful in achievement as those suitable for wandering and living.

Guo Xi, 'The Significance of Landscapes' (*Lin quan gao zhi ji: Shanshui Xun*), 9th century.[12]

In his text *Lofty Record of Forests and Streams* (*Linquan Gaozi Ji*, c.1117), Northern Song painter Guo Xi expressed that the most outstanding among all landscape paintings are the ones that represent landscapes in which one could dwell and wander, as if one were really there. Many scholars also argue that long takes in films could generate similar effects, through the prolonged duration of a shot supplemented with slow-panning or stable camera movements (Lin, 1991; Hao, 1994; Ni, 1994; Udden, 2002; Silbergeld, 2012).[13] To them, long takes embody an aesthetic that quintessentially mimics Chinese scroll paintings. Film theorist Lin Niantong, in particular, formulates the aesthetics of 'unrestrained roaming' (*you*游) found in Chinese films, associating them with classical landscape aesthetics, and suggests that roaming long takes also allow viewers to dwell in and tour therein. According to James Udden, the character '*you*' is usually translated as to swim, to float, to waft or to drift. Udden also points out that in an aesthetic sense, 'it is broadly applied to include the development of events, continuity, and the layout of things'.[14] Very often, the roaming long takes would also be extreme long shots that depicted outdoor physical landscapes, showing human figures in miniature as in classical landscape paintings, in order to highlight the significance of physical environments to human beings. Consequently, the emphasis in the use of roaming long takes and the merging of spaces of substance and void, both suggesting that representation of physical environment in film can allow an openness and space for imagination and reflection.

A number of Chinese animations have used long shots, still images, and long takes with slow and stable camera movements, to linger on the physical environments and provide time for the story to unfold and for viewers to contemplate on what is seen on the screen. Such film techniques certainly facilitate the expression and exploration of relationships between human beings and physical landscapes in filmic representations, more so than with the use of close-ups, shorter cuts and faster-paced narratives. Additionally, since classical landscape aesthetics is one that stresses harmony between human and the environment, contemporary filmmakers' or artists' attempts to mimic, appropriate or recreate such atmosphere and visual presentation in their works should also be regarded as a means to explore whether film as a modern technology can examine and reflect relationships between people and physical environments in similar ways in the world today.

Animating harmony: Landscapes in water-and-ink animation

Since classical Chinese landscape aesthetics' rise to prominence in the fifth century, there had been changes in Chinese painting styles and techniques over the centuries, reflecting influence from the West. In landscape painting, however, it has maintained the essence of its tradition, as seen in the general characteristics of blandness and philosophical ideals behind, the projection of the longing for spiritual unity of human and nature that remain distinctive from Western aesthetics. Into the twenty-first century, there is still a strong impulse in Chinese films to persist in the exploration of relationships between humans and the environment, often in the fashion of classical landscape paintings that generate a deep ecological aesthetic, best exemplified in the water-and-ink (*shuimo*水墨) animated films.

In 1960, Te Wei (特偉, 1915–2010) produced the first Chinese water-and-ink animation in film history, and revitalized traditional aesthetics in innovative ways. Based on Chinese painter Qi Baishi's painting, *Where Is Mama* (*Xiaokedou Zhao Mama*小蝌蚪找媽媽,1960) the animation portrays live movements of ink-painted fish, shrimps, crabs, tadpoles, frogs and similar little water creatures on screen, successfully fusing classical painting techniques with animated motion pictures. From 1960s to late 1980s, Te Wei created two other landmark films in the fashion of classical *shanshui* painting tradition, stressing the ecological ideals contained within Confucian philosophy. Inspired by paintings of renowned artist Li Keran (1907–1989), *The Cowboy's Flute* (*Mu Di* 牧笛1963) portrays the extent of harmony between humans, animals and nature. A cowboy herds his water buffalo in the field. He falls asleep in the forest and dreams about his buffalo that has wandered off, having been attracted by a thousand-feet waterfall. Inspired by the sound of fluttering bamboo leaves from wind blowing, the cowboy makes a flute with his hand-knife and begins blowing out songs of nature. Attracted by sounds from the flute, birds and animals of all kinds, large and small, as well as the lost buffalo, all come towards the cowboy. He wakes up from his dream, mounts his buffalo and rides leisurely across the fields in the dusk. As he makes his way through a forest of willow trees, across paddy fields in the setting sun, the boy and the buffalo's reflections from the water in the field are fused with scenes of the surrounding landscape into a holistic picture. *The Cowboy's Flute* uses typical sceneries of Jiangnan with flowing rivers and small bridges, lines of willow trees, thick bamboo forests and paddy fields, and through the cowboy's journey in search of his buffalo, the animation reveals fascinating settings of mountains with unusual looking peaks, flying waterfalls and deep valley streams.

Soon after *The Cowboy's Flute*'s release, Mao Zedong and the ruling party launched the Socialist Education Movement, also known as the Four Cleanups Movement, which aimed at reasserting the importance of revolutionary spirit against traditional Chinese beliefs and cultural practices. Consequently, writers and all art workers were encouraged to uphold the principle of privileging the present rather than the ancient/traditional in their creations; emphasizing depictions of life in the thirteen years after liberation; and to portray the living and not the deceased or the ancient, in all literature and art works. It was believed that only through such portrayals of life in *new* China could the doctrines of socialism be promoted.[15] At the time of the Cultural Revolution, most of Te's animations were labelled counter-revolutionary and were banned for screening.

Because of the decade-long political turmoil, it took Shanghai Animation Film Studio seventeen years to resume productions of water-and-ink animations. In 1982, Wu Qiang and Tang Cheng's *The Deer's Bell* (*Lu ling* 鹿鈴) was produced. It depicts the story of a genuine friendship between a young peasant girl and a small deer. Portraying landscapes of peaceful and serene forests, mountains and rivers in water-and-ink, the film expresses the grace and lyrical elegance of the landscape convincingly. However, water-and-ink animations had never been a dominant form of expression in China due to its complicated production process, as well as the influence of Western animation aesthetics. In China's reform era in the 1980s, with urbanization being a major concern, there was little interest in representing the great beauty of natural environments in films and animations. Classical Chinese landscape aesthetics, enhanced by water-and-ink painting techniques, stresses the balance of substance and void, light and darkness, in the depictions of natural landscapes, thus posing some restraints to the animations' themes and settings.

However, in 1988, Te Wei resisted committing to mainstream animation productions, and returned to create his final and internationally acclaimed water-and-ink animated film, *Feeling from Mountain and Water* (*Shan shui qing* 山水情). It tells the story of a fisher-girl and an old guqin master. One day, the old master falls ill in the wilderness and the fisher-girl takes the old man back to her thatched home to rest. When the old master recovers, he begins teaching the girl to play guqin. With the passing of autumn and winter comes spring, by which time the girl's skill in playing the instrument has much improved. To make her improve further, the old master takes her on boat rides through rivers large and small and on climbing expeditions up mountain cliffs. They become fascinated by nature's enchanting sublimity, majesty and magnificence. Crucially, the old master encourages the fisher-girl to understand nature and, through which, to appreciate how best to express the wonders of nature in her music. Before the old master leaves, he gives his much-treasured guqin to the girl. As the sight of him vanishes in the expanse of the distant mountains, it prompts the girl to play, on the cliff top, a tune from her heart. The melody of the song resounds throughout the mountain air, reflecting her feelings of admiration and adoration for the beauty of nature and its pursuit of spiritual unity between human and nature.

Although from the 1960s to the 1990s, Shanghai Animation Film Studio produced merely four water-and-ink animations, all of them received positive acclaim and numerous awards, so much so that these four productions have become acknowledged as definitive of Chinese animation in the twentieth century. As renowned filmmaker Zhang Songlin suggested:

The techniques used in water-and-ink animation have changed the long established method of production for moving pictures. Moving pictures are painted on individual transparent celluloid plates for the production of filmstrips and, for every 10-minute of screening, some six to seven thousand painted plates were required. To ensure consistency and stability of images and avoid jumps and disruptions, all such plates were painted with outline sketches and colouring where lines are considered the basic component of an image, with colouring playing a complementary role. In contrast, water-and-ink painting relies on its use of ink and water with brushstrokes to highlight ink shades to produce effects of focused or real and distant or virtual objects. Such a painting technique, without clear edge lines and space colouring, is incomprehensible for application on tens of thousands of celluloid films.[16]

With the blending of classical landscape painting aesthetics with the narrative and editing techniques in modern animated films, the four animated short films serve, in the history of Chinese animation, as irreplaceable foundations. Despite being created twenty-five years apart, during which time the many turbulent years of political and cultural changes had come to re-define everyday life, the underlying design of the shorts appear to convey a similar message: to demonstrate the kind of human sentiment towards the natural environment, which in turn generates an ecological aesthetics that is exemplified by the atmosphere of blandness; the construction of spaces of substance and void; and the unrestrained roaming movements within the landscapes.

In *The Cowboy's Flute*, Te Wei uses blankness on the screen to construct spaces of void. Without the need for meticulous brush strokes, he effectively presents scenes of the lifelike activities of the cowboy and his buffalo. Through his use of space and void, he emphasizes the subjects' – the cowboy's and the buffalo's – freedom and mobility of their activities in the vast and boundless expanse of water. Later, when the cowboy finds his buffalo missing, he climbs up to the highest peak in his search and we are shown a panoramic scene of the vast mountain areas with a sea of clouds (represented by blankness) blurring all beneath the cliff top and, in response to this situation, the boy's expression of helplessness. Through his prompt clarification of the missing buffalo sequence as being nothing more than a dream, Te Wei intentionally mixes scenes of reality and dreamscape, making it difficult for viewers to distinguish between the two – so as to reveal our capacity for imagination. By introducing the element of substance to balance that of void, *The Cowboy's Flute* follows traditional Chinese aesthetics, aiming to achieve a state of harmony as depicted in Confucius's *The Doctrine of the Mean*. In *Feeling from Mountain and Water*, with the departure of the old master, the fisher-girl tries in vain to spot the trail of the vanishing master, hindered by the mist in the forest. The film makes use of void and abstractions to create an airy, dream-like environment. This is similar to how blank spaces were used in classical Chinese paintings, where such spaces of void 'function both as a code and as specific ideological connotation, reflecting the ancient Chinese philosophical, as well as religious, consciousness'.[17] Finally, the old master vanishes in the manner of an illusion, and thereby increases his sage-like image, fusing him with nature as one; in Confucian terms, an anthropocosmic harmony and unity between humans and nature (*tianren heyi*) is thus attained.

To invite spectators to psychologically roam, tour and dwell in the represented natural landscapes, *Feeling From Mountain and Water* depicts the old master and his pupil's journey in nature by adopting relatively long takes and slow pans over the background sceneries, which are landscapes painted in water and ink. These images, though not exactly roaming long takes as defined by Lin Niantong, nonetheless project the subject's intended movements into the natural context. The protagonists' journey in nature starts with several shots from different perspectives (each shot a different landscape painting) to represent the young girl taking her boat through the imposing valley gorges. The backdrop of each image is painted with different texture strokes, and with intensifying use of chiaroscuro to portray their gradual progression from a relaxing trip along the river bank, to one down the majestic and enchanting gorges. With such portrayal of people in nature, the images emphasize the diminished human significance, in the blending of the protagonists into the magnificent, enchanted natural landscapes, creating harmony between humans and nature.

Following this, we track the old master and his pupil with a panoramic shot that tilts up from the foot of the mountain, as if we are seeing a crane shot rise vertically, to reveal the rugged features of the peaks to the vanishing point of a mountain path in the mist. In juxtaposition, another shot tilts downward from the top of a waterfall, following the water as it flows to the bottom where we see the two protagonists, awestruck at the sight of the powerful waterfall. What makes both *The Cowboy's Flute* and *Feeling from Mountain and Water* deeply ecological is the belief in submitting oneself to the way of nature in order to achieve spiritual unity with all living creatures and the physical environment. Towards the end of the two stories, both protagonists realize nature is the guiding principle in creating the best music. The cowboy's buffalo finally returns, only when it hears the boy's music inspired by the sound of wind, and produced by the flute made of bamboo. The sound of nature, at the same time, attracted all animals in the wild to gather and listen. In *Feeling from Mountain and Water*, the Old master knows that only by taking his pupil on a journey in nature, can she be inspired to play greater music. Like the ancient Chinese landscape painters would agree, Te Wei's animated films reassert the importance of understanding and experiencing nature, as a means to create greater art, be it a painting or a piece of music. Such advocacy of linking human beings' artistic expressions with the principle of nature facilitates the establishment of emotional bonding between human beings and the physical environments. For several decades, Te Wei's water-and-ink animations have continued to be regarded as a significant step for Chinese animation's development, for they turned static sceneries in classical Chinese paintings into animated landscapes in which stories among human beings, animals and nature could take place.

Animating modernity: Digital *Shanshui* in contemporary art and performance

Since the 1990s, many of the major animated films that have been produced have made little reference to classical water-and-ink aesthetics, and nature is no longer shown as pure and idealistic as depicted in Te Wei's animations. With natural habitats gradually replaced by skyscrapers, shopping malls, congested and polluted urban environments, our relationship with mountains and water, and our ability to roam in an unrestrained manner through natural landscapes has become less and less significant. Instead, there is an increasing awareness of the huge discrepancy between the ideals represented in classical landscape paintings, and the realities one sees in our physical, lived environments. Classical eco-aesthetics and the ideal of *tianrenheyi* have been brought into question.

Chinese animated films produced in the past few decades have lacked clarity of position and direction of development, as well as the capability to compete in the international market. However, in the past decade or so, animation has asserted its presence in various other contexts, reflecting the changing relationships between humans and the environment, as shown in recent media art installations and performances, rendering animated media art an important tool in the development of China's soft power.[18] In terms of representations of *shanshui* and urban landscapes, in particular, we see a number of interactive media representations of digitally animated landscapes that invite viewers to re-approach and experience environments – both natural and urban; past and present. In 2010, the animated art exhibit 'River of Wisdom: Animated Version of the Riverside Scene of Qingming Festival' became a major highlight in the Shanghai World Expo. Transforming Northern Song Dynasty Chinese painter Zhang Zeduan's painting 'Riverside Scene at Qingming Festival' (*Qingming Shanghetu*) into a multimedia installation, the 120 m × 6 m animated painting depicts meticulous details of human life in the prosperous township of Bianjing, the capital of Northern Song Dynasty, some nine hundred years ago. The long-scroll animated painting is formed by twelve high-resolution projectors that use computer geometric transformation and correction technology. It retains the colour tone, style and details of the original painting. In addition, the animation has added scenes of transition from day to night and vice versa, to portray the economic prosperity of the time. With the aid of digital animation technology, 'River of Wisdom' brings classical painting aesthetics and traditional artwork to the attention of present-day viewers. It presents China's image as an emerging nation of economic and technological advancement, while retaining its rich cultural and artistic traditions.

Since the early 2000s, prominent film director Zhang Yimou has incorporated computer animation technology into his large-scale outdoor performances. From his films *Raise the Red Latern* (1991), *Hero* (2002) to the opening ceremony of 2008 Beijing Olympics, Zhang's works have been recognized internationally for their strong visual impact. Since 2003, he has created the 'Impression' series (*yinxiang xilie* 印象系列), a series of outdoor performances using natural landscapes in different parts of China as theatre stages. Being some of the world's largest natural stage shows, these performances are popular among visitors from all around the world. They have been marketed and praised for their successful attempts in portraying beauty and harmony in Chinese natural environments. To enhance the visual impact of the performances, various forms of multimedia, animation and lighting effects have been used to produce a mediated and simulated nature.

In one of these shows, *Impression Hainan* in Haikou, the semi-open stage was built within a sheltered auditorium fronting a sandy beach along Qiongzhou Strait. Animated images are effectively projected onto a constructed stage floor to simulate natural landscapes. Instead of being set on the actual beach, the performance takes place on a greyish cemented stage floor on which different colours and patterns of lighting effects are projected, simulating different natural landscapes in the dance performance. At times, the colourful projections turn the stage floor into an animated sandy beach and, at others, into a forest of green coconut trees. In one scene, blue lights are projected on to a huge piece of cloth held over the heads of some fifty performers, through whose movements, wave after wave of currents are created, resulting in a highly realistic portrayal of a roaring sea upon which animated jumping dolphins are projected.

Elsewhere, in the Buddhist Mount Putuo, Zhejiang, *Impression Putuo* presents the audience with an example of a skilful integration of natural real-life landscape with cinematic digital animation. In one scene, the large screen shows an animation of an old and young monk in conversation about Buddhist philosophy. The young monk relates a story of his encounter with a woman in need of help to cross a stream in the forest. A vivid scene of the animated forest and stream is then represented with the use of projection mapping, designed to fuse animated landscape on screen with the real-life landscape behind, juxtaposing the uphill climb of the animated young monk with the movement of the screen, giving the audience an impression of the animated characters going up the real-life mountain in the distance. Through the fusion and overlapping of natural evening scenery with animated images, *Impression Putuo* enriches the faint-looking real-life landscape, turning it into a visual spectacle. A later scene opens with an all-encompassing screen projecting the view of a graceful traditional Chinese garden with pavilions, a stream and willow trees. With the spectators immersed in the exquisite images of the garden landscape, part of the screen is withdrawn, exposing a view of the natural landscape behind, which, assisted by colourful artificial lighting and the presence of a 'real' landscape, greatly enhances the viewer's impression of the garden setting.

Within a decade, these multimedia performances have developed into major tourist attractions in various Chinese cities. Those who praise them consider the animations complementary to real-life landscapes. They facilitate and stimulate a re-discovery of the natural landscape, addressing peoples' diminished attention to the appreciation of the natural. Others, however, have criticized the performances for exoticizing and commoditizing natural landscapes with excessive artificial lightings and computer-generated effects. In any case, the juxtapositions of and interactions between real-life natural landscapes with virtual, animated landscapes have offered people new ways to contemplate the varied relationships between human beings and the environment in the world today.

Over the past few decades, the true cost of economic progress has become increasingly apparent. Industrialization, modernization and extensive urban development have brought about many positive changes in human life, but, at the same time, no less negative consequences in the forms of environmental degradation, extinctions of non-human species, natural and human-induced disasters, toxic waste and contamination, new diseases and epidemics, illnesses and deaths.

In recent years, we begin to see sceptical representations of uncanny, 'post-natural' landscapes in the works of contemporary artists. Since 2007, Shanghainese artist Yang Yongliang has created several series of animated video art installations that depict Chinese landscapes fused with digitally mastered, exaggerated modern cityscapes. Viewing it from a distance, his works appear to be images of classical Chinese *shanshui* paintings, with their black and white, ink-like compositions. However, taking a closer look, one sees that the 'natural landscapes', the mountains and water, are in fact a bricolage of images of construction sites with large cranes, skyscrapers, shopping malls and signboards for commercial corporations, factory buildings, crumpled bridges and roads, and area-wide traffic congestion, giving industrial pollution, excessive urban development and environmental destruction their due criticism.[19] In the century, it is now clear that the modernization process, used simply for the utilitarian ends of development, is insufficient to support a full range of human flourishing'.[20] Globally, people are disillusioned by the so-called progress brought about by modernization and overdevelopment. The kind of transcendental experience and spiritual connectedness between human beings and nature, or between humans and the idealized landscapes portrayed in *shanshui* paintings, is becoming increasingly difficult for contemporary people, who lack the training and cultivation, to perceive and attain. Yang's animated landscapes effectively criticize the staggering speed at which the city grows and engulfs the environment, and highlights our contemporary collective sense of detachment from nature. Towards the end of *The Day of Perpetual Night* (2012), one of Yang's animated installations, a UFO flies over the landscape and pauses in the sky – this interesting twist gives the animated Chinese landscape a surrealistic touch, thus blending classical water-and-ink aesthetics into recent techno-cyber culture.

From the portrayal of human–nature relationships in Te Wei's short films, to the interactive media representations in contemporary art and performance, animation has transformed and evolved, but never ceased to be an important artistic expression for depicting Chinese people's complex relationships with the environment. Despite the diminishing emphasis on the unity between human and nature in recent animated representations, with the disruptions and violations of the rules of blandness and tranquillity in classical landscape aesthetics, and the expression of uncertainty and anxiety in modern, uncanny landscapes, the impulse to reference classical water-and-ink painting aesthetics is recurrently seen in the various forms of animated landscapes of Chinese media and art. From feature film to outdoor live performance, digital media artworks for museum and art exhibitions, to moving billboard advertisements on the streets, the broadening usage of animation technology has provided innovative ways to represent and shape landscape in the constantly changing China of today.

Notes

1   Burton Watson, *The Analects of Confucius* (New York: Columbia University Press, 2007), 45.

2   Wei-ming Tu, 'An "Anthropocosmic" Perspective on Creativity', in *Dialogue of Philosophies, Religions and Civilizations in the Era of Globalization: Chinese Philosophical Studies, XXV*, ed. Zhao Dunhua. (Washington, DC: The Council for Research in Values and Philosophy, 2007), 143–153.

3   Jerome Silbergeld, *Chinese Painting Style: Media, Methods, and Principles of Form* (Seattle: University of Washington Press, 1982), 1.

4   François Jullien, *In Praise of Blandness: Proceeding from Chinese Thought and Aesthetics*, trans. Paula M. Varsano (New York: Zone Books, 2004), 37.

5   Jullien, *In Praise of Blandness*, 25, 125.

6   Confucius, *Daxue Zhongyong*, ed. Zhong Mang and Wang Guoxuan (Hong Kong: Chung Hwa Books, 2012), 49. (Chinese, translation by author.)

7   Wucius Wong, *The Tao of Chinese Landscape Painting: Principles & Methods.* (New York: Design Press, 1991), 20.

8   Silbergeld, *Chinese Painting Style*, 48.

9   Jerome Silbergeld, 'Cinema and the Visual Arts of China', in *A Companion to Chinese Cinema*, ed. Yingjin Zhang (London: Blackwell Publishing Ltd, 2012), 405.

10 Jullien, *In Praise of Blandness*, 132.

11 Baihua Zong, *Meixue Sanbu* (美學散步) (Shanghai: Shanghai Renmin Chubanshe, 2007), 115. (Translation by author.)

12 Guo Xi, 'Kuo Hsi's The Significance of Landscapes (*Lin quan gao zhi ji: Shanshui Xun* 林泉高致集:山水訓)' (ninth century), in *Early Chinese Texts on Painting*, trans. Susan Bush and Shih, Hsio-yen (Hong Kong: Hong Kong University Press, 1985), 151–152.

13 Niantong Lin, *Zhongguo dian ying mei xue* (中國電影美學) (Taibei: Yun chen wen hua shi ye gu fen you xian gong si, 1991), 41–42; Hao, Dazheng (trans. by D. Wilkerson). 'Chinese Visual Representation: Painting and Cinema', *Cinematic Landscapes: Observations on the Visual Arts and Cinema of China and Japan*, eds. Linda Ehrlich and David Desser (Austin: University of Texas Press, 1994), 52; Ni, Zhen. 'Classical Chinese Painting and Cinematographic Signification', *Cinematic Landscapes: Observations on the Visual Arts and Cinema of China and Japan*, 73; Silbergeld, 'Cinema and the Visual Arts of China', 403.

14 James Udden, 'Hou Hsiao-hsien and the Question of a Chinese Style', in *Asian Cinema*, 13.2 (Fall/Winter, 2002): 57.

15 Songlin Zhang and Jianying Gong, *Shui chuangzao le 'Xiaokedou Zhao Mama': Te Wei he zhongguo donghua*/ 誰創造了'小蝌蚪找媽媽'：特偉和中國動畫 (Shanghai: Shanghai Renmin Chubanshe, 2010), 127.

16 Huilin Zhang, *Ershi shiji Zhongguo Donghua Yishushi* (Shaanxi: Shaanxi Renmin Meisu Chubanshe, 2002), 84.

17 Zhen Ni, 'Classical Chinese Painting and Cinematographic Signification', 73.

18 Developed in the 1980s, 'soft power' is a concept coined by Joseph Nye to refer particularly to 'the ability to achieve goals through attraction rather than coercion', in *Soft Power: The Means to Success in World Politics* (New York: PublicAffairs, 2004), x.

19 Yang Yongliang, previews of the series of animated landscape video art works, accessed 2 December 2014, http://www.yangyongliang.com/video.html.

20 Tu, Wei-ming. 'The Ecological Turn in New Confucian Humanism: Implications for China and the World', *Daedalus*, 130.4, *Religion and Ecology: Can the Climate Change?* (Fall, 2001): 251.

7

Latvian Animation: Landscapes of Resistance

Mihaela Mihailova

Introduction: The post-Soviet production context

During the past two decades, Hollywood's embrace of three-dimensional computer animation has contributed to CGI's rise as a dominant technological and aesthetic paradigm worldwide. This development lends new urgency and relevance to the question of aesthetic and ideological alternatives – both traditional and newly created – that can help elucidate, complicate and contextualize the oft-discussed digital turn by exploring the range and diversity of global approaches to creating animated landscapes. This issue has been addressed in the context of national cinemas, notably vis-à-vis Japan (where hand-drawn animation is still widely used), as exemplified by the scholarship of Thomas Lamarre, Marc Steinberg and Susan Napier, among others. Partially inspired by such studies, the following pages focus on contemporary Latvian animation, highlighting the ways in which Latvian animated landscapes resist and experiment with computer-generated imagery and negotiate related issues of cartoon realism.

Subsumed under the category of Soviet film from its infancy in the mid-1960s until the collapse of the USSR, Latvian animation has, in the past two decades, emerged from relative obscurity in the early twenty-first century to make its mark on the international festival circuit, thanks to a number of award-winning shorts and international co-productions.[1] Still, unlike its neighbour Estonia, whose animation is highlighted in a number of English-language articles and a book-length study,[2] Latvia has received comparatively little attention in the Anglophonic branch of Animation Studies, being limited to a book chapter on filmmaker Signe Baumane[3] and a short entry in Giannalberto Bendazzi's *Cartoons: One Hundred Years of Cinema Animation*.[4] Partially compensating for this dearth of scholarship and opening up avenues for future study are among the goals of this chapter.

Latvian animation underwent a seismic shift in the early 1990s. During the Soviet period, in Latvia, as in the rest of the Soviet Bloc, the film industry was heavily state-subsidized and dependent on government distribution mechanisms.[5] This meant that financial profit was not a high priority and indeed a culture of commercial animation was largely absent. With the collapse of the Soviet Union, this model fell apart and state subsidies were drastically diminished, forcing the Latvian film industry to develop new modes of production and attitudes towards filmmaking. Documentary filmmaker Antra Cilinska's account of the situation recalls 'a sharp decrease in state funding, empty studios looking to attract foreign crews, the disappearance of domestic films from the circuits, armies of idle film professionals, and the redefinition of concepts like "copyright", "entertainment", and "audience".[6] To add to this, the absence of independent production pathways, the competition from foreign productions (now much more readily available), and the temporary shrinking of the market (due to the loss of the built-in audience of fellow Soviet states) further contributed to the stagnation which marked the immediate post-Soviet period.

Despite this crisis, by the turn of the century, Latvian animation had managed to adapt to its new circumstances and come up with solutions, some of which hinged on the continuation of familiar practices. Much of animation production today is still largely dependent on government support provided by two main funding bodies, the National Film Centre of Latvia and the State Culture Capital Foundation.[7] Still, new trends have emerged as well, such as Latvian animators' increased participation in international co-productions, including the features *Lotte from Gadgetville* (2006), directed by Estonians Heiki Ernits and Janno Põldma and *The Three Musketeers* (2006), a Latvian/Danish/UK co-production. This rise in collaborations is likely due to the availability of European Union support through the EURIMAGE and MEDIA Plus funds, which Latvia joined in 2001 and 2002, respectively.[8]

At home, Latvian animation is represented by a variety of new and already established studios. Rija Films, founded in 1995, is perhaps the most internationally recognizable studio, predominantly focusing on drawn animation. Until a few years ago, studio Dauka also remained a strong presence in traditional animation. Animācijas Brigāde, along with the Juris Podnieks studio, produces stop-motion films. Other studios, including Studija Centrums, Jet Media, Urga and Atom Art, to name a few, have released shorts representing a wide variety of techniques and modes: documentary animation and musical films, cutouts and textiles, etc. An interesting product of the meeting between the country's strong animation auteur traditions and the requirements of the free market are the independent studios founded and operated by a single animator, such as Vladimir Leschiov's Lunohod and Aija Bley's A. Bley Film Studio. Thus, while Latvia now has a developed studio system, this system remains fundamentally different from the profit-oriented Western model, as Latvian directors compete for subsidies both at home and abroad while continuing to emphasize individualistic and traditional approaches to animation.

While the historical development, labour organization and business imperatives behind this production environment are fascinating in their own right, they provide a contextual framework for examination of a major distinguishing feature of Latvian animation – its persistent resistance of the increasing proliferation of computer-generated imagery and the obsession with photorealism oftentimes associated with this technology. With a few exceptions, the balancing act between the realities of a market economy and the reluctance to fully abandon the models of the past has given birth to films which engage and reinvigorate traditional animation techniques (stop motion, pencil drawing, watercolours, cutouts, etc.) or favour less conventional ways of incorporating computer animation. Keeping in mind the complex economic and sociopolitical processes that have shaped this corpus of films, the rest of this chapter is devoted to a close reading of their aesthetic, thematic and emotional landscapes. Using a representative selection of shorts, the following pages will tease out common trends, features and cultural tropes, consider the historical, stylistic and ideological implications and reasons behind this adherence to a traditional look, and put these diverse films in conversation with each other and with a larger Eastern European animation tradition. Despite drawing parallels with dominant Hollywood trends, this text does not aim to propose a simple West v East binary opposition, but rather to encourage a more globally oriented conversation about contemporary animation landscapes that takes into consideration the variety of discourses that are shaped by and intern shape today's international animation production.

Embracing traditional techniques

Contemporary Latvian animators work in a wide range of classical techniques, creating a truly diverse corpus of films. Still, a few common trends unify these seemingly disparate works. Among them, a chief concern is the emphasis of medium alongside content – indeed the harmonious, symbiotic relationship between the two. Oftentimes, Latvian animation's resistance to the encroaching presence of the digital finds expression in pieces which seek to emphasize and explore the specific characteristics of a given technique and find its resonances with the emotional landscape of the film.

Reinis Pētersons's directorial debut, *Ursus* (2011), offers a productive case study. This charcoal-on-paper short tells a poignant, atmospheric tale of a circus bear's pursuit of a freedom that is represented by the landscape of the forest. The director himself has emphasized the handmade aspect of his film, pointing out that *Ursus* is 'deliberately created with this likely *classical* [emphasis in original] method as it tries to avoid the temptations of the digital world'.[9] This quote introduces two key ideas that will continue to resurface throughout this chapter, namely, the value of animation craftsmanship and the notion of digital technology as potentially corrupting. Here, craftsmanship and digital animation are implicitly coded as incompatible with each other, while the computer is understood to represent a threat to artistic expression, or even a potential crutch. Pētersons's choice of technique becomes an expression of intent, namely, the intent to resist the appeal of the digital.

There is a romantic flavour to his praise for the 'textures and delicateness' of charcoal and a nostalgic desire to hold on to the tactile quality of traditional animation that can get lost amidst the polished perfection of the computer-generated image.[10] Pētersons's background as a painter, graphic artist and illustrator is strongly felt in the style of his wordless, melancholic piece. His landscapes come alive through their pervasive sense of texture; the image vibrates with inner power as moody shades of grey and specks of white dance across the overwhelmingly dark screen, turning *Ursus* into a moving lithograph. The charcoal technique effectively captures the bear's tumultuous feelings; the small, yet perpetual and incessant fluctuations of form create a vision of a world atremble with conflict and uncertainty. Emotional conflict plays out through the contrast between light and darkness. Thus, when the bear comes out into the whiteness of the circus ring, outlined clearly at the centre of the frame, the crowd of spectators, rendered in dark hues, appear to surround him on all sides, with the menacing, inescapable darkness of the charcoal becoming a visual shorthand for the oppressive and stifling gaze of the humans.

While *Ursus* provides a glimpse into the lyrical aspect of Latvian animation, on the opposite side of the emotional spectrum rests the light-hearted atmosphere and humour typical of the country's puppet tradition. Director Jānis Cimermanis's stop-motion shorts represent a gleeful celebration of gag-oriented laughter, visceral slapstick, frantic energy and perpetual chaos. Many of his films are dedicated to the antics of the three well-meaning, yet chronically inept members of Rescue Team, who inevitably exacerbate every problem they are called upon to fix. As his characters flail around, bump into each other and drop objects, the director takes advantage of the limited jerky movements of the puppets to emphasize the physical comedy and amplify the absurdity of his situations. The signature design of the puppets – complete with bushy hair, oversized bulbous noses and googly eyes – further reinforces the zany, light-hearted atmosphere of these pieces, while the busy, cluttered spaces enhance the sense of chaos. Cimermanis's humour is particularly effective in self-reflexive shorts which parody his own medium, such as *Film Studio* (*Kinostudija*, 1993) and *Hunting* (*Medības*, 2007). The former, an amusing take on the inner workings of a film studio, lovingly pokes fun at puppetry, as one of the employees mistakes an animatronic dragon for a real monster and a number of sets end up destroyed as the Rescue Team attempts to wrangle with the beast. In the latter, the puppets themselves build comically fake wooden animals in another clever nod to the animation process. Like Pētersons, Cimermanis emphasizes a unique characteristic of his medium – specifically the nature of movement in stop-motion – in order to establish a mood. His approach is likewise an act of resistance to the digital, as it embraces the irregularity of motion instead of treating it as a limitation of traditional stop motion easily overcome with a computer.

Another stop-motion director, Nils Skapāns, has expressed a similar attitude, describing the movements of a puppet animated with a computer as 'too perfect'.[11] Skapāns, who works predominantly with plasticine, identifies his films as continuing 'the conservative, in a positive sense of the word … classic puppet animation traditions where each of the film's characters is created by hand'.[12] Here, the refusal to adopt recent technology is once again explicitly framed as conscious artistic choice. While Cimermanis takes advantage of the inherent uncanniness of moving puppets to create comedy, Skapāns – specifically in his adult-oriented shorts – builds alien landscapes inhabited by otherworldly creatures. As with Pētersons, an authentic sense of palpable texture becomes crucial in shorts like *Flap Your Wings!* (*Sasit spārnus!*, 2008), a pre-historic tale about evolution, and *Brickannia* (*Klucānija*, 2000), a bizarre cyclical story about birds set in outer space. The organic nature of the landscape in *Flap Your Wings!* is conveyed through the director's use of actual found materials (such as seashells) and choice of texture, especially for the bodies of the evolving bird-like creatures, which are scaly and rough, as befitting the dinosaur age. In *Brickannia*, the uneven texture and jagged shapes of the plasticine mountains and the emptiness of the space create an otherworldly setting, while the wooden birds, with their visible connective hinges and clearly delineated separate parts, look unsettlingly robotic and (un)dead.

This preoccupation with the materiality of the image is central to a definition of animated realism espoused by some Latvian puppet animators, based on the notion that puppet animation is inherently more realistic compared to a drawn image. Animācijas Brigāde producer Māris Putniņš summarizes this philosophy as follows: 'The puppet animation deals with realistic things – space, volume, and texture and in comparison to the drawing [sic] animation, it can create illusions'.[13] Thus, tangibility is privileged among the true measures of realism in an animated landscape. This is an interpretation of animated realism that emphasizes touch along with sight, sense along with vision – in contrast to digital animation, which favours appearance.

As these case studies show, Latvian animation's commitment to handcrafted art and its awareness of medium are common features of its landscapes of resistance, but they manifest in a variety of ways with unique aesthetic and thematic effects and implications. In order to explore this diversity further, the following pages will highlight several notable trends in contemporary Latvian animation output, reading the aesthetics of resistance as a product of the interplay between artistic and social concerns and ideologies.

Metaphorical landscapes

Latvian animators' resistance to computer technology has engendered a range of approaches to creating traditionally animated landscapes. While many contemporary animators strive to recreate the surrounding world by accurately rendering texture, light and weight, some Latvian directors reject the ordinary world altogether, defying physics, logic and conventional rules of representation and narrative. To quote director Vladimir Leschiov, 'why create a copy of reality when you can invent your own world'.[14] Leschiov, who has drawn with pencil, watercolour and even black tea, chooses his technique in correspondence with the mood of the piece. One of the most versatile and singular contemporary Latvian animators, he has produced a body of work described as 'philosophical, visually exquisite, poetic and with a surreal touch'.[15] His work exemplifies the strong metaphorical current within today's Latvian animation, characterized by phantasmagorical, surreal landscapes marked by idiosyncratic symbolism and inhabited by mysterious characters.

His film *Insomnia* (*Bezmiegs*, 2004) is a dreamy, mystical tale of a man wandering through an urban night-time landscape that is more psychological than physical, featuring bizarre occurrences – a man scaling a building downwards, a shepherd inside the moon, a cat which might be an alter ego to the protagonist's wife – which remain open to interpretation. In accordance with the logic of dreams, glimpses of meanings and connections are tantalizingly offered, yet ultimately left out of reach. Instead, visual rhymes, such as the image of the full moon, suggest a perpetual subliminal cycle of symbols. Leschiov's decision to draw with coloured pastels on grey paper in order to convey a 'night-time feeling'[16] further reinforces the atmosphere evoked by the title, with the muted greys and blues of his colour palette evoking a foggy dream landscape, capturing the elusive sheen of pale moonlight. The soundscape, with its muffled, distant sounds and echoes, likewise suggests a state between slumber and wakefulness, completing the vision of a man imprisoned within his own psyche.

Leschiov returns to the idea of a personal journey in *Wings and Oars* (Spārni un airi, 2009), in which a former pilot remembers his life and relationships. Like *Insomnia*, this film lacks a conventional narrative. Instead, it offers a series of reminiscences conveyed through a complex web of visual motifs and metaphors. The motif of flying permeates the film: a plane takes flight, the protagonist himself sprouts wings, flying fish jump out of the water and even a pair of pants rides the wind (Figure 7.1). Disjointed and fluctuating like

Figure 7.1 Images of flight dominate the visual landscape of *Wings and Oars* (Lunohod, 2009)

memory itself, his imagery – centred on travel and marked by almost incessant metamorphosis – conveys a sense of constant movement, a desire to escape and an insatiable longing for new horizons.

Like *Insomnia*, here Leschiov infuses his landscapes, rendered in watercolours with a warm brownish-yellow colour scheme punctuated by vivid red, with a consistent mood. His natural spaces are seemingly serene: a field covered in vibrant poppies, a sea under slowly moving white clouds. And yet, a wind disturbs the grass and agitates the waves, creating a dynamic, restless world. The watercolours, which Leschiov describes as an unpredictable medium, reinforce the sense of perpetual flux.[17] In close-up, the red poppies appear to change every second, as shadows and hues dance across their surface with a quiet intensity. Like the films discussed earlier, Leschiov's work is not confined by visual realism. The sense of truthfulness to reality in his films derives from capturing the wonderful weirdness of mental states and accepting the inexplicable as part of everyday life.

Another traditional animator notable for her use of visual metaphors is émigré filmmaker Signe Baumane, who has been working in Brooklyn since 1995.[18] Her film *Woman* (*Sieviete*, 2002), produced at the Latvian studio Rija, reflects the connection with nature and the influence of animism that she describes as having shaped both her work and Latvian animation in general.[19] This animistic spirit finds expression in the fusion between the human and natural world and the harmonious, sometimes even symbiotic co-existence of people and animals in Baumane's work. In this short, the titular Woman is entirely at peace with her wild surroundings. She is literally born out of the Moon: the celestial body transforms into a water jug and pours the woman into existence. Her connection with wildlife is constantly reinforced throughout the film; framed by Baumane's lush forest landscape (painted in watercolours), the Woman is carried on the back of a large red bull, the shape of whose horns mirrors the crescent of the moon, enhancing the visual harmony of the landscape.[20] Eventually, she seems to absorb the bull's primal energy and is reborn, ritually emerging out of the water, now red like the animal and adorned with the same pair of crescent-shaped horns. The notion of the female as simultaneously sensual and wild, animalistic and loving, which is present in all of Baumane's work, is here illustrated via the metaphor of the bull-woman.

Woman – like the Leschiov films mentioned above – exemplifies Latvian animation's love for rich metaphors, motifs and visual symmetry, as well as its gleeful defiance of common narrative strategies. At the same time, it engages another key side of Latvian animation's spirit of resistance, namely, the embrace of female sexuality and the creation of feminist spaces and erotic, sensual landscapes – a trend largely affirmed by Baumane herself.

Feminist spaces, erotic landscapes

Baumane is known for her feminist provocations that challenge traditional gender norms and roles and conservative views on sexuality through a combination of verbal and visual humour and explicit imagery. The female characters in her films are empowered, unapologetic and aware of their bodies. They are proactive and outspoken, posing a 'threat to the so-called rules of masculinity'.[21] For example, her hilarious series *Teat Beat of Sex* (2008) explores a range of issues related to sex and sexuality, such as the pros and cons of large penises, the implications of not wearing underwear and the benefits of masturbation. It showcases Baumane's singular brand of humour based on visualizing concepts through visual puns and metaphors. Oftentimes, she gives a literal illustration of a metaphor or simile for comic effect; thus, a well-endowed man whose penis is compared to a squash by the protagonist is drawn holding a giant squash growing out of his pants. The immediately recognizable simplistic, cartoony and unapologetically erotic aesthetic of her films conveys a sense of personal touch and frankness. While challenging digital animation's cult of perfection with her unembellished drawings, Baumane also defies the notion that explicit sexual content belongs in a masculine landscape.

Aija Bley's hand-drawn short *Island of Doctor D* (*Doktora D. Sala*, 2005) is likewise infused with unbridled female sexuality. The female character, a beautiful nurse, has inherited her curves and her sumptuous hair from the fairy-like women of Art Nouveau. She is coded as a seductress via her association with the colour red through her hair, dress and her work collecting donated blood. Throughout the film, the nurse's flowing red tresses, which take on a life of their own, become a metaphor for her wild sexual energy (Figure 7.2). Growing ever longer, the hair curves itself into inviting gestures and even wraps itself around a man's ankle, becoming an expression of sexual agency and desire. Thus, by drawing the female as an aggressor, this film reverses traditional gender norms,

Figure 7.2 Red hair becomes synonymous with overwhelmingly powerful female sexuality in *Island of Doctor D* (Rija Films, 2005)

creating an erotic space controlled by the woman – both the woman on screen and the one at the animation stand.

Mara Linina's *Comet* (*Komēta*, 1997) offers an extremely minimalist take on the Adam and Eve myth. In this delicate hand-drawn piece, the Biblical characters are simply outlined, their bodies not coloured in. Despite not being fleshed out, however, Eve is represented as a sensual being. She is not a woman unaware of her nakedness, but one who is comfortable in her skin. The camera lingers on her naked form as she strikes a pose, hand on hip, and cooks the bears Adam killed for her, while he uses their skins to make her a fur coat. Moments later, this fur coat is already on her shoulders, but is quickly allowed to slip off, and the couple gets intimate. Their first sexual union is ingenuously visualized by using the transparency of their forms, as their bodies literally overlap on screen, the outlines of hers visible and superimposed on his form. They briefly become a fused being, recalling the erotic drawings of Sergei Eisenstein. Like Eiseinstein's sketches, Linina's technique, in transcending the boundaries of the solid outline, achieves 'freedom from the rules of drawing'.[22] This is a freedom attained and celebrated through eroticism – a feminine sexual energy that leaks away from Eve's transparent body to permeate the entire landscape.

Computers in Latvian animation:
Digital landscapes with a twist

While the films described so far present alternatives to the computerized look, perhaps the most fascinating form of Latvian resistance to the visual clichés of digital animation is their subversive co-option of the digital turn. Indeed, not all Latvian animators exclusively favour traditional techniques; some choose to adapt computer-generated imagery to their own styles. Thus, among those who do make extensive use of computer technology, there is a tendency to avoid the well-rounded, polished appearance characteristic of mainstream computer animation and resist the appeal of imitating live action in favour of highly stylized imagery that approximates the look of classical animation. The idiosyncratic painter Kārlis Vītols, who oftentimes creates animation for exhibition, exemplifies this trend, using computerized collage to animate a variety of materials, such as paintings, posters and photos.[23] While the intervention of digital technology is visible in his animation, his landscapes defiantly evoke the sense of solid, three-dimensional materiality characteristic of cut-outs. Thus, films like *Devil's Fuji* (*Velna Fudži*, 2008) recall the explicitly hand-crafted look of television shows like *South Park* or the overly angular cartoonishness of *Samurai Jack*. A colourful, overly stylized pastiche which combines echoes of video game aesthetics with allusions to classical Latvian writer Rainis, this film places new technologies in the service of traditional aesthetics, adapting the new tool to the desired artistic style and not vice versa.

While Vītols's digital landscapes remain firmly rooted in fine art, graphic designer Egils Mednis's 2007 machinima piece *The Ship* (*Kuģis*), rendered using the toolset of the game *Unreal Tournament 2004* (Epic Games, 2004), embraces computer technology, by virtue of the set, animations and character models having been created using *Maya* before being imported into the *Unreal* editor.[24] Both the desert icy landscape and the characters are designed with attention to photographic likeness. However, this film is notable for its use of computer animation to destabilize this illusion of reality even as it is supposedly sustaining it. The convincingly recreated arctic landscape is suddenly disrupted by a hallucination of a giant ship. In contrast to the surrounding landscape, this ship is an abstraction: a moving dark mass of flickering lights, at once threatening and disorienting because it is hard to classify. Eventually, it transforms into the side wall of a building, and this sudden return to a familiar computer-generated reality is even more jarring because of the contrast it establishes, making the viewer question the place of these events in the narrative and the nature of the narrative itself (is it all a dream or a hypothermia-induced vision?). In that sense, while the dominant aesthetic of *The Ship* remains realistic, the film takes advantage of its technology to interject a dream or hallucination at a key moment, thereby undermining its own reality and questioning if and how this world – a computer-generated world – can negotiate a sense of realism.

Resistance is not futile: The roots of a trend

As the previous pages have shown, contemporary Latvian animators are finding myriad creative ways of resisting or adapting computer animation and its underlying aesthetics and ideology. What remains to be seen is, why? Rather than a simple set of reasons, the answer may emerge from the complex interplay between numerous aesthetic, social, historical and economic factors and imperatives that have shaped and continue to shape the national landscape of Latvian animation to this day.

To go back a full circle, the contemporary production context in the country plays an important role. The fact that, due to their reliance on subsidies, Latvian animators are not forced to optimize for profit, has been seen as creatively liberating. As Vilnis Kalnaellis, managing director of Rija Films, has put it, 'the question of investment returns does not concern us'.[25] Thus, freed from the necessity to cater to the mass taste by following popular trends or otherwise submitting to business imperatives, Latvian directors have more room for experimentation. The fact that individual auteurs have historically been able to secure funding in the country means that singular animation styles have been – and continue to be – encouraged to flourish.

Another contributing factor is the importance of honouring the existing national tradition in animation filmmaking. In local film publications, it is not rare to see a director praised for his or her commitment to the legacy of the past. For instance, a special issue of *Film News* introduces puppet director Dace Rīdūze as someone who 'respects the traditions of both the studio [Animācijas Brigāde] and the Latvian animation films in general'.[26] The tone of press releases also betrays a strong sense of pride in this tradition. The aforementioned *Film News* article begins with the following proclamation, 'The masters of Latvian animation are proud that animation – both the drawing [sic] and puppet animation – is, was, and will be the most competitive Latvian film genre'.[27] Likewise, many Latvian animators place great importance on being true to their roots. The desire to preserve a national tradition, establish a stylistic continuity and also honour Latvian culture is often explicitly stated in interviews. Roze Stiebra, one of Latvia's pioneering animators who is still active today, has said the following: 'The U.S. style of animation is not necessarily a good thing. We believe it is possible to do something else, to use stories and a style inspired by our own national culture.'[28] Evidently, a resistance to globalization and outside influences is also part of the equation. In many ways, Latvian animation remains inwards-looking, as evidenced by a statement from Kalnaellis, according to whom, 'to save one's identity and culture, we need to look for good animators, interesting designs and find good stories that are based in our own countries'.[29]

All of this ties into the notion, espoused by some animators, that there are essential qualities directly related to national character and circumstances that set Latvian animation apart and make it unique. For instance, Leschiov believes that Latvian animators' penchant for surrealist landscapes and bizarre metaphors is a function of living in the country. He has stated a preference for working in Latvia because everything there is 'absurd and illogical', to quote him, for '[f]oreigners think my films are strange, but I'm not making it up. I show it like it is'.[30] This idea of the essential Latvianness of Latvian animation is echoed by Signe Baumane, who argues that 'Latvian filmmakers operate on a notion of visual metaphors, some of which translate outside of the Latvian context, but some of which don't, [while] American films are more literal. You get what you see.'[31]

However, the preference for traditional animation techniques is not simply a question of national pride. Largely due to the fact that, until recently, there was no dedicated animation program in the country, a number of Latvia's leading contemporary animators are trained as fine artists and predominantly self-taught in the field of animation.[32] For instance, Kārlis Vītols and Reinis Pētersons hold degrees from the Art Academy of Latvia.[33] Keeping this in mind, the embrace of classical art approaches and techniques in their films can also be read as a product of an artist's, as opposed to an animator's, sensibility.

Finally, the resistance to computer animation could partially be attributed to the vision of computer technology as creatively stifling and limiting. In that sense, it is a form of resistance to the power held over the creator by the tool. As previously discussed, the ideal of craftsmanship is highly valued in Latvian animation, and the reliance on software is often seen as its antithesis. Being able to animate with a variety of techniques is seen as a sign of authentic artistry, while reliance on the computer is interpreted as a sign of weakness and dependence on one's tool. The following quote by Leschiov summarizes this attitude, emphasizing the dangers of artistic stagnation in a digital production context, and pointing to the shift of focus away from the creator and onto the machine: 'You can experiment with other animation methods and figure out new ways, but with this it isn't possible – your new animation medium is your newest *super* [*sic*] computer, and you have to buy an even newer and better one next year. That's simply the development of equipment, not animation.'[34] This philosophy inscribes Latvian animation in an ongoing debate about the possible danger of technology undermining animators' labour and making it obsolete in the context of contemporary production practices, which the author has addressed elsewhere.[35] This is hardly surprising: in a creative environment which emphasizes artistry, individualism and respect for tradition, the impersonal conveyer belt efficiency and the constant need for innovation that has become synonymous with computers may indeed seem to pose a threat.

Latvian animation in the contemporary Eastern European context

To contextualize the phenomenon discussed in this piece, it is crucial to keep in mind that Latvian animation developed – and continues to develop – as part of a larger Eastern European tradition shaped by a constant exchange of ideas, collaboration and creative cross-pollination. As already discussed, Latvians actively participate in co-productions, especially with neighbouring Estonia. Moreover, many young animators cross the border to Tallinn in order to study at the Estonian Academy of Arts, which offers a two-year degree in animation.[36] Others, such as Edmunds Jansons, hold animation degrees from the Moscow Gerasimov Institute of Cinematography.[37] Indeed, Latvia's ties to Russian animation remain strong as well. When asked to list her influences, Baumane mentions Lithuanian painter Stasys Eidrigevičius, Polish and Eastern European poster art, and Russian animator Yuri Norstein.[38] Similarly, Leschiov singles out Russian animation as his main source of inspiration.[39]

Moreover, the economic, social and political changes that shaped post-Soviet Latvian animation affected many Eastern European or former Eastern

Bloc countries in equal measure and with similar results.[40] In Bulgaria, after the existing system – which relied on the same model of total government control over funding and distribution – collapsed, animation switched to a mix of private production and state subsidies.[41] In Russia, too, the 1990s was a time of instability and stagnation, but since then a model that combines commercial animation with largely state-sponsored independent works has been operating.[42] In Estonia, animation studios, despite being ostensibly independent of the state, likewise receive funding from the Ministry of Culture.[43] Other features of the Latvian production landscape – such as the rise of one-man studios and international co-productions – are also visible across Eastern Europe. In that sense, insofar as Latvia's resistance to computer animation is at least partially a product of the country's post-socialist sociopolitical landscape, contemporary Latvian films can be seen as representative of a set of approaches and attitudes towards filmmaking born out of the historical and economic circumstances in this geopolitical region at the turn of the new century.

Indeed, contemporary animation produced in many former Eastern Bloc countries, as well as non-Soviet socialist countries like Bulgaria, exhibits a similar resilience in the face of technological and aesthetic change. In Estonia, the country's signature brand of hand-drawn surrealism continues to flourish, largely due to the enduring influence of renowned directors like Priit Pärn and Ülo Pikkov.[44] In Russia, animation auteurs like Aleksandr Petrov continue to work with traditional animation techniques, while large studios such as Mel'nitsa produce two-dimensional animation.[45] Likewise, in Bulgaria, the legacy of hand-drawn animation continues to endure, thanks to the short works of Anri Koulev, Ivan Rusev, Pencho Kunchev, Andrey Tsvetkov and Kalina Vutova, among others.

Thus, as fascinating as it is to study the Latvian adherence to traditional animation in the national context, the trends discussed in this text are by no means part of an isolated phenomenon, but rather a glimpse into a complex larger picture. These landscapes of resistance form part of a bigger map that extends across national borders and unites several animation traditions through a shared history and a common struggle to rediscover an artistic identity while regaining a political one. In that sense, while looking at Latvian animation is valuable for its own sake, it opens up a conversation about the unique features and artistic roots of Eastern European animation at large.

Conclusion: The future of animated landscapes in the digital age

In conclusion, the question of the place of computer technology in Latvian – and indeed Eastern European – animation is worth briefly reconsidering with an eye on the future. While the majority of animated work produced in the country remains true to classical animation, films like Pēteris Noviks's *View Finder* (*Skatu meklētājs*, 2010) and Aija Bley's *The Prickly* (*Eža Kažociņš*, 2004), which employ three-dimensional computer imagery without subverting its technology and brand of realism, point to the penetration of digital aesthetics in contemporary Latvian production. These are relatively isolated cases, but instead of dismissing them as exceptions that reinforce the rule, one might instead read them as the harbingers of a changing artistic climate. It is possible that, as business models and animation practices continue to evolve further towards internationally oriented production and distribution, even nations with long-lasting traditions in classical animation will increasingly look outwards to other parts of the world, their animated landscapes evolving to incorporate a new variety of forms and influences. One need only look as far as Russia, where traditional-looking cartoons are competing at the box office against recent commercial features such as *Space Dogs 3D* (Inna Evlannikova and Svyatoslav Ushakov, 2010) and *The Snow Queen* (Vladlen Barbe and Maksim Sveshnikov, 2012), which represents a rising trend of embracing the dominant Hollywood style of three-dimensional digital animation. As Eastern European countries struggle to compete against American imports that dominate their domestic screens and strive to develop their commercial animation industries, computer animation may be seen as a way of remaining relevant in the digital era. While this poses a threat of *de facto* legitimizing a particular style as the new norm and encouraging derivative, standardized animation, it also holds the promise of enriching both the art of digital animation and the discourse surrounding the functions and properties of digital media with fresh approaches. As the Latvian example shows, adoption of digital animation need not involve an outright erasure of older forms, just as adherence to tradition does not necessarily equal complete denial of the digital. Instead, the animated landscape could become a site of aesthetic and ideological cross-pollination – a space for conversation, not contest.

Acknowledgements

This research would have not been possible without the generous support of the Keggi-Berzins Fellowship for Baltic Studies. Additionally, I would like to thank Vladimir Leschiov, Signe Baumane, Edmunds Jansons, Iliana Veinberga, Ieva Viese, Marina Gevorgian and Juris Freidenbergs.

Notes

1 For a historical overview of key studios and films in Latvian animation, see *Film News from Latvia* (2009), Special Issue: Latvian Animation.
2 Chris Robinson, *Estonian Animation: Between Genius & Utter Illiteracy* (Eastleigh, UK: John Libbey Publishing, 2006).
3 Chris Robinson, *Unsung Heroes of Animation* (Eastleigh, UK: Hohn Libbey Publishing, 2005), 198–210.
4 Giannalberto Bendazzi, *Cartoons: One Hundred Years of Cinema Animation* (London: John Libbey Publishing, 2004), 378.
5 Kevin O'Connor, *Culture and Customs of the Baltic States* (Westport, CT: Greenwood Press, 2006), 145.
6 Antra Cilinska, 'Making Films in Latvia: Producers' Challenges', *KinoKultura* 13 (2012), accessed 15 July 2014, http://www.kinokultura.com/specials/13/cilinska.shtml.
7 Uldis Dimiševskis and Simon Drewsen Holmberg, *Audiovisual Production in Latvia: A Nordic Context* (Riga: National Film Centre Latvia, 2007), 10.
8 Cilinska, 'Making Films in Latvia'.
9 Agris Redovičs, *Ursus* (Riga: National Film Centre Latvia, 2011), 4.
10 Ibid., 4.
11 Nils Skapāns, 'Alone with Puppets', interview by Zane Balčus, Wonderful Day (Riga: National Film Centre Latvia, 2010), 3.
12 Ibid., 2.
13 Dita Deruma, 'Production Company AB', *Film News from Latvia* (2003), 20.
14 Vladimir Leschiov, interview by Mihaela Mihailova, Riga, 29 July 2013.
15 Vladimir Leschiov, 'Some Notes on Animation', interview by Kristīne Matīsa, *Film News from Latvia* (2009), 2.
16 Leschiov, interview.
17 Leschiov, 'Some Notes', 3.
18 Signe Baumane, interview by Mihaela Mihailova, New York, 21 April 2014.
19 Ibid.

20 Ibid.

21 Robinson, *Unsung Heroes*, 209.

22 Joan Neuberger, 'Strange Circus: Eisenstein's Sex Drawings', *Studies in Russian & Soviet Cinema* 6.1 (2012): 16, doi: 10.1386/srsc.6.1.5_1

23 Ieva Viese, email message to author, 10 August 2013.

24 Friedrich Kirschner, 'Toward a Machinima Studio', in *The Machinima Reader*, ed. Henry Lowood and Michael Nitsche (Cambridge, MA: The MIT Press, 2011), 59.

25 'Latviiskaya animatsia nabiraet oboroty', *Delfi*, 9 February 2006, http://www .delfi.lv/showtime/news/picsnsounds/pics/latvijskaya-animaciya-nabiraet -oboroty.d?id=13566717 (accessed 20 July 2014).

26 Dita Rietuma, ' "Firefly", Keeping on the Tradition of Bugs', *Film News from Latvia* (2003), 4.

27 Ibid., 4.

28 Shahla Nahid, 'What Is the Future for Animated Films in Latvia?' *FIPRESCI*, 15 February 2009, http://www.fipresci.org/festivals/archive/2006/riga/riga_latvian _animation_films.htm (accessed 20 July 2014).

29 Ibid.

30 Leschiov, 'Some Notes', 4.

31 Baumane, interview.

32 The author would like to thank Rachel Walls for pointing out the significance of this.

33 Redovičs, *Ursus*, 2.

34 Leschiov, 'Some Notes', 3

35 Mihaela Mihailova, 'The Mastery Machine: Digital Animation and Fantasies of Control', *Animation: An Interdisciplinary Journal* 8.2 (2013): 131–148, doi: 10.1177/1746847713485833.

36 Leschiov, interview.

37 Edmunds Jansons, interview by Mihaela Mihailova, Riga, 5 August 2013.

38 Baumane, interview.

39 Leschiov, interview.

40 For an overview of the post-1990 changes in the animation industries of the Czech Republic, Poland, Slovakia, and Hungary, see *Homo Felix: The International Journal of Animated Film* 5.1 (2014).

41 Nadezhda Marinchevska, *Bulgarsko Animatsionno Kino 1915–1995* (Sofia: Colibri, 2001), 277.

42 Natalia Lukinykh, 'Inspired by the Oscar, Hardened by the Marketplace: On the Everydays and Holidays of Russian Animation', *KinoKultura* 13 (2006), accessed 15 July 2014, http://www.kinokultura.com/2006/13-lukinykh.shtml.

43 Robinson, *Estonian Animation*, 150.

44 Ibid.

45 Birgit Beumers, 'Folklore and New Russian Animation', *KinoKultura* 43 (2014), accessed 15 July 2014, http://www.kinokultura.com/2014/43-beumers.shtml.

Part Three

Form: Journeys through Animated Space

8

The Landscape in the Memory: Animated Travel Diaries

María Lorenzo Hernández

Animation, as the enduring reproduction of a movement or of a fleeting instant, has a privileged relationship with memory. This memory can be registered in the artist's notebook as a shape or a sketch, which anticipates a future animated gesture, a character or scene. Moreover, the relationship between animation and a specific kind on graphic diary, the *travelogue*, has led to an interesting short film sub-genre: the *animated travel diary*, a storytelling form where the landscape becomes central in the revival of the animator's experiences of a now-distant country. Animated travelogues are, then, close to documentary films, yet influenced by personal expression and the artist's subjectivity.

Three films that operate in this way, and which provide the focus for this chapter, are the Oscar-nominated *Madagascar, carnet de voyage* (Bastien Dubois, 2009), *Ámár* (Isabel Herguera, 2010) and *Viagem a Cabo Verde* (José Miguel Ribeiro, 2010). To briefly introduce these films, *Madagascar, carnet de voyage* describes the Famadihana, a fascinating Malagasy celebration that sees families exhume their dead relatives in order to rewrap their decomposing bodies in fresh funeral shrouds; *Viagem a Cabo Verde* recounts director José Miguel Ribeiro's personal experience of his unplanned pathfinding as he explored the island country of Cape Verde; finally, *Ámár* is inspired by Isabel Herguera's sketchbooks, which were composed during four years in India, and which record her rediscovering the pleasure of drawing in the streets.

The success of these animated travelogues demonstrates the vitality and attractiveness of a new animated genre that brings together a journalistic

This chapter is based on research presented at the 2nd International Conference in Illustration and Animation CONFIA, held in Porto, Portugal, November 29, 2013, under the title 'Animated Travel Diaries. Memory, Transit and Experience'.

perspective with an artistic desire. Accordingly, the following analysis of these films will review the qualities of the animator's sketchbook as a memory archive, capable of recording the impressions of the people, their traditions and their urban and natural sceneries. Additionally, these animated travelogues share a certain documentary gaze, with their authors' testimonies actively negotiating the middle ground between the biographical and the anthropological. Moreover, although these films bring to the screen many forms of traditional drawing and painting, the use of digital media as tools for animation is essentially linked to the filmmaking process, finding new and stimulating form to re-imagine drawing for animation. Lastly, we will also consider how animated travel diaries suggest new narrative and aesthetic forms that, in addition to fulfilling their own artistic agendas, have arguably *contaminated* other contexts and spaces, such as the art gallery.

The sketchbook as memory

Animated travel diaries represent something of a crossroads in terms of aesthetics and genre, with their close relationship to *hand-made* drawing challenging the current dominance of digital animation and their autobiographical point of view serving to enhance the documentary quality of these narrated trips. The idea of *animated diary* has diverse and distinguished precedents, such as the chronicle drawn by Nedeljko Dragić in his film *Dnevnik* (*Diary*, 1974), where the author's identity is dissolved in the metamorphoses of the self through the use of different techniques, languages and aesthetics, which in combination provide a defamiliarized portrait of urban life. Following in the footsteps of Dragić's movie, Vuk Jevremović's short film *Tagebuch* (*Diary*, 2000) develops a subjective approach to the animated travel diary, with the eyes of the protagonist providing the source for the film's POV style. Michaela Pavlátová's *This Could Be Me* (1995), a film commissioned for television, could be also mentioned in this category, as the documentary focuses on the author's identity and circumstances: the city of Prague, her studio and the places where she observes people.

However, in the three animated films analysed in this essay, the idea of a *sketchbook* – as a record of visual memory – prevails over the idea of a spoken *diary*. The animator's chronicle takes the form of images and marginal texts, creating dialectics between animations and drawings in order to build ideas and memories. Even in the digital age, nothing replaces the artist's observations and analyses that have been carried out by simply drawing in a sketchbook: as Nina Paley suggests about drawing, it 'is an aid to thinking. It's a way to work out ideas, just like writing an outline or notes'.[1] Moreover, as Peter Parr explains, the sketchbook attests to the artists' learning process and demonstrates their constant exploration; and more applicable for the animator who travels, the sketchbook can be understood as a *navigation* instrument itself: 'Your sketches will support each other in charting your search'.[2]

For artists who express themselves through drawings, the painted shapes do not only prevail over any written idea or annotation: drawings are the true treasures rescued from their trips to distant lands. One of the essential features that make this treasure richer is variety. When you see any of Dubois's, Herguera's or Ribeiro's sketchbooks, what is immediately evident is the multiplicity of approaches, subjects and techniques: charcoal, ink, crayon, collage and gouache, to name but a few of the material properties evident in the works of the artists in question. Drawing becomes the more dynamic, creative force for the artist, since it can be done everywhere. Very often, artists start a drawing from life, but they are forced to abandon the place and they must colour it from their own memory, or rather they complement the initial impression by adding elements of a different nature (like photographs). A sketch can be as realistic or inventive as the artist wishes: if Dubois's or Ribeiro's drawings attract us for their virtuosity, Herguera tends more to rework reality in a comic or metaphorical style, transforming the process in such a way so as to suggest a playful counterpoint to the artist's imagined/remembered dialogue. As a result of this variety, their films defy the convention of aesthetic unity that can at times characterize the more mainstream quarters of the animation industry, instead favouring a bewildering diversity of strokes, designs, colours and procedures. In animated travel diaries, artistic drawing is released from its confinement as a preproduction framework, since their 'concept art' – the phase of production that precedes the realization of a film – reaches the visible surface of the film, making it appealing for an audience rarely confronted with the spontaneity that is captured in those drawings that are typically used to prepare for *the animation*.

In addition, the presence of elements such as notes by hand, glued boarding passes, labels and reminder stickers, reinforces the testimonial character of the travel books that inspired these films, and the corporeal presence of their pages, which permeate through the scenes of these films, and which have become, in the process, flash-back narrations of sorts. Herguera, considering how the notebook is essential as an object that supports and gives texture to the drawings, reflects:

'I write in the striped notebook that I bought this morning. I liked it because it was old and I thought that everything that I did in it would have a lustre of wisdom, a patina of mystery to keep your interest.'[3] Unlike the motion picture – which only exists as a projection and may be seen either in theatres, on screens or via interfaces – the sketchbook is a genuine and unique object, which belongs to the physical world and only acquires value as it is used by the artist; the signs of its employment, its own wear, not only make it unique, but also truthful.

In this sense, *Ámár* deeply respects the essence of the book as a memory, showing in many moments Herguera's original drawings from her sketchbooks – not animating them, just adding ambient sounds and camera movements. As a consequence, these pictures are stylized, gestural, with vibrant and even arbitrary colours, encouraging a sense of abstraction and symbolism (Figure 8.1). Contrastingly, the animation of the film is mainly done through a technique of black inked drawings that move onto backgrounds of hand-cut colour paper. It could be said that though Herguera's adoption of this visual code to represent that moment when the present life and the past collide in a film, she inverts the received hierarchies of temporality through an atypical use of colour, since the almost monochromatic scenes from the film correspond to the present, while the colourful, synthetic shapes from the sketchbooks are flashes from the past.

In Ribeiro's movie, by contrast, his drawings are detailed, realistic, and with elaborate depictions of those who are portrayed. *Viagem a Cabo Verde* shows the animator's inks and washes from two notebooks used during the course of his trip to Cape Verde, which, some three years later, he decided to base a film upon, therefore prompting him to travel again to the African island to re-enact some of his experiences. Very often, a single drawing from the sketchbook becomes an entire scene – like the eloquent drawing of his broken boots. Moreover, in *Viagem a Cabo Verde*, many of these sketches suddenly come to life through

Figure 8.1 Image from *Ámár* (Isabel Herguera, 2010), courtesy of the artist.

subtle, selective animations of the portrayed characters – who suddenly turn to the camera or perform their daily tasks.

Differently to Herguera and Ribeiro, Dubois did not develop his story from a previous travel, but he did intentionally visit Madagascar to research the Famadihana and start making art for the film. As a sign of this intent, to pre-produce *Madagascar, carnet de voyage* Dubois travelled to the island country with more than ten kilos of drawing and painting material (with the cardboard of the boxes, he made the covers of his own hand-made sketchbooks). Unlike Herguera and Ribeiro, Dubois was not an experienced animator when he planned this film, although he was experienced in the field, having been travelling internationally since 2004, including hitchhiking to Istanbul when he was just 21. Throughout these travels he developed his skills as a landscape designer. For the artists in question, it is clear that the sketchbook became their best travel companion; enabling them to draw (and record) daily scenes in a non-photographic way: the passer-by, the buildings most beloved by the people that surrounded them, and more abstract experiences, such as the relationships that were formed with the local inhabitants. As such, the sketchbook promotes dialogue and an interchange of information, better conveying the knowledge acquired about the places visited. Using determined strokes of gouache and watercolour, framed in a virtuous line, Dubois portrays the people he meets, always looking directly into their eyes, whilst also drawing the bustle of the capital, and the almost silent solitude of the rural landscape.

Clearly, animated travel diaries are a potentially rich genre for artists who would became animators, and not simply because these films highlight the enjoyable side of their creative process. What these films celebrate above all else is the act of drawing for its own sake, because the trace represents the animator's voice. These films bring to the foreground the physical presence of the sketchbook, and everything that is commited onto its pages like a moving collage – nothing less than the animated memory of the artist.

Experience and exoticism: The documentary gaze

Annabelle Honness Roe argues that: 'Both moving and still images have a capacity, in their ability to replay the past, to revive and reanimate the temporal instant and physical bodies that have long since been lost. In their capacity to play with time, these media remind us of the ephemerality of our own existence.'[4]

In a very direct sense, the travelogue records the animator's journey both *inside* and *outside*. On the one hand, the diary records the encounter with Otherness when entering a different culture; and on the other hand, it serves as a reflection of one's own voice, confronted with the unknown.

Frequently, trips allow travellers to meet themselves, to mature their ideas, lose prejudices and to conceive new projects. Dubois's, Ribeiro's and Herguera's movies all started from a more personal rather than objective position in the recording of their travels, yet all three came to gain at least some degree of journalistic tone. Their observations are defined by their personalities and background, as well as how they understand their new scenery: a context where they actively seek to know themselves.

Animated documentary could be regarded as an oxymoron, since some contradiction can be detected between animation – as a *fabricated* form – and documentary – a genre founded on the ambitions of filmmakers who have sought to portray *reality*, which, as an idea, has apparently been better sustained by using live-action film. Israeli animator Yoni Goodman notes that 'animation is all about fooling the eye – making the eye see what's not really there',[5] and this is a quality that he tests in interesting ways when attempting to animate Ari Folman's memories of the Libanon war in *Waltz with Bashir* (Ari Folman, 2008). Paul Fierlinger offers another perspective, believing that 'any story can be told with objectivity. The act of selecting scenes and the way in which they're put together *is* putting in a point-of-view. You can't make a purely objective film, and if you could, it wouldn't work'.[6] Perhaps most pertinently, Paul Ward points to a decisive contribution of animation to non-fiction film when he argues that:

> Animation and documentary are diverse discursive categories rather than simple entities, and it is instructive to examine the points of contact between them. As I have stated in detail elsewhere, it is something of a myth that animation is a mode that somehow cannot be used by documentary practitioners. Such a way of thinking is based in naïve and simplistic notions of how documentary functions, and in a misguided belief that documentary is somehow 'capturing' reality rather than offering an analysis of it.[7]

In the animated travelogues considered in this text, such *analysis* of reality, combined with the *visualization* of emotional states, prevail over the mere documentary depiction, giving as a result the *evocation* of 'ideas, feelings and sensibilities' – as suggested by Roe – in their experience of the Otherness.[8]

None of the films in question has been explicitly presented as *documentaries*, yet, through their relationships to reality and to non-fiction forms, this distinction is subject to significant slippage. The three films submit to Roe's aforementioned observations regarding animated documentary, and, furthermore, their authors are 'filmmakers trained in the craft and art of animation, who have chosen to turn their attention to non-fiction subject matter'.[9] The journey of self-knowledge that Herguera, Ribeiro and Dubois undertook in their voyages runs underneath the documentary view of their travel books and the resulting films. *Madagascar, carnet de voyage* uses strongly evocative images to describe the Famadihana, a tribal tradition that can rarely be recorded, photographed or accessed by a Westerner; *Viagem a Cabo Verde* sums up Ribeiro's travel to Cape Verde in an analytical and comprehensive way that recalls strongly Guy Delisle's[10] comic book diaries; and Herguera's *Ámár* pictures an imagined India and is lived through others, plotting inside this visualization a painful story from her own stay there. Since the documental source of the three works is mainly the memories recorded in the sketchbooks, the storytelling develops the events *as these persons are*, as Anaïs Nin would say, and not merely as a camera would register them. Additionally, the appearance of the authors in these films, adding their voices to the soundtrack, further extends the look (and feel) of autobiographical confession. Despite this association with reality, it is important not to confuse these *animated animators* with their real persona, since only in *Madagascar, carnet de voyage*, and in *Viagem a Cabo Verde*, is the animated self-portrait of the filmmaker deliberately used to construct a tone closer to reportage than to fiction.

In *Ámár*, the sketchbook tells a story of loss and desolation: Inés (Herguera's alter ego) visits her friend Ámár because she wants to retrieve the memories of a trip they did together in the past, but Ámár is being held in a mental hospital. There, Inés confronts the memory of that trip, of which all that is left are the drawings and annotations stored in their sketchbooks. After seeing Ámár, who fails to recognize his friend, Inés endures the bustle of the populous city, reflecting her feeling of confusion, mixed with wild visions of buskers and dances of Hindu deities. In the final scene, drawing serves as a powerful visual means through which to reconcile the remembered past with the present life: Inés is drawing again on the streets of India, sitting on the cart Ámár gave to her.[11] The focus of the film is clearly personal and subjective, with little concern for the documentary or anthropological; however, the film was produced mostly in the country it describes (between the National Institute of Design in Ahmedabad and a small study in Goa) and with the participation of Indian artists.

Meanwhile, *Viagem a Cabo Verde* condenses two months of marching through the former Portuguese colony, with Ribeiro facing inaccessible landscapes and sharing experiences with friendly natives. The pilgrim – just a black silhouette, with no individual traits emerge, and thereby recalling one of Giacometti's walking figures – travels without cell phone, clock or preconceived plans, carrying only what is necessary in his backpack. He examines the mountains, the people, the sea, the music, the people of Cape Verde and, above all, an essential part of himself. There he learns simple but fundamental things, like shaking his boots before putting them on (to dislodge hiding creatures that might otherwise bite or sting the would-be boot-wearer), or not to plan the next day. One of the most striking values of the film lies in the use of metamorphosis to illustrate changes of scenery and time lapses, taking advantage of the main character's stylized design that helpfully provides a large capacity for transformation: for example, when the time comes to leave, his profile melts to become the sea waves. In one of the film's most notorious twists, the barefoot and cracked heels of a native become the rocky slope of the same mountain they are climbing. Ribeiro talks with the people of Cape Verde and he conveys their reality using animation as a means to visualize complex situations, such as how many times you have to climb a mountain with a mule loaded with bricks to build a house. Undoubtedly the most symbolic moment of the film comes when the traveller exchanges his notebook with a child's and they draw in each other's pad.

Madagascar, carnet de voyage tells us about the Famadihana or 'return of the dead', a Malagasy tradition that highlights the importance of deceased ancestors and is an important occasion for festivities: when the unearthed relative has already lost the corrupted flesh and is reduced to bones, only then do they become an *ancestor*, a mediating spirit who gives advice in exchange for gifts.[12] Their shroud is renewed and they are offered dances and sacrificial cattle, an idea that appears in the film with a high degree of abstraction: under the rhythm of the drums, a mountainous landscape becomes a zebu hump and out of its severed head comes out a beautiful flower, and off this, the skull of the animal itself emerges, establishing a visual connection with the ancestor's unearthed bones. This cathartic sequence, which reflects the animator's outburst during the celebration – fostered by the intake of rum Toka Gasy – is followed by the film's conclusion: a dizzying camera move that collates a series of scenes, including the farewell to the dead, important landscapes like the forest inhabited by lemurs, and to finish, the traveller picking up his backpack before boarding the plane. The stay in Madagascar has been completed, leaving behind a series of unique imprints.

In these films, the narrators surrender towards a daily routine unrestricted by the rush of Western life. For instance, *Viagem a Cabo Verde* underlines this contrast when the main character takes the bus line: while in Europe people wait for the bus, in Africa it is the bus that waits for the passengers – significantly, *Madagascar, carnet de voyage* describes exactly the same scene when the animator crosses the island to attend the Famadihana.

But, while the general tone of Ribeiro's film is educational, using the voice-over to convey information alongside schematic visuals, *Madagascar, carnet de voyage* transmits this through images, texts and music, subjectively channelling this experience of collective celebration. The focus of *Ámár, Madagascar, carnet de voyage* and *Viagem a Cabo Verde* reminds us that memory is fluctuating and the truthfulness of non-fiction films is questionable, but there is always a residue of authenticity even in what is reinvented.

The digitalization of the memory: production processes

The animation of artistic drawing and the multiplicity of graphical techniques that have been discussed thus far would not be possible without the technologies of today; although the sketchbook is the essential part of the concept art and supports a significant part of the animation – since many scenes of these films are developed from a single image – digital tools are indispensable to capture, re-work and transfer into film the original aspects of hand drawings. Moreover, as I have argued elsewhere, many digital applications have been proven to complement the traditional tools of drawing and painting, because their development and refinement tend to imitate hand-made aesthetics, emulating the properties such as pencil strokes, the watered-down look and the smearing of pencil graphite.[13] Furthermore, contemporary filmmaking technologies are more portable than ever, allowing the animator to work almost anywhere with a laptop or tablet (and a freely accessible plug socket). It seems that this particular moment, with technology adapted to both drawing and mobility, has created a particularly supportive environment in which to animate travel diaries.

In this context, the presence of the sketchbook takes many forms. In *Ámár*, it is a quiet presence at the beginning and the end of the film; it only acquires movement when Inés abandons the hospital and she confronts the bustle of the city, and as a result, completely changes the syntax of the movie. However, in most of the film, the animation evokes her ink drawings, with the characters appearing as ink stains on different coloureds. Digital compositing, where masks and multiple layers are created using software such as Adobe After Effects, also helped make possible one of the most striking images from the film: the dense and chaotic urban landscape, where in one establishing shot of the city we see the roads full with cars moving through the concentric walled space. In *Viagem a Cabo Verde*, the book provides a heterogeneous look to the film. On the one hand, most of the film is animated digitally, mixing highly stylized characters with watercolour backgrounds. A texture of watercolour paper is present throughout the entire film, like a layer – superimposed digitally – serving to remind us of the physical presence of the sketchbook. Undoubtedly, *Madagascar, carnet de voyage* is technically the more complex of the three films, since it uses 2D and 3D animation, traditional and digital animation, drawing both across flat surfaces and in volumetric depth. Using a mixture of 3D animation and hand-painted textures, the smallest details – irrelevant to the story, but that nonetheless enrich the atmosphere – are offered in three dimensions: the woman who sells fruit to the bus travellers, a wader in a pond, a young girl bathing in the water. Very often, the technique used is camera mapping, allowing the fixing of a drawing or painted texture onto a three-dimensional volume.

Digital compositing was also used extensively in this film. Working from an inspirational image taken from one of the sketchbooks, many scenes were divided into layers such as backgrounds, shadows, animated elements and effects. This process is little different from that followed in more conventional productions, but from a procedural perspective, the presence of the sketchbook as an on-going feature of the visual composition serves to distinguish these productions from their mainstream cousins. In *Viagem a Cabo Verde*, it is possible to see in the entire movie as a floating texture that varies in every scene, encouraging the viewer to recall that what they are seeing is *an animated book* – the borders of the paper, the joint between the pages, different kinds of paper, all serve to heighten this effect. As a consequence, the film landscapes range between realistic representations and mere silhouettes on neutral backgrounds, with many of these scenes created using rotoscope. While rotoscope is conventionally considered a method of saving labour, by Dubois filming himself and different characters during the rotoscope process, this gives the film an additional indexical connection with *reality*.

Since the country Dubois describes is not a 'developed' Western nation, to re-create Madagascar it is necessary to borrow elements that represent life and culture in that country. The little, remarkable toy car stop-motion scene makes use of the same models produced by the orphans from the orphanage where Dubois had his accommodation. Likewise, the astounding market scene made with embroidery – patiently sewn by a lady from Madagascar – weaves this original craft with the digital codes of the film's production.

The works contained within the sketchpads not only remains as relevant today for the animator as it was prior to the digital age, but it is experiencing a striking revalorization that has made it a central object of exhibitions and animation compilations interested in materiality. During the Mostra de Cinema d'Animació, ANIMAC 2010, in Lleida (Catalonia), an exhibition of animators' sketchbooks was held, where original drawings by artists such as Maureen Selwood, Sekhar Mukherjee, Izibene Oñederra or Laboratorium were brought together. Dubois also contributed with original art from his film, giving visitors the chance to investigate both the physical object and conceptual realization of his work.

Later, in October 2010, an exhibition titled 'Cuadernos de viaje (Travelogs)' by Herguera was held at the Arteko gallery of San Sebastian (Basque Country). Alongside the sample rescued notebooks with sketches made during her years in India, which had allowed her to come up with *Ámár*, the audience also had the opportunity to see an installation at the gallery, for which the entire space became an ephemeral three-dimensional sketchbook. As in Herguera's own scrapbook, the walls offered a place to improvise, revise perspectives and incorporate new objects, images, textures and messages. As a result, a collage about India, unique and unrepeatable, was displayed. Herguera observes:

> The notebook is a game space where there is no supervision, no trial, no you have to show anyone .... All this comes with the same attitude: there are a number of drawings, of items that I have, how to configure them to compose a narrative? ... Every day I dared to bring another element, to add one more thing, without thinking, actually again recovering that attitude with the notebook .... It worked because I wanted to put it in at that time.[14]

In this confluence of arts, genres and spaces, the notebook is no longer merely a physical object, but a concept, a way of understanding and recording reality. In animation, the drawn diary helps to create a particular atmosphere or tone to engage the viewer in what is told. But as a non-narrative form, the drawn diary takes centre stage by itself, providing innovative solutions to overcome staid conventions in the creative process, making improvisation and chance two valuable allies of inspiration.

Conclusions

As aesthetic pretext, the storytelling basis of animated travel diaries can also be used to create a false documentary vision, establishing new rules on the approach to staging. As well as mock-documentaries demonstrating how easy it is to fake the documentary codes – like 'shaky camerawork, talking-head interviews, grainy image quality, production sound and a filmmaker positioned as impartial observer'[15] – the visual codes identified in animated travel diaries may serve the fictional mode, to re-create stories told in first person. The variety of techniques, the marginal notes, the co-existence of animation and physical elements like sticky notes, the use of pro-filmic material like live-action film or rotoscoping, and above all, the presence of the sketchbook pages themselves, are, in summary, the main features that establish the animated landscape of an imaginary story.

The notebook of the artist, as an element for reflection and creation, is still the basis for the boldest animated actions, providing formulas that support fresh imagination whilst renovating different arts form. Despite the accommodation of a limited number of resources and materials, the sketchbook continues to offer the animator a window into a variety of styles, techniques, media, graphics and findings, without neglecting the trials and errors that occur during the search for creative freedoms.

Moreover, the travelogue allows the animator to confront their own self with the Otherness they find in their travels: the fascination with the new and the unknown that renews the will to live and to draw. The notebook also supports a stimulating narrative format, involving the introduction of the animators in their own films, and even dissolving fiction into the real, enabling the creation of an alternative reality. As shown by Dubois's, Herguera's and Ribeiro's films, what ultimately counts is the passion with which they are made: the enthusiasm committed to the page by their authors when they started to sketch the events of their experiences, serves to revive their memory when they return to the sketchbook after leaving the animated landscape long behind.

Notes

1 Paul Wells, Joanna Quinn, and Les Mills, *Drawing for Animation* (London: AVA Publishing, 2009), 146.

2 Ibid., 102.

3 'Escribo en el cuaderno de rayas que me compré esta mañana. Me gustó porque estaba viejo y pensé que todo lo que en él hiciera tendría un lustre de sabiduría, una pátina de misterio con la que mantener vuestro interés.' In Isabel Herguera, 'Un experimento en el jardín de la ley', *Animac Magazine 11. Escrits sobre animació*, no.

10 (2011): 3, translated by author.

4　Annabelle Honness Roe, *Animated Documentary* (Basingstoke: Palgrave Macmillan, 2013), 141.

5　Judith Kriger, *Animated Realism: A Behind-the-Scenes Look at the Animated Documentary Genre* (Oxford: Focal Press, 2012), 6.

6　Ibid., 187.

7　Paul Ward, 'Animated Interactions: Animation Aesthetics and the World of the "Interactive" Documentary', in *Animated 'Worlds'*, ed. Suzanne Buchan (London: John Libbey, 2006), 114.

8　'Certain concepts, emotions, feelings and states of mind are particularly difficult to represent through live-action imagery …. Animation, however, is increasingly being used as a tool to evoke the experiential in the form of ideas, feelings and sensibilities. By visualizing these invisible aspects of life, often in an abstract or symbolic style, animation that functions in this evocative way allows us to imagine the world from someone else's perspective.' See: Roe, *Animated Documentary*, 25.

9　Roe, *Animated Documentary*, 2.

10　Canadian animator Guy Delisle, who supervised several outsourced productions in the Far East, recorded his experiences in several graphic novels, the second of them, *Pyongyang* (2003), is his most acclaimed work – and, interestingly, one of the most revealing documents we have of life in the secretive North Korea. Delisle has continued drawing chronicles of his travels through politically controversial countries, such as Myanmar or Israel, writing his diaries and drawing in his sketchbooks.

11　'In India, to draw comfortably and undisturbed, it is important to find a place to sit. This is always difficult because the ground is full of rubbish, and the spacious, comfortable, and well located stones are scarce or they are already occupied. The first years I used to go out to draw with a mop bucket, that I employed to load both notebook and brushes and I could turn it around to sit in any corner … Ámár, the real person, never gave me that car – a very personal and valuable object that I have never get rid of it – but it was he who introduced me to the animation when we were both students of Nam June Paik in Düsseldorf.' Isabel Herguera, e-mail message to author, 2 June 2013. ('En la India, para dibujar a gusto y sin molestias es importante encontrar un lugar donde sentarse. Esto es siempre difícil pues el suelo está lleno de basuras, y las piedras cómodas, amplias y bien localizadas escasean o están ya ocupadas. Los primeros años solía salir a dibujar con un cubo de fregar, que me servía tanto para cargar el cuaderno y los pinceles como para darle la vuelta y sentarme en cualquier esquina … Ámár, el personaje real, nunca me dio ese carrito – un objeto muy personal y valioso y del que no me he desprendido – pero fue él quien me introdujo a la animación cuando ambos éramos estudiantes de Nam June Paik en Duesseldorf.' Translated by author.)

12　As anthropologist Encarnación Lorenzo explains about this Malagasy tradition,

'When a person dies, they must be buried temporarily in the place of their death. The Merina folk think, until the flesh is completely corrupted, the dead keep wandering and they have power to harm their families. By contrast, once their remains have been reduced to bones, they become benefactors and it is time to honor them properly to ensure their protection. We must not overlook the structural contrast between these two pairs of concepts: the wet (rotten meat) and the dry (bones), as usual in the organization of the social life of the native peoples.' ('Cuando muere una persona, se la entierra provisionalmente en el lugar de su fallecimiento. Los Merina piensan que, hasta que no se descompone por completo la carne, los muertos vagan errantes y tienen poder para causar daño a sus familiares. Por el contrario, una vez que sus restos han quedado reducidos a los huesos, se transforman en sus benefactores y es el momento de honrarlos adecuadamente para asegurarse su protección. No debemos pasar por alto la contraposición estructural entre esos dos pares de conceptos: lo húmedo (la carne putrefacta) y lo seco (los huesos), tan habitual en la organización de la vida social de los pueblos nativos.' Lorenzo Hernández, 'Madagascar: antropología y animación documental.' Translated by author.)

13 'These digital tools reproduce the visual imprints and even the names of the traditional ones: brush, airbrush, colour palette, canvas, etc. Digital art does not interrupt hand-made processes and aesthetics, but rather, has given them a new life.' See: Sara Álvarez Sarrat and María Lorenzo Hernández, 'How Computers Re-Animated Hand-Made Processes and Aesthetics for Artistic Animation', *Animation Studies* 7 (2012): 1, accessed May 2014, http://journal.animationstudies .org/sara-alvarez-sarrat-and-maria-lorenzo-hernandez-how-computers-re -animated-hand-made-processes-and-aesthetics-for-artistic-animation-2/.

14 'El cuaderno es un espacio de juego en el cual no hay ningún tipo de supervisión, ni de juicio, ni lo tienes que mostrar a nadie … Todo esto surge con esa misma actitud: hay una serie de dibujos, de elementos que tengo, ¿cómo componerlos para que configuren una narrativa? … Todos los días me atrevía a traer un elemento más, a incorporar una cosa más, sin pensar, realmente otra vez recuperando esa actitud del cuaderno … Funcionaba porque me apetecía ponerlo en ese momento.' Herguera, 'Cuadernos de Viaje', documentary in Eitbkultura, Eitb.com, 21 October 2010, accessed June 2013: https://www.youtube.com/watch?v=z1epJ7aeNjQ, translated by author.

15 Roe, *Animated Documentary*, 43.

9

Off the Rails: Animating Train Journeys

Birgitta Hosea

In 2012 the average resident of the UK spent 361 hours travelling a total of 6,691 miles. Of this travel, 11 per cent was done by public transport.[1] During their travels, the experience that these average residents have of landscape is in movement, of passing through places before arriving at their final destination. This is an important point to stress, as the mobility paradigm in urban geography and sociology proposes that cities and society can be studied in terms of travel rather than stasis – through the movement of peoples, resources, data, finance – in order to better understand the formation of identity, ideology, power and society.

In accord with these ideas about mobility, this chapter will focus on animations that move between locations and are concerned with trajectory and locomotion rather than landscape as a static entity. After considering the connections between early cinema and the train, we will examine a body of works that are all thematically linked through their association with animated train journeys, although the individual pieces of work may take different forms – from pre-filmic moving panoramas, to phantom rides, to *Ivor the Engine*, *Thomas the Tank Engine*, *Madame Tutli-Putli*, transport information films, post-filmic subway zoetropes and railway simulation games. Through a discussion of diverse approaches to animated – and animating – train journeys, this chapter will explore the implications of the mobility paradigm in urban geography for animation, not just in terms of visual content or subject matter, but in terms of animation as a concept and the politics of animation.

Landscape and the railway

It is no exaggeration to say that the advent of the railway fundamentally transformed the landscape. The thousands of miles of railway lines built all over the world traversed deserts, mountains, forests and prairies; the result of countless hours of backbreaking and sometimes fatal work blasting through rocks and exposing layers of ancient, geological time.[2] Railway tracks, tunnels and bridges scarred the landscape and new station buildings were erected. In the United States, the construction of the Union Pacific Railroad through the territory of indigenous peoples led to raiding parties, sabotage, massacre and the displacement of the original inhabitants as well as the near extinction of vast herds of buffalo.[3] The experience of the countryside was brought within the reach of town dwellers, as tourism and walking for leisure began to emerge as forms of leisure and the land began to lose its meaning as a purely functional resource to be bought, sold and to bear fruit, instead being reinterpreted as 'landscape', scenic, to be looked at and contemplated for leisure purposes.[4] In our new millennium, it is easy to forget the extent of this feat of engineering and the impact that it had on people. Much smoother and faster than a horse-drawn carriage, the sustained speeds experienced in the journey by train were unprecedented and there was a seismic shift in the perception of speed. In 1830, the actress Fanny Kemble described her experience of travelling thirty-five miles per hour during her thrilling preview of the UK's first passenger railway from Liverpool to Manchester thus, 'When I closed my eyes this sensation of flying was quite delightful, and strange beyond description.'[5] Before the railroad, the extremely difficult journey across the continent of America had taken months by horse-drawn carriage – with the fastest times achieved being six to seven weeks. After the opening of the Transcontinental Railroad in 1869, the same distance could be covered in under a week. Rebecca Solnit rightly claims that this achievement 'changed the scale of the earth itself'.[6]

It was not only the human experience of travelling through space that changed with the railway, but also time. Traditionally, time was measured by the position of the sun in the sky and was subject to regional variation. The demands of national rail timetables, the need for competitive trade networks and streamlined schedules for efficient factory work led to the introduction of a standardization of time around 1847, when railways, Post Offices, towns and cities across the UK adopted Greenwich Mean Time, known colloquially as 'Railway Time'.[7] In 1883, four different time zones were introduced by North America's railroad companies to rationalize the difference in time between the vast territories they covered. Before this, a total of 200 time zones had to be traversed during the train journey from San Francisco to Washington, DC.[8] The four time zones adopted by the railways were made official US policy in 1908.[9]

Before mechanized transportation systems, distance was conceptualized by the physical limitations of the human body or the animals that people used to transport them – a week's walk from here, a day on horseback. Zygmunt Bauman argues that the separation and abstraction of time and space from lived experience defines the emergence of the modern era.[10] This sense of new way of being in the world can be seen in contemporary accounts from the 1800s, in which the railway was popularly seen as an 'annihilation of space and time' a transformative technology that changed the way people experienced the world in which they lived.[11]

Early cinema and the train

Film can also be seen as a transformative technology. In his books on cinema, Giles Deleuze argues that the cinema is a technology that fundamentally changes how things are, because it changes the way that people think and engenders a new perceptual model, a new way of thinking.[12] The train ride and the film: both of these experiences mark a shift in our relationship to space and time; both of these experiences involve watching moving images. In the cinema and on a train, the viewer or traveller sits still while, caused by a mechanical process, an image moves in a rectangular frame before her eyes. She is mentally or physically transported to another location. However, it is important to note the different perceptions of time and space involved in these two different experiences. During the train journey, this encounter with moving landscape is synchronous: it happens now. There is a linear relationship to time and space (unless she falls asleep or her attention lapses) as she travels to a different geographical location. Her body moves in accord with the vehicle that is carrying her. She knows she is travelling *here* and *now*. While watching a film, her relationship to space and time is different. The experience of film is asynchronous – it was made in another location, *there*, and in the *past* to be recalled for viewing *now*. Unlike the train journey, film time and space can be presented non-linearly (i.e. time periods can be shown non-chronologically and multiple locations can be shown non-consecutively). Whereas the train journey offers the view of real, continuous landscape, with the live-action film, although continuity of setting is an illusion, there is an assumption that there is an indexical link to a 'real' believable location, to a landscape that really exists or once existed before the camera during some pro-filmic event. What animation promises beyond the photographed, realist film is the representation of imagined landscapes with no indexical link to a pre-existing location being necessary.

It could be surmised that the novel experience of seeing moving scenery through the Victorian train window awakened a popular desire for moving images as a form of entertainment. Tim Cresswell suggests that the new experience of watching scenery moving past outside the windows of trains in motion coincided with the emergence of a 'new panoramic perception of space'.[13] Panoramic representations are, however, considerably older than this and yet did come into contact with the train.

The use of long linear paintings to represent historical and mythic narratives goes back at least 2,000 years, with examples found in ancient China, Egypt, Babylon and Rome.[14] Emerging in the late 1700s in the form of backgrounds to peepshow boxes and toy theatres, moving panoramas became a popular form of entertainment in the English-speaking world around the mid-1800s as a sideshow in travelling fairs. Moving panoramas were painted on canvas like theatrical scenery and were moved through by being rolled and unrolled like horizontal rollerblinds. They were not only displayed, but also performed with variable speeds of hand-cranked unrolling, sound effects and the voice-over of a showman accompanist.[15] In his book, *Illusions in Motion: A Media Archaeology of the Moving Panorama and Related Spectacles*, Erkki Huhtamo considers the possible Asian influences on this tradition, including *wayang bèbèr*, a Javanese form of storytelling in which a series of panoramic scrolls are believed to have been unfurled to the accompaniment of music and a sung narrative; however, as Huhtamo warns, this remains in the realm of conjecture with no direct evidence found to date.[16]

Gaining in popularity during the 1800s, moving panoramas began to be displayed in theatrical presentations, such as Phillipe Jacques de Loutherbourg's Eidophusikon, which in 1871 combined moving panoramas, clockwork automata, lighting and sound effects to depict dramatic scenes on stage such as shipwrecks.[17] At the Paris Exposition of 1900, a Trans-Siberian Railway Panorama commissioned by the Compagnie Internationale des Wagon-Lits enabled visitors to sit inside one of three train carriages and view the scenery traversed during a fourteen-day trip move past the window in the compressed time of one hour. The scenery was created by theatrical scene painters Marcel Jambon and A. Bailley with three separate levels of distance moving at different speeds – going from foreground to background – and, thus, created a parallax effect familiar to viewers of contemporary animation. The seats in the carriage were mechanically manipulated so that they would jiggle up and down as if in motion and could stop and start in accord with the scenery seen outside.[18] A Trans-Siberian Railway Panorama by Pavel Pyasetsky has recently been preserved in the Hermitage State Museum, St Petersburg.[19] Interestingly, Huhtamo contends that two such attractions were on display at the Paris Exposition: the smaller-scale watercolour panorama by Pyasetsky, which won the Exposition's Grand Prix, in the Siberian section of the Russian Pavilion and the larger-scale version by Jambon and Bailey as a passageway between the Russian and Chinese Pavilions. With the emergence of the cinema, popular forms of entertainment, such as the moving panorama, fell out of favour with mass audiences and yet the connections between trains and moving images continued.

The link between the advent of the train and the development of cinema is not only metaphorical. The railway informed not only the subject matter of early films, from the earliest shorts *A Kiss in the Tunnel* (1899) to the more fully developed narrative of *The Great Train Robbery* (1903), but also the technology of the early cinema in many different ways. For example, Eadweard Muybridge's zoopraxiscope, arguably one of the earliest examples of the recording and playback of actual motion, was due in part to funding he had received from the railroad tycoon, Leland Stanford, for his motion studies of racehorses.[20] Travelling by train also helped Albert E. Smith solve the technical problem of image flicker in films. Lynne Kirby cites an anecdote of how the solution came to him as he was looking out from a train window at a sequence of picket fences and telegraph posts. This inspired him to add extra blades to the shutter and he discovered that by multiplying the flicker, it would actually be eliminated.[21]

The experience of travelling by railway directly contributed to the subject matter of early films. In phantom ride films, which were created from 1898, the spectator sees from the point of view of a camera attached (with the cameraman) to the front of a moving train and feels as if, in the words of a contemporary review, they are 'part and parcel of the picture'.[22] The train itself is not seen. Starting out with local views, cameramen were soon dispatched to distant lands to create these popular films,[23] a precursor to the travelogue. As if gazing out of the window of a railway carriage, the viewer would watch the landscape passing by.

Reminiscent of the Trans-Siberian Moving Panorama, moving image footage was also combined with physical sensation to create popular attractions. In 1905, George C. Hale, a mechanical engineer, applied for a patent for a 'Pleasure

Railway'. The visitors would enter a railway carriage and watch phantom ride films of train journeys that were rear projected onto a large screen.[24] The carriage that they were sitting in would be jolted, sway from side to side and they would feel puffs of air – all synchronized to simulate the experience of what was happening in the film they were watching. Venues for the Hales Tours opened in amusements parks throughout America and there were four in the UK, including one in Oxford Street, that allowed visitors the virtual experience of travelling through far-away places like Tokyo, Switzerland, Ceylon and Lourdes until the novelty ran out around 1912.[25] Phantom ride films shot from moving trains contributed to the development of cinematic tracking shots, with mobile cameras mounted on wheels that could move across tracks and were, thus, able to film while moving through space.

In the apocryphal tale of the origin of film, at the Lumière brother's first screening of film clips that took place in an underground billiard hall at the Grand Café in 1895, the audience fled screaming from the auditorium at the sight of a train hurtling towards them as it approached the station. They had confused the moving images of *Arrival of a Train* (1895) with real experience. It didn't take long for this founding myth to establish itself. As early as 1901 British filmmaker, Robert W. Paul created the satirical film *The Countryman's First Sight of the Animated Pictures: A Farmer Viewing the Approaching Train on the Screen Takes to His Heels* (1901).[26]

Film historians argue that there is no historical evidence for this extreme reaction of panic and that these stories have become exaggerated.[27] Advertised as 'living photographs', what appeared initially as a static image on screen began to move, but not for long. The *Arrival of a Train* was a short, black-and-white, silent film with a great deal of flickering lasting just fifty seconds. The astonishment of the spectator was more likely to be for the 'unbelievable visual transformation', the sophistication of the visual trickery, rather than the spectator's inability to tell fact from fiction.[28] Martin Loiperdinger and Bernd Elzer consider the whole story to have been manufactured as part of marketing hype – indeed, in a New York publicity stunt, paramedics with stretchers were stationed by the entrance to the place where the films were shown. Furthermore, there is no factual evidence of the *Arrival of a Train* even being included in the programme for the first film screening in 1895.[29]

Rather than being naïve, the audience for the 'cinema of attractions'[30] – the films of 1895–1904 – were actually accustomed to theatrical illusionism in the magic shows, waxworks, panoramas, dioramas, magic lantern and lightning sketch performances shown at fairs and variety theatre and craved ever more spectacular entertainment. Indeed, following the first head-on train crash in 1896 at Crush City, Texas, train crashes became not only the subject matter of films such as Edison's *The Railroad Smash-Up* (1904), but train wrecks, for which 30,000 paid to see, were staged for the purpose of entertainment at county fairs in the United States from 1896 to the 1920s.[31] Factual and fictional accounts of train journeys continue to the present day as subject matter for both film and animation.

Animation and trains: Data visualization

The earliest example of an animation about a train journey that I have been able to find, *Cartoon Train Journey 1910–1920*, dates from just after the cinema of attractions period and is in the British Pathé archive.[32] A short clip, under two minutes, was designed to be shown as part of a programme of newsreels. This stop-motion animation depicts a train journey from London to Edinburgh. It uses the train journey as a device to explore the geography of Britain and depicts the earth in cross section to describe the difference in geological make-up of the land traversed on this journey. The miniature steam train, which emits puffs of animated yarn to stand in for steam, is shown from above in plan view for the final section of the journey from Berwick to Edinburgh. Animation is used as a tool to express factual data in a diagrammatic form, thereby expressing information about British geology that would have been much harder to communicate in the form of live-action footage of a train journey. A purely quantitative/instrumental approach to the depiction of transport geography, however, gives a limited and narrow account of the rich experience of travelling by railway.

As previously discussed, a train journey involves much more than travelling from A to B in the quickest time possible. The passenger watches moving landscape out of the window. She eats, sleeps, reads, talks and daydreams. She has a time-based, qualitative experience. With the short film, *European Journey 2030* (2013), co-directed and animated by Birgitta Hosea and Steve Roberts, a team of researchers aimed to express the affective impact of a journey through the form of animation.[33] The SYNAPTIC project (Synergy of New Advanced Public Transport Solutions Improving Connectivity in North West Europe) focused on the qualitative experience of international rail travel and made suggestions as to how this could be improved in a future journey from Preston (UK) to Delft (the Netherlands) in 2030. Animation was chosen as the ideal medium in which to collate the findings of the four different research projects that made up the SYNAPTIC project into one seamless narrative – in the form of a journey. Using animation to disseminate the research findings enabled a complex collection of multiple data sets to be depicted audiovisually in order to make the research coherent and accessible to specialist and non-specialist audiences alike. The aim was to represent the process and experience of travel, in particular to emphasize the quality, comfort and convenience of the journey.

When presenting research findings, the use of diagrams to communicate instrumental data has value for the comprehension of quantitative, numerical information. However, it is a challenge to represent action, process or experiential data using a graph, a map or a scale diagram.[34] Animation as a form has more potential to describe the affective and qualitative experience of a journey than a static information diagram. In *European Journey 2030*, the technique of character animation was chosen as opposed to motion graphic moving diagrams. In the animation, painterly backgrounds created in Photoshop, humorous illustrations created in Illustrator and a rich soundscape heighten the sensual nature of the journey that is being depicted. Operating at a subliminal level to contribute to the atmosphere, the soundtrack comprises samples of real-world sounds, including recordings made at UK and European train stations.

In addition to having the potential to express an affective and sensual landscape, animation has a capacity for the visualization of proposals or hypothetical findings that have not yet been realized. The scenario in this animation is based in 2030. The background designs were inspired by architects' plans for buildings that have not yet been built, such as Delft Station, and imagined re-developments of existing buildings, such as Tulketh Mill and Preston Station. Using the device of train travel to structure the narrative, the film visualized the journey of Suravi Dumill-Douze as she travelled from Preston with her young daughter to a work meeting in Delft, enabling the traveller character to operate as an agent of focalization[35] through whose subjective perspective the journey can be experienced by the viewer. This extended researcher Peter Hall's use of a fictional family in his work on transport planning to serve as a narrative device for a human-centred description of the process of making a journey.[36] In the next section, I will consider animations in which the central agent of focalization for the narrative is not a human character, but the train itself.

Train as character: Regulation and rebellion

Although both animations are series designed as entertainment for children and both are named after the trains that serve as their main characters, *Thomas the Tank Engine* and *Ivor the Engine* provide two very contrasting worldviews.

Thomas the Tank Engine was first shown on ITV in 1984. It was based on the Railway Series books by Reverend W. Awdry that were inspired by a wooden train set he made for his son and the stories he made up about trains when his son was sick. These stories were so popular with his family that, at the insistence of his wife and son, he eventually sent them off to be published. TV producer Britt Allcroft was inspired to create the books as an animated series for children. Originally created in stop motion, the series continues its third generation and is now made in CGI by Hit Entertainment. It continues in popularity with a theme park in Japan and has spawned a number of games and toys.[37]

In the *Thomas the Tank Engine* stories, the trains operate in a milieu of strict rules and regulations on the island of Sodor. Watched over by the Fat Controller, these animations explore themes of hard work, compliance, orderliness and knowing your place. Life is not about enjoying the ride, but following the rules and being securely back in the station at night. For example, in *Thomas Comes to Breakfast* (1986), Thomas arrogantly assumes that he does not need his driver, to the great concern of his friends who ultimately have to haul him out of the Station Master's House that he crashes into after a careless cleaner meddles with his controls. He is in disgrace and in trouble with the Fat Controller, who temporarily replaces him with a much more obedient and compliant diesel train. In *Thomas and Gordon* (1984), Thomas cheekily shows off about being the most hard-working engine. The young upstart is taught a lesson by Gordon, another train, who drags him along so fast that his wheels hurt. 'Now you know what hard work means', says Gordon. 'Maybe I don't need to tease Gordon to feel important', Thomas thought and, life lesson learnt, he puffed slowly home.

These animations show a world in which the vehicles have more personality than the human beings. In the limited stop-motion technique used in the original series, use of camera movements, real smoke and water breaks up shots of static models. There is more motion used in the animation of the trains, particularly their faces, than in the human characters who are static figures without articulation. The personality of the locomotives and their movement through space (integral to the staging of adventure in each episode) therefore become the features that are foregrounded.

A very different world is shown in another classic British animation, *Ivor the Engine*. Created from painted cut-outs animated by Oliver Postgate and Peter Firmin's Small Films Co, the series was originally made in black and white for Rediffusion in 1958 and then remade in colour for BBC in 1975. Adding to the charm of Firmin's designs, Postgate made the sounds of the train puffing himself. The series is now available as an iPad game. Whereas *Thomas the Tank Engine* largely focuses on trains as primary characters with narratives of compliance and control that end up with the steam locomotive firmly quartered back in his shed at night, *Ivor the Engine* is used as a delightful narrative device for exploring a range of characters that are encountered on journeys through the Welsh countryside, such as Idris the Dragon, the local choir and Dai Station, the station master. It is an ensemble piece with a large cast of characters exploring the interconnected rural lives of Welsh villagers.

Ivor the Engine as a character is not as visually anthropomorphosized as the trains shown in *Thomas and Friends*, which typically have faces on the front of their boilers. An omniscient narrator has access to Ivor's feelings and Mr Jones 'the Steam' (his driver) can talk to Ivor, with Ivor's replies taking the form of tuneful sounds from his steam whistles. In the series, Ivor is shown as rebellious, kind and community spirited. He does not want to be constrained by the timetable, interacts with the local community by helping animals, doing favours and battling with the problems of health and safety regulations for the conveyance of dragons. The structuring narrative thread that runs through the series is that Mr Williams wants to make Ivor's branch line part of the national Welsh railway and follow conventional rules and timetables. Luckily for our hero, by the end of the series Mrs Potty, a rich local eccentric, buys the line so Ivor can continue to defy conformity and regulation to benefit others, for example, by changing his route to stop and help an elephant.

Evoking a nostalgic vision of a bygone era of steam in which communities helped each other out, the episodes of *Ivor the Engine* focus on the experience of mobility – the journey itself rather than the end destination. Through the movement of the train through the landscape, different characters and stories in different locations are brought together. In the next section, the train will be considered as a location rather than as a central character.

Train as location: Moving through the non-place

The tourist, the travelling salesman, the itinerant circus performer, the tax exile, the cleared slum dweller – in our contemporary world, people are on the move. In his study of mobility, Cresswell relates how in the field of anthropology it is recognized that communities grow, change and move. They may be diasporic and live in exile, holding a common cultural identity, but no longer living in the same mythic place of origin. In opposition to a fixed permanent place of residence, he cites Marc Augé's suggestion for a new type of place – a place of travellers and transients, a temporary place that people just pass through and do not live in – the non-place.[38] In the non-place, tradition and heritage are no longer relevant. It is a place of transit, to be occupied briefly and then passed through: like a train.

On the train, events, stories and strangers are brought together in a confined space for a limited period of time – the duration of the journey. Rather than being restricted to one social milieu, passengers on public transport encounter people from beyond their normalizing geographic, professional, class, gender and race boundaries (within the restrictions of the class of carriage they have bought a ticket for). Doreen Massey argues that space is an open system, in which layers of co-existing stories coincide by chance.[39] This chance encounter of multiple narratives is particularly apparent in the non-place that is the train. Exploring this temporary clash of cultures in close proximity has provided a rich vein of storylines for film and animation.

Clearly inspired by *The Lady Vanishes* (1938), *Madame Tutli-Putli* (2007) is a stop-motion, film noir pastiche in which strangers are brought together on a train. In this National Film Board of Canada animation directed by Chris Lavis and Maciek Szczerbowski, a female traveller boards a train. The main character is given an uncanny, emotional depth through film of real human eyes being skilfully composited onto the puppet's face. The subtle atmosphere of claustrophobia and unease is further heightened by a dramatic use of sound. The old-fashioned compartment, reminiscent of *The Lady Vanishes*, has a retro, nostalgic design undercut by the use of a modern, plastic, disposable coffee cup as a prop. The carriage is packed with strangers and their possessions. The train is delayed during the night and two strange people get on, gas the passengers, steal their possessions and then start removing their organs. *Madame Tutli-Putli* wakes up and escapes to the restaurant car. However, the ending is left open and unresolved. Does she escape or do they find her? Is it real or a dream? Is she doomed to stay onboard the train for all eternity? We don't find out. This film portrays a nightmarish sense of the train as an unfamiliar, non-place from which you cannot escape. As in Jean Paul Sartre's play *Huit Clos* (translated in English as either *No Exit* or *In Camera*, 1944), hell is the ultimate horror of being trapped with other people in a state of limbo for all eternity.

This state of being in a non-place, forever on a journey, not arriving or beginning but in an 'in-between' state of becoming is also explored in *Traion II (Train)* (2014). The *Traion* series of works use drawing to explore the trace of presence in motion. In *Traion II (Train)*, the train journey is used as a metaphor to explore different aspects of movement. The animation loops continuously, so the journey never ends. The process of making this animation, designed for gallery installation, involved the artists, Maryclare Foá and Birgitta Hosea, sitting on a moving train and on each consecutive frame digitally tracing around a still photograph of themselves sitting on the very same train. As the motion of the train effects the accuracy of the drawing, adding unintended hand shake and variation, the resulting animation is a recording of the motion of the train itself. This process was inspired by the work of artist, William Anastasie. Starting in 1977, Anastasie started a series of drawings that used moments of chance motion from everyday life as the basis for mark making. Travelling on the New York subway, he would hold a pencil in each hand and lightly touch the surface of paper on his lap. As the subway moved and his whole body responded, he would create inadvertent marks on the paper.[40] In both *Traion II (Train)* and the work of Anastasie, the surrounding landscape of the train carriage becomes an animating force in itself.

In the windows of the train carriage depicted in *Traion II (Train)*, hand-drawn scenery passes by as if landscape is being travelling through. This was created by the artists making very long, abstract, action drawings on the walls while walking around the studio, which were subsequently divided into foreground, mid-ground and background and then animated. Thus, in this work, different levels of motion within the train carriage are evoked: the motion of the passenger's body while sitting on a moving train and the motion of an imagined landscape moving past the window in parallax. The irony being that, as the train itself is a location from whose perspective the viewer looks out, the motion seen out of the window is an illusion. It is not the landscape that actually moves, but train itself. This perspective is considered in the next section, where we will focus on what is outside the train carriage: the landscape that travellers are transported through.

Speculative landscapes

Landscape is often thought of as eternal and unchanging, but in reality it is changing all the time due to changing patterns of habitation, agriculture, industry and climate change as well, of course, as the slow shifts of the tectonic plates that hold our continents together. In her work on space, Massey argues that space is not fixed, essential and eternal, but plural, relational, in a state of flux, always in the process of being produced, subject to the result of interrelationships.[41] Using animation, future changes to the landscape as a result of its relationship with human beings can be hypothesized and depicted.

In the short animation *Speculative Landscapes* (2010), which was inspired by a journey on the futuristic Maglev train in Shanghai, original live-action footage from this journey was reconstructed and re-imagined by specialists in architectural visualization, Factory Fifteen. The rail journey is used as a premise for the depiction of imagined landscapes. A hyper-real combination of matte painting and CGI with live-action footage is used to present a landscape that becomes increasing industrial, barren and devoid of natural vegetation, until it degenerates into apocalyptic piles of industrial waste. Thus, the film makes a poignant and effective comment on the ecological issues that could affect a hypothetical future society.

CGI animation can be used to portray photo-real journeys through hypothetical landscapes and, in combination with games engines, this can be extended to allow the viewer control over user-generated journeys. In *Train Simulator 2014*, for example, the fantasy of being a train driver is offered with the opportunity to experience limitless travel throughout a virtual model of worldwide, iconic train routes. The virtual landscape that is being travelled through is modelled with extreme attention to the detail of actual locations. Although reminiscent of the phantom ride films discussed earlier, *TS2014* offers much more than a fixed view of a journey. Multiple viewpoints are available while driving the train – from inside the driver's cab, the passenger's view from inside the carriage or helicopter views from above. Marketed as much more than a game, rail fans can make and share routes and components. They can contribute improvements to the scenery and customize their journeys. On fan forums there is great importance placed on making minor amendments to routes in order to improve their veracity to real-world locations.

The voice-over for *We Are Rail Fans* (2013), the promotional film for *TS2014*, offers a seductive glimpse into the pleasure afforded from playing this game:

> They take you for granted, the travelling hordes. To them, you're just crowded and dirty, functional, a means to an end... Their lives move too fast to stop and look, to sit back and enjoy the view. It all flies past in a blur... They want the destination: we want the journey... We look at the world outside, along the backs of other lives: a face at the window, a broken bike in the yard, vast fields, rivers wide, in and out of cities, towns and countryside... We have a place where time is our own, where steam, diesel and electric are king.[42]

The experience is one of being mobile, of enjoying the encounter with different types of landscapes and, yet, like in model railway building, being in control of the landscape, able to alter and perfect the model to make it more 'realistic'. This is a continually evolving process with new versions of the game and new add-on routes or train models being offered for sale. Updates will always be needed to satisfy the demand of fans for a real-world experience as the railway environment itself changes over time.

This section has considered the animated encounter with train travel through landscape as subject matter. In the next section, it will be through the motion of the actual train journey itself from which the animation is created.

Screen-less animation[43]

From the earliest optical toys (such as the zoetrope) to the work of contemporary artists, screen-less methods of creating animated images have been explored that work on the principle of optical illusion. When travellers on the Manhattan-bound B or Q train in New York pass DeKalb Avenue station, they are confronted by animation in the subway tunnel itself. Bill Brand's artwork *Masstransiscope* (1980) consists of a 300-feet painting illuminated by fluorescent light and encased in 228 metal slits. It is located on the platform of the abandoned Myrtle Avenue station.[44] The animated images are not mediated by film or video – the passengers see the original painting rather than a photograph or digital scan of it. Based on the principle of the zoetrope, the conventions of the cinematic context are reversed when these moving images are viewed. As opposed to a sequence of images moving through a film projector, the painting is still and it is the audience who move past a sequence of images. As the images are viewed by the passengers through the metal slits that stand between the painting and the subway train, there is an illusion of motion created by the actual motion of their bodies through space. Rather than landscape seen as continuous space outside the train window, graphic forms appear to dance and change form on the subway walls in real time.

Conclusion

The theme of trains connects a body of animated work that is extremely diverse in approach and form. What is central to each of the works discussed in this chapter is the journey. The animated railway journey can be read as a metaphor for the transience and flux at the root of contemporary society that Bauman has termed liquid modernity. Our contemporary world is fluid, flexible and globalized. We consume mass media, cheap flights, the Internet, global brands. People eat international cuisine, experience media or buy goods from around the world, travel for work or pleasure, change their jobs, become obsolete, re-train, move between professions and disciplines, relocate for economic reasons or because of political conflict or slum clearance. Multinational corporations take advantage of trading around the world to defy national laws and tax regulations. National borders are disputed, leading to war and the displacement of people. Bauman suggests we are in an age of flux, change and continuous obsolescence. As opposed to the solid, modern age held together and made coherent by belief in grand narratives, we are in a new age of liquid modernity where interdeterminacy and uncertainty are key to our consumerist state: 'Liquid modern life is a daily rehearsal of universal transcience. Today's useful and indispensible objects, with few and possibly no exceptions, are tomorrow's waste. Everything is disposable, nothing is truly necessary, nothing is irreplaceable.'[45]

Our societies have global issues, but these, Bauman suggests, are drifting, aimless without vision. Perhaps we are in a transitionary phase between epochs or perhaps we have lost our way:

> I am increasingly inclined to surmise that we presently find ourselves in a time of 'interregnum' – when the old ways of doing things no longer work, the old learned or inherited modes of life are no longer suitable for the current condition humana, but when the new ways of tackling the challenges and new modes of

life better suited to the new conditions have not as yet been invented, put in
place and set in operation.[46]

It's a constant process; there is no goal of 'progress' and we haven't reached the
'future'. In the age of Modernism, there was a goal in sight, the ideal future, but
liquid modernity is a state of constant change for change's sake: 'To "be modern"
means to modernize – compulsively, obsessively; not so much "to be", let alone
to keep its identity intact, but forever "becoming", avoiding completion, staying
undefined.'[47]

Power has become disassociated from politics, the individual feels
disenfranchised, unable to influence world events or the flow of capital. Notions
of territory, disciplines, meaning and boundaries are permeable. Since the
advent of the computer, this sense of change and fundamental, ontological
uncertainty has been apparent in the field of animation.[48] At the crossroads of
many art forms, traditional techniques and rapidly evolving technical processes,
animation is an ideal candidate to be considered as a liquid art form.

Using the thematic taxonomy of train journeys permits a comparison of a
range of practices that might be considered pre-cinematic animation, cinematic
animation and post-cinematic animation. The breadth of these practices show
that the idea of animation is in flux, not static, an intermedial cross roads reinvented by each successive generation. From moving panoramas and phantom
rides through to children's TV series, subway zoetropes and railway simulation
games, what these works all have in common is that artificial movement is
recorded/encoded, stored and then played back.[49] They do not all use film as
their medium of encoding, storage and playback. Considered in relation to the
processes of mobility, the reproduction of artificial movement via animation can
be seen to have implications for a consideration of time and space, whatever the
form by which this movement is stored.

Animation visualizes mobility and yet also has mobility at its core as a form.
Beyond relating to a discipline changing how it sees itself, the mobilities paradigm
raises other issues for animation. Cresswell argues that geographical concepts are
not neutral, but are both social and political. They have consequences for how
we conceptualize the world that surrounds us, for how we 'structure and enable
practice in the world'.[50] Although the ability to move is at the basis of all humanity,
mobility is 'socially produced motion' and requires detailed interrogation. While
mobility may appear to be at the very heart of what freedom means, Cresswell
warns us that there are restrictions as to how mobile we can really be according

to class, race, gender and physical ability.[51] To have mobility – to be free to move as we choose – implies economic, political and gender privilege – to afford the cost of a ticket, to have the correct visa or travel permit, to be able to roam freely in the city at night without fear.[52]

As we theorize and gaze at the navel of our liquid modern art form, it is easy to neglect the political implications that result from a mobilities perspective on animation. We all need to take a global perspective on our industry and its use of resources: the outsourced 'cheap' labour-forces who make our animations for wages that would not be acceptable in the Western world; the mountains of discarded plastic cartoon toys that are currently not biodegrading on rubbish heaps around the world; the electricity used to power our gadgets and cloud computing; the wars fought over the rare mineral coltan used in our electronic devices and the dire conditions of the workers who make these devices for us. I would like to argue for more politics in animation. Not a politics at the level of representation, but at the material basis of what we actually do, at the level of tools, supplies, technology and distribution. For the responsibility we bear for the global patterns of production and consumption that result from animation.

Notes

1 Department for Transport, National Travel Survey: 2012 (UK Government, 2013).
2 Cf. Henning Mankell's chilling account of the contribution of indentured Chinese labour to the building of the American railroads in his novel *The Man from Beijing* (2011).
3 Rebecca Solnit, *Motion Studies: Time, Space and Eadweard Muybridge* (London: Bloomsbury Books, 2004), 62–65.
4 John Urry, *Mobilities* (Cambridge: Polity Press, 2010), 102.
5 Solnit, *Motion Studies: Time, Space and Eadweard Muybridge*, 9.
6 Ibid., 4.
7 Urry, *Mobilities*, 97.
8 Tim Cresswell, *On the Move: Mobility in the Western World* (New York and London: Routledge, 2006), 6.
9 Solnit, *Motion Studies: Time, Space and Eadweard Muybridge*, 61.
10 Zygmunt Bauman, *Liquid Modernity* (Cambridge: Polity Press, 2013), 9.
11 Solnit, *Motion Studies: Time, Space and Eadweard Muybridge*, 11.
12 Gilles Deleuze, *Cinema I: The Movement Image*, trans. Hugh Tomlinson and Barbara Habberjam (London: Continuum Books, 2012), 8.

13 Cresswell, *On the Move*, 5.

14 William Uricchio, 'A "Proper Point of View": The Panorama and Some of Its Early Media Iterations', *Early Popular Visual Culture* 9.3 (2011): 3.

15 Erkki Huhtamo, *Illusions in Motion?: A Media Archaeology of the Moving Panorama and Related Spectacles* (Cambridge, MA and London: MIT Press, 2013), 8–15.

16 Ibid., 32–34.

17 Uricchio, 'A "Proper Point of View"', 5.

18 Cf. ibid., 6; and Huhtamo, *Illusions in Motion*, 310–311.

19 State Hermitage Museum, 'Restoration of Pyasetsky's Great Siberian Railway Panorama (1894–1899)', *Hermitage News*, 2007, http://www.hermitagemuseum.org/html_En/11/2007/hm11_3_35.html.

20 Solnit, *Motion Studies: Time, Space and Eadweard Muybridge*, 4–5.

21 Lynne Kirby, 'Male Hysteria and Early Cinema', in *Male Trouble*, ed. Constance Penley and Sharon Willis (Minneapolis: University of Minnesota Press, 1993), 68–69.

22 Lynda Nead, 'Velocities of the Image C. 1900', *Art History* 27.5 (2005), 758.

23 Christian Hayes, 'Phantom Rides', *BFI Screen Online*, accessed 7 July 2014, http://www.screenonline.org.uk/film/id/1193042/.

24 Raymond Fielding, 'Hale's Tours: Ultrarealism in the Pre-1910 Motion Picture', *Cinema Journal* 10.1 (1970): 39.

25 Ibid., 44.

26 Martin Loiperdinger and Bernd Elzer, 'Lumiere's Arrival of the Train: Cinema's Founding Myth', *The Moving Image* 4.1 (2004): 91.

27 Cf. Tom Gunning, 'An Aesthetic of Astonishment: Early Film and the (In)Credulous Spectator', in *Viewing Positions*, ed. Linda Williams (New Brunswick, NJ: Rutgers, 1995), 116; and Loiperdinger and Elzer, 'Lumiere's Arrival of the Train: Cinema's Founding Myth', 94.

28 Gunning, 'An Aesthetic of Astonishment: Early Film and the (In)Credulous Spectator', 119.

29 Loiperdinger and Elzer, 'Lumiere's Arrival of the Train: Cinema's Founding Myth', 99–102.

30 Gunning, 'An Aesthetic of Astonishment: Early Film and the (In)Credulous Spectator', 121.

31 Kirby, 'Male Hysteria and Early Cinema', 74.

32 The British Pathé archive gives only an approximate date and the original title is unknown.

33 Robin Hickman et al., 'Animating the Future Seamless Public Transport Journey', *Built Environment* 39.3 (2013): 370–371.

34 Edwards Tufte, *Visual Explanations: Images and Quantities, Evidence and Narrative* (Cheshire, CT: Graphics Press, 2005).

35 This concept is taken from Mieke Bal's work on narratology Mieke Bal, *A Mieke Bal Reader* (Chicago, IL: University of Chicago Press, 2006), 270.

36 Peter Hall, *London 2001* (London: Unwin Hyman, 1989); and Peter Hall, *London 2000* (London: Faber & Faber, 1963).

37 'The Story of Thomas and Friends', *Thomas & Friends*, accessed 7 June 2014, http://www.thomasandfriends.com/en-gb/About/index.html.

38 Cresswell, *On the Move*, 44.

39 Doreen Massey, *For Space* (London; Thousand Oaks, CA; New Delhi: Sage Publications, 2005), 111.

40 William Anastasi and Margaret Iversen, 'Interview with Thomas McEvilley//2005', in *Chance, Documents of Contemporary Art* (London; Cambridge, MA: Whitechapel Gallery; MIT Press, 2010), 107–108.

41 Massey, *For Space*, 9.

42 Train Simulator 2014, *We Are Rail Fans*, 2013, http://youtu.be/C12ayclepqA?list=PL vUwWjZgALPWvOt-_ZIl0T-eT5-89yw7b.

43 I have taken the term 'screen-less animation' from the spectacular work of Trope, who works in this area by animating light over sequential kinetic sculptures to create animation in the environment. Cf. http://www.trope-design.com.

44 Jo Brand, 'Masstransiscope', *Bill Brand* (2013), Artists website http://www.bboptics.com/masstransiscope.html.

45 Zygmunt Bauman, 'Liquid Arts', *Theory, Culture & Society* 24.1 (2007), 123.

46 Bauman, *Liquid Modernity*, vii.

47 Ibid., viii.

48 Birgitta Hosea, *Substitutive Bodies and Constructed Actors: A Practice-Based Investigation of Animation as Performance*, PhD diss. (London: University of the Arts, 2012), 11–23.

49 This idea is further developed in my PhD thesis, Hosea, *Substitutive Bodies and Constructed Actors: A Practice-Based Investigation of Animation as Performance*.

50 Cresswell, *On the Move*, 21.

51 Ibid., 265.

52 Ibid., 3.

10

Between Setting and Character: A Taxonomy of Sentient Spaces in Fantasy Film

Fran Pheasant-Kelly

Introduction

With reference to Aylish Wood's concept of 'timespaces', this chapter explores the sentient spaces of fantasy film.[1] It suggests that digital technologies, in producing either computer-generated or computer-assisted effects, have extended the capacity and significance of film settings by endowing them with a cognitive awareness and physical articulation more in line with film characters than with backdrops for action. Wood contends that 'digital effects produce spaces with the ability to transform, or [...] have a temporal quality', thus adding an extra dimension to the narrative progression'[2] and designates these temporally extended special-effects spaces as 'timespaces'. However, the digitally generated/ assisted landscape often moves beyond Wood's notion of a temporally extended space, and rather, constitutes an enhancement of setting to the level of a sentient being. Moreover, this sentience invests the narrative with a causal as well as a temporal element. In other words, sentient spaces contribute towards narrative progression in ways beyond temporal extension. Trees are especially amenable to such effects, evident, for example, in *Harry Potter and the Goblet of Fire* (2005) when animated tree roots malevolently ensnare one of its characters, Cedric Diggory (Robert Pattinson). The sentience of landscape is not in itself a new phenomenon, being evident in early fantasy film – for instance, the forest of *The Wizard of Oz* (1939) similarly assumes cognitive qualities. Yet, new animation and digital techniques facilitate a more credible anthropomorphism of settings, to the extent that they are either little different from animated characters or are conflated with them. Analogous to Wood's contention for convergence between time and space in 'timespaces', this chapter therefore argues that settings have become credible sentient entities, with digital technologies effecting a diminishing/absent margin between character and setting. In so doing, it utilizes the description 'animated settings' in relation to sentience in both the genres of animation and fantasy. Textually analysing a range of fantasy films, including the *Harry Potter* series (2001–2011), Peter Jackson's *The Lord of the Rings* trilogy (2001–2003) and Steven Spielberg's *The Kingdom of the Crystal Skull* (2008), amongst others, and referring to Wood's 'timespaces' as well as Sigmund Freud's theory of animism and studies of animation by Paul Wells and Chris Pallant, this chapter posits a concept of sentient computer-generated imagery (CGI) as marking setting-character convergence.

Sentience and cinema

In discussions of CGI and animation, characters (as conventionally perceived) generally predominate, illustrated, for example, by scholarship on motion-capture and digital techniques involved in the characterization of Gollum (Andy Serkis) in *The Lord of the Rings*,[3] the skeletal pirates in *Pirates of the Caribbean* (2003–2011)[4] and the animated figures of *Toy Story* (1995).[5] Currently, anthropomorphism in animals, as animated cartoon figures (*Shrek* [2001]), digital constructions (*Jurassic Park* [1993]) or as digitally manipulated 'real' characters (*Cats and Dogs* [2001]), is attracting particular academic interest.[6] This is not only a result of developments in digital technology, but also because of the rising representation and agency of animals in film, the latter likely stemming from a more generalized sensitivity to animal welfare and recent animal studies which identify various humanoid attributes in animals, such as intelligence and complex emotions.[7]

Film landscape, by contrast, generally garners scholarly attention for its aesthetics, by providing a spectacle either to be physically overcome within the narrative, as in *The Perfect Storm* (2000), or one to be admired and contemplated from a distance, although, more recently, ecological perspectives of landscape have also become prominent.[8] Otherwise, studies of landscape and cinema are wide ranging and variously consider inscriptions of nostalgia, deviance, nationhood, cultural identity, heritage, social meaning, tourism and myth.[9] Overall, with the exceptions of Kirsten Thompson (2006),[10] who focuses on special effects and spectacle in *The Lord of the Rings*, and Scott Bukatman (2000),[11] who discusses artificial spectacle as an example of the technological sublime (and therefore retains a focus on aesthetics), there is limited analysis of digital and/or animated landscapes, or the capacity of settings to assume sentience.[12] The dramatic scenery of *Avatar* (2009) provides a recent example of the latter, with its digitally constructed aspects (as well as its associated September 11 meanings) enhancing its sublime effects. Here, the spectator is constantly invited to view wondrous, often surreal panoramas from extreme long shots that cause characters to appear diminished within the frame and seem dwarfed by their grandeur. An interesting paradox occurs in *Inception* (2010), which likewise presents digitally assisted and digitally generated cityscapes as sublime spectacle. However, part of the film's sublime impact stems from the fact that the cityscape is physically mobile, and appears to rise up and fold over itself, an action that positions the spectator, along with the characters, at the foot of an immense awe-inspiring vista. Yet, despite its dynamism, the cityscape in *Inception* lacks any anthropomorphic or sentient qualities and we do not get a sense of its livingness. Arguably, this is because its movement lacks obvious psychological or narrative motivation other than one of display. Rather, like the contemplative views of landscapes in *Avatar*, the scene corresponds to Bukatman's description of the technological sublime. Taking these two digitally dependent films as examples, a clear differential would therefore seem to exist between the computer-generated landscape and the digitally enhanced character.

Indeed, in his study of digital and animated landscapes, and corresponding with these observations concerning *Avatar* and *Inception*, Pallant likewise notes, 'our collective conditioning in the visual grammar of cinema supports an immediate understanding of what constitutes character and what constitutes landscape when we see a mainstream animated film'.[13] While acknowledging such a distinction, Pallant then goes on to describe potential convergences between setting and character, referring to a scene in the 1951 animated cartoon *Gerald McBoing Boing* in which 'landscape is endowed with the same metamorphic potential typically associated with character animation'.[14] He further considers two short films, *The Sand Castle* (1977) and *Bottle* (2010) in which the first displays the emergence of 'sand characters' that remain distinct from the landscape and the second exhibits a constant fluctuation between the landscape and setting. The latter, according to Pallant, 'prompts continued spectatorial re-evaluation of what constitutes landscape and what constitutes character, and on what basis such distinctions can be made'.[15]

Even as digital technology fosters a more seamless congruence between landscape and character, anthropomorphic tropes are evident in films as early as *The Wizard of Oz*, in which a forest scene not only conveys certain moods and emotions through eerie diegetic forest sounds and frightened reaction shots of the characters, but also features sentient, talking trees (the special effects in this case involve flexible 'tree suits' worn by actors). Certainly, fantasy is a genre that is especially amenable to such congruence, for, as Katherine Fowkes notes, 'one central aspect of fantasy stories is that each feature a fundamental break with our sense of reality'.[16]

Sentient spaces in fantasy film

Whereas studies of anthropomorphism tend to focus on animals, Wood explores more fully the concept of the animated landscape to consider the impact that the digitally contrived setting may have on narrative. More usually, attention centres on the contribution of digital effects to spectacle, which many scholars[17] suggest detracts from, or arrests the narrative. Conversely, others argue that CGI spectacle may actually enhance or contribute to the narrative.[18] In this vein, Geoff King proposes that certain editing techniques augment spectacular special effects and further the narrative by lengthening the time over which the action occurs, particularly when the event involves an explosion. King describes how an initial explosion is presented in a series of rapid shots from different angles and positions that suggest it is happening more than once. He contends that this impact or explosive editing approach is close to one of montage, with editing creating a fuller impact than the actual content of the individual images.[19] Explosive activity may also be depicted twice in rapid succession, which clearly breaks the rules of continuity editing, and is used again to heighten the effect of spectacle.[20] For different reasons, Wood agrees, but her argument rests on the claim that digital effects may extend the narrative in the way that they 'produce spaces with the ability to transform, or which have a temporal quality, thus adding an extra dimension to the narrative progression'.[21] Like King, Wood's approach focuses on the debate concerning the disruption of narrative by spectacle, with her main contention being that spectacle may, in fact, contribute to the narrative. She clarifies this by explaining the time–space distinction conventionally associated with the interactions between spectacle and narrative, stating that whether such arguments 'suggest that spectacle provides cohesion, interrupts the narrative or acts as an integrated, if distinct, element of a film, [they] affirm the separation of the spatial and the temporal.[22] Wood goes on to propose that 'digital effects, however, most specifically when they extend the duration of spectacle or give extended movement to spatial elements, introduce a temporal component to spaces.'[23] In other words, she suggests a conflation of time and space in certain animated settings involved in dynamic activity. She also implies an effect on narrative, stating that

> If such elements are, however, made to act (though not *react* [original emphasis] as they are not necessarily animate), or move within the space, then they too can have the effect of modifying the situation, and as such can operate as mobile agents of the narrative. I am not suggesting that such elements are in any sense the equivalent of characters, only that characters are not the only means through which situations can be modified.[24]

Ultimately, because her focus lies on digital effects rather than on animated settings, Wood does not address the notion of agency behind the formation and physical intervention of 'time-spaces', nor the characterization inherent in such effects.

Motivation and agency are significant to a claim for the characterization of settings, for, in considering the principles of narrative construction, Bordwell and Thompson note how characters 'create causes and register effects ... they make things happen and react to the twists and turns of events.'[25] These traits 'are designed to play a causal role in the narrative'[26] and, whilst the authors also acknowledge that such features may be located in either events (such as the burning skyscraper in *Towering Inferno* [1974]), or other entities – they illustrate this point by reference to the shark in *Jaws* (1975) – arguably, the way that certain digital landscapes are animated to mimic human emotion aligns the anthropomorphic setting closer to the digital character than previous examples. The contention here, therefore, is that particular animated settings do not arbitrarily move and change form merely to extend the narrative – rather, they act as if motivated by human emotions.[27] Ostensibly, the sophistication of digital effects enables the convergence of setting and character to the extent that the metaphoric symbolism of certain landscapes and backdrops has evolved to encompass an increasing array of features more associated with characters than settings. Just as inanimate objects are readily endowed with sentient or animistic capabilities, so are settings therefore increasingly anthropomorphized.

If animism explains such effects as the result of the belief that all living entities possess a soul,[28] then landscape too is starting to command a sense of its 'livingness'. Freud contends that animism is a primitive belief in the existence of 'spiritual beings both benevolent and malignant … [and that] all the inanimate objects in the world are animated by them'.[29] In fantasy film, such animism often arises as a result of the performance of magic or enchantment, and gives rise to instances of the uncanny. As Freud further explains, 'we appear to attribute an uncanny quality to impressions that seek to confirm the omnipotence of thoughts and the animistic mode of thinking in general'.[30] In a related way, the notion that landscape possesses an inner personality or will resonates with contemporary environmental concerns, and certainly, as Sean Cubitt argues, *The Perfect Storm* might be explained in terms of nature's retribution for overfishing and global warming.[31] David Butler too identifies a spiritual ambience and a 'primacy of spirit' in certain Chinese depictions of landscape.[32] Yet, there are instances of a more obviously animistic trend within film. Examples abound in fantasy cinema (partly because of its affinity for the incredible and magical), particularly those films produced since 2000, which was a pivotal year for the advancement of digital technologies. Specifically, the development of digital high-definition cameras, the first of these being Sony's F900 in 2000, and enhanced post-processing techniques have facilitated more credible and spectacular visual effects.[33] Indeed, digital techniques have expressly enabled the feasibility of the animated landscape. Wells elaborates on the precise features of animism and anthropomorphism, and contends that, 'Animism, a concept which may be defined as a pre-rational, pre-scientific state of relatedness to the organic inter-connectedness of the natural world and primordial conditions, may be seen to inform the animation which prioritises subjectivity and resists orthodox modes of representation'.[34] Wells further stipulates a set of criteria for identifying anthropomorphic qualities in early Disney cartoons – and even though he proposes these in relation to humour, they also provide a basis upon which to analyse the anthropomorphic features of sentient digital spaces. For Wells, the key aspects are as follows:

1. The necessity for the illusion of eye contact between the character performing and the audience watching
2. Facial gestures which obviously signif[y] particular thought processes
3. Physical traits and behavioural mannerisms common to, and recognised by, the audience, which remain largely consistent to the character
4. The direct expression of *motivation* [original emphasis] in the character and the immediate execution of the narrational action which achieves the objective signified …

5. The creation of a particular *rhythm* [original emphasis] for the character which expresse[s] a specific attitude or purpose
6. The overall treatment of the character as if it were an actor playing a role[35]

A further point that both Wells[36] and Pallant[37] highlight in relation to Disney cartoons is the use of exaggeration, again, relevant in theorizing the way in which animated landscapes are depicted. Although actions that are executed by sentient settings may not necessarily be exaggerated *per se*, the cinematography, perspective and framing which are deployed may act to generate hyperbole or emphasis. For instance, following Wells's classification above, the deployment of close-up enhances the potential for eye contact between the sentient setting and spectator while the use of long shot may accentuate a physical 'bodily' rhythm – exemplified by the restless motion of the castle in *Hauru no Ugoku Shiro/Howl's Moving Castle* (2004), or the gigantic striding movement of the Ents in *The Lord of the Rings: The Two Towers* (2002).

Taking Wells's framework as a guide for analysis, several categories (and therefore degrees) of sentience in film settings are proposed, of which most entail the display of emotion or agency that impacts the causal logic of the film. This taxonomy includes discrete settings that are intrinsically and consistently sentient and animated and which are central to the narrative, for example, the castle and the fire in *Howl's Moving Castle* and the house contents of *Poltergeist* (1982); the recognizably humanoid features or forms that emerge from a non-human or inorganic setting and which often possess verbal capacity, for example, the character of Wyvern, one of The *Flying Dutchman's* crew in *Pirates of the Caribbean: Dead Man's Chest* (2006), the Rock Monster in *Galaxy Quest* (1999) and the appearance of Voldemort's face in the clouds in *Harry Potter: The Goblet of Fire* (2005); settings that assume certain human traits and verbal capacity but essentially retain their original form (the Ents in *Lord of the Rings: The Two Towers*); fourthly, settings that lack demonstrably human features or the ability to speak but, nonetheless, act as if motivated by human emotions, and, in some way, still affect narrative progression (examples include the moving tree roots which ensnare Cedric in *Harry Potter and the Goblet of Fire*, and the passage through the labyrinth that spontaneously appears in *Pan's Labyrinth* [2006] to enable Ofelia's [Ivana Baquero] escape from her stepfather); a fifth category involves less obvious landscape mobility that does not entail vocalization or movement unusual to the landscape, but regardless, seems to occur of the setting's own volition and has benevolent effects that impact narrative causality, for example, the closing scenes of *Indiana Jones and the Crystal Skull*; and finally, the digital landscape that may move spontaneously, but does not appear sentient in any sense, and merely functions as a form of display, as in *Avatar* and *Inception*.

Digital capacity (sometimes combined with conventional animation techniques and special effects) has particularly facilitated sequences that entail the apparent livingness of non-human structures, enabling these to perform as characters. The castle in the animated fantasy *Howl's Moving Castle* epitomizes such personification in that the structure is mobile and 'walks' on 'legs', has facial features and emits steam as if respiring, while its multi-jointed form facilitates a physical flexibility normally found in living organisms. The castle is integral to the narrative, since it provides refuge for Sofî, its protagonist, who is transformed from a young girl (Chieko Baishô/Emily Mortimer) to an old woman (Baishô/Jean Simmons) by a witch's curse, and also provides portals to different realms. Aside from offering a safe haven for Sofî, the castle is home to a wizard named Howl (Takuya Kimura/Christian Bale), his young apprentice, Markl (Ryûnosuke Kamiki/Josh Hutcherson), and a fire demon named Karushifâ (Tatsuya Gashûin/Billy Crystal). In the spectator's initial encounter with the castle, enabled via Sofî's viewpoint, the itinerant structure suddenly appears over the brow of a hillock and the first impression that one has is of two eyes, represented by cannon ports positioned appropriately on its approaching front. Just as the castle emits a growling sound, its 'mouth', containing rows of jagged teeth, gapes open and its tongue extends. Despite the castle's technological construction, which consists of metal plates bolted together, its physical flexibility (facilitated by multiple joints that allow the movement of its components in all planes simultaneously) and facial features endow it with anthropomorphic qualities. Its apparent and persistent elasticity gives the impression that it is constantly inhaling and exhaling, thus enhancing a sense of its livingness. Not only does it seem to act benevolently in its rescue of Sofî from the cold (it flies low to the ground and scoops her up to enable her to board), but it also exhibits signs of emotion – one such scene occurs when Sofî, as an old woman, is flying through the air on an aircraft to escape from the King's palace. As they approach Howl's castle, just visible in the distance, she exclaims 'the castle is coming to meet us'. The castle then appears to smile in response (Figure 10.1), and seems to jump up and down, its movements becoming even more exaggerated, as if pleased to see Sofî return.

Figure 10.1 Howl's Moving Castle (*Howl's Moving Castle*, Studio Ghibli, 2004)

Other usually inanimate aspects of the *mise-en-scène* also assume sentience, including a fire that must be kept constantly alight within the castle (narratively, to provide energy and magical power to sustain the castle). The anthropomorphic form of the fire is explained by the presence of a demon named Karushifâ, who is also first viewed by the spectator from Sofî's perspective. Like the initial sight of the castle, the appearance of the demon's 'eyes' (conveyed as two bounded holes in the fire) suggests its sentient qualities, followed by the materialization of a mouth, and then a voice while the purposeful articulation of the flames serve as arms which the fire uses to express humanoid gestures.

A second mode of presentation occurs as a character (humanoid or otherwise) appears to materialize from landscapes and settings in scenarios where character and landscape are physically integrated but transiently become distinguishable from each other. This category might encompass the short films, *The Sand Castle* and *Bottle*, to which earlier reference was made. Typical mainstream examples include a sequence in *Pirates of the Caribbean: Dead Man's Chest* when Will Turner (Orlando Bloom) boards the *Flying Dutchman*, a ship whose crewmembers variously resemble semi-human sea-creatures. Turner has a heated exchange with one such character, 'Bootstrap' Bill Turner (Stellan Skarsgård), the scene being set against what appears to be a seaweed-and-barnacle-encrusted rock surface. Bootstrap explains the history of the *Flying Dutchman* and its crew: 'once you've sworn an oath to the *Dutchman*, there's no leaving it. Until you

end up like poor Wyvern there', he tells Turner, nodding towards the rocky
backdrop. Turner turns to look at the seemingly innocuous encrusted rock
surface, and then turns back towards the spectator, the camera framing Turner
and the rock surface behind him in which a face is now just discernible. When
Turner makes reference to a missing key, an extreme close-up discloses the face
suddenly becoming animated and its eyes opening. Eye contact is therefore
established between Wyvern (John Boswell) and the spectator, facilitating a
more credible anthropomorphic character, in line with Wells's categorization.
Moreover, Wyvern's shocked facial expression clearly signifies thought processes
concerning the whereabouts of the missing key. A cracking sound occurs as the
creature attempts to extract itself from the rock, the remains of its face encrusted
with sea creatures and crystallized sea-plants, while its body appears to remain
integrated physically with its surroundings. These cracking sounds continue,
occurring with every movement of the character/setting, creating a particular
set of characteristics and rhythm. Upon questioning about the missing key,
Wyvern instructs Turner to 'open the chest with the key and stab the heart … no
don't stab the heart, the Dutchman needs a living heart, and if there's no captain,
there's no-one to have the key', thus providing important narrative information
concerning the whereabouts of the missing key, which drives the plot onwards.
In other words, the creature, part-inanimate and part-human, functions beyond
contributing a temporal dimension to space but rather, facilitates the narrative
through the expression of motivation.

A third way that animated settings communicate agency is through the
assumption of a limited set of human features whilst essentially retaining their
original form. The 'Ents' scene in *Lord of the Rings: the Two Towers* typifies
such an effect. Here, two Hobbits, Merry (Dominic Monaghan) and Pippin
(Billy Boyd), attempt to escape a tribe of cannibalistic semi-human beings,
the Orcs, by climbing a tree, when a close-up discloses two eyes suddenly
opening. In a similar manner to the eye contact established with Wyvern in
Dead Man's Chest, the tree's gaze is directed towards the spectator. A mouth then
appears, and, as the tree loosens its roots, it steps intentionally on the Hobbits'
pursuer. Low-level close-ups of the vegetation reveal that the tree-roots have
become 'legs' which stride relentlessly through the forest, before an overhead
perspective sees the tree's branches grasp the Hobbits and lift them up to safety.
The actions of the tree, together with its 'facial' features, clearly suggest traits of
determination, benevolence and wisdom (features carefully articulated by J.R.R.
Tolkien in relation to the Ents in his original writing). Indeed, the tree's gruff,

kindly voice and long mossy tufts hanging down from its face are suggestive of an old, bearded man, an impression further enhanced when we learn that the tree is named 'Treebeard'. The close-up panning camerawork that frames the two hobbits as Treebeard transports them through Fangorn Forest indicates its rapid and relentless mobility (which establishes a rhythm to its behaviour and further consolidates a sense of a coherent identity) while a cut to a long shot discloses the walking tree in its entirety amidst the forest. 'Nobody cares for the woods anymore', declares Treebeard, indicating the environmental concerns that underpinned the original novels, but which may also resonate with contemporary audiences in respect of climate change issues. As Cubitt notes, 'Treebeard belongs to the ancient days, and he speaks for what might today be accounted a deep ecology; an absolute valuation of the green world as a world apart.'[38] In this sequence, the animated landscape is further indicated to be motivated by benevolence, as Treebeard tells the hobbits, 'I told Gandalf I would keep you safe and safe is where I'll keep you.' Thematically, the sentient setting is significant in respect of environmental destruction and, narratively, crucial, first in rescuing the two Hobbits and later, in the destruction of Isengard.

Such sentient portrayals of flora and vegetation, discernible across a range of fantasy films, reinforce the prominence of environmental concerns. Absent from C. S. Lewis's novel, from which it was adapted, Andrew Adamson's 2006 film, *The Chronicles of Narnia: The Lion, the Witch and the Wardrobe*, also features anthropomorphic trees. One such scene discloses tree blossom blown by the wind until it assumes human form. Later, the tree blossom as sentient entity is relevant to narrative causality as a means to communicate Aslan's (an anthropomorphized lion voiced by Liam Neeson) death to the eldest of the four Pevensie children, Peter (William Moseley). Close-ups of individual leaves blowing laterally and purposefully through the air, and overhead long shots, which show the woods appearing to sway in unison, signal the trees' animation and motivation. The sound of the leaves and blossom blowing becomes more pronounced before they re-assemble into a human form and a voice informs Peter and his younger brother Edmund (Skandar Keynes) of Aslan's death. The blossom figure has distinct facial features, and, as she relays the news to the boys (the blossom speaks with a female voice), a medium close-up frames the character/setting frontally. Even though her eyes appear merely as black holes, an equivalent of eye contact occurs in this frontal address to the spectator. Again, there is a characteristic rhythm to the movement of the blossom that is more in keeping with a character than a setting. In a similar vein, the livingness of plants is made palpable in *Harry Potter and the Chamber of Secrets*, and *Pan's Labyrinth*, where, in identical scenarios, mandrake roots are visualized in close-up and are animated to appear like screaming babies. Also in the *Chamber of Secrets*, the cityscape of London becomes animated, as, for example, one scene discloses the enchanted 'Knight Bus', emergency transport for stranded witches and wizards, appear to 'breathe in' in order to squeeze through the traffic.

A sequence in *Pirates of the Caribbean: At World's End* further illustrates the sentient setting which has limited humanoid features and which retains its original form. The highly surreal scene witnesses the film's protagonist, Captain Jack Sparrow (Johnny Depp) alone on a beach, which is revealed to be Davy Jones's Locker. The hyper-reality suggests that Sparrow is suffering from hallucinations, indicated by a prior sequence when he envisions a crew comprising identical copies of himself and it is therefore unclear whether he also imagines the subsequent events. He first picks up a smooth white stone, and hurls it, for it to transform into a crab-like creature. A rapid zoom in from long shot discloses the 'crab' extend first one claw in a sudden single action, accompanied by a cracking sound, followed by the extension of a claw on its opposite side. Its eyes then project out on stalks, to gaze directly at the spectator. Sparrow subsequently attempts to move his beached ship, *The Black Pearl*, by himself, clearly an impossible task (though it remains uncertain whether this is still part of the hallucination). The crab looks on, the camera positioning the spectator at an extreme low level, just behind the on-looking crab, thus encouraging identification with the crab/stone, as if it were a living entity. Thereafter, Sparrow turns around to see the beach now littered with hundreds of similar smooth white stones – the 'crab' turns to address them, and clicks its pincers in a Morse-code type of signal, the staccato nature of its claw actions replicating those displayed earlier and its instructional connotations suggesting the 'crab' as a leader. The rest of the stones subsequently also transform into crabs in an identical manner to the first, creating a distinctive bodily rhythm which expresses a specific purpose, namely, to manoeuvre the gigantic ship towards the shore. They therefore display obvious motivational qualities since their combined action enables Sparrow to eventually escape from the afterlife of Davy Jones's locker.

A fourth manifestation of the animated setting occurs when the landscape remains in its original state and does not display any overt physical humanoid characteristics yet appears as if mobilized by emotion. Typical examples include the writhing tree roots in *Harry Potter and the Goblet of Fire*, which ensnare Cedric. Here, Harry and Cedric are competing in a school tournament and their final task is to find their way through a hedge maze to access a golden Triwizard Cup. The trees of the maze become animated, and, although the facial features and voices that characterize other sentient cinematic trees (such as the Ents) are absent, the tree roots snake along the ground in rapid serpentine fashion to ensnare the two. As Cedric falls to the ground, Harry looks back to see the roots quickly envelop and bind him in malevolent fashion. The impression of an evil presence is accentuated as the trees begin to crack and groan and a gale gusts through the maze. In this case, as in Voldemort's appearance in the clouds, the trees' sentience is a manifestation of evil. Conversely, the labyrinthine setting of *Pan's Labyrinth* facilitates the escape of young female protagonist, Ofelia, from her cruel stepfather when she returns to an enchanted garden labyrinth carrying her young infant brother. Entering the labyrinth she comes to a dead end, with the Captain in pursuit. Frantic to escape the latter, she looks round desperately, when the walls of the labyrinth suddenly move to provide an escape route. The stone walls retract and tree roots and branches then separate to enable her to pass through, as if by divine intervention. As Ofelia runs through the passageway, the tree branches continue to move purposefully, as if alive, before the route re-seals itself to secure her escape, albeit transiently. Even as the animated setting in this case functions as a timespace by temporally extending the narrative, just as Wood explains, it also displays benevolence in keeping with human motivations.

However, when Harry Potter (Daniel Radcliffe) and Ron Weasley (Rupert Grint) crash their magical flying car into the bewitched Whomping Willow tree in *Harry Potter and the Chamber of Secrets*, the tree reacts violently (again it does not speak and lacks facial features). Its branches attack the car, as the entire tree becomes animated, each bough swaying and smashing through the car's windows. Long shots display the tree filling the frame, whilst close-ups of the vigorously moving branches heighten their threat, and point-of-view shots from the perspectives of Harry and Ron further convey a sense of imperilment. As the car containing the two boys crashes to the ground, a long shot from a low-angle perspective reveals the tree bend over as if towards the spectator, and again attack the car. The effect of action towards the screen has a similar outcome to King's description of the impact aesthetic, whilst the violence is displayed from various angles, the editing thereby temporally extending the action. The combined result is one of temporal lengthening of the scene as well as narrative implication in that the actions of the tree signal that unknown forces are contriving to keep Harry and Ron away from Hogwarts.

As an example of the fifth category of sentient setting, a similar scenario of temporal extension occurs in the final scenes of the *Kingdom of the Crystal Skull* when Indiana Jones (Harrison Ford), Marion Ravenwood (Karen Allen), Henry Oxley (John Hurt) and Henry Williams (Shia LaBeouf) escape from the underground kingdom of Akator to observe a spaceship emerging from the valley below. The frame is constructed so that the group views the spaceship and the crater from which it emerges from a high-angle perspective, thereby enhancing elements of the sublime. A maelstrom of rocks and debris encircles the rising craft before crashing downward, devastating a vast area of valley landscape. Thereafter, torrents of water from the surrounding rivers and lakes cascade down into the crater left by the spaceship, covering over the scarred landscape, and visually serving to submerge the violated setting, as if restoring order. Thus, rather than either merely serving as sublime spectacle or motivating causality, the implied healing power of the landscape, also indicated by Oxley's comment, 'like a broom to their footprints' (in itself suggesting psychological motivation), has narrative import in that it both secures, and corresponds with the film's closure.

Conclusion

Film settings, whether of home or of landscape, have longed displayed sentience and human form. However, digital technologies have expressly enabled the increased credibility of such sentience, endowing spaces and landscape features with physical mobility, humanoid facial expression and human-like emotion. In this way, there is a diminishing margin between setting and character. Wood argues that one effect of digital technologies is to expand the temporal dimension of such settings and spaces, and ascribes the term 'timespaces' to these animated settings. This chapter suggests a further aspect to the animated setting because of the latter's capacity for displays of psychological motivation and, consequently, causal impact on the narrative. Just as Wells indicates a number of markers to identify the anthropomorphic cartoon character, similar criteria may be applied to sentient settings to produce a taxonomy of such spaces, the voice being especially important in marshalling a credible subjectivity. One obvious cause of this heightened personification of the setting, in particular, trees and the natural landscape, is the effects of environmental damage and climate change. If the *Wizard of Oz* was unaffected by such concerns, these surely come to the fore in recent productions such as *The Lord of the Rings* and *Avatar*. Arguably, an awareness of landscape destruction (similar to an increased sensitivity to animal welfare) is therefore intensified by the credibility of animated settings, which encourage the spectator to identify with the setting *as* character, or otherwise to view the animated landscape as centrally implicated in the narrative trajectory.

Notes

1   Aylish Wood, 'Timespaces in Spectacular Cinema: Crossing the Great Divide of Spectacle versus Narrative', *Screen* 43.4 (2002): 374.

2   Ibid., 371.

3   Cf. Jacqueline Furby and Claire Hines, *Fantasy* (London and New York: Routledge, 2012), 119; and Tom Gunning, 'Gollum and Golem: Special Effects and the Technology of Artificial Bodies', in *From Hobbits to Hollywood: Essays on Peter Jackson's Lord of the Rings*, eds. Ernest Mathijs and Murray Pomerance (Amsterdam and New York: Rodopi, 2006), 319–349.

4   Cf. Frances Pheasant-Kelly, *Fantasy Film Post 9/11* (London and New York: Palgrave Macmillan, 2013), 75.

5   Cf. Clinton Lanier, Scott Rader and Aubrey Fowler, 'Anthropomorphism, Marketing Relationships, and Consumption Worth in the *Toy Story* Trilogy', *Journal of Marketing Management* 29.1–2 (2013): 26–27.

6   Cf. Sean Cubitt, *EcoMedia* (Amsterdam and New York: Rodopi Press, 2005); Anat Pick and Guinevere Narraway, *Screening Nature: Cinema beyond the Human* (New York and Oxford: Berghahn Books, 2013); and Michele Pierson, 'CGI Effects in Hollywood Science-Fiction Cinema 1989–95: The Wonder Years', *Screen* 40.2, (1999), 158–176.

7   Cf. Bekoff Marc, *The Emotional Lives of Animals* (Novato, CA: New World Library, 2007).

8   Cf. Cubitt, *EcoMedia*; Robin Murray and Joseph Neumann, *Ecology and Popular Film: Cinema on the Edge* (New York: New York University Press, 2009); Anil Narine, ed. *Eco-Trauma Cinema* (London and New York: Routledge, 2014); and Stephen Rust, Salma Monani and Sean Cubitt, eds. *Ecocinema Theory and Practice* (London and New York: Routledge, 2012).

9   Cf. Robert Fish, ed. *Cinematic Countrysides* (Manchester and New York: Manchester University Press, 2007); Catherine Fowler and Gillian Helfield, eds. *Representing the Rural: Space, Place and Identity in Films about the Land* (Detroit, MI: Wayne State

University Press, 2006); Graeme Harper and Jonathan Rayner, eds. *Cinema and Landscape* (Bristol and Chicago, IL: Intellect, 2010); Martin Lefebvre, ed. *Landscape and Film* (London and New York: Routledge, 2006); and Alfio Leotta, *Touring the Screen: Tourism and New Zealand Film Geographies* (Bristol and Chicago, IL: Intellect, 2011).

10 Kirsten Moana Thompson, 'Scale, Spectacle and Movement: The Massive Software and Digital Special Effects in *The Lord of the Rings*', in *From Hobbits to Hollywood: Essays on Peter Jackson's Lord of the Rings*, eds. Ernest Mathijs and Murray Pomerance (Amsterdam and New York: Rodopi, 2006), 283–300.

11 Scott Bukatman, 'The Artificial Infinite: On Special Effects and the Sublime', in *Post-War Cinema and Modernity: A Film Reader*, eds. John Orr and Olga Taxidou, (Edinburgh: Edinburgh University Press, 2000), 208–222.

12 One example includes the work of Pallant (2013) who discusses hand-drawn, stop-motion and computer generated animated landscapes.

13 Chris Pallant, 'Animated Landscapes', in *Film Landscapes: Cinema, Environment and Visual Culture*, eds. Graeme Harper and Jonathan Rayner (Newcastle: Cambridge Scholars Publishing, 2013), 183.

14 Ibid., 189.

15 Ibid., 192.

16 Katherine Fowkes, *The Fantasy Film* (Malden, MA and Oxford: Wiley-Blackwell, 2010), 2.

17 Cf: Andrew Darley, *Visual Digital Culture: Surface, Play and Spectacle* (London and New York: Routledge, 2000), 104; Tom Gunning, in Janet Staiger, *Perverse Spectators: The Practices of Film Reception* (New York and London: New York University Press, 2000), 12; and Vivian Sobchack, *Screening Space; The American Science Fiction Film* (New Brunswick: Rutgers University Press, 1987), 262.

18 Warren Buckland, 'Between Science Fact and Science Fiction: Spielberg's Digital Dinosaurs, Possible Worlds and the New Aesthetic Realism', *Screen* 40.2 (1999): 178.

19 Geoff King, *Spectacular Narratives: Hollywood in the Age of the Blockbuster* (London and New York: IB Tauris, 2000), 94.

20 Ibid., 95.

21 Wood, 'Timespaces', 371.

22 Ibid., 373.

23 Ibid.

24 Ibid., 376.

25 David Bordwell and Kristen Thompson, *Film Art* (London and New York: McGraw Hill, 2001), 63.

26 Ibid., 63.

27 The responsive landscape might also be a consequence of actorly choices, which would certainly be the case in green screen performance.

28 Sigmund Freud, *Totem and Taboo and Other Works, The Standard Edition of the Complete Psychological Works of Sigmund Freud*, Vol. 13. Trans. James Strachey (London: Vintage, 2001), 76.

29 Ibid., 76.

30 Ibid., 86.

31 Cubitt, *EcoMedia*, 65.

32 David Butler, *Fantasy Cinema: Impossible Worlds on Screen* (London and New York: Wallflower Press, 2009), 84.

33 Christopher Kenneally, *Side by Side* (USA, 2012).

34 Paul Wells, *Understanding Animation* (London and New York: Routledge, 1998), 32.

35 Ibid., 129–130.

36 Ibid., 131.

37 Pallant, 'Animated Landscapes', 194.

38 Cubitt, *EcoMedia*, 23.

Part Four

Form: Peripheral Perspectives

11

The Metamorphosis of Place: Projection-Mapped Animation

Dan Torre

In this chapter I will look at a number of theoretical considerations concerning the rising trend of large-scale projection-mapped animations, which signals an emerging and unique form of site-specific animation. This type of cinema involves the production of location-inspired animation that is then projected, often outdoors on to specific structures – buildings, bridges or other monumental constructions. Although the origins of this type of cinematic experience date back several decades, more recently increased 3D mapping proficiency and improved multi-projector synchronization have given the process far greater accuracy. Not only can the animator now produce animation made specifically to fit every curve, crevice and outcropping of a structure, but the projectors have also become powerful enough to make these extremely complex, large-scale presentations possible. The result is a unique type of *situated animation* that is an animated form custom made for a particular location, unquestionably anchored to it, and fully integrated into that specific real-world architectural landscape.[1]

The process of most animation generally involves distinct phases. One of these is its actual making and construction; another is its presentation. There are, of course, numerous different methods by which to create animation (including a wide range of digital, traditional and hybrid practices), but generally the presentation phase involves a fairly predictable display upon a rather innocuous screen. However, projection-mapped animation requires a very exact production process, in terms of both its construction and its presentation. Importantly, the real-world landscape always plays an integral role in *both* of these phases. This chapter, while analysing projection-mapped animation from both perspectives, will place particular emphasis upon the presentation process – the precisely mapped projection that is displayed onto actual physical spaces. There is, perhaps, no other form of animation in which the process of display plays such an integral role in the realization, and again in the ultimate manufacture of the imagery and content. This process goes beyond merely making visible the movement of the recorded animation; it also situates and further constructs the animation into a real-world space.

From this practice, a number of intriguing conceptual ideas emerge that help to define the unique properties of the process and the experience of projection-mapped animation. Taking into account several contemporary projection-mapped animation examples, this chapter will focus on the following factors: site specificity, movement, metamorphosis, visual layering, sound and the materiality of light. In turn, these distinctive analyses will be set within a larger 'theoretical landscape' of process philosophy and contemporary animation studies.

Situated animation

The group *Urbanscreen* is one of many studios that have produced projection-mapped animations. These artists normally create their situated animations first by creating a precise 3D model of the real-world landscape or building, before creating an animated sequence that adheres to the surfaces of the 3D model. The animation is then rendered and readied for projection (sometimes being split into different sections so that different projectors can display separate sections from different angles). The result is a precise projected display that is meticulously mapped to the actual physical surfaces. For example, in 2009, they projected a work titled *555 Kubrik*, on to the side of the *Galerie Der Gegenwart* building in Hamburg, Germany. Its imagery was so exactly mapped to the building that the effective transformation was highly dramatic (Figure 11.1).

Windows appeared to be carved out of the solid walls; the large stone bricks of the building were made to protrude outward, then be pulled back in – complete with animated shadows. In addition, bold colour patterns of motion graphics appeared to paint themselves upon the walls, then to move in a very dynamic manner. The animation and projection were so seamlessly composited on to the building that, regardless of the angle from which the spectators were to view it, the illusion would still be convincing. Music and sound effects also helped to underscore many of the animated movements; for example, the sound of scraping concrete could be heard as the stone bricks began appearing to protrude.

Figure 11.1 Still image from *555 Kubrik* (Urbanscreens, 2009)

The practice of projection-mapped animation has evolved from a number of different mediums, including magic lantern performances, traditional cinema and animation, installation video art, experimental film, and even VJing. Though it does owe a great debt to each of these practices, it has emerged with a number of its own distinct attributes. Some of the earliest permutations of projection-mapped animation can actually be found in turn-of-the-century stage productions that incorporated projected lightning sketch performances. For example, one of Australia's pioneering animators, Alec Laing, would draw his lightning sketches directly onto frosted glass plates while the magic lantern projected them onto the stage. The lead actress on stage, who happened to be his wife and went by the stage name of 'La Milo', would get into position and hold a motionless pose (usually semi-nude) that was reminiscent of a particular well-known European painting or sculpture. His sketches would adhere precisely to the forms on stage, and also link them visually to those well-known art works. Later, in about 1907, he animated some of these lightning sketches and instead of live sketching he projected the movie-films onto the stage. More recently, the practice of VJing can be seen as a contributing influence on contemporary projection-mapped animation. Historian Bram Crevits writes: 'The experience is composed in an inextricable way out of different, separate particles: the DJ spins records, the VJ triggers [visual] loops and someone else manipulates the strobe light, mostly without any form of pre-arrangement...It is again postmodern: the deconstruction of the whole – there isn't one right way to look at things.'[2] Generally, VJing has encompassed rather fluid and intuitive live performances and, although there might be a number of pre-composed sound and visual materials comprising motion graphics and found footage, the mixing and somewhat capricious flow can make the production and experience quite different with each performance.

Some contemporary VJing does incorporate the more precise practice of video mapping but, on the whole, it still tends to emphasize the *performance*, while projection-mapped animation focuses primarily on pre-constructed animations that are precisely linked to a specific location. I suggest that 'situated animation' is an appropriate term by which to describe this form as it defines some of its most important aspects – that it is both site specific and size specific in nature. It is animation that is undeniably part of the landscape. In fact, projection-mapped animation must involve the same real-world space in both its production and presentation.

Traditional live-action cinema and traditional animation tend to engage with landscape in differing ways. Live-action cinema generally involves the selection and isolation of real-world spaces. In turn, these photographed physical places constitute a 'spatial predicate' upon which the scenes are built,[3] whereas the landscapes of most traditional animation tends to be 'ontologically indefinite',[4] these constructed spaces serving to locate the equally ontologically indefinite animated characters. (For example, Willie E. Coyote and the Roadrunner are set within a *stylized* desert-themed background; Wall-E, the robot, is set upon an *imaginable* alien landscape.) Nevertheless, these painted or constructed landscapes of animation do serve to anchor the characters and props, substantiating these characters and providing them a great deal of presentational believability. In fact, as Chris Pallant notes, these 'can be much more than a surface upon which characters come to life',[5] for in animation the landscape actually has the power to define the scale, perspective and 'place' of the animated character. However, projection-mapped animation is made both *from* and *for* a specific landscape and therefore constitutes its own unique reading of the 'spatial predicate'. It requires the real world as its inspirational base; it then requires that same real-world space for its exhibition.

Fundamentally, there can only be a single location in which a projection-mapped animation can be displayed, whereas traditional cinema (be it digital or analogue) facilitates duplication and widespread distribution. Thus, a traditional animated movie can play simultaneously on 3,000 cinema screens anywhere in the world, and thanks to the generic nature of the screen (being smooth, flat and white) the movie will look more or less comparable regardless of where it is shown. Some films, of course, have been made with a specific type of venue in mind (particularly some of the large-format films – the cinemascope films of the 1960s or the more contemporary Imax films), but even so there have been enough venues of this type to allow the films to be easily distributed from one location to another without affecting their presentation. Many instances of installation art and 'expanded cinema' are also site specific, but because of their comparatively modest scale, many of these could be packed up and relocated into another gallery or exhibition space in another city on the other side of the world. Simply put, traditional films and animation, in terms of their presentation, are not site specific; they embody an inherent presentational ambiguity. In addition, these films can either be made for, or be scaled and transferred to the small screen – be it a television, a computer or a mobile device, their meaning and content remains more or less intact since there is also an ambiguity of scale inherent to most cinema that allows for this conversion – we tend to accept and recognize Mickey Mouse or Bruce Willis as themselves, no matter what their cinematic size may be. But with projection-mapped animation, the movie is made specifically for a single venue (such as the west side of the Sydney Opera House). And because the movie was made specifically for that façade, it cannot be distributed or transferred or scaled to any other site (without actually scaling down and transporting the Opera House as well) and therefore is exclusively a *situated* animation.

I consider it appropriate to compare these site-specific, projection-mapped animations to site-specific, stop-motion animators such as Blu, who also work on a large architectural scale in very specific locations. 'Blu' has produced a number of animated films such as *Muto* (2008) and *Big Bang Big Boom* (2010), which are composed of massive graffiti-painted images (some so large that they cover entire sides of buildings). His working process is, of course, quite different since he works directly on the building, painting and repainting his imagery in preparation for the next sequential photograph. With projection-mapped animation, the animator generally creates the animation while working with a 3D virtual model of the specific building, then *translates* this into a projection-able image. But both approaches have in common a degree of deference to the specific location. Blu, for example, could have made his animated film, *Muto*, virtually anywhere; however, it would have been a very different film if it were set anywhere but in that particular location. Even though Blu may enter into a space with definite plans as to what sort of imagery he wishes to create and what stories he wishes to tell, inevitably his ideas and visual imagery will be dramatically altered by the dominance of the physical space. Similarly, *Urbanscreen* group may have a fairly set idea, or possibly a generalized repertoire of motion graphic designs prepared when they approach a project, but these too will most definitely be altered in order to conform to the unique physical structure of the building. This is a key distinction that defines both the work of Blu and the process of projection-mapped animation – the animator must respond to what is already there, thus giving the *place* a definitive power over the proceedings of the animation.

Though movies and animation can have a very real impact on the audience, traditional cinematic works are not concrete and do not possess the same physicality as things that reside within the actual world, they remain very fluid in nature, and it is this that enables them to be replicated and screened anywhere. I believe that animation in particular, because of its construction process, encourages an abstraction and invariably provides a decontextualization of time, image and motion. Even when animation does achieve a certain level of realistic effect, behind it lays an array of distortive processes: for example, the process of imposing external movement to the form, distancing it quite firmly from actuality. Since animation is not actuality, it could be located in the realm of what philosopher Nicholas Rescher refers to as the 'irreal'. According to Rescher, the primary difference between actuality and irreality is that the irreal lacks 'specificity and concreteness' and is resistant to 'individualization'.[6] By contrast, real things possess a definiteness of detail: 'A leaf cannot lack a more or less definite shape, a flower cannot lack a more or less definite color, [and] a [particular] building cannot lack a more or less definite height'.[7] Animation, because it is not actuality – nor even a direct recording of actuality – always tends to be non-definite in nature.

Projection-mapped animations are composed of two integral but contrasting parts: the concrete physical structure of the building and the irreality of the animated projection. Once the final projection-mapped animation is completed, the animation will only be successfully actualized if it is projected upon the intended building. The specific building limits the projected animation to a particular location; it also ties the animation to a particular scale, giving some of the irreal aspects of animation a much more real context. Some might refer to this merged form as a type of *augmented* reality, but I would think a better description would be *concretized animation*[8] because the animation is utterly dependent upon the specific site – and is, in fact, nothing without it. The building fixes and actualizes the projected image, giving it a very *specific* and unique physical presence. Augmented reality is a term that privileges actuality, whereas concretized animation biases the animated form.

But at the same time that the buildings are concretizing the irreal nature of animation, I would propose that the projected animation is also serving to *abstract* and transform the real world. When the projected layer of animation – or what we could also think of as projected abstraction – is overlaid upon the concrete form, it works to obscure the explicit detail of the real. It serves to de-specify that space, transforming the site into the more abstracted realm of the irreal, and in doing so, *absorbs* the specific building into the diegesis of animation. A good example of this is the projection-mapped animation that was made to commemorate the 800th anniversary of Santiago de Compostela Cathedral (Improbable Films, 2012), in which the building was transformed and made to move in remarkable ways. The turrets appeared to spin around and columns appeared to grow and shrink with remarkable plasticity. In fact, the projected image was so exact that it blended in precisely with the real structure, making it impossible to tell where the real building stopped and the animation began. Once the actual had entered into the animated realm it was then able to engage in an animated act of extraordinary movement and metamorphosis.

Metamorphosis of place

Metamorphosis is an essential structure within the animated form that provides 'the ability for an image literally to change into another completely different image'.[9] Concrete things in the real world also go through a continual process of metamorphosis, but they normally transform at such a slow rate that we are not usually witnesses to their change. We might see the effects of real-world metamorphosis, but not the actual occasion. We can see the butterfly, but not the caterpillar changing into it; we can see the ruins, but not the process that slowly turned the ancient structure into rubble. However, the actual conception of metamorphosis can be made dazzlingly visible through animation and is something in which the medium truly excels.[10] Metamorphosis is also very common in projection-mapped animation, but here we don't see just animated images morphing into other images: we also see (what appears to be) the actual buildings and spaces first becoming animation, and *then* morphing into other forms, creating a uniquely *situated* concept of metamorphosis. The abstract overlay of animated light partly obscures the concrete forms, appearing to transform them from the specific to the abstract. Once the building has become abstracted, it can then freely engage in animation's metamorphic conventions.

All real-world buildings have an evolutionary history: they were constructed, they might have begun to deteriorate somewhat, they might have been extended further and built upon, and one day they will be either demolished or reduced to ruins. And this seems to be a recurring narrative that is presented through the use of projection-mapped metamorphosis. As an example, we are presented with a true documentary history of the Prague Clock Tower (2010) through the projection-mapped animation that was used to commemorate its 600th anniversary. At one point in this animation, the current aged state of the building is highlighted, before a younger version is then overlaid – capturing a moment of stark visual contrast as the transformation takes place. At another point we see the building affected by an accelerated deterioration and subsequent hyper-reclamation by nature of the building's ruinous state as it is quickly overgrown with vines. Still later we see a fantastical deconstruction of its form. Thus, the Prague Clock Tower is transformed into the animation state, and then morphed into new abstract shapes – it becomes a different historical construct from one moment to the next.

And all the while that we are watching the animated display of metamorphosis, we are constantly aware of the underlying pre-transformative form and are always conscious that, regardless of its transformations, it will always at some point revert back to its original pre-metamorphic state. That is, the animation will cease, or at least diminish in prominence, allowing the viewer once again to see the original building. I believe that this idea of being aware of the actual, even when confronted with the irreal, is analogous to Whiteheads consideration of the interplay between the actual and the abstract when he observed that 'abstraction may misdirect us as to the real complex from which it originates. But, in the dim recesses behind consciousness there is the sense of realities behind abstractions … [which] points back to its origin'.[11] We know that the building is there and will always be there, but we also delight in the entertainment of the transformative spectacle.

In 2010, an animation by Fernando Salis was projected onto the Christ the Redeemer statue in Rio de Janeiro, Brazil. The statue stands at a colossal height

Figure 11.2 Images from Christ the Redeemer projection (Fernando Salis, 2010)

and is posed with its enormous arms outstretched wide. The brief projected animation included a variety of images and abstract forms – and towards the end, a simple animated butterfly was projected onto the surface of the statue and appeared to gently flutter about it. Then, as a finale, the Christ figure apparently folded his colossal arms to his chest (reminiscent of a grand 'hugging' action). Although the illusion is not perfect (the viewer is still partly aware that the real arms remain outstretched), it is a reasonably convincing effect. In terms of animation, it is a rather simple movement, yet it represents a mammoth transformation of the real-world space (Figure 11.2).

Visual layers

Another important aspect of animation is the manner in which it can be layered and composited, which helps to describe its general constructive nature. 'Compositing' notes Thomas Lamarre, 'is what makes for a sense of the coherence of the image under conditions of movement in animation'.[12] Many forms of animation, from traditional cel animation to various kinds of digital animation, all actively utilize layering and compositing as a method for building up the imagery and the movement of the animation. At the very least, it might involve the placement of animated characters onto a separate background or landscape or, quite plausibly, hundreds of layers all working together. The interplay between the layers can be a vital strategy of the animated form, which can allow for incredibly complex narrative information, intriguing juxtapositions of imagery and movement, and even multiple representations of time. This practice of layering in animation can be furthered substantially through the projection of the imagery onto the architectural forms. Because this type of animation is 'situated' upon recognizable structures, the projected image and the display surface become inextricably linked in visual and narrative dialogue. With most animation it is the moving image alone that provides us with the narrative content (the screen merely serves as a facilitator of this content). However, with situated animation, the 'screen' can contribute, quite literally, a large share of narrative information and its visibility and tactility become essential to this narrative. Many projection-mapped animations will directly reference the physical materials and construction of the building – we might see bricks move or crumble, windows and doors open and close. The contours of the building might be outlined, or particular sections exposed or obscured.

There are many different approaches to how the animated layers might interact with the landscape. More often than not it will involve a type of dialectic – a continual pointing and counter-pointing between the actual physical building and the animated overlay. For example, in the previously mentioned projection-mapped animation that commemorated the 800th anniversary of the Santiago de Compostela Cathedral, we see an intriguing dialogue between the two layers during its nearly fifteen-minute display. Initially we see a vine-covered building, with giant butterflies fluttering about it, only portions of the real building being visible. Then suddenly a fantastical dragon emerges and appears to burst through the wall (bricks can be seen shattering and crumbling as the dragon traverses the façade, breathing fire and destroying sections of the building). Later, the full building is illuminated and revealed but, almost instantaneously, parts of it begin to move. Some elements appear to spin on their base, and columns and protrusions appear to slide up and down. Then we see portions of the wall slide back to reveal an array of giant clockwork gears, which are implied to be the source of this new movement. The gears move in seemingly choreographed time with the movement of the building. Still later we can see symbols of religious ritual precisely placed and animated upon various sections of the cathedral.

Another thing that occurs in this building's animation (also in a number of others) is a dialectical display of both the interior and exterior spaces of the building. The audience is afforded a view of the actual exterior of the building while at the same time seeing an animated view of its interior. This is something that Paul Wells would refer to as the penetrative property of animation: its capacity to reveal the unseen – in this case the interior of a building. However, this is a unique embodiment of Well's idea of penetration, for not only does the animation allow us to see a representation of the interior spaces – simultaneously we are able to see the physical exterior spaces as well.

Situated soundtracks

Sound can be an essential component within all forms of animation and it often plays an important role in regard to projection-mapped animation as well. The soundtrack can work in a number of different ways in situated animation, quite often being used to underscore the spectacle or metamorphic illusions of the projected display. Thus, when we see an animated brick apparently protrude from the side of the building, we will hear a loud scraping sound. Or, we might hear the sound of pencil sketching on paper as the building is transformed into an architectural diagram (as was depicted during one sequence in the 800th anniversary of Santiago de Compostela Cathedral). Additionally, thunderous music will often accompany the animation. This musical track helps to structure the often graphical and rather non-linear moving imagery of many situated animations (perhaps also pointing back to its VJing roots).

As with all animation, sound is normally an imposed element.[13] However, because these animations often take place in large, outdoor spaces, the sound must be very loud so that it can be heard through the roars of the crowd and the general ambient noise of the urban landscape. Thus, the sound effects and music often echo around the space and, in a sense, become part of the real-world diegesis. It is sound that is not only synchronous to the animation, but also synchronous to the space. By contrast, the sound in a traditional cinema (or even in a lounge room) will generally be attuned to surround the viewer, but it cannot actually surround the cinematic space represented on the screen. Yet, the situated sound of projection-mapped animation can take advantage of the large eclectic space. Invariably, the sound will reverberate off of the surrounding structures (that are essentially the animation) accentuating the very real expansiveness of the landscape.

One particularly novel use of sound can be found in *Perspective Lyrique: An Interactive Architectural Mapping* (2010), which was produced by 1024 Architecture, and which was presented at the Fete des Lumieres that took place in Lyon, France. The ornate building façade was animated so that it appeared to

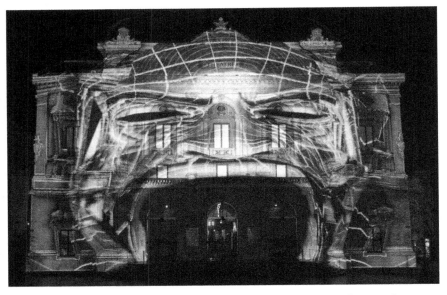

Figure 11.3 Still image from *Perspective Lyrique: An Interactive Architectural Mapping* by 1024 Architecture (2010)

warp and transform radically until, finally, a giant face appeared. At this point the audience was invited to step up to a microphone and speak into it. Their speech was manipulated into non-verbal grunts and tones, which then activated the 'mouth' of the animated face. The building seemingly roared and bellowed out into the space and created a uniquely situated form of lip-synched animation (Figure 11.3).

Light and shadow

Throughout this chapter I have examined the dichotomy surrounding the actual concrete building and the irreal nature of animation. Light, which is the basis of projected animation, also embodies an oppositional state: light is on the one hand composed simply of waves of energy, and on the other hand light is composed of photon particles that exhibit a true physical mass when they are activated. It is this physical presence, the materiality of light and its active processes, which create the incredible spectacles of projection-mapped animation, taking it, I believe, far beyond the current technologies of mobile screen overlays or even augmented reality goggles which appear to superimpose imagery over real spaces. With projection, the light actually interplays with the concrete structures, the photon particles literally penetrating and bouncing off the physical building materials. And, according to Whitehead, it is such interactions – in fact, the interaction of all matter down to the smallest particle level – that pervades and constitutes the very nature of actuality.[14] In this manner, the projected light edges the experience closer to the actual – and for the audience, promotes a visibly and equally shared experience.

Such a display also showcases the Deleuzian concept of the fold – a concept that Deleuze used widely, but we might think of it as simply a way to describe the relationship that something has with itself (for example, the interior of a form is merely the folding of its exterior). The fold expresses a logical and fluid interconnectivity that some theorists have applied to the consideration of architectural forms.[15] As Greg Lynn notes in his discussion of contemporary architecture, 'If there is a single effect produced in architecture by [the Deleuzian concept of] folding, it will be the ability to integrate unrelated elements within a new continuous mixture.'[16] And if architecture, with its combined construction materials and adornments, can do this on its own, then this construction can arguably be compounded further by the addition of projection-mapped animation. Thus, not only does light add visually or phenomenologically to the building, but it also adds physical materiality and in turn creates new kinds of fused interconnections. Simultaneously, light is concretized by the building, whilst also serving to transform the building; and is further both absorbed by, and reflected off, the building.

Cinema has always been about light and shadow. In traditional cinema, light is generally used to display images, and shadow (or the absence of light) to hide images. This is most obvious, for example, in the Film Noir genre where, if it was necessary to obscure the face of Orson Welles in *Citizen Kane*, shadows, or the absence of light, would achieve this. Projection-mapped animation can utilize light and shadow to reveal and obscure particular elements. But, outside of the dark, controlled cinema space, with its flat textureless and colourless blank screen, it is impossible to create a totally black shadow that would truly conceal the façade of a building. So in the non-blackness of outdoor spaces – *light* is often used to *conceal*.

As an analogy as to how this technique might be used, we can look to the humble squid. The common squid that lives in relatively well-lit shallow waters uses ink to hide itself. When it feels threatened it squirts out a large cloud of black *shadowy* ink and then scurries off, well hidden behind it. By contrast, the vampire squid (*Vampyroteuthis infernalis*), which lives nearly 1,000 meters below the surface in very dark water, is able, as with many creatures that live in these depths, to produce its own illumination. So when it feels threatened it squirts out a thick cloud of bioluminescent mucus containing masses of particles of blue light that lasts for several minutes. It hides behind this cloud of *light* and then scurries off.[17] Similarly in projection-mapped animation, light (and its constituency of colour) is often used to obscure the building so that only the projected animated imagery can clearly be seen; in other cases, light is used simply to reveal the building. So, light is used to both reveal and to obscure, and to transform the background structures.

Another exceptional quality of projection-mapped animation is that light is often used to generate artificial *shadows* and, as with traditional animation, it is the use of shadows that help substantiate a character's or an object's being grounded in a particular place – just as animated shadows in traditional cel animation serve to 'break down the division between foreground and background', helping to create 'a unified visual world'.[18] That is, shadows help to anchor the character to the ground – so they do not look, for example, as if they are floating in the air above the ground. Shadows can also help to substantiate the perspective of the background itself and are essential elements of most realistic visual landscapes. A well-lit landscape with clear visibility but without shadows can seem very artificial. Shadows can sometimes be a challenging element for the animator to produce effectively. Particularly in traditional cel animation, as Donald Crafton has noted, 'creating shadows within cinema posed special problems for animators'.[19] As a result, a number of unique techniques such as the shadowgraph were developed to create convincing semi-transparent shadows.[20]

The use of shadows becomes a doubly difficult problem in projection mapping as the animated shadows must both place the animation, and also displace the actual shadows that are created by the intensely bright projectors. Quite often these shadows will also be animated – as in the afore-mentioned commemorative celebrations of the Prague Clock Tower, the shadows can be seen alternately to shorten, elongate and then travel from left to right. This use of animated shadows provides a simulation of a hyper-speed trajectory of the sun passing overhead. Of course, these were not real shadows, but computer-generated animations that over-power the real-world nighttime: projected light is utilized to create purely simulated shadows in real spaces.

Conclusion

In this chapter, a number of concepts have been articulated that are essential to the form of projection-mapped animation: site specificity, metamorphosis, visual layering, sound and the materiality of light. And though most animation benefits from a perceptible landscape, situated animation represents a very unique approach to the animated landscape – for it truly does appear to animate the actual, real-world landscape. It requires the real landscape both to create and to display the animation; and without these real-world spaces, these animations could not exist.

Though most of the projection-mapped animation that has been made in recent years has been very much about spectacle, there is vast potential for further development and we should look forward to seeing what might emerge from this evolving medium of 'animated landscapes'.

Notes

1 Though projection-mapped animations are best seen on location, hundreds of video documentations of these displays are available on-line.
2 Bram Crevits, 'The Roots of Vjing: A Historical Overview', in *Vj: Audio-Visual Art + Vj Culture*, ed. Michael Faulkner (London: Laurence King Publishing, 2006), 14–19, 15.
3 Martin Lefebvre, 'Between Setting and Landscape in the Cinema', in *Landscape and Film*, ed. Martin Lefebvre (London: Routledge, 2006), 51.
4 Tyrus Miller, ' "Cut out from Last Year's Moldering Newspapers": Bruno Schulz and the Brothers Quay on the Street of Crocodiles', in *Screening the City*, eds. Mark Shiel and Tony Fitzmaurice (New York: Verso, 2003), 83.
5 Chris Pallant, 'The Animated Landscape', in *Film Landscapes: Cinema, Environment, and Visual Culture*, eds. Graeme Harper and Jonathan Rayner (Newcastle: Cambridge Scholars Publishing, 2013), 190.
6 Nicholas Rescher, *Imagining Irreality: A Study of Unreal Possibilities* (Chicago, IL: Open Court, 2003), 75.
7 Ibid., 71.
8 George Griffin has used the term 'concrete animation' in his discussions of flipbooks and other physical forms of animation.
9 Paul Wells, *Understanding Animation* (London: Routledge, 1998), 98.
10 Dan Torre, 'Cognitive Animation Theory: A Process-Based Reading of Animation and Human Cognition', *Animation: An Interdisciplinary Journal* 9.1 (2014): 47–64.

11 Alfred North Whitehead, *Modes of Thought* (New York: The Free Press, 1968), 124.

12 Thomas Lamarre, *The Anime Machine: A Media Theory of Animation* (Minneapolis: University of Minnesota Press, 2009), 124.

13 For example, Wells, *Understanding Animation*; and Torre, 'Cognitive Animation Theory'.

14 Alfred North Whitehead, *Process and Reality* (Corrected Edition) (New York: The Free Press, 1978), 67.

15 Gilles Deleuze, *The Fold* (Minneapolis: University of Minnesota Press, 1992): *passim*.

16 Greg Lynn, *Animate Form* (New York: Princeton Architectural Press, 1999): 8; cf. Paul Harris, 'To See with the Mind and Think Through the Eye: Deleuze, Folding Architecture, and Simon Rodia's Watts Towers', in *Deleuze and Space*, eds. Ian Buchanan and Gregg Lambert (Edinburgh: Edinburgh University Press, 2005) for more on Deleuze's concept of the fold and its application to architecture.

17 Bruce H. Robinson, Kim R. Reisenbichler, James C. Hunt and Steven H. D. Haddock, 'Light Production by the Arm Tips of the Deep-Sea Cephalopod Vampyroteuthis Infernalis', *Biological Bulletin*, no. 205 (2003): 102–109.

18 Donald Crafton, *Shadow of a Mouse: Performance, Belief, and World-Making in Animation* (Berkeley: University of California Press, 2013): 191.

19 Ibid., 183.

20 Ibid., 190.

12

Plasmatic Pitches, Temporal Tracks and Conceptual Courts: The Landscapes of Animated Sport

Paul Wells

A Country Road. A Tree. Evening – The animated moment

The opening descriptor from Samuel Beckett's seminal theatre piece, *Waiting for Godot* (1953), may seem an unusual starting place and touchstone for a discussion about the relationship between animation, landscape and sport. Its citation and use here, however, merely seeks to immediately demonstrate the cross-disciplinary method of analysis I wish to adopt in the following discussion. Simply, I will be drawing from a number of contexts in the theoretical ideation of this relationship, principally to look at 'animation' not merely within the framework of Film and Media Studies, but a broader artistic, cultural and practice-based palette that helps differentiate its distinctiveness and credentials in both addressing 'landscape' and 'sport'. Leaving aside Beckett's own passion for cricket, for example – the metaphoric and choreographic principles of which, he surely adopted for some of his later plays – his dramaturgical precision offers an immediate point of access in defining time and space in animated landscapes.

When I first saw *Godot* its relationship to animation to me was obvious. The empty stage, a blank page; the selective and particular choice of an image (the tree) bequeathing it immediate literal *and* associative weight; the absolutely precise and limited choreographies of the performances both a vindication of specific motion in the service of narrative *and* symbolic ideas; the use of sound and light a model of art direction prompting emotive stimulus and response. This sheer *distillation* of theatre seemed to me to be completely correspondent to the core principles of animation. Drawing *Godot* and animation into relief again here, though, affords the possibility of seeing the stage and the animation space as a place of a variety of landscapes – 'the stark but richly articulated exterior scene we see before us on the stage; landscapes that serve as the setting for offstage action; pictures of some other world that can only *be* imagined; and the landscapes from the past, which serve to illuminate the characters (more or less) remember'.[1] Landscapes then, are literal, suggestible, imaginary and mere acts of memory – and crucially, in animation, often extant in these states at one and the same time.

Beckett's minimalist styling – a piece of theatre delivered only by a mouth (*Not I*), for example, or by someone buried up to their waist in sand *(Happy Days)* or by an old man merely in dialogue with a tape recorder (*Krapp's Last Tape*) – is perhaps only made radical by its re-definition of Chekovian naturalist spaces or Shakespearian spectacles. Read as *images* though, it defines not merely spaces to be looked at, but specific temporal choices that also determine how the ostensible 'story', or more precisely, the conceptual premises of the sharing of 'experience' (psychological, emotional, physical) might be understood. It is in this particular relationship between space and time that Beckett's theatre speaks directly to animation, and significantly, in this instance to sporting landscapes. Pursuing this idea further reminded me of three texts that share close proximity on my desk: Kenneth Clark's *One Hundred Details from Pictures in the National Gallery* (2008), written in 1938; David Thomson's *Moments That Made the Movies* (2013); and, selected by a rarefied cast of sports writers, *1001 Football Moments* (2007). I have always been interested in the status of 'the moment' going back to my PhD thesis dealing with Virginia Woolf's 'moment of being' and D. H. Lawrence's 'living moment', right through to the 'micro-narrative' paradigm I have used in animation screenwriting,[2] but crucially, I wish to suggest here that animation, both in its execution and exhibition, insists upon the impact of the temporal to help articulate the sense of place and context.

Though Clark's work has been much discredited by the Marxist intervention of John Berger, his approach to neglected details in the National Gallery's masterpieces is still highly instructive. By homing in to things that are not at the focus of the picture, Clark draws attention to the artefacts, buildings and figures that populate the composition and add layers of meaning to the image, often unnoticed in even highly reflective approaches to the work. As in the observation of Beckett's theatre, then, this re-positioning of the gaze as a more holistic and inclusive apprehension of the *literal* choices in making the image, insists upon an understanding that they play a bigger part in speaking to *dramaturgical* moments of significance, and potential *metaphorical* implications.

Less fundamentally becomes more. Crucially, in relation to animation, this way of seeing is important because all aspects of the *mise-en-scène* are specifically chosen and may have a dramatic and symbolic function. The landscape here is not merely a location that is chosen and recorded, but a space that is deliberately composed and constructed, and populated by elements – central and peripheral, foreground and background – that potentially work as 'characters', or more commonly, in helping to define them.

Crafton has also identified the importance of *uniplanar* and *cross-planar* movement in determining animation space, the former left-to-right or right-to-left sequential movement in which the character does not change scale; the latter, background-to-foreground or foreground-to-background movement that necessitates a change of size, definition and scale in the character as it corresponds to changing perspective and depth of field.[3] This does not merely apply to the motion of the character, though, but the delineation and nature of the environment it exists within. Simply, the environment – 'the landscape' – may have as many dramatic characteristics as the primary performances by obviously configured characters. Clark's work points to the importance of this, and this helps to privilege animated space and time as a *confluence* of deliberately designed aspects with specific dramatic purpose rather than the partially configured, discovered, accidental or additional affects that attend most live-action shooting and cinematography. Even in the most mannerist of *mise-en-scène* composed by filmmakers like Alain Resnais, Peter Greenaway or Wes Anderson, their work does not fully take into account this absolute specificity in the performance and the pure principle of motion itself as it is harnessed to narrative and metaphoric purpose. Animation apprehends the *whole* moment through the very necessity of its construction.

If Clark's work helps to draw attention to the complete agency of the animated landscape, Thomson seeks to locate the specific qualities of film practice in creating significant moments. As Roland Barthes thinks of the 'punctum' in a photograph, Thomson, however, homes into the moments that are defined only by their status in *movies*: 'doing something that could be managed in no other medium – the look, the pace, the movement, the texture, the context, all these things are vital'.[4] This, in principle, is encouraging in that given the points I have raised above, this allows for the notion of *particularity* in the medium of expression, and a specific outcome accordingly. Interestingly, though unsurprisingly, given the consistent marginalization of animation in film criticism and theory, Thomson does not include a moment from an animated film. This may be because 'moments' in traditional cinema are a narrational or aesthetic 'peak' but in animation are the constituent elements in the very construction of the piece. This is not to say that animation shorts and features do not have narrational or aesthetic peaks, but rather that such peaks in animation are prompted by different means, and that the 'moment' is sometimes best revealed by viewing animation through a different critical, conceptual and material lens. This is where it becomes clear – to me at least – that animation is not favourably viewed in relation to the dominant practices of 'live action' cinema, but through other artistic and cultural *practices* that inform elements of it, or *resemblances* that best reveal it.

Cinema, of course, seems a natural ally because there is a related – if wholly different – model of film that has been defined as 'animated'. The particularity of this difference it seems, though, has either been of no major practical or critical consequence throughout the history of cinema – thus animation's intrinsic marginalization in that history – or conversely, necessitated the championing of the form as an alternative practice in order to insist upon its significance and achievement. Equally, one might naturally conclude that to look at 'landscape' might immediately catalyse the idea of looking at 'landscape painting', and while this might be pertinent and enabling, it is important not to be drawn into potentially inappropriate art historical focus since an animated landscape is not necessarily a 'landscape painting' that moves. Rather, it is important to view 'landscape' in animation as a theatrical space with mobility and purpose, rather than a vista or geographical configuration that is apprehended and comprehended principally through stillness. To this end though, the animated landscape should also not be understood as something that apes the landscape in the traditional filmic or painterly sense – a 'background', for example, or the consequence of layout, or even an obvious depiction of the countryside or a city skyline. *It is ultimately a specifically imagined and constructed environment dramatized through its plasmatic motion in the moment, and revealed by the cognate disciplines it relates to or represents.*

1001 Football Moments then ultimately confirmed my view that sport was an ideal cognate discipline by which to define the specificity of animation, and also to engage with the animated landscape. Many of the 'moments' delineated in the book are not surprisingly key 'events' in the game itself – goals, saves, fouls, etc. – but these are all the consequences of the conduct of the sport, and the context in which it takes place. Simply, the execution of sporting practice is determined by its regulatory frameworks, however informal, which are in turn defined within specific spatio-temporal conditions. The infrastructural dynamics of sport then immediately echo what are the infrastructural dynamics of animation as a form; both sport and animation are defined by their material codes and their practice conventions. Each is engaged with *a complex and highly specific preparatory and developmental process in the creation of a particular sequence of pre-choreographed movement in the service of a pre-determined outcome.*[5] This choreography, though, also functions as the visualization of temporal and spatial flow within the formal parameters yet fluid landscapes of the places in which sport is played. As Connor has aptly expressed it, 'there are what I want to call spaces of play – stadia, arenas, sports grounds … [Thereafter] there is the play of space that is initiated within the space of play'.[6] This sense of space, then, is inextricably defined by motion – movement expressed simultaneously as narrative and aesthetic combined – *and* as it is delineated by the *imposition* of sporting practice upon a space both within the narrative itself, and as an act of animating an environment.

Games without frontiers

This is initially best illustrated by looking at the Beckettian minimalism in two examples. In *War Game* (2001), a film based on the Christmas truce between the British and German soldiers during the First World War, the action literally plays itself out in a 'no man's land' not dissimilar from *Godot*'s country road. The barren ground that stretches between the enemy trenches is initially defined as a geographical territory, thereafter a battlefield, but only at the moment when a football is introduced into the space is the ground defined as a potential 'pitch'. Goalposts are improvised by using coats, equipment and trees, and so expansive does the game become there are at least five 'pitches' in use as all the soldiers join in. The landscape is literally animated by the sport that takes place within it, and which in turn is defined by the shared understanding of the core principles of how football is played. Crucially, then, the choreography of the game dictates the choreography of the animation, which then reconfigures the space *not* as a site of war but a place of peace – not as the scene of brutality and fatality but an arena of joy and life. The landscape is literally and metaphorically changed by the imposition of sport. This speaks in a small way to the way in which a landscape is determined by 'belief'. Simply, sport – in this instance, football – is only created and sustained by the belief that it is 'serious'; this becomes relative though when it is diminished or dismissed as merely a game, and not significant in the broader schemes of human behaviour. Even professional sport can be relegated in this way, but this is to ignore the important role sport plays in representing emotional, spiritual, intellectual and physical ideas. When the lead characters in *War Game* – Will, Freddie, Billy and Lacey – volunteer to go to war they only see it in the light of taking on opposition as if they were playing a game of village soccer. The hardcore reality of their experience in the trenches inevitably changes this perspective, but the football match with the Germans at least becomes a symbol of hope; an event that promises that anywhere can be transformed into a preferred and privileged reality. It is the promise of animation itself.

The embedded metaphors in sporting activity, then, speak directly to the rendering of landscapes. The village football the boys play is the embodiment of their innocence and the wider parameters of family and community; the match during the truce a reminder that this is what both sides are ironically seeking to preserve in their homelands. While the game is maintained it is 'serious'; its symbolic function both to the characters and to the viewers, a significant intervention into the trauma of war. When the truce is over though, the football match is seen to be 'only a game', its import of no consequence when set against the seriousness of warfare. It is clear that the landscape defined by the football match is one more broadly fulfilling to a moral imagination that rejects the tragic waste of lives in seemingly pointless conflict. The 'playful' confrontation of sporting conduct then rationalizes the landscape insisting upon the literal and material becoming in some way symbolic and metaphorical. Both the imposition of sport and animation thus also necessitates a shift from the political and the ideologically charged to the philosophically and ethically engaged – the limits of localized national confrontation repositioned as a universal humanitarian issue. Crucially, too, the concept of 'no man's land' has been reconfigured as a shared and collaborative space no longer informed by the incipient promise of fighting and colonization. The temporary interlude of sporting conduct dilutes the idea of a theatre of war and amplifies the potential grounds of peace. To be able to play sports and games is to cast spaces as civilized; landscapes as the preserve of organized competition rather than chaotic conflict. Sport – intrinsically associated with leisure (though clearly not to those for whom it is work) – becomes a rhetorical model of a managed contest to be enjoyed by participants and spectators. In *War Game*, this is presented through the inherently rhetorical language of animation in both re-imagining the original Christmas Eve truce, and in offering alternative modes of reality. Animation interprets and interrogates as it plays out its illusionism; sport reveals this through the nature of its kindred constructed-ness.

This might be further illustrated by addressing the near Beckettian black humour of *Sports Cartoons* (1986). One of the episodes deals with ice hockey. It is immediately pertinent to suggest that if the 'no man's land' of *War Game* is in essence the neutral and associative space of Beckett's near-empty stage, then more particular 'real world' environments, affected by specific climates and conditions, may prompt more specific kinds of sporting activity. *Pingu* (1986–2006), for instance, in being set at the South Pole, means the environment inevitably underpins episodes such as *Pingu Goes Fishing, Pingu and the Race on Barrel Planks, Pingu Plays Fish Tennis, Pingu Goes Skiing, Pingu is Tobogganing, Pingu's Sledge Race, Pingu Plays Ice Hockey, Pingu's Curling Game, Pingu Goes Cross-Country Skiing, Pingu the Mountaineer, Pingu the Snowboarder* and *Pingu Makes a Big Splash*. Pingu's snowbound Antarctic context is in once sense a permanent Winter Olympic park because the social community and its infrastructure will play out activities in the snow, a good number of which will be sporting, since the cultures that created such sports had to necessarily base them on, and develop them through, the environment. Pingu would *naturally* swim, sled, toboggan, fish, snowboard, climb and curl as a consequence of exploiting the limits of his context for maximum social effect, and with some degree of intuitive expertise. Janet Perlman and Derek Lamb's address of ice hockey, though, is a far cry from this contextual logic, and for that matter, from both the real execution of the sport, or the *Peter the Puck* series (1973–1975) illustrating its professional rules, regulations and conduct.

In the ice hockey episode, a hippo goalkeeper is isolated on an ice island and brushes ice from his goal area while other hippos stand on other islands waiting as the puck is played between two players on another isolated isle. This complete deconstruction of the game in this fashion points to its context and the significance of the environment in articulating the landscape in which it exists. The landscape ultimately operates as a meditation on the purpose of the game. The vibrancy, speed and violence of ice hockey has been deconstructed in a way that renders the ice, the isolated players and the purpose of the game (to score goals) redundant and pointless. Such activity, then, only works as 'sport' if its rules, principles and environment function in a cogent and coherent way. Denied this, the elements that combine to make it work become quickly meaningless; their fragmentation mere evidence of their need to be constructed, and to once more, stimulate and inspire 'belief'. This then is sport and animation defined as pure artifice, with the disruption of the environment being the very opposite of the improvised if imaginary 'pitches' in *War Game*. The landscape here works not as the purposive construction in the symbolic apprehension of memory and hope, but as an oblique observation on the contrived and habitual ways humankind seeks to pass time. This is a place as an engagement with the nature of *pastime* – and in a true Beckettian sense, its sense of estrangement presents the attempt to find meaning in existence as knowingly absurd.

Sporting place and animated space

So far, I have addressed the animated sporting landscape as a consequence of the natural environments it might be played within, and ostensibly as a metaphor for human identity and purpose. These observations chime with the early emergence of sport as a vernacular, largely rural activity played out through activities such as hunting and fishing. This was to change with the onset of modern industrialized sport, which spoke directly to an urban working class, and necessitated the emergence of national organizations who would determine its rules and conduct. As Lincoln Allison notes, though, it 'was confined to precise, small slices of time and space'.[7] This shift, of course, points to the emergence of nominated and specific places dedicated to the conduct of sport – gyms, custom pitches, pools, courts, grounds and stadia. Though this standardization effectively embedded sport as a core social and commercial activity, it also served to promote a greater attention to the terms, technologies and transmission of sport as a cultural practice. Further, the sense of place dedicated to sport inevitably began to nuance the particularities of its new landscapes. As John Syer and Christopher Connolly have pointed out:

> The concept of 'place' varies according to the sport. Indoor competitions are affected by floor surface, lighting, surrounding space, height of the ceiling, air currents and temperature. Outdoor conditions vary according to weather, ground conditions and setting. There are also other variables that are outside the structure of the competition which affect your concentration and should be considered. For instance, you may be affected by spectators and officials, and all venues have some tangible 'atmosphere' which might easily intrude upon your awareness.[8]

Animated films that embrace sport pay considerable attention to this concept of place as it usually operates as the contextual stimulus for the animator in exploring and populating what J. P. Telotte describes as the 'animated space'. Telotte explores this 'animated space' in relation to its shifting parameters using

Anthony Vidler's concept of 'spatial warping' and Paul Virilio's concerns about the increasing social dissonance in framing and understanding 'reality', to suggest that animation offers a re-conceptualization of the seemingly 'flattened' and 'depthless' mediated representation in numerous visual texts.[9] This analysis speaks mainly to a discourse about animation's relationship with 'reality effects', both as graphic interpretations and as photo-real imitations, but here I wish to suggest that in using sporting place as the subject and object of animated space, a different model of landscape is suggested.

Syer and Connolly, noted earlier, are actually interpreting sporting place from the perspective of the athlete, and as such, they are in effect insisting that the context the sportsperson inhabits is as much a psychological place as it is a material one. If the 'no man's land' of *War Game* and the absurdist fragmentary ice rink of *Sports Cartoons* are essentially external visual metaphors, the internal visualization of the physical context of play is in effect a visual simile for not merely what the landscape looks like, but how it is experienced and how it feels. Animation is especially persuasive at apprehending this model of visualization.

The following script is from *2DTV* (2001–2004), a topical satirical show that poked fun at well-known public figures and celebrities. One of the show's targets was British tennis player, Tim Henman, who in spite of his undoubted talent and quality could never quite succeed at the highest level, and was often accused by the press of 'choking' in key moments of important matches. 'Choking' is essentially a form of psychological disintegration in which the previous calm, controlled application of the athlete gives way to panic and anxiety. In recent times, this has also be colloquially described as the 'yips', but in whatever way it is viewed it has been acknowledged as evidencing just how significant psychological and emotional preparation is in sport, alongside the more obviously physical and technical practice. As such, 'visualisation' strategies have been employed to enable athletes to engage in a level of mental rehearsal to enhance the processes of execution in the real event. 'Choke', the scenario, presented below addresses the psychological space of Henman as he serves for a match point against Andre Agassi:

Exterior – Day – A tennis court at Wimbledon

British tennis hopeful, Tim Henman stands preparing to serve. The crowd dressed in British 'fan' regalia sit watching. The scoreboard in the background records that Henman is two sets, five games, and forty-love up against rival, Andre Agassi.

Commentator: So Tim Henman now leads two sets to love; five games to
                love; and forty love.

We hear arbitrary cries of 'Come on, Tim!' from the crowd. A mole with a Union
Jack top-hat emerges through the grass, saying 'Come on, Tim!'.

Umpire: Quiet Please.
Commentator: Match Point. If he can just hold his nerve ....

We see Henman's serve from his point of view, from behind the ball and racket,
and looking towards Agassi in the distance. There is an advertising hoarding
behind Agassi with the words 'Coke', 'Sprite' and 'Lucozade' advertised. His racket
suddenly becomes molten; the tennis ball metamorphoses into a heavy bowling
ball. Agassi's racket becomes huge, and the tennis net rises up on its own. The
camera moves past the net and Agassi, towards the words on the advertising
hoarding, 'Coke' changing to 'Choke', 'Sprite' to 'Shite', and 'Lucozade' to 'Give Up
Now You Big Girl's Blouse'. On the soundtrack, there are 'sci-fi' sounds signifying
'interior noise' in Henman's mind, and a pulsing heartbeat. Cut to Henman in
close up, sweating profusely, his teeth chattering.

Commentator: The title is Henman's, just so long as he doesn't go to pieces ....

Henman breaks into hundreds of china-pieces, 'Tom & Jerry' style.

Commentator: ... again .... [Crowd groans][10]

Once again, this should be viewed as a concentrated 'moment' extending the few
seconds of Henman's serve into a protracted engagement with his response to
'place'. The pressure exacted by the fact that this is Wimbledon, one of the oldest
and most iconic venues for the sport, and his 'home' tournament is exacerbated
by the encouragement of the crowd. Such an 'atmosphere' is inevitably affecting,
and Henman's perception of the court and the action of his serve begins to
change. Sporting 'place' literally becomes 'animated space' here, as the action
is imagined from Henman's point of view. This is an iteration of the serve as he
thinks, feels and executes it, revising what was previously a physical, material
landscape into a mobile quasi-solipsistic one. In relation to what the viewer sees
though it is no less a landscape, since its constituent elements – the grass surface,
the scoreboard, the net, the advertising hoardings, the playing equipment, the
crowd, etc. – all become vehicles for the metamorphosis that symbolizes the
psychological and emotional transition Henman experiences. It is further an
animating space both for Henman's actions and the crowd's expectations. Sound

is also used to suggest his inner state. Crucially, then, even though this sequence is played out as what is arguably a cruel joke, it reveals a model of psychological reality that challenges the 'depthlessness' of normal tennis coverage, in which commentators can only imagine what Henman might be thinking. Animation, here, not merely plays with the idea of perceptual experience and visual interpretation, but challenges the conventions of broadcast sport, which for all its literalness and constructions of 'liveness' does not penetrate the inner landscape of personal sporting visualization. 'Choke', for all its playful satire, does this, literally showing the shifts in an animated landscape that turns it from a tennis court into a mental picture. Only when Henman's body fragments does the piece overtly play out a 'cartoon' gag, privileging the freedoms of the form over its capacity to apprehend the perceptual specificity of Henman's gaze.

This model of 'world building' is predicated on the capacity for animation to visualize interior spaces as they process and interpret the external environment. More often, though, animation re-interprets and re-visualizes exterior spaces as they extend the parameters of the core story concepts and reflect the development of the characters. These details – like those noted by Clark in paintings earlier – serve to enhance what might be termed the *ideation* of landscape. Andy Schmidt, supervising animator at Pixar Animation, for example, notes, 'When we were doing *Cars 2* (2011) it was important to think as much about the environments as the characters. We basically began a "car-ification" of the buildings, landscape, everything.'[11] Pixar's Nascar-inspired racing-cum-road trip narratives, *Cars* (2006) and its sequel, speak to the perennial issues in animated sports stories, namely, the extent to which the animation itself apes and imitates sporting action, how far it extends, distorts or revises sporting practice, and crucially, how much it plays out tensions between the organic and mechanical. As is clear from my previous remarks, this extends to the ways in which the environment takes on narrative and symbolic purpose. In the context of sporting animation, the location normally has significance as it is usually the place where the sporting activity is conducted, but it does not operate as mere 'shell' for the action to take place within, but lives as part of a wider set of parameters that synthesize the purpose of the narrative.

In *Cars*, Lightning McQueen, a rookie race-car has ambitions to win the Piston Cup. On his way to the Championship finale at the Los Angeles International Speedway, as a result of an accident, he finds himself in Radiator Springs, a hick town off the main highway. His adventures there serve as a reminder of small town values set against the glamour and greed of the highly commercial professional racing circuit – the off roads and broken paving of the run-down town on Route 66 an instructive comparison to the shining stadium tracks and their extraordinary banks of anthropomorphized car spectators. McQueen's arrogance and ambition to win the Piston Cup is ultimately revised when he becomes aware of Doc Hudson, actually the 'Fabulous Hudson Hornet', a three-time Piston Championship winner, who was forced out of racing following an accident in the early 1950s. Hudson's retreat in Radiator Springs is essentially the consequence of being abandoned by the sport itself; winners and losers are often quickly forgotten with the passage of time and social change – a theme echoed in the way the small town has fallen into neglect and faces economic challenges following the construction of Interstate 40, which by-passes Radiator Springs. The animated landscape here has embedded within it some of the coruscating critique suggested by Perelman concerning the 'insidious infiltration [and] innocent seeming mischief' of sport in the vanguard of 'plundering financial capitalism' and 'this almost invisibly, because the degree and scale of its invasion (of all space) and its occupation (of all time) are such that we no longer see it, because we see nothing else'.[12] Though in my opinion, extreme in its outlook, Perelman's view is advanced on the basis of seeing sport as the embodiment of questionable ideological imperatives, systematic corruption and moral and ethical ambivalence. It is useful as a perspective here, because of its post-structuralist claim that sport invisibly and totally consumes space and time at the expense of knowing and perceiving its affect. It is ironic, then, that animation too has become all pervasive socially, yet seemingly remains invisible as the core cultural mediator, and as a distinctive visual language. On these terms and conditions, then, the animated landscape reinforces Perelman's claims, rendering invisible the oppressive imperatives of late industrial capitalism amidst the gloss of shining race cars, and, in *Cars 2*, the global vistas in a World Grand Prix, which echoes the multi-nation presence of Formula One, and appositely, sees 'all space' (actually Japan, Italy, the UK and Germany) and 'all time' (three races), all 'car-ified'.

Cars partially seeks in some ways to challenge the values Perelman suggests are inherent in contemporary sport and its commercial agenda, though, by showing McQueen remaining with his sponsor Rust-Eze instead of the more influential Dinoco, and when McQueen demonstrates sportsmanship in helping 'the King' Strip Weathers, following an accident in the final race. The same kinds of ideological tensions inform *Cars 2*. As Pixar's Ellen Moon Lee remarks:

The World Grand Prix is the equivalent of the Olympics or the World Cup to our *Cars* characters. With that spirit, we set out to design an identity/brand system that would denote not only a grand scale international event, but also something specifically for race enthusiasts. In our story, this race relates to alternative fuel, so that also influenced our choices of colors, symbols and overall presence.[13]

On the one hand, then, the World Grand Prix epitomizes the triumph of the commercial brand, while on the other seeking to recognize the obvious impact such racing has by making the very subject of the film an eco-themed narrative about the use of Allinol, a bio-fuel, and conventional oil resources. The animated landscapes of each race are informed by different surfaces and challenges that come to represent sport as an environmental issue. As Allison has noted: both the 'environment' and 'sport' have been institutionally raised in status above the level of mere marketable commodities and assumed to consist of activities that are ends in themselves or of public benefit, or both. The questions of principle concern why this should be so, how the boundaries of the activities should be drawn and how their worth can be assessed against each other.[14] The animated landscapes of *Cars* and *Cars 2* then can be read as inherently provisional places, drawing upon established geographical spaces and known iconographies to test the parameters of social value and behaviour. Those who invest in the spirit of place in both films seek to demonstrate a sense of social responsibility through sport. The crucial point here, though, is that the provisional yet formalized parameters afforded by animation and sport as forms can test the 'land' in landscape without impinging upon it in reality. These virtual landscapes are testing places for the discourses that are current and challenging, but seemingly beyond resolution. Again, at the deepest level, the animated sporting landscape is the epitome of Beckettian absurdism in providing agency to quasi-utopian dialogues in dystopic times.

Sportscapes

Bale has suggested that what he usefully terms *sportscapes* can prompt *topophilia* (love of place) or *topophobia* (fear of place), depending upon points of recognition, identification and community.[15] It is clear that the animated sporting landscape is usually an attempt to inspire topophilia and to rationalize topophobia. *War Game*, for all its tragic loss, shows 'no man's land' as a place of temporary reconciliation and joy in sport; *Sports Cartoons* point to the imaginative folly of sport as one of its endearing ways in which humankind copes with the meaninglessness of existence; *2DTV* playfully satirizes the psychological landscapes of sport; while *Cars* and *Cars 2* test the external landscapes of sport to address some of the value-laden meta-narratives of contemporary life. Most sporting animation uses its virtual landscapes to employ both the freedoms of animation and the choreographies of sport to provide both spectacle and speculation. Crucially, too, these landscapes normally demonstrate the significance of technology and the contemporary media in advancing new approaches and ideas. It is in this, though, that sport and animation come together in a highly self-reflexive model of intervention, in that they are the subject and object of progressive technologies and cross-platform mediation. I wish to address this issue by making some final remarks about *Tooned* (2012) and *Tooned 50* (2014), sporting vignettes made by Framestore and the McLaren Formula One team, promoting the history and achievements of McLaren motor racing (Figure 12.1).

As is also the case in the examples discussed earlier, there are times when there is a realization that animation is an attractive language of expression to portray the world afresh and, yet, with a certain appealing familiarity. This is certainly the case in relation to the way in which the Formula One motor-racing team, McLaren, wished to represent itself not merely to committed 'petrolheads' and

Figure 12.1 Lewis Hamilton in the pits (*Tooned 50*, Framestore, 2013)

sports fans, but to younger viewers already engaging with Sky Sports' coverage of the grand prix season, and a more global audience attuned to the celebrity culture engaged with Formula One worldwide. This is not to say that McLaren viewed animation as a children's medium, but rather one that would playfully revise the idea of motor-racing as a 'dirty' industry, characterized by grease, oil, car parts and sweat-strewn mechanics.[16] Equally, there was the sense that humour would do much to leaven the earnestness and competitive edge of real-world sporting endeavour, and promote a more idiosyncratic approach based on the personalities of the drivers. To this end in the first series, Lewis Hamilton and Jensen Button are effectively presented as child-like siblings competing under the watchful paternal gaze of Professor M (Alexander Armstrong) as they test McLaren's new technologies. It is in this, though, that the animated landscape is best identified since the Technology Centre – partly modelled on McLaren's actual headquarters – is a pristine, principally white, modernist space, in which the progressive paraphernalia of motor-racing meets the freedoms of animation in enabling Hamilton and Button to re-invent the *attractions* of the sport by replacing the idea of the old school mechanical with Bond-style futurism.

This is a place where one drop of Mobil oil can cover a floor and last a whole season; where vehicles can be thought controlled and raced backwards; where a whole technology centre can be re-configured into a space craft to chase a new rocket-powered Formula One car. It is also a place that can re-cast past legends into genre-types: Emerson Fittipaldi as a side-burned werewolf with a split personality correspondent to his real-world affability outside the car, and his unfettered competitiveness within it, or James Hunt as James Bond, a clever family-friendly analogy, enough to acknowledge Hunt's well-known hedonism beyond racing, but his style and efficiency as a driver, too. Importantly, then *Tooned* uses its animated landscapes to maintain a relationship between tradition and modernity; to look nostalgically back at past achievements but to look forward to a progressive and successful engagement with the future.

This is best epitomized in *A Glitch Too Far*, which introduces a state-of-the-art driving simulator – essentially a generator of multiple landscapes – which Button and Hamilton are asked to test on the basis that 'what happens in the simulator can be extremely significant for next season'. Button and Hamilton are distracted texting, and brace themselves for what they assume will be an advanced theme park ride – again, both aspects that cast the drivers as figures engaged in youthful recreation rather than systems checking. Button and Hamilton sit on raised seats with nothing around them, and mock the 'advice for landing', before the simulator proceeds to go wrong and they travel through a variety of landscapes on golf carts, spacehoppers, champagne bottles and stop mid-air 'to buffer'. The pair is now trapped in the computer; ultimately, both a self-reflexive reminder of the animation process itself, and the idea of the virtual environments they exist within. The drivers have the opportunity to abort the simulation – itself reminiscent of a computer game – when a sign emerges asking if they want to continue. In a knowing reference, Button says 'Lewis, you're going to have to make up your mind soon', and when Hamilton presses 'No' to continue, the couple go through multiple metamorphoses and transitions, at one point swapping identity, and becoming grids, wireframes and data bytes. The animated sporting landscape then ultimately defines all animated landscapes as imaginary sites composed of representation phenomena that suggest revisions and re-configurations of place.

The Professor meanwhile has gone to see Ron Dennis, the CEO of McLaren, to tell him what has happened, and when Dennis suggests that M should turn the simulator on and off again, the Professor warns that such a procedure could result in losing the drivers. In a surprising conclusion, Hamilton metamorphoses into Sergio Perez, McLaren's new driver following Hamilton's real-world departure to the Mercedes team. Animation sustains the continuing simulation of people and place, but more importantly, the inner logic established in the landscapes of the McLaren Technology Centre. Hamilton and Button are part of a virtual world that resembles the real world, but one that has infinitely more narrative and metaphoric possibilities in defying the laws of physics and gravity, so normally valued by engineers. The representation of technology in sport then also foregrounds the capacity of computer technology in animation – the animated sporting landscape or sportscape, a topophilic vindication of projection and possibility that changes and advances the perception and understanding of both forms.

Notes

1   Enoch Brater, *10 Ways of Thinking about Samuel Beckett* (London: Methuen Drama, 2011), 34.
2   For a discussion of 'micro-narrative' see Paul Wells, 'Boards, Beats, Binaries and Bricolage: Approaches to the Animation Script', in *Analysing the Screenplay*, ed. Jill Nelmes (London and New York: Routledge, 2011), 89–105.

3 Donald Crafton, *Shadow of a Mouse: Performance, Belief and World-Making in Animation* (Berkeley: University of California Press, 2013), 170.

4 David Thomson, *Moments That Made the Movies* (London: Thames & Hudson, 2013), 10.

5 For an extensive discussion of the relationship between animation and sport, see Paul Wells, *Animation, Sport and Culture* (Basingstoke: Palgrave Macmillan, 2014).

6 Steven Connor, *A Philosophy of Sport* (London: Reaktion Books Ltd, 2011), 50.

7 Lincoln Allison, *The Changing Politics of Sport* (Manchester: Manchester University Press, 1993), 10.

8 John Syer and Christopher Connelly, *Sporting Body, Sporting Mind* (London: Simon & Schuster, 1987), 12.

9 J. P. Telotte, *Animating Space: From Mickey to WALL-E* (Lexington: University Press of Kentucky, 2010), 5–14.

10 Script written by Paul Wells; original production script now lost.

11 Personal Interview with the author November 2012

12 Marc Perelman, *Barbaric Sport: A Global Plague* (London: Verso, 2012), ix–x.

13 Ben Queen, *The Art of Cars 2* (San Francisco, CA: Chronicle Books, Ltd, 2011), 26.

14 Allison, *The Changing Politics of Sport*, 207.

15 John Bale, *Landscapes of Modern Sport* (Leicester: Leicester University Press, 1994), 132–140.

16 This is discussed by McLaren CEO, Ron Dennis, in the 'making of' documentary on the DVD release of *Tooned*, the first collection of vignettes about McLaren.

13

The Zombiefied Landscape:
World War Z (2013), *ParaNorman* (2012) and the Politics of the Animated Corpse

James Newton

The landscape of a live-action film, in being captured by the photographic process, is transformed from a once living, active entity, into one which is fixed, still and dead, through the effect of being 'shot' by a camera's lens. The animated landscape, by contrast, is a zombiefied landscape. At its birth, either through computer generation (CG), through model making in the case of stop motion, or images drawn by hand in traditional cel animation, the (pre) animated landscape is static and lifeless, composed of inanimate objects. But through the methods of animation it springs to life; animated by its creation as a filmic object. Thus, the zombie – familiar to us from numerous horror movies, its incarnation as a reanimated body composed of a moving formation of dead tissue – proves an apt metaphor. Upon further examination, it becomes clear that the connections existing between animation and the zombie genre extend beyond metaphoric associations. In particular, the relationships between them are cemented through the now widespread use of CG to create the zombies and the cinematic landscapes in which they roam and terrorize. This stands in contrast to the methods used in analogue-era zombie films, where they are created by actors, costume and make up, and the landscapes via set design and location photography.

The relationship between character and landscape is integral to an understanding of the zombie genre, reflected in the dominance of images of zombies taking over various landscapes. When introducing animated production processes to a zombie film, this relationship is indelibly affected. In this chapter I explore the politics of the zombie genre, and how the increasing use of animation within it alters the nature of the established political interpretations surrounding zombies and the films in which they appear.

Zombie politics and the impact of animation

The city of Jerusalem, entirely cut off by 100-foot walls, is besieged by thousands of rabid, lightening quick, super-strong zombies. Inside the walls the Israeli authorities are busy processing scores of refugees, Israelis and Palestinians alike. Outside is chaos. Israeli military hardware, helicopters supplied by America, circle in the sky. They shoot machine-gun fire indiscriminately into the hordes of zombies below. It has little effect on their advance. Suddenly there is a pile up beside one of the walls; zombies crawling over each other, on top of each other, higher and higher, forming links and chains to take them closer to the top. They work together instinctively, resembling a colony of attacking ants (Figure 13.1). In moments the chain reaches the top and they begin to spill over into the settlement below.

The preceding passage describes the most striking scene from *World War Z* (2013), a big-budget zombie film which utilizes computer-generated images to often startling effect. Clearly, it is a scene that demands to be read politically. The presence of an explicitly identified Israel, Palestine and 'Other' – in the shape of the zombie horde – presents the potential for a political and allegorical interpretation of the scene. That the Israelis have defended themselves by walling off the city, yet do not display any discrimination by allowing thousands of Palestinians refuge to escape the apocalypse – yet, it should be noted, it is the noise of these refugees which ultimately triggers the zombie assault on the wall – accentuates the scene's blatant (and complex) political implications.

Since George Romero's *Night of the Living Dead* (1968) included barely hidden critiques of the social context in which it was made, the zombie film has

Figure 13.1 A mass of animated zombies (*World War Z*, Paramount Pictures, 2013)

developed as a liberal, and in some cases explicitly left wing, example of genre filmmaking. In Romero's ground-breaking film, a small group of survivors battle the newly risen dead, and in turn transform into zombies once they themselves die. It works as an allegory of a country tearing itself apart in an era of civil rights clashes and opposition to the Vietnam War; underscored by the black hero being mistaken for a zombie and then shot and slung on a bonfire by a lynch mob at the film's cynical conclusion.

Robin Wood's *Hollywood from Vietnam to Reagan* (1986) provides an excellent example of this form of allegorical reading of the horror movie. In his analysis of American horror films from the 1970s, Wood outlines the concept of the 'return of the repressed'. Here, Wood claims that the horror is generated by the growing prominence of social groups that had been oppressed or made abject by their relationship to mainstream society. Most notably, these groups include 'The Proletariat', 'Alternative Ideologies or Political Systems' and 'Other Cultures'. At the top of his list of these groups are 'Quite simply, other people'.[1] He writes that, 'it is logical and probable that under capitalism all human relations will be characterized by power, dominance, possessiveness, manipulation: the extension into relationships of the property principle'.[2] The zombie represents the ultimate expression of the return of these 'others'; it transgresses the social boundaries that keep these groups repressed and oppressed by returning to life to attack those that have rendered it abject. By refusing to properly die, the zombie rejects its status as the abject.[3]

In 1978, Romero released *Dawn of the Dead*, a keystone movie in the genre and the foundation on which both zombie film production and an understanding of their ability (as allegorical films) to offer social critique was built. In this sequel to his earlier film, Romero sets the majority of the action in the commercial landscape of a generic shopping mall, with zombies and humans descending there on instinct, so that the commentary shifts from civil rights and the Vietnam war to consumerism and capitalism. In his later two films from the same series, *Day of the Dead* (1985) and *Land of the Dead* (2005),[4] the targets are primarily Reaganite militarism and the Bush administration's 'War on Terror', respectively. Each film in the series tackles what is deemed to be the key political issues relevant to the United States at the time of production.

Returning to the scene from *World War Z* described earlier, we can see that the recent zombie movie continues this trend of social critique and invites allegorical interpretation from the viewer. However, there is a sharp distinction in the way we should understand the film, and other recent examples, such as the *Resident Evil* franchise (2002–2012), in comparison to the left-leaning social critique of the Romero movies. But this difference comes not from a reinterpretation of the narrative content, but through an understanding of their formal properties. The distinction is rooted in the CG rendering of the zombies in *World War Z* and *Resident Evil*, rather than how they are played by actors and stunt performers in films made in the pre-digital era. That is to say that the material aspects of the recent zombie films, which may be described as digital or CG-animated zombies, affect allegorical interpretation of them. Instead of dozens of extras in zombie make up and costume enacting the end of the world, performing as zombiefied versions of us and taking over the locations in which they were shot, the apocalypse of the CG-animated zombie film is depicted digitally. The zombies are no longer real people, extras or stunt performers, but digital, CG creations that number in the thousands. Crucially, the landscape itself is similarly animated, both created and enhanced through the digital process, extending its ability to both carry and shape meaning.

Arguably, in those films where humans portray the zombies, the zombies retain a greater sense of individuality. Therefore, if a revolution or revolt by the oppressed horde is to be understood politically, it is as a collective group of individuals forming a union to strike back against the economic and political systems that governed them when they were alive. With CG animation the zombie horde can easily become faceless. In *World War Z*, for example, they are not presented as a collection of individuals, but as an indistinguishable mass. This is largely because of the animation process itself, whereby the software engine Massive was used to generate the collective behaviour of the zombies mass, but at the expense of time-consuming and expensive singular design choices that might otherwise have been made on a zombie-by-zombie basis. In the Romero movies, the analogue nature of production means we can clearly detect individuality in each zombie, precisely because a human individual portrays each zombie. In the CG-animated zombie film this is not often the case. The zombies, by virtue of being so indistinguishable, are clearly coded as a homogenized 'other'; they no longer serve as horrific, corporeal avatars into which we can project ourselves as spectator, but something digital, multiple and vast. The zombies and the landscapes merge. In being so plentiful, enabled only through the ability to replicate so many of them, the zombies *become* the landscape – a reanimated landscape.

What I wish to consider in this chapter is the proposition that the technological developments of computer-generated imagery and digitally animated special effects have, in fact, transformed the left-wing inflection of the zombie movie into one which is reactionary and conservative. By way of contrast, I also provide an analysis of the stop-motion animation *ParaNorman* (2012), a family film that nevertheless sits within the zombie movie tradition by virtue of its narrative and formal references to the genre. *ParaNorman* avoids the reactionary connotations suggested by films such as *World War Z* as much by its stop-motion form as by the elements embedded in its plotline. The stop motion of *ParaNorman* enforces a connection between the living characters and its zombies because they are produced by the same methods: through model making. Any similarity between the two is extinguished in a CG process, which creates a material distinction between them; the emphasis is placed on physical difference rather than likeness. With this comes the suggestion that the conservative implications of the CG zombie movie are engrained in the specifics of the digital animation prevalent in their depictions of a world taken over by the living dead; an implication not present in other types of animation.

Us and them: The polemics of analogue and CG zombies

The tradition of sympathy for the figure of the zombie, based on metaphorical and allegorical interpretations, pre-dates the politicization of horror from the 1970s onwards which Wood discusses. Prior to Romero's flesh-eating creatures, the zombie's origin and principal reference point is in voodoo.[5] The voodoo zombies, in Kevin William Bishop's words, 'act primarily as cultural metaphor for enslavement'.[6] Reduced to the status of a slave, voodoo zombies 'blatantly lose their independence and autonomy', and epitomize 'the depiction of a human subject as nothing more than an object, a dumb tool to be used and abused by others'.[7]

Ultimately, there is something radical about the depiction of slaves turning against their oppressors. This narrative subtext is made explicit in *The Plague of the Zombies* (1966), the last major voodoo-themed zombie film prior to Romero's reinvention of the genre with *Night of the Living Dead*. The film conflates capitalist exploitation and British social class divisions by featuring a resurrected zombie workforce destroy the Cornish tin mine where they are forced to toil by their aristocratic master.[8]

The zombie as a slave metaphor is given a radical reinterpretation by the Romero films (and those inspired by them) by depicting them instead as highly aggressive with a compulsion to consume human flesh. No longer enslaved, with no direct masters, the post–Romero zombie instead has the power to destroy those more fortunate than themselves: the economically advantaged living. The variants on the genre that followed, including those that came from Europe in 1970s and 1980s, were almost invariably indebted to the aesthetic and political traditions that Romero started – specifically the flesh-eating zombie and the explicit, if occasionally clumsy, social commentary.[9]

Todd K. Platts continues the understanding of the genre as a political one, by attempting to locate the zombie film within the field of sociology, proposing that it is based on what he considers an 'emerging field' of study into the popular phenomena surrounding zombies.[10] Aside from the films he considers the recent craze of the zombie walk as an important aspect of this culture. The zombie walk, flash mobs where significant numbers of people gather in a public space made up as physically damaged or decomposing walking corpses, is an important indicator of the influence of the Romero films.[11] They invoke the sense of collectivism and solidarity, and therefore the left-wing revolutionary potential of the zombie masses as created in the Romero series in particular. The joy of the zombie walk comes in the taking over and reclaiming of the public landscape (parks, shopping malls, streets, etc.) as a collective group. Platts underlines the left-leaning nature of the zombie film by highlighting how many of the zombie walks take place in aid of progressive causes, such as 'hunger' or homelessness.[12] Therefore, the fans who take part in these walks are specifically entering into the social critique of institutions that permeates through many of the most notable examples of the genre. They are imposing a political position based entirely on reclaiming dominance over the landscape.

As has been hinted, the most crucial aspect that informs the left-leaning critique of the analogue zombie film is the use of actors, stunt people and extras playing them. In doing so, the focus is on their humanity, and not on the differences from those still living. The central trope is their identifiable human traits and characteristics. Across the genre there is the recurring idea that the zombies are more benign than many of their living counterparts. While the zombies present a physical danger within the narratives, the worst aspects of humanity, such as selfishness, jealousy, racism and/or the institutional and hierarchical structures of society, form a far greater threat – all of which are frequently played out through the characters' negotiation of their immediate, and shared/contested, landscape.

The title 'zombie' infers an unthinking being, blindly or unconsciously following a pattern. In *Dawn of the Dead*'s very explicit critique of consumerism the message is clear that the zombies are returning to the commercial environment of the shopping mall because, according to one character, 'this was an important place in their lives'. And yet the film does not ask us to scorn the zombies. It presents them as simultaneously distinguishable as individuals, and as part of a mass group. Their unique characteristics give them personality and evoke sympathy. Among those we encounter are a nurse, a baseball player, children, businessmen, a nun and a Hare Krishna monk in full robes, in addition to dozens of regular citizens. They represent a cross section of society, brought together and made equal in status by their shared zombification – echoing the ritualized, trance-like consumerism that frequently characterizes the weekend shopping trip; in this sense, it is possible to see a powerful relationship emerge between the individual and such marketized landscapes, where the ceaseless hunger to consume shapes not just the individual's behaviour, but also the surrounding landscape. The zombie of the Romero films fills the dual role of being both a threat, and the reminder to the living characters of what they are and what they could still be. All of which are underlined by the refrain voiced by characters across the series: 'they're us, that's all'.

Dan O'Bannen's the *Return of the Living Dead* takes these sympathetic and empathetic incarnations of the zombie further. As stated, they are a more explicitly collectivized group that can communicate verbally and organize with intelligence. It too demonstrates a continuum between the living and the dead, defined by resemblance, in the way they can speak to those still alive, and in their physical deterioration and decomposition; one zombie is played by an actor with no legs, and shows amazing ability to shift quickly across the ground on his stumps to chase away the living. His physical limitations prove no hindrance as a zombie. However, because he is played by a real person, what the film actually reveals is the triumph of the human spirit over potential disability – the ability to transcend any physical impediments – rather than merely show off a zombie's dexterity. A CG legless corpse would not be able to do this because the human element is reduced or removed entirely.

The *World War Z* zombies also have incredible physical ability, but this is almost entirely artificially created via digital effects and the algorithmic simulations of Massive's software engine. The zombies are creature-like in their animated depiction, displaying quick, reptilian movements. They are able to pounce through the air to attack and the soundtrack echoes with a croaking hiss whenever they appear in close up. Together, they are presented as a swarming mass. In this, there is a rejection of the progressive nature of the zombie walk, of a collective group reclaiming a public landscape. The scenes in *World War Z* of cities being taken over are depictions of pure apocalyptic horror; large in scale, which emphasize the panic and terror of those still alive by employing high-angle shots of the city landscape with people fleeing in all directions. In many of the shots the landscape and the zombies are materially the same, created entirely via a digital process. The individuality of each zombie is lost in their homogenization and their lack of separation from other elements of the frame. The zombies featured in *World War Z* and the *Resident Evil* series of films look alike and move alike.

Fittingly, the zombies in *World War Z* were designed and differentiated according to stages of decomposition, 'ranging from one that had just been infected by a bite to one that had been undead for a very long time',[13] rather than through any 'human' characteristics. This homogenization is technically sophisticated. Jody Duncan, in *Cineflex*, reveals how animators would create each individual zombie from a combination of twenty-four varying body types, mixed with 'digital costuming', and then each would be 'built to match up to different zombification levels', one of four stages of decomposition.[14] These digital creations either stand alone as entirely CG zombies, or augment physical performers so that materially the effects, the locations and actors merge. Digital effects in this instance have replaced what would previously have been the responsibility of a number of film crew departments, including casting, acting, costume and make up, set design, and location management. The separation of these elements in the analogue zombie film means each is interpretable based on its own merit, and the zombies maintain autonomy and a distinction over the physical space that surrounds them – a status not possible when they are digitally augmented.

One example of this differentiation between computer animation and the analogue can be found in two superficially similar images, one from *Resident Evil: Retribution* (2012), and the other from J. R. Bookwalter's zero-budget super 8-mm zombie film *The Dead Next Door* (1989). Both contain short sequences where zombies attempt an attack on the White House in Washington, DC.[15] In Bookwalter's film the camera is behind the zombies as they claw at and climb on the White House gates. Because the camera is behind them and at street level it shows an affinity with those zombies (representing an underclass) locked out of the gates of power. This crucial element gives the shot a subversive quality. This is replicated in the analogue process of production. Essentially, Bookwalter has replicated the zombie walk. He has located himself and his crew, with extras dressed and made up as zombies, and has temporarily taken over the politically symbolic landscape. The contrasting image from *Resident Evil: Retribution* achieves the opposite effect. It reverses the image of *The Dead Next Door* by placing the camera behind the humans – military types and those working for the evil corporation responsible for the viral outbreak in the first movie – as they stand on the White House roof surveying the zombiefied landscape; ready to defend humanity from the vast throng of the living dead that is locked outside the gates. Had this image been created through analogue methods, with each zombie a literal individual, this would have presented a revolutionary statement and a strikingly subversive image. It would have been an image of the oppressed and repressed turning on those who have created the material conditions for their now miserable existence; and by closing in on the White House they would be taking revenge on the last vestige of capitalist and imperialist iconography. Instead, in its CG manifestation, *Resident Evil: Retribution* sides with the corporation and the government, as they consider a solution to the ultimate problem; that of the revolting underclass – visually encoded as a disgusting, unsympathetic mass. As in the scene from *World War Z*, there are so many zombies in each frame that they seemingly morph into the other elements, becoming an extension of the CG materiality that links every aspect of the image. What was once character, now becomes the landscape.

Re-animation: Stop motion and the animatronic corpse

Other forms of animation, such as stop motion or animatronics, do not suffer from the same issues as computer-generated imagery because the process of creation eschews mass replication for individualistic design. This means it is possible to uphold the utopian principles of the analogue zombie film. One feature of the *Return of the Living Dead* is the use of animatronics to create certain important zombies.[16] Its most notable moment of animatronics is when a half corpse, hideously decomposed, is strapped to a table and explains the true horror of her condition – that being dead is agony and that eating brains takes away the pain. It is a poignant moment in the film, one that helps to transcend its status as a shallow piece of comedy.[17] If we are to treat the formal aspects as vitally as the film's content, then we can conclude that it has taken that which is animated – an animatronic puppet – to give humanity to the zombie. It is a process of animation that brings to life a physical and existential pain, and one of the principal moments where a sympathetic – if not symbiotic – connection is established between the living and the dead.

The stop-motion animation *ParaNorman* follows a similar path in using the artificiality of its formal process to reinforce the continuity between humans and zombies. It is the closest completely animated feature film yet to address some of the themes prevalent in the zombie movies of George Romero and those that followed in their wake.[18] The storyline is one of an 11-year-old boy who can communicate with ghosts, who has to save his small American town when zombie judges from the eighteenth century are resurrected by a witch's curse. Though marketed as a family film, *ParaNorman* revels in its placement within horror movie tradition, and contains a number of amusing references to famous examples of the genre.

The process of stop-motion production, the taking of individual photographic shots, draws a connection with Cameron's work in *Zombie Media*. He references Roland Barthes and Andre Bazin to make a connection between the physical materiality of photography and his own treatise on how the zombie film's foregrounding of grain and pixelation mirrors the physical deterioration associated with zombie movie content.[19] He discusses how they consider still photography's 'deathly ontology',[20] and how this notion is continued in the work of Laura Mulvey and Garrett Stewart. Mulvey and Stewart examine how much of moving-image production tends to ignore or hide its origins in the still photograph.[21] In stop motion, the stillness and photographic origins are not hidden, despite the image appearing to move. There is a physical vulnerability and inherent imperfection present in stop-motion animation. The movements of the characters on screen are necessarily defective replications of real life – being able to see visible fingerprints remains one of the appealing qualities of stop-motion animation in the face of the digital perfection encouraged by CG and hand-drawn animation. By embracing this, *ParaNorman*'s predominantly stop-motion form emphasizes the 'deathly ontology', providing an appropriate harmony with the zombie film. In *ParaNorman*, the sense of decay and imperfection is ever present. Its meaning, the way it is to be understood, is as intrinsically linked to its form as its narrative content.

ParaNorman also emphasizes the continuity between the living and the dead. The zombies are a shambling, physically imperfect, mess. Numerous visual jokes are made at the expense of their bodies falling apart. In this, they more closely resemble the dishevelled and lumbering dead of the Romero movies. The living humans, too, are defined physically by imperfection and exaggeration. In its re-creation of the body, the stop-motion process celebrates human physicality and fallibility. The characters are intentionally created to be asymmetrical.[22] Norman's ears jut out and his nostrils are unbalanced. In one moment, a close up of his face is framed on both sides by the jutting, overweight midriffs of his parents. There is also a grotesque quality to those characters intended to be attractive within the narrative diegesis. His cheerleader sister has oversexualized and exaggerated hips, while the jock she romantically pursues has a preposterously large chest-to-waist ratio. Both work as a parody of stock characters from horror and are characterized here as much by their physicality as by any other unique characteristic.

With landscapes, the stop-motion film retains the distinction between character and setting present from the analogue zombie film, based on its foundation on a 'creative procedure that resembles that of live-action set design'.[23] Chris Pallant discusses how this is often seen as a necessary approach in stop motion to foreground character over the set or 'location'; a separate aesthetic defines both character and landscape forged out of the differing materials used to create them – supple and flexible materials for characters, and more solid materials used to fashion elements of the landscape.[24] This gives *ParaNorman* a distinction between its characters and the space they inhabit familiar from the zombie takeover of landscape in analogue examples from the genre.

ParaNorman opens with a 'FEATURE PRESENTATION' title card familiar from Quentin Tarantino's Grindhouse homages,[25] complete with mock-degraded film stock effect. The image exists as a reference point for informed, mostly adult, members of the audience, problematizing the demarcation of animation as a children's genre. It then immediately cuts to a scene from an imaginary zombie film being watched by Norman and his deceased grandmother. What follows is a homage to the comic splatter of the *Return of the Living Dead* and other assorted horror movies. While younger viewers may understand the homage as vaguely associated with horror, the specifics of these references are aimed squarely at those familiar with the genre, reinforcing how *ParaNorman* attempts to locate itself within the historical traditions of analogue horror movies. It begins with a close up of a human brain discarded on the floor, a huge chunk bitten out of it. Two female feet stagger backwards into shot, resplendent in red stilettos, one of the heels inadvertently puncturing and squashing the brain. The woman in the stilettos is fleeing from a zombie, and she continues her flight with the brain still attached to her shoe. The walking corpse cries out for 'brains'; an exclamation first uttered by the dead in O'Bannen's film. As he lurches forwards the soundtrack fills with her incessant screams. The low-budget origins of many horror movies are affectionately parodied. The entire scene is filtered through fake and very noticeable 35-mm film grain. At one point, a microphone and boom pole hover into view, only for the animated 'actress' to push it back out of shot. The lumbering zombie also takes so long to reach her she has to take a deep breath to renew her screaming, but not before she shares an exasperated glance down the camera lens. As with the creation of Norman's cheerleader sister, her physicality is sexualized. She wears knee-high socks and also has exaggeratedly shapely hips covered by tiny shorts, reminiscent of the first female victim in Tobe Hooper's *The Texas Chain Saw Massacre* (1973). Her stilettos hark back to the blatant fetishistic use of red high heels in Dario Argento's *Tenebrae* (1983). The sexualized image is played for laughs when at one point she looks affronted that the zombie might have been admiring her behind as she bends over to remove the brain stuck to her foot. The scene's playful yet gruesome violence reminds us not only of O'Bannen's film, but also of the inventive splatter of the Romero movies, to say nothing of the comic style (and stop-motion special effects sequences) of Sam Raimi's *Evil Dead* series (1981–1992). The sequence ends with the zombie pitching forward to bite her, but cuts to Norman watching the film at home on VHS before the full horror of the scene plays out.

In its opening sequence *ParaNorman* is using stop-motion animation to align itself with the pre-digital horror film tradition. It affiliates itself to the zombie movies of Romero and O'Bannen, and other assorted horror films, by faking those formal aspects that betray their analogue production traditions; film grain and degraded stock, more primitive special effects, and VHS home video distribution. In its emphasis on the content, such as the bad acting, extreme violence and fetishism, *ParaNorman* reveals its pleasure and joy in these elements of horror. It rejects the implications of the digital horror movie – the slickness and sheen of the camera work and effects – and locates itself within the utopian historical landscape of the analogue zombie film.

Conclusion

There is no doubt that the scene from *World War Z* discussed at the start of this chapter uses computer-generated animation to 'raise the bar' in terms of imagined visions of zombie apocalypse. The scenes in Jerusalem are spectacular and thrillingly shot, edited and visualized through its digital form. Indeed, it would be practically impossible to create the same scene using analogue methods and real-life performers playing the zombies. There are simply too many of them, moving too quickly, performing feats which are too dangerous. The landscape also would require set building on a scale too large for it to be financially feasible. The power of the scene comes from the capabilities of its digitally animated effects.

Also, its concoction of elements – set in Jerusalem, the advancing zombies, Israel protecting Palestinian refugees, plus the film's Hollywood production context – make it a potent, complicated and extremely problematic scene to analyse allegorically. It is not my intention to provide such an interpretation, but to point out that the CG animation has to be considered as relevant to a political reading of the scene as its content – a consideration that can be overlooked in live action–minded approaches to Film Studies.

My hypothesis is not meant to propose any inherent conservatism in the use of computer animation, only to examine the way it has been used so far, and of how it has altered the implications of the zombie genre. A look at the recent upsurge in zombie-themed video games, for example, suggests the possibility that with careful consideration a social critique can be transposed to an entirely digital format. Certainly, the aesthetic traditions leftover from Romero, that of the zombies taking over the city landscapes, is replicated in the *Resident Evil* (Capcom, 1996–2012) games (on which the film series of the same name is based), as well as other games such as *Left 4 Dead* (Electronic Arts, 2008, 2009), and *The Last of Us* (2013). In fact, in the first instalment of the *Dead Rising* series (Capcom, 2006) the action is located predominantly in a shopping mall to imitate the main landscape of *Dawn of the Dead*.

In a hidden Easter Egg from *GTA V* (Rockstar Games, 2013), the zombie is used as an arbiter of satirical content when one of the central characters of the game happens across the 'Vinewood Zombie', an actor playing a member of the living dead, who hangs around on street corners calling repeatedly for 'brains'. The actor/zombie is culturally self-aware, and is using the image of the zombie to satirize modern city life, but his attempt is a clear failure. He undoubtedly reclaims part of the city landscape, but it is a zombie walk undertaken only by one. His zombie walk fails because it lacks sufficient support and numbers in which to truly take over the landscape, or indeed to become the principal feature of the landscape of 'Vinewood'. If we were to compare it to the zombie walks of real life and those of the analogue zombie film, it fails as a performance because it is only through the group dynamic that it achieves its progressive nature.

If we compare it to the digital and CG zombie film it fails because he exists in insolation, remaining a singular character, unable to transcend the boundary between characters and setting that comes when there are so many zombies that they *become* the landscape. In this instance, *GTA V* is using the figure of the living dead as a social critique, and also satirizing the pop-cultural use of zombies in which to do so. Indeed, the interactivity over its animated landscape extended to players of *GTA V* underlines the impotence of the Vinewood Zombie. In the world of *GTA*, zombies are not necessary to return as the 'other' to take over the landscape because the player is urged to do that for themselves by being handed the autonomy to break laws, drive on pavements and on the wrong side of the road, attack bystanders, and generally occupy civic spaces in ways not afforded to members of the public in real life.

What I have attempted to highlight in this chapter is that by using computer animation to reproduce what was once the work of multiple departments in a film crew (casting, set design, costume, make up, actors, stunt performers, etc.) to bring to life a zombie takeover then there has to be a consideration of how such images should be interpreted in critical and academic circles. By simply replacing the analogue with the digital does not mean that our previous ways of understanding an image should remain. Form is as essential to understanding a film as its content. In the case of the zombie film, a careful re-thinking of how computer animation is to be used needs to happen if the perception of its progressive social commentary is to continue as before.

Notes

1   Robin Wood, *Hollywood from Vietnam to Reagan* (New York: Columbia University Press, 2003), 66–67.
2   Ibid., 66.
3   Ibid., 103.
4   Romero also released *Diary of the Dead* (2007), and *Survival of the Dead* (2009). For an understanding of the complex relationships and associations connected to the Romero series see http://www.popmatters.com/column/159439-legacy-of-the -living-dead/.
5   *I Walked with a Zombie* (Jacques Tournier, 1943) and *White Zombie* (Victor Halperin, 1932) are two of the most noteworthy examples of this cycle.
6   Kyle William Bishop, *American Zombie Gothic* (Jefferson, NC: McFarland & Co, 2010), 131.

7 Ibid., 131.
8 Cf. Andy Black, refers to how the film foregrounds the concept of the former working classes raised from the dead to continue slaving in even more exploitative conditions than they did when alive: Andy Black, *The Dead Walk* (Hereford: Noir Pubishing, 2000), 24.
9 Two examples Black highlights are the Spanish-made *The Living Dead at Manchester Morgue* (1974), which features a counter-cultural left-wing biker as its hero, up against a reactionary cop as well as a zombie horde, and the Italian *Hell of the Living Dead* (1979), where zombies in the Third World fight against the Western scientists and military who have polluted their land and caused the outbreak.
10 Todd K. Platts, 'Locating Zombies in the Sociology of Popular Culture', *Sociology Compass* 7.7 (2013): 547–560.
11 The zombie walk movement is now worldwide, with events being held in many towns, advertised via their own websites or social networks. One of the earliest of the organized walks was World Zombie Day, information for which can be found here http://worldzombieday.co.uk/.
12 According to Platts the walks 'spread awareness of local and global issues; the major theme at Zombie Walk Detroit 2012 was "walk against hunger"', 556.
13 Jody Duncan, 'World War Z: Zombie Wars', *Cineflex Issue* 135 (2013): 17.
14 Ibid., 26.
15 Cf. The White House was also intended to be a reference point for Romero in the script for what became *Day of the Dead*. Kim Newman, *Nightmare Movies* (London: Bloomsbury, 1988), points out that the unproduced screenplay was originally titled *Zombies in the White House*, and would have ended with 'the establishment of an ambiguously utopian new normality after the overthrow of the repressive old order', 209.
16 Christian Sellars and Gary Smart, *The Complete History of the Return of the Living Dead* (London: Plexus, 2010).
17 Jamie Russell, *The Book of the Dead: The Complete History of Zombie Cinema* (Surrey: FAB Press, 2005) interprets *Return of the Living Dead* as nihilistic, an interpretation of the film rejected by Bishop, 155.
18 *Corpse Bride* (2005) and *Frankenweenie* (2012) also feature reanimated corpses, but their reference points are from the gothic horror tradition, rather than the American films of the 1970s and 1980s referenced in *ParaNorman*.
19 Cameron is referring to Roland Barthes, Camera Lucida, trans. Richard Howard (New York: Hill and Wang, 1981); Andre Bazin, *What Is Cinema?*, Vol. 1, ed. and trans. Hugh Gray (Berkeley: University of California Press, 2004), 14.
20 Allan Cameron, 'Zombie Media: Transmission, Reproduction, and the Digital Dead', *Cinema Journal* 52.1 (2012): 66–89, 73.

21 Cameron refers here to Laura Mulvey's *Death 24× a Second: Stillness and the Moving Image* (London: Reaktion Books, 2006), and Garrett Stewart, *Between Film and Screen: Modernism's Photo Synthesis* (Chicago: University of Chicago Press, 1999).

22 See http://www.cartoonbrew.com/feature-film/meet-paranorman-character -designer-heidi-smith-67775.html for an interview with character designer Heidi Smith.

23 Chris Pallant, 'The Animated Landscape' in *Film Landscapes: Cinema, Environment and Visual Culture*, ed. Jonathan Rayner and Graeme Harper (Newcastle: Cambridge Scholars Press, 2013), 194.

24 Ibid., 195.

25 Used to open *Kill Bill* (2004) and to introduce Tarantino's 'Death Proof' segment in *Grindhouse* (2007), his double-bill anthology co-directed with Robert Rodriguez.

Part Five

Function: Interactivity

14

Evoking the Oracle: Visual Logic of Screen Worlds

Tom Klein

Imagine if humans were different in form: one very long leg and one very short. At first glance this might seem just a permutation, one of the many possible arrangements of a body, but with further consideration it can lead to a world so vastly different from the one that exists. To accommodate walking, sidewalks might require raised platforms for the shorter leg, while the longer leg took strides on the ground. Perhaps this platforming would need to extend to every walkable surface, including the architecture of buildings. This one simple change in practical terms would not only alter the designs of entire cities, but would also impact the economy, transportation, cultural traditions and certainly sports and leisure. In effect, this one change would be magnified deeply into the human landscape.

Such a thought experiment offers a glimpse at the magnitude of possible transformation in an animated *mise-en-scène* and of the power of cinema to carefully frame a narrative in the context of fantastical realms. In the hands of ambitious and visionary directors, audiences watch stories through radical new prisms. Handled as a novelty it can be a gratifying thrill or a clever trick, but brought to light as an allegory it can seem like a transcendent journey. Both ranges of audience reaction are the result of a projected wonderment from invented screen worlds: animation, live action with effects, interactive new media or games.

Among these, the mechanics of an invented space are most apparent in games because rules exist for players to interact meaningfully with the landscape. Therefore, a look at the visual logic of gamespace is a good entry point to a larger discussion of its role in cinema. If a game can be won or completed then its designer has established a set of rules that form the basis of its system of play.

These should logically make sense and show consistency so that a player can deduce outcomes and solutions. Yet this does not mean such a world, based on a rational premise, needs to be ordinary. Quite to the contrary, gamers are conditioned to the thrill of spectacle and danger.

Oftentimes the landscape of games achieves a grandiosity of violent intensity, with warriors shaped by superhuman muscles and overwrought weaponry and armour. Yet these things do not necessarily stretch the boundaries of visual invention, as most games remain within familiar fantasy, sci-fi and action genre conventions. The more dynamic ones that will be considered here, however, employ a novel 'game mechanic', defined for videogames as 'an action invoked by an agent to interact with the game world, as constrained by the game rules'.[1] This term has gained wide currency among both designers and game enthusiasts, and the notion of visually based logic presented herein is largely the same concept as mechanics, yet intrinsic also to cinema. These are like 'rules of nature' that manifest themselves as the workings of the innovative space within a game or a film.

As with the first example (long leg/short leg) a game mechanic imposes itself on the virtual landscape because it is a defining conceit of this imagined space. A player holding this knowledge can use it like a Rosetta Stone to unlock the meaning of what otherwise appears strange to an outside observer, such as the blocky environment of *Minecraft* (2011). The rules of play require each cubic piece to be discerned, so the block-like aesthetic is imposed for practical reasons, and a player can engage with the space by mining, smelting and building. In any game, good design logic rewards a reasoned inquiry into its mechanics. Responses to players' actions reveal how landscapes react to input. Over time, as predictive patterns emerge, these learned results lead to a deeper understanding of the rules in such a world.

For instance, in *Portal* (2007) the puzzle solving is an extension of one's growing familiarity with the central dynamic of the game: a portal-jump. Players first set an in-point (a) and an out-point (b). Then by jumping into one portal they emerge from the other. If players leap down from high above into a, then they fling out from the other end b, with all that linear momentum carried in a new direction. This can be used to cross wide distances or to leap over tall obstacles. Creative applications of this concept are subsequently applied to solve more and more intricate puzzles, and it becomes a tool of innovative process like a wheel or a gear.

The notion of a portal has traditionally had a simpler context as a doorway between two worlds, such as Lewis Carroll's 'looking-glass'. While this is not a new concept, it is an evolving one, due to its protracted leap from the pages of literature to its visualization in comics, cinema and now videogames. Long since Alice found herself in Wonderland, portal-travel has endured as a fantasy and sci-fi trope. Audiences have grown familiar with various iterations over time as its conceptual complexity has grown. For instance, in the Pixar feature *Monsters, Inc.* (2001) the climax shows an enormous factory of suspended doors through which the monsters engage in a fanciful high-speed chase. As they leap through door after door, they are portal-jumping into a number of alternate worlds. Considering the breakneck pace of this chase and the degree of visual reasoning required to connect these disparate locations, it is hard to imagine a Victorian audience making sense of this action sequence. And, yet, a century and a half after *Alice's Adventures in Wonderland*, children watch *Monsters, Inc.* and routinely understand its sophisticated mélange of portal-connected realms (Figure 14.1).

This is the visual logic of the animated world of Monstropolis, where the need to produce 'scream energy' necessitates an unusual corporate enterprise: building these doors to send monsters to the human world. Such a contrivance, appearing in a film, serves as a good example of visual logic: *a visible expression of the mechanics that operate a defined system, especially a fictional conceit; it is bound by rules that manifest in rational observed patterns, even if at first sight its rules are unclear and its meaning must be interpreted and solved; it may take the form of an image which illustrates a cause and/or effect, a cinematic sequence which reveals an action and/or result, or an interactive experience that allows an inquiry and response.*

Figure 14.1 Portal-travel (*Monsters, Inc.*, Pixar, 2001)

An important distinction for the concept of visual logic is that the designer must imbue the resulting work with its operating principle, generally something unusual and unique. Correspondingly, the ability of a viewer to interpret that principle might be seen as central to its fulfilment as a work of art or as popular entertainment. Just as videogames often take players through a series of progressive steps that serve as a tutorial, a film like *Monsters, Inc.* uses an opening scene to serve the same purpose. In it, an automated training simulation reveals how 'scarers' cross through special doors to collect children's screams in pressurized tanks. This kind of instructive scene is characteristic of films that employ visual logic. By conveying what are essentially the rules required to understand the movie, it shows the gamification of cinema.

In contrast, something made to be intentionally ambiguous or nonsensical, even when the result is pleasing or possibly profound, would be judged to *not* display visual logic. Of course, to define art, cinema or games by such rigid parameters is problematic and one must inevitably submit to exceptions and 'grey area', which will not only be acknowledged here but will form the basis for 'Evoking the Oracle', the titular thesis of this piece, that an underlying human awe can be produced by intimating the workings of a thing without actually revealing its true nature.

This might sound like spirituality or faith, but it can actually be a number of things. And, working in reverse, if the operating principle is known by a few but difficult for them to convey then a visual metaphor can function as a bridge for others to understand it. For example, a notable achievement of modern science is a theory of quantum physics that in real terms is expressed as math, but which is largely explained to the public with a cartoon-like allegory known as 'Schrödinger's cat'. The cat is the brainchild of physicist Erwin Schrödinger, who devised it as a thought experiment to suggest the implications of quantum superposition. Much of the appeal of this story is not only the paradox of the cat existing in two states, but also the suspense that the cat could die under the arranged mad-scientist conditions.[2]

Proposed by a colleague of Einstein, it has the glimmer of genius yet sounds like the premise of an Edward Gorey cartoon. The desire to understand something that eludes normal comprehension is intriguing – and then, to hear the story told with a cat has made this an enduring icon of physics since 1935. However, a thing can be appealing for different reasons. Let us consider the story of Schrödinger's cat but without the credibility of its mathematical proof or the showmanship of letting on about a mysterious subatomic paradox. In that case, wouldn't the story lose a great deal of its wonderment? Yes, it arguably would. But if it was presented in a compelling format, perhaps as a videogame with rules that were learned experientially, then it might not matter at all. Through gameplay this paradox might seem wondrous on merits other than its actual proof. That is, the virtual simulation might provide a sense of otherworldly appeal to a player whether it had basis on fact or not.

A modern inventory of screen worlds comprises many different media and devices to view them, but there were also pre-cinema examples, such as nineteenth-century panoramas. In these, landscapes were painted across giant cylindrical surfaces and then displayed in rotundas for paying audiences. The landscapes would typically show a colossal sight, like a view from a promontory or a vast naval battle. The artist Robert Barker built a structure in London called The Panorama for a rotating display of his installations that, when properly lit and then framed top and bottom with black paint or drapery, would make it seem like a window to a world floating in a void. These were spectacles that drew considerable crowds and became popular throughout Europe. Such a setting invites obvious comparisons to a theatrical experience. It can even be seen as a projection of imperial power through depictions of military victories.[3] The awe-inducing imagery chosen for panoramic entertainment – Lord Nelson's fleet, glorious mountaintop vistas, great cities of the world, armies clashing on battlefields – brings to mind the calculations of Hollywood that an audience will more readily watch an overblown epic than an understated drama.

The studio ethos to promote this type of fare and the vast expense and complexity of producing epics is the long road travelled from the earliest days of cinema when the initial draw was simply 'moving pictures'. Now, with the vast toolset of digital manipulation insinuated so deeply into screen worlds, the capacity for building towards spectacle has never been more pronounced. In the course of pursuing these entertainments of the future, the allure of presenting wondrous realms will arguably facilitate the wider use of visual logic in cinema.

Spectacles

Newspapers captured the flurry of excitement as the first Lumière films arrived in London in 1896. This French invention was promoted as a cinematograph. It was hailed by reporters as a remarkable photographic instrument, and the articles about it were written as news and opinion, not critical assessments of the films as art, with a notable exception. That distinction belongs to Alfred Octavius Winter, the first formal movie critic whose essay 'The Cinematograph' appeared in London's *New Review* in response to the Lumière films. Winter judged them artless and began his review with the curious statement, 'Life is a game played according to a set of rules'.[4] He demurred that these short films were a document of everyday events such as factory workers taking lunch or passengers disembarking a train, which stripped them of artistic possibility:

> The dominant lesson of M. Lumière's invention is this: the one real thing in life, art, or literature, is unreality. It is only by the freest translation of facts into another medium that you catch that fleeting impression of reality, which a paltry assemblage of the facts themselves can never impart … Has then the Cinematograph a future? Artistically, no.[5]

The first movie review not only panned its subject, but also condemned the future of cinema, implicitly disparaging every movie that might come thereafter. However, Winter offered the small prospect that beauty could prevail only when the 'casual, unconscious life of the streets learns to compose itself into rhythmical pictures'.[6] This is even more interesting in regard to how he finishes the review, comparing motion pictures to another invention that was released to public astonishment in the same year: the X-ray. When he concludes that the 'curiosity-monger may find it profitable to pierce through our "too, too solid flesh" and count the rattling bones within', one can only wonder if he deems X-rays to have real commercial value as a spectators' attraction.[7]

The revelation of an X-ray was in showing a 'living' skeleton. It went deeper than a photograph, exposing a parallel world within everyday lives. In a sense, it was an audacious special effect and a compelling example of visual spectacle. It was also virtual reality. The correspondence between a man and his X-ray 'avatar' is analogous to a motion-capture rig and its computer model. In either case, the illusion needs electricity to vitalize the resulting landscape – bright translucence within blackness. Like the virtual worlds of *Tron* (1982) or *The Matrix* (1999) these are borne of energy, sustained in a flickering current.

If Winter could imagine X-rays as a public attraction, then was there something meaningful beneath this impression? The notion of a revealing 'ray' enables any number of unseen things to be seen. For example, when Gandalf's magic in *The Hobbit* (2013) reveals a legion of orcs hidden by Sauron's spell it is not unlike antecedents such as seeing ghosts or angels living among us. The wondrous capacity of X-ray vision, even when figuratively used in cinema, is to show an impression of a simultaneous reality, one that exists in the same space.

The advent of computers opened the human imagination to the many possibilities of virtual reality, and writers and directors began to conceive what those spaces might look like even before computer graphics were capable of rendering credible dimensional worlds. Despite those shortcomings, early games could be enthralling just on the merits of their gameplay. William Gibson, describing events that led him to coin the term 'cyberspace', observed teenagers in an arcade obsessively playing what he regarded as crudely visualized games, and he noted that 'even in this very primitive form, the kids who were playing them were so physically involved, it seemed to me that what they wanted was to be inside the games, within the notional space of the machine; the real world had disappeared for them'.[8]

This demonstrates the power of visual logic to captivate, even in the absence of sophisticated imagery. The aspect of player control in a videogame, of manipulating the primitive graphics to win, could manifest a sensation of being inside the game. Gibson, a literary progenitor of 'cyberpunk', had an influence on cinema through his published work, but the efforts of twentieth-century film directors to advance virtual reality as a genre were often sensationalist and even lurid, in examples such as *Looker* (1981), *Total Recall* (1990), *Lawnmower Man* (1992), *Virtuosity* (1995) and *Johnny Mnemonic* (1995). It seemed as if the spectacle of what could be done in this creative landscape largely fell short of expectations, even during this period's unabated rise in the popularity of computers and games, but that changed with *Ghost in the Shell*/攻殻機動隊 (1995) and especially *The Matrix*, the most consequential and influential film within the genre. Among the reasons for its impact were the millennial advancements in digital effects and its arresting 'cyberpunk' style. Its temporal shifts and innovative use of 'bullet-time' photography were a studied mix of Anime conventions and technical artistry. However, beyond its raw visual splendour, what made this film stand apart as a Hollywood feature was a game-like structure that served as an intricate puzzle. *The Matrix* required moviegoers to interpret its complexity, to distinguish the 'worlds' and to decode how things related.

Narratives like this fall within a growing trend that Thomas Elsaesser describes as mind-game films. He states that 'these show how the cinema itself has mutated: rather than "reflecting" reality, or oscillating and alternating between illusionism/realism, these films create their own referentiality, but what they refer to, above all, are the "rules of the game".[9] For a film that questions the notion of perceived reality, *The Matrix* does not diegetically indulge in tropes of madness or an unreliable narrator. Instead, it establishes its landscape through a set of rules and then it resolutely adheres to them. There is a certainty to the mechanics of its universe, and viewers who might be confused by any parts of the movie are left inclined to feel that they simply did not 'keep up' with the story (Figure 14.2).

The wonderment of *The Matrix* comes not from contemplating 'Am I even real?' but rather from being challenged by the visual logic of the film and then, in effect, solving the puzzle. Watching virtual reality does not generally throw into question our own human existence. It only just reasserts how our suspension of disbelief requires conviction to believe in the artifice of the screen world. When the Matrix-hackers working for Morpheus provide Neo's wish for 'lots of guns', the audience see a stockroom of weapons slide in, suddenly populating the white expanse with seemingly endless rows. Seen out of context, this environment of sliding gun racks is miraculous, but within the rules of the film it makes sense. It is meant to be logical. As well, it relates to the concept of weapon inventories, showing how a familiarity with videogames plays a role in priming moviegoers for the growing complexity of visual logic in cinema.

Hollywood has turned films like *The Matrix* into global franchises with sequels and transmedia spin-offs. Elsaesser notes that their global appeal and profitability has had a transformative effect on the movie industry, stating that:

> what makes the mind-game films noteworthy in this respect is the 'avant-garde'
> or 'pilot' or 'prototype' function they play within the 'institution cinema' at

Figure 14.2 Weapon inventories as 'visual logic' (*The Matrix*, Warner Bros., 1999)

this juncture, where they, besides providing 'mind-games', 'brain-candy', and, often enough, spectacular special effects, set out to train, elaborate, and, yes, 'test' the textual forms, narrative tropes, and story motifs that can serve such a renegotiation of the rules of the [Hollywood] game.[10]

Fans scrutinize the smallest details of these films on message boards and forums, presupposing that these screen worlds are to be discussed as if they were real. Scenes are re-watched and they are freeze-framed. Every aspect of the landscape is open to scrutiny and is expected to comply with the established storyline. The fans themselves enforce the orthodoxy by questioning or even ridiculing anything that is inconsistent or appears to be outside of those rules. Therefore, as studios propagate a franchise across multiple platforms, its core defining traits had best remain congruous. Adjustments, when they are made, should be gradual and well considered. The obsession of a fan-base to have such a strong regard for these details not only creates fresh topics of debate but also bolsters its loyal cult following. This makes the landscape of the franchise more meaningful, both inspiring and renewing a subculture's deep connection to it.

One can find examples of this even long before the rise of 'fan-boys' and gamers. During the active period of his work in the twentieth century, M. C. Escher was a meticulous designer of peculiar illusions. His were deceptive drawings that relied on false perspective to create paradoxes. These kinds of spaces, when rendered in 2D, are either challenging or impossible to build in 3D, but within a flat drawing the ambiguity of depth could be manipulated to make overlaps appear variously foreground or background. Stairways could be made to accommodate any different orientation. And waterfalls could marvellously be their own source of water. Although the puzzle-like novelty of his artwork made it a widely popular phenomenon, Escher's landscapes resonated deeply with mathematicians. In fact, if one could replace the attendants of the math conference mentioned in the next paragraph with fans at a Star Trek convention, this would serve to frame how these two like-minded subcultures were galvanized by creative expressions of things that were previously or otherwise confined to being 'technical'.

On the occasion of the 1954 International Congress of Mathematicians, for which a gallery show of Escher's work was sponsored, N. G. de Bruijn wrote that it was not only Escher's geometric patterns that had long captivated him, but also that he was fascinated to realize that the artist shared the 'same imagination' with him. He contended 'that the congress participants would find themselves surprised to recognize their ideas expressed in such a different form from the usual …aware of the fact that Escher was no mere illustrator of scientific and mathematical ideas, but expressed something at a deeper level in an unusual way'.[11]

Visual logic can be adapted from image to motion to interactivity, and *Monument Valley*, released in 2014 by Ustwo, is a perfect example of how the pleasures of an Escher drawing can be ported over to a game. In it, a princess named Ida must be navigated through a whimsical series of architectural spaces. Players soon come to learn that the touch screen-control allows them to rotate and slide sections of buildings. Movements of these pieces through the game space allow for Escher-like distortions. The workings of this environment make sense once players have recalibrated their expectations of perceived depth. Things that were in front can be made to go behind. Ida can be made to cross a gap simply by lining up two edges, making a 'bridge' with a tricked perspective. Once this Escher-esque operating principle is grasped, each new obstacle blocking Ida's progress can be cleverly overcome by applying visual logic. Even when played on the small screen of a smartphone, *Monument Valley* instils a sense of wonderment because the 'looking-glass' illusion is made real as one actively plays it. Prodded by finger swipes, the resulting motion of the graphics makes the isometric perspective more convincingly dimensional. This is a charming spectacle to see, but even more so to unlock. The game enables a dynamic unfolding of what Escher could only produce in static.

Douglas Hofstadter, the author of the groundbreaking book, *Gödel, Escher, Bach*, wrote:

> Each time I looked at [Escher's] *Up and Down*, in my mind's eye I would see the boy stand up, walk down a few stairs, then turn right and go down the little flight leading to the basement of the tower, open the door, and then start to climb inside the tower …and then –in some indescribable manner –would find himself upside-down, below ground level, in the basement of the tower he'd just climbed.[12]

Substituting the boy for Princess Ida, this is a reasonable description of gameplay in *Monument Valley* and Hofstadter had already day dreamed it decades earlier. If there is a clear basis for how something imaginary might work then it can be logically extended from one media to another.

Building from this, imagine that the game mechanic of long leg/short leg is now attributed to Ida. In addition to navigating the false perspectives of the landscape, a player could also make Ida step down into any gap or hole to cross them with her one very long leg. The sliding and rotating mechanisms would serve both the Escher-obstacles and the leg-obstacles. Obviously in this scenario the screen world is more complex, but one can still reasonably combine them and imagine how they can both operate together at the same time. Using digital tools, a development team could then make a simulation. And although it might be a heady environment through which to walk a game avatar, surely some nimble gamer would be able to make that leap and meaningfully engage with this new landscape.

This is an aggregate way of thinking about future entertainment, of piling separate concepts together in one space. Whether or not that would make for sensory overload depends not only on a viewer's spatial reasoning but also on how those concepts would reduce to an easily observable action. The best innovations to come will be simple enough to convey at a glance but will have a depth of meaning. These elegant new realms will 'create their own referentiality', as Elsaesser observed of mind-game films.[13] Visual logic in cinema is a visual spectacle – the audacious originality of seeing something that appears strange until it suddenly comes into focus and then makes sense by its own rules, like an X-ray.

One hundred years after Winter wrote that motion pictures captured a life that was 'as flat and fatuous as the passing bus', cinema was inexorably shifting to its digital future.[14] Computer graphics have given rise to the unseen and made possible fantastic voyages. The new millennium has largely closed the door on the long-held practice of shooting to film, perhaps giving vindication to Winter. His dismissal of film and realism can arguably be seen as forward-looking, as if he saw ahead to the wonders of glowing screen worlds and all of their potential for 'unreality'.

Oracles

An animator with a pencil is free to imagine any space. Animated films have enabled the kind of infinite prospects that software presently confers to makers of digital cinema. It is just that paper drawings are limited by (1) style, (2) breadth of detail and (3) a lack of verisimilitude. However, those are aesthetic issues. At any period in the history of cartoons, ambition could be availed by what an animator might *draw* – dinosaurs, dragons and phantasmagoria. Visual logic has long had a place within the animated *mise-en-scène*, but usually it was for the purpose of comedy, taking the form of 'sight gags'. These have been a staple of American studio cartoons. For instance, in the MGM cartoon *Deputy Droopy* (1955), a pair of robbers repeatedly runs to a nearby hilltop to scream because Droopy keeps administering some minor torture upon them. Eventually the gags become elaborate, but the first one is simple. It exists just to establish the pattern: the robbers, afraid to wake the sheriff, hold their screams until they can first race up the hill. This conveys the rules of the cartoon landscape, that each successive scream is a variant of the first. Desperately facing new pratfalls and continuously getting hurt, the robbers inventively find ways to keep rushing the hill delivering more screams. The ability of the viewer to interpret the visual logic is central to its fulfilment as humour. If you 'get it' then you laugh.

This notion of a repetitive formula was widely in use at the studios, and as practiced by directors such as Tex Avery and Chuck Jones, the escalation of gags to outrageous heights was the common template for narrative progression. Development of the cartoons by storyboards and sketches only reinforced the visual basis for the gags, but dialogue was also used to carry the humour. There were pantomime cartoons that relied on pure visual logic, but generally a main character in a cartoon had a speaking role, for both comic effect and narrative exposition. In *Deputy Droopy*, the slapstick premise is clarified when the sheriff verbally gives instructions that he will be in the next room: 'Now remember the signal, *any kind of noise*, drop a pin, let out a yell, anything, and I'll come a-shootin'.'

In contrast to American studio animation, there was a stronger tendency in Europe for short animated films to have no dialogue, rooted in the continent's diversity of language. After World War II, independent animators in Europe often received government funding and, as a measure of success to substantiate the investment, they competed for selection at film festivals. To ensure a film's reception by international audiences, it was desirous to find non-verbal ways to tell a story. Independent animators around the world will often still forgo dialogue as a practical consideration.

Of course, this can open a film to different interpretations when a character does not speak to clarify intention. Additionally, in the twentieth century, Cold War political censorship and the rise of abstraction and graphic stylization all played a role in making films more subjective or even intentionally open to interpretation. JiříTrnka's *The Hand/Ruka* (1965) was an allegory about one man's resistance to oppression. The Czech authorities were pleased when they presumed that the film implied a strong anti-American message, but Trnka later asserted that the film's message was pointedly aimed at the communist Czech government instead. In a sense, it did not matter. The film's sparse and allegoric setting allowed viewers to imagine that the antagonist, a human hand, symbolized any domineering power at all.

The short film *Balance* (1989), animated with stop motion by Wolfgang and Christoph Lauenstein, also employs a figurative setting. It shows an escalation of greed among men who reside on a levitating square plank. Their survival depends on spacing their weight evenly across the surface so they do not tip off when it teeters dangerously. Once the mechanics that impel this landscape are made clear to a viewer, the sparseness of the screen world puts a focus on its visual logic. The ground plane continues to pivot while the men walk precariously upon it. Then a new object is introduced, a music box that slides around among them. As they grow to covet the music box, the balance they have maintained is completely undone and they exploit the shifting angles to knock each other over the edge.

It is a poignant story about obsession and violence told through the prism of its minimalist setting. By observing how this small world operates, we infer the desires and emotions of the characters living there. *Balance* is not fixed in a specific place or time. In fact, the abstraction can be seen as obscuring the sense of 'otherness' we may instinctively apply to a faraway geography that we actually recognize. In a film allegory, the screen becomes a mirror and we can imagine ourselves operating and navigating within those same constraints.

That inclination to find meaning in the abstract has parallels to the ancient practice of consulting an oracle. When the leadership of Athens went to the Oracle of Delphi to seek advice for fighting the Persian Empire, the Athenians were cryptically told that they would be safe only behind 'wooden walls'. By heeding that advice and interpreting it to mean they should take refuge on their fleet of wooden ships, they famously defeated the Persian armada in 480 BC. To truly evoke the Oracle, a modern film should be more than a clever allegory. After all, the Athenians held the conviction that just one insight into the future would provide their salvation. While that does not have to be the threshold for oracular ambitions in cinema, it at least suggests that a viewer should believe that the imparted message holds an underlying truth. Contemporary moviegoers, just like the peoples of antiquity, can accept meaning divined from the mysterious.

James Whitney's animated film *Lapis* (1966) is a meditative flow of geometric patterns based on the ritual symbology of Hinduism. When the symmetry of dots keeps shifting like a kaleidoscope, it shows the power of abstraction to imply meaning. These movements, both emanating from a centre and flowing to it, are drawn from the concept of the *mandala*, a metaphysical encircling image. In Whitney's film the *mandala* feels like a cosmic entity that weaves and morphs to the rising intensity of Indian sitar music. The turning rings have the hypnotic effect of drawing a viewer downwards as if through spirals to an origin point.

A Hindu practitioner would recognize the animated *mandala* in relation to its traditional forms, so *Lapis* has a specific cultural and spiritual reference. However, the notion of a circle has been theorized by Jung to be evocative of a sensation of completeness.[15] If symbolic meaning in the Jungian interpretation of dreams compels it a primordial place within human consciousness, then Whitney's *mandala* cannot be characterized as simply a cultural appropriation. Its visual substance can be said to resonate deep within us, awakened as a cellular memory.

This is fascinating to ponder as a code or imprint that has some basis as a rule within a larger game that we 'play'. It allows that visual logic does not just work as an operating principle for a contrived screen world, but that it also informs the deepest mechanics of human life. *Mandalas* have been used in meditation for the purpose of internalizing the image of a perfect circle. This requires clearing one's mind and drawing an inward focus, yet a film like *Lapis* can facilitate a similar experience through nothing more than passive viewership. The film can be seen as both an aesthetic aspect of Hindu ritual – like flowers, incense, lamps – or it can be the entire experience in itself. By referencing what might be visual semantics from a human or cosmic dreamscape, it becomes universal in its mystical appeal.

To animate the *mandala* in *Lapis*, James Whitney carefully designed its patterns of dots and hand painted them on to cels. He then 'filmed them using a computerized animation stand (the first "Motion-Control" camera, invented by his older brother John) which could shoot very precise multiple exposures in calibrated displacements that turned 100 dots into thousands of dots in variegated colors with intricate changing patterns created by transitory trajectories'.[16] It is evident that to choreograph all this motion he needed an underlying algorithmic framework imposed with machine-like order. In effect, Whitney was a mathematical artist whose work was complex enough to require analogue computing. Yet, when audiences respond to the precision and integrity of his math-based animation, do they then perceive its perfect order as 'god-like' or divine? Elegant geometry can be wondrous, seeming to impart a truth that is greater than what algorithmic expression should warrant. By visualizing the math, the constraining rules show how beauty must abide the unwavering mechanics of the universe.

Another animator whose renowned technical skill informed his creative work was Norman McLaren. He based his experimental film *Canon* (1964) on the musical technique of playing a melody against itself in overlapping intervals. Each of three sections in the film employs a different rendition of a canon. It culminates in a remarkable sequence produced with an optical printer to superimpose the same film clip of a man in a hat. He crosses a stage from left to right with a series of actions along the way. By printing the clips to run simultaneously on staggered delays, the copies of this single performance begin to curiously relate to one another. After a short time, the man in the hat engages meaningfully with himself at different beats in time. The delays allow him, for instance, to kick a version of himself that is doing exactly what he did eight seconds prior: taking a bow and doffing his hat. At that point (189 frames earlier, according to McLaren's technical notes) he was greeting the man he is presently kicking, but at this new interval that same man is bowing to yet another arriving 'clone'.

This is the nature of *Canon*, a recursive and self-referencing visual paradox. From its chain of images arises a distinctly mathematical structure. The filming and optical processing had to be carefully planned and timed to enable the interlocking performances to synchronize. McLaren's clever directing yields an example of what Douglas Hofstadter calls a 'strange loop'. It was, after all, the looping nature of canons that touched off Hofstadter's intellectual excursion through the shared terrain of Gödel, Escher and Bach. He describes it as a phenomenon that 'occurs whenever, by moving upwards (or downwards) through the levels of some hierarchical system, we unexpectedly find ourselves right back where we started'.[17] Then, alluding to M. C. Escher's *Waterfall*, he suggests a reader 'compare its six-step endlessly falling loop with the six-step endlessly rising loop of [Bach's] "Canon per Tonos". The similarity of vision is remarkable'.[18]

Such a puzzle-like quality in art can be a source of amusement or it can activate a primal sense of wonder, disputing notions of sequencing and order and scale. Within an atom, is there a galaxy? Does time ever end? Will the universe repeat? Why am I here? *Can I really see a world in a grain of sand?* Even as physicists knit together a wider fabric of human understanding, the soul-searching questions of individual purpose and mortality will always persist. There will never be a shortage of yearning to know things whose answers seem to lie in the stars.

Audiences may come to regard the increasingly challenging narratives of digital-age cinema as enlightenment-by-oracle. The interpreted outcome of Athens' wooden walls is a metaphor for any oblique or puzzling landscape. As the viewer interacts with such a space, it can lead to personal meaning and ultimately a level of fulfilment through a spiritual or intellectual journey. However, a cinematic oracle should demand something of the viewer in the same way that a mind-game film requires a viewer to unlock the mystery of a screen world.

The feature film *Life of Pi* (2012) offers such an experience (Figure 14.3). In the aftermath of a tragedy at sea, a boy named Pi must share a lifeboat with a deadly tiger. Within this limited 'stage', the film plays as an allegory. It posits that the vigilance Pi must maintain to stay alive is its own unlikely reward because it sustains him from later succumbing to the hidden danger of a floating mangrove island. However, the earlier occupants of the boat – a zebra, an orangutan and a hyena – have no lessons learned to take away from the ordeal. They are all killed, victims of the lifeboat's desperate game of survival. Like *Balance*, each murder changes the 'equation' of the locale. A series of moves and countermoves leaves the boy and the tiger in a draw.

Figure 14.3 The stereoscopic ocean (*Life of Pi*, Fox 2000 Pictures, 2012)

The simplicity of the minimal setting is deceiving. To believably render the animals trapped on this small boat, it took the resources of multi-continental film production and visual effects technologies. The struggle of the boy to overcome each new setback was a careful orchestration of logic puzzles, each solution followed by a further complication. The visual effects made possible a fantasy that looked real, availing its director of an epic animated parable. The stereoscopic landscape was a culmination of painstaking efforts to track the spatial depths of on-set cinematography made difficult by shooting in a large tank of water. Real footage was composited with highly detailed 3D animation of the shipwrecked animals, ocean waves and bioluminescent marine life to create a menagerie of ethereal sights.

Life of Pi demonstrates how digital-age cinema allows the improbable to feel authentic, achieving this in spite of classical allusions to mariners' odysseys and even Aesop fables. As a narrative conceit it is really not much less contrived than, for example, the dreamscapes of Christopher Nolan's *Inception* (2010). When the protagonist in that film appears to lose touch with reality, professing he might stay within the dream, this manifests as an ambiguous ending. The hierarchy of dreams in *Inception* serves as an oracle, an illusory architecture that impels a journey.

Life of Pi also 'evokes the oracle' by posing two different versions of its survival story. Like a mind-game film, it is a puzzle that leaves viewers to ponder what they have seen. Yet, as an exemplar of new possibilities in cinema, it convincingly offers the grandeur and mystery of the universe. This is articulated by Pi when he says, 'And so it goes with God.' The paradox of faith is that it offers no proof. The miracle of the human condition is the inclination to believe. Consequently, a spiritual quest can seem much like Hofstadter's 'strange loops', where we unexpectedly find ourselves right back where we started when the journey is over. Yet by a different measure we are *not* right back where we started. We have engaged with an opportunity to evolve and spiritualize.

If an oracle is a vessel for personal reflection and interpretation, then screen worlds are a place for oracles to flourish in a modern context. Visual effects in cinema will only grow and necessitate different narrative trajectories to support them. As many aspects of games find greater currency in all media, the allure of visual logic will likely expand. And, in so doing, landscapes as stirring as an Escher tower or a *Portal* maze can offer inspiration for directors to envision new kinds of film mechanics. At their finest, such premises and realms will fill us with the awe of a great journey and the wonder of discovery.

Notes

1 Miguel Sicart, 'Defining Game Mechanics', *Game Studies: The International Journal of Computer Game Research* 8.2 (2008): 1.

2 Jim Al-Khalili, 'The Paradox of Schrödinger's Cat', in *Paradox: The Nine Greatest Enigmas in Physics* (New York: Crown Publishing, 2012), 179–180.

3 Denise Blake Oleksijczuk, *The First Panoramas: Visions of British Imperialism* (Minneapolis: University of Minnesota Press, 2011), 5–7.

4 Alfred Octavius Winter, 'The Cinematograph', in *The New Review*, Vol. XIV, ed. W. E. Henley (London: 1896): 507.

5 Ibid., 512.

6 Ibid.

7 Ibid., 513.

8 William Gibson, 'The Art of Fiction No. 211', interview by David Wallace-Wells, *The Paris Review*, no. 197 (2011), 132.

9 Thomas Elsaesser, 'The Mind-Game Film', in *Puzzle Films: Complex Storytelling in Contemporary Cinema*, ed. Warren Buckland (New York: John Wiley & Sons, 2009), 39.

10 Ibid., 38.

11 Michele Emmer, 'Art, Math, and Cinema', in *M. C. Escher's Legacy*, ed. Doris Schattschneider and Michele Emmer (Berlin: Springer-Verlag, 2003), 143.

12 Douglas R. Hofstadter, 'Mystery, Classicism, Elegance: An Endless Chase After Magic', in *M. C. Escher's Legacy*, ed. Doris Schattschneider and Michele Emmer (Berlin: Springer-Verlag, 2003), 28.

13 Elsaesser, 'The Mind-Game Film', 39.

14 Winter, 'The Cinematograph', 511.

15 Louise Child, *Tantric Buddhism and Altered States of Consciousness: Durkheim, Emotional Energy and Visions of the Consort* (Farnham: Ashgate Publishing, 2007), 11.

16 William Moritz, 'James Whitney', in *Articulated Light: The Emergence of Abstract Film in America*, ed. Bruce Posner and Gerald O'Grady (Boston, MA: Harvard Film Archive/Anthology Film Archives, 1995), 11.

17 Douglas R. Hofstadter, *Gödel, Escher, Bach: An Eternal Golden Braid* (New York: Basic Books, 1979), 10.

18 Ibid., 11–13.

15

Beyond the Animated Landscape: Videogame Glitches and the Sublime

Alan Meades

This anthology is ostensibly concerned with landscape – with its depiction, presentation and animation within a range of media, and the complexities of representation and meaning that this raises. This chapter approaches landscape from the animated context of the contemporary videogame, where its visual depiction, the challenges it presents and its gradual exploration and navigation is not only instrumental in forming the way that players play, but the way that gamespace and landscape are understood.

While it may seem initially curious to talk of our understanding of landscape, we should remember that landscape and its depictions are steeped in meaning and significance. Our depictions of landscape speak of our human relationship with our surroundings and to a lesser extent, with nature, an example of which is to briefly consider what it means to hold a scalable, interactive global animated landscape, in our hands, as we casually browse and trace our fingers across a Google map on a smartphone. This is a message of technological mastery and visibility, where the enormity and scale of the world is literally reduced and simplified so that it not only fits into our pockets but also responds to our whim. We may feel confident, secure and knowledgeable, and landscape conceptually becomes more like a background, merely something that exists, to be traversed or navigated in order to reach a destination.

We should recognize that perspectives like these are as much the product of the prevailing rhetoric of human mastery (covering progress, technology and attitudes of civilization) as they are about landscape, and therefore are subject to change. We now find ourselves in a culture that subordinates, simplifies and makes landscape *visible*; the landscape is visually awesome, but subordinate to human whim – to be navigated, carved or protected. This is in contrast to historic landscape depictions, such as those seen within the landscape painting of the Romantic period, which often contained a rhetoric of *inscrutability* and as a result the natural world and the landscape took on a feeling of awesome unknowable hostility. This meaning/feeling, understood as the *sublime*, has had such a significant impact upon our understanding of landscape through painting and other cultural outputs from the eighteenth century onwards that its representational style – its aesthetic conventions – have become central to our depiction of landscape to this day. While we have retained its conventions of representation, such as the emphasis of scale, spectacle and awe, over time the aspect of inscrutability (and the unease this fostered) has diminished. As a result, we now look back at a Romantic landscape painting that looks awesome, but to us does not feel inscrutable. It looks the same but our relationship to it has changed: it has lost the terrible spectacle, that is, the sublime.

The reason to point this out is not simply to highlight that things have changed, reducing our ability to access the sublime, but also to emphasize that our depictions of landscape are meaningful: not simply on account of saying things about the world, but crucially our relationship with it. Landscape paintings, animated landscapes, videogame landscapes, each attempts to position the human (both as in humankind and as in spectator) in relation to landscape and therefore contains an underlying rhetoric that seeks to bifurcate our understanding of this relationship.

However, this chapter does not approach animated landscape from a passive stance, exploring landscapes simply as designed, but introduces the added complexity of player action, specifically an exotic mode of play, glitching, where players actively seek out and employ mechanisms to subvert and exploit game code.[1] Glitching presents an even more interesting context against which to reconsider the animated landscape – as we begin to explore the subverted, remediated animated landscape, we begin to interrogate our constructed understanding of landscape.

This chapter explores the impact of glitching, *the intentional triggering of software fail-states*, upon the coherence of representation and meaning in videogame animated landscapes. It argues that the glitch-induced code-spasms, the incoherent visual artefacts and errata that erupt through exploitation, alter our understanding of animated landscapes. Initially, glitches challenge and subvert what we will call the 'operatic sublime', the aesthetic vocabulary of landscape representation, originating from Romantic landscape painting, and now more generally employed to present awesome gamespaces and vistas. And secondarily we will explore the ways that through introducing more extreme fail-states glitches, we reconnect animated landscapes with the inscrutability and terrifying awe traditionally associated with the sublime, as understood as the 'technological sublime'. This chapter therefore explores the relationships between the animated landscape, the sublime and unexpected and often censured play styles in contemporary videogames.

Landscape and the sublime

Prior to the development of the sublime as an identifiable cultural motif landscape was various approached as decoration, as documentation or as a meaningful signal of ownership, power or geopolitical situation. For example, throughout the fourteenth to sixteenth centuries, landscape is used primarily as backdrop to religious scenes and portraits. In the seventeenth-century *Dutch Golden Age* we see landscape as political discourse, with the intentional depiction of northern European pastoral landscapes utilizing the conventions of Italian painting regarded as a statement of rejection of Catholic rule. While in the eighteenth century we begin to see the emergence of 'capricci' – landscapes for decoration that depict imaginary yet appropriately modelled architectural features in picturesque settings.

The sublime is a concept closely associated with landscape painting in the mid to late eighteenth century, particularly the work of the Romantic landscape painters including J. M. W. Turner, Caspar David Freidrich and John Constable. These works differ from the previous use of landscape by giving the landscape itself a character. It is not merely backdrop, status symbol, political statement or pleasant image, but an image where the landscape takes a stance in relation to the viewer, often highlighting the scale, vitality, mystery and spectacle of space it depicts. In landscape paintings, such as those by Turner or Freidrich, we feel the sublime through the enormity and power of nature (and often the corresponding fragility of the human), such as through witnessing the swirling mists that overpower and engulf Turner's steam trains or warships, or perhaps through the sheer scale of snow-capped mountain peaks and sunsets, and the tiny terrorized silhouetted figures that cling onto the rock faces in Freidrich's work. These paintings were created to unsettle the viewer, to make them pause and feel humbled by the scale, hostility and power of the (super) natural character of the landscape, that allude to the colossal unknowable aspect of the eighteenth-century natural world. At its core the sublime refers to a humbling feeling of awe and wonder in the face of greatness, perhaps highlighted by magnitudes of scale, which in turn communicates an impression of unknowability and even spirituality.

More broadly, the sublime also became an important concept in philosophical aesthetics. According to Edmund Burke, whose *A Philosophical Enquiry into the Origin of Our Ideas of the Sublime and Beautiful* is regarded the canonical text on the matter, the sublime was dependent on the judicious application of seven aspects: Darkness, Obscurity, Privation (or depravation), Vastness, Magnificence, Loudness or Suddenness.[2] By carefully utilizing these motifs within their paintings, embracing dark and light contrasts, obscuring elements, focusing on subject matter of toil and strife, and through offering spectacular magnificence opulence or beauty and order, the artist offered an image that not only depicted landscape but had a grander, sublime resonance. The landscapes took on additional character, presenting something awesome and frequently unknowable – beyond normal experience, perhaps even beyond the reach of human understanding, and the notions of omnipotence and spirituality that this entails.

Aesthetic attitudes and tastes have changed enormously since the eighteenth century, and so too have our relationships with nature and the meaning of landscape. As a result, over time the seven aspects have become part of a generalized visual language that we associate with landscape. We perceive that we live in a world where digital technologies have simultaneously mapped, shrunk and reconfigured the landscape expanse. We now hold scalable interactive maps in our hands, and the natural wilderness – the awesome mountains, plains and geological forms – no longer resonate with the awesome terror of the unknown, but are reassuringly docile in their simulated form. However, when the technology fails, the battery dies, or the signal is lost, the landscape is suddenly untamed. It shatters pretence of our technological mastery of space, destroying our imagined and digitally supported synthesis with landscape. It is perhaps no wonder that the operatic sublime no longer holds its terrifying aspect so central to the landscape paintings of the eighteenth century, and we now gaze at these images as neutered 'awesome' representations. They look impressive, but our version of impressive lacks the vertiginous terror that it once held. The sublime becomes a mode of description, or another technique to employ in order to create 'awesome' landscape depictions. We read these depictions as 'awesome', but dislocated from the terrifying and spiritual associations that Burke and the Romantic painters were preoccupied with.

The sublime 'as process' is now employed whenever an awesome landscape is required, whether static or animated, and we now see its use in paintings, photography, the filmic and the animated, including the animated landscapes of contemporary videogames (something we will touch upon in more detail shortly). In *Beauty and the Contemporary Sublime* Jeremy Gilbert-Rolfe argues that over the twentieth century as the sublime appeared to diminish within landscape painting, it was not that it ceased to exist as an aesthetic dynamic, but that it shifted location and manifestation.[3] Gilbert-Rolfe suggests that what was once seen in imposing inscrutability of painting shifted on a contemporary notion of 'blankness'. As Gilbert-Rolfe puts it, we live in a culture where 'the terrible infinity or obligatory inscrutability of the sublime [is] now being a property of technology rather than nature'.[4]

While specifically talking about a televisual, or video graphic, context, Gilbert-Rolfe's observations apply even more fittingly to the everything machines of digital culture, and the ways in which the brushed aluminium laptops or black gloss videogame consoles that project animated landscapes onto screens offer no insight into their operation or potential. Whereas the Romantic operatic sublime existed in the swirling noise and cacophony of nature—of obscure mists, dark chasms and colossal mountain ranges, the awesome inscrutability of the sublime now exists in the blankness of technology. To put it more directly: we now feel a sense of awe, unknowability and the presence of non-human consciousness when confronted by the power of a computer, and especially when looking at the immutability of silicon and computer chassis. These technologies appear capable of unpredictable and powerful things, yet offer no real indication to their process to all but the most technically adept. For the majority they are awesome, unknowable and intimidating.

From the context of the technological sublime, blankness 'is now the sign of an invisible and ubiquitous technological presence'.[5] This is at once the cold black blankness of the unpowered or faulty mobile phone, and sensed in the rising anxiety that comes with the loss of a GPS or mobile phone signal when we have become subordinate to networked technologies to navigate and get our work done in the world. In this respect our contemporary attitude towards the technological sublime reconnects with the spiritual aspect of the operatic sublime, notably the notion of it having logic beyond our comprehension, and the resultant expectation that there is the possibility of another possibly inhuman intelligence that is capable of understanding it. In the eighteenth century this manifested itself in a sense of spiritual otherness, the power of a creator, while from Gilbert-Rolfe's secular position the technological sublime suggests an 'ungrounded intelligence, electronically supported'.[6]

> Technology has subsumed the idea of the sublime because it, whether to a greater
> extent or an equal extent than nature, is terrifying in the limitless unknowability
> of its potential, while being entirely a product of knowledge – i.e., it combines
> limitlessness with pure ratio – and is thus at once unbounded by the human,
> and, as knowledge, a trace of the human now out of the latter's control.[7]

From such a perspective we can trace the sublime within technology and by extension within the products of this technology. In the case of the computer it is therefore possible to glimpse the blank technological sublime in the computer itself, *its blank case, the inscrutability of its components, or the way that the separate modules work as a whole*, but also in the software that it executes, *the uncanny output of a speech recognition system, the behaviour of an artificial chat-bot, or the autonomy of a videogame landscape.* The technological sublime can then be felt in the materiality of technology, and in its products, in the case of videogames these are the white and black console boxes, and the games that operate upon them, however, software and hardware is designed to be user-friendly, to wield to the demands of the human. In this respect we might argue that the design of user-interfaces, of games, controllers and interactive experiences, is done to minimize inscrutability and incoherence – in other words, to hide the technological sublime. When using computing technologies in their normal or optimal operational conditions, the technological sublime is not felt.

The technological sublime within the videogame therefore derives its awe not from the landscape artfully depicted on the screen, but by the very method of depiction itself, the awesomeness of the technology—its ability to conjure up the animated landscape itself. The technological sublime is the unknowability, the sense of power, and the feeling of enormity that is situated in the technology itself and in the case of these animated landscapes is visible when one is able to see beyond the representation, beyond the familiar textures, the 3D models and the animations, when one fleetingly glimpses the entropic void beyond.

Before we explore the nature of videogame animated landscapes it is worth considering the impact of the glitch (an intentionally triggered and exploited error), and fail-states, upon the coherence of a computing technology and the visibility of the technological sublime. In an essay on videogames and the technological sublime Eugénie Shinkle characterizes the impact of a fail-state, suggesting that such events 'shatter the bond between player and technology, disrupting the flow of the game, leaving the gamer powerless, and foregrounding the complexity of the underlying technology, its distance from the human'.[8] The player is exposed to the digital sublime as opposed to software designed to offer coherence and to minimize affect. Thus, exposed to the technological sublime the player experiences 'not a logical, reasoned perception' but 'a visceral response that exceeds the powers of reason – an estimation of magnitude through intuition'.[9] Or, returning to Gilbert-Rolfe's non-human intelligence, 'the player is confronted by an inexpressive intelligence, a pure, depersonalised power, a technological other'.[10] Failure events therefore subvert the mechanisms of coherence and highlight the sublime.

Thus, within a videogame we see a hollow application of the aesthetic language of the operatic sublime in the depiction of awesome landscapes; this uses the conventions but does not aim to contain an added layer of inscrutability. We also see the technological sublime in the potential of the hardware platform and in the power of the landscapes it conjures, but each of these are partially neutralized by intuitive user-interface design that attempt to make the technology work on a human level. It is therefore when error states are introduced we are able to more clearly see the 'technological other' free from the camouflage of coherence. It is in fail-states, induced by critical failure or by intentional glitching, that we view the sublime in a videogame animated landscape.

Videogame animated landscapes

Mainstream contemporary videogames often make use of an 'open-world' model of game design, where the player navigates a 3D animated landscape through their play. Examples vary, including Rockstar Games' faithful recreation of post-war LA in *LA Noire* (2011), a post-millennial pastiche of the same metropolis in *Grand Theft Auto V* (2013), the generic distillation of the cinematic Western into fifteen square miles of digital terrain in *Red Dead Redemption* (2010). Useful contextual information about the nuance of navigating and populating Rockstar Games' worlds, specifically *LA Noire* and *Red Dead Redemption* can be found in the work of Chris Pallant.[11] Open world games are particular in the sense that they explicitly present a navigable animated landscape that works upon the mantra that if something is visible it should be accessible, by contrast other games that present animated landscapes, such as the *Call of Duty* (2003–2014) franchise offer restricted sections of larger landscapes, where the player is limited by the design of the space – stopped by obstacles or the dreaded invisible barrier. While both the open and linear game models present navigable landscapes the former attempts spatial and contextual coherence, while the latter affords a more abstract gamespace – perhaps more akin to a carefully disguised chessboard than a landscape per se.

Each of these videogame animated landscapes also adopts a certain character, which is evidenced through its level of hostility towards the player, and which becomes critical in motivating and rationalizing the player's actions. Through navigating and interacting with the animated landscape we come to understand *Red Dead Redemption*'s picturesque brutality, *LA Noire*'s sun-drenched and only partly rotten post-war metropolis, or *Grand Theft Auto V*'s parody of a Los Angeles where the American dream has soured into a cut-throat landscape of poverty and excess. Each of these characters becomes apparent through the opportunities that the animated landscape offers us, and this in turn is instrumentally influenced by its design and presentation, whether it is the placement of an out-of-town general store calling to be held-up in *Grand Theft Auto V* or the vantage points in *Red Dead Redemption* from which to survey the bandit camp before seeking the bloody bounty.

Each of these is a sculpted landscape, carefully created to entertain, motivate and captivate players, their character contextualizes play and frames meaning— we feel the hostility of the frontier, the simmering perversion beyond the picket fences, or the enabling indifference of the metropolis. In each case the character of the animated landscape is felt as much as it is seen, the player is an antagonist working in relation to this character, and it is partially the navigation of, orientation with and eventual mastery of these landscapes that adds profound meaning to the played experience.

The characterization is the product of careful modelling, design and simulation, resulting in sprawling, semi-autonomous coherent environments. Game designers produce this through the application of a number of techniques: *rapid iteration and analysis* to test and fine-tune the landscape for coherence and opportunity; *evocative narrative elements* that present recognizable iconography and signs that reassure players and encourage certain ways of interpretation and response; and *focalization* techniques to draw attention and lead players to certain sequences of events. This is in turn based upon extensive research conducted to ensure that the generic expectations, geographical qualities and visual motifs within the landscape are consistent and correct.

The efforts taken to create this coherence can be seen in the steps taken to distil the entire Californian repertoire into forty-nine digital square-miles of animated landscape in *Grand Theft Auto V*. Aaron Garbut, art director at Edinburgh-based Rockstar North, detailed the extent of the research exercise, 'we've shot over 250,000 images and hours of video. We've driven all over Los Angeles and out into the surrounding desert, towns, and forests'.[12] In addition, this research was then coordinated with the various art teams and with the studio heads and series producer – the point here is that this enables animated landscapes to best capture the essence of the real-life referents, best straddling the relationship between reality and the spaces then simulated. While in the case of an entirely imagined landscape, and alien landscape, in *Mass Effect 2* (2010) for example, the research simply takes a different form, relying upon the existing cultural expressions, films, television programmes, books and artwork.

Once videogame landscapes begin to take form they are subject to rigorous iterative challenge in order to maximize coherence and enjoyment. Garbut's team challenge their prototypical spaces with the following criteria:

> [D]oes it look good enough? Does it play well enough? Does it feel distinctive? Does it sit well with its surroundings? Does it get across the character of the area we're trying to create? How does it sit in terms of vistas and general sculptural composition? Do we need more color, contrast, branding, or lighting? Does it feel weathered? Does it have a sense of place and history? Can we layer story over it, whether through ambient, 'generalized story' …or whether it's layering our actual story over it: mission detailing, filling out areas that belong to characters, random events or beats, and random characters you might meet.[13]

It is worth noting Garbut's '*vistas and general sculptural composition*', '*sense of place and history*' and the tension between '*generalized story*' and '*actual story*'. These are the primary concerns of the open world gamespace in terms of meaning: the way it looks, the way it seems to work, what the game needs you to do to progress, and what you might spontaneously get up to as a diversion. All of these concerns, so instrumental to establishing the meaning and interpretation of the game are situated within a relationship to the animated landscape. As Garbut points out: 'We've considered the placement of every tree'.[14]

Michael Nitsche calls the various objects and signs that a designer carefully places within an animated landscape 'evocative narrative elements'.[15] These evocative narrative elements are then carefully arranged (as with Garbut's trees) to ensure that certain sequences and activities appear more natural, leading to certain ways of playing. This range from a player spontaneously attempting to jump a river in a car, perhaps making use of a natural ramp made by the curve of the land, or a construction site offering pyrotechnical opportunities for a scripted gangland fire-fight. Alternatively, lines of sight and the opening-up of vistas encourage progress in certain directions, or orders of progression. This placement of objects, lines of sight and opportunities is considered 'focalization' – it draws focus to certain interpretations and uses. The animated landscape is therefore characterful, giving the impression of a living, breathing, ecosystem and contains additional triggers that invite spontaneous and scheduled play interactions.

Nitsche explains the use of evocative narrative elements thus:

> The elements are not 'stories' but suggestive markings. They are clustered in certain ways and aimed to trigger reactions in players in order to help them create their own interpretations …Evocative narrative elements encourage players to project meaning onto events, objects, and spaces in game worlds. They help to infuse significance. Their value is not realized on the level of the element itself but in the way players read and connect them.[16]

Nitsche asserts that the connections and meanings are made with the player, and therefore it is essential that the spaces are tested for coherence (hence Garbut's criteria) lest something about the space present incongruity that challenges the growing understanding of the landscape and its character. In an open world gamespace where the player simultaneously traverses and makes sense of the landscape, the order and nature of the interactions that they have translate directly into the way that they understand the character of the gamespace and the game itself. The narrative is constructed in the players' minds; it becomes a response, triggered by the comprehension of signs and interaction with them (including the sequence and type of interaction). This is in effect the layering of coherence over a gamespace, and an attempt to hide the technological sublime, but perhaps less grandly – it is the process of designing an enjoyable gamespace. Much of the challenge and fun of the game is learning what to do, the patterns, causality and rules, as much as then doing what we believe are required, and the trick of a superb designer is to manage the balance between instruction and inscrutability.

While animated landscapes can certainly be imposing, breath-taking and awesome, as anyone who has taken the time to climb *Grand Theft Auto V*'s

Mount Chiliad range, or experienced *Red Dead Redemption*'s 'ride to Mexico', would attest, videogames are designed to present a narrative of personal mastery as opposed to domination. The vast majority of games hide a narrative of mastery – mastery as the player deciphers the processes that underpin the game, or develops the twitch muscle-memory and gameplay tactics to beat the game. Open world games present a landscape book ended with the assumption that, providing the player invests sufficient time to develop understanding and expertise, they will be able to master and dominate the landscape. This might take the form of galloping across the prairie on a jet-black warhorse and a fully filled dead-eye gauge, or screaming under the Vinewood Boulevard highway bridge in a *P-996 Lazer* attack fighter. The animated landscape is a challenging invitation to explore and to understand. In so doing the videogame animated landscape intentionally avoids inscrutability, it is instead a puzzle to be solved, and thus cannot connect with the technological sublime in any way other than being an awesome picturesque that presents an impressive landscape.

Glitching

While most players will enjoy navigating and traversing an animated landscape as they slowly become aware of the structures, processes and demands placed upon them by a videogame, there are other forms of play that intentionally subvert this process. Glitching, for example, is a process by which players, *glitchers*, identify weaknesses in the simulation of a game that can be exploited to alter the play experience. Glitches are truly protean, taking advantage of a poorly defined videogame object characteristic or a flabbily handled line of code, and therefore can manifest themselves in any aspect of the videogame that is dependent on code. Glitches that are generally sought out are those that offer some level of competitive advantage within a videogame, typically by enabling players to navigate animated landscapes in irregular ways – such as enabling a player to reach an intentionally unobtainable location in a landscape, or even falling beyond and under an animated landscape. Glitchers who find themselves outside of the normal boundaries of the animated landscape are generally no longer subject to the same restrictions as within, they then are free to explore and exploit this position. One salient example would be to attack other players from an unexpected and invisible vantage point under the map, but equally the same process may be used to explore and to see what the videogame engine creates.

Those who use glitches to go 'under the map' are presented with shifting incoherent vistas that shimmer, fracture and break, as planes and objects are pushed in-and-out of system memory. We see areas of vastness, geometric geological outcroppings and swirls of emptiness that not only closely resemble the works of Romantic landscape painters but also expand upon the concepts they proposed.

Glitches are generally discovered by an individual or small team of glitchers and then shared with the general public on video- sharing sites such as YouTube, including detailed instructions allowing replication. For those interested in using glitches identified by others it is simply a case of searching the web, while for those wishing to identify glitches themselves there is a relatively small set of processes that can be done to expose latent flaws within a game. This is a result of commercial videogames being produced on a small number of middleware game engines, each of which has its specific weaknesses. Once the glitcher knows of these weaknesses, such as an inconsistent handling of overlapping objects within an animated landscape that the game engine attempts to overcome by pushing an object upwards, creating an 'elevator glitch', all they need do is set up these conditions repeatedly until a glitch becomes apparent. As videogame engine middleware is iteratively updated exploitable flaws have remained broadly consistent over multiple releases, with many engines remaining susceptible to the same glitches irrespective of the engine build. What this does not expose is the time required to identify glitches and the dedication and focus required of those identifying them. In my experience of attacking newly released games in an attempt to discover glitches before others it is common for prototypical glitches to become apparent every half-hour or so, often depending on the budget of the game and the amount of quality assurance bug testing it has utilized. These prototypical glitches are often frustratingly partial, often allowing the player to access an unanticipated area, but not to trigger full game-failure, or to venture into the truly abstract spaces under the map. Glitch knowledge is incremental and prototypical glitches occasionally do yield game-breaking full glitches, but while the time required varies, it often takes multiple hours. I've certainly been part of an unsuccessful hunt with three other glitchers on a newly released Call of Duty expansion pack that lasted for four hours before I retired, and for the other more dedicated glitchers, went on for eight. I would consider it a very good day if I found a glitch in an hour.

Needless to say, despite the time taken to identify glitches there are many players willing to do so, and many more who are keen to use them to help beat games, to antagonize and dominate other players, or to subvert game spaces. While it is likely to be a somewhat esoteric and peripheral use of glitching, I find it especially interesting to use glitches from an aesthetic perspective, exploring what animated landscapes the videogame produces while under fail-states. For me this has the capacity to enrich the experience of the videogame text by offering a different perspective, and, returning to the theme of this chapter, to also afford a glimpse of the technological sublime.

If we remember that videogames are designed to minimize exposure to the incoherent inner workings of the algorithmic technological sublime, then using glitches begins to undermine this process. Employing glitches or exploits one is able to intentionally remediate and challenge the relationship between the represented sublime – the animated landscape – and the technological sublime beyond. The glitch enables us to force the game into a fail-state and tease at the relationships between animated landscape and the sublime. This is illustrated through the following glitching vignette from Rockstar Games' *Grand Theft Auto V*.

A glitch vignette

I pull my cherry red Bullet muscle car to the curb on El Burro Boulevard, stepping out onto the hot asphalt. In the distance I can make out the seaport, its loading cranes shining a curious baby-blue against the plum dusk sky. I walk round the front of the car and onto the scrub at the curbside, heading towards a road bridge that spans a cliff running down to the sea below. I walk past a palm tree growing at the cliff edge and step right up to the bridge, the hard concrete inches away from my face. I stride forwards, colliding with the solid wall. Yet, instead of being stopped, I pass straight through the barrier finding myself in a sarcophagus-like space under the bridge, surrounded by concrete walls on all sides. The sound of passing cars reverberates in the hollow and I walk towards the next concrete surface to test its permeability. I push through this one as easily as the last, but find myself falling down, screaming as I hurtle towards water far below. The impact with the water rips the scream from my lungs and I struggle up towards the surface, taking a deep breath when I finally break through. I recognize my surroundings, a strangely inverted version of El Burro Heights – somehow I'm beneath it looking upwards. Up above me mundane life continues, I see a line of cars snaking their way along the freeway in the far distance, oil derricks, industrial units, a trailer park, all being slowly lit by streetlamps as the night begins to close in. Police sirens wail somewhere in the city, there's the hum of traffic off of the bridge somewhere up above me, and the gentle click-clacking of an unseen train, mixed with the splashes and ripples as I tread water in this strange subterranean lake. I cautiously paddle forwards pausing to gaze up at the spectacle above me, as I move, sections of floor, wall, and landscape blink in and out of existence and I am struck by the juxtaposition of the mundane, and the swirling vastness where the objects are translucent or missing. I swim until I reach a strange maritime object – the water stops at a hard edge, elevated in space, as if within a colossal glass tank. I touch the edge and once again fall through, this time into the swirling pitch darkness that I glimpsed through fractures in the animated landscape. As I plummet I flip over onto my back, watching as El Burro Heights, Los Santos and then the State rush away from me as I fall deeper into the abyss. I scream and begin to tumble, spinning head-over-heels into the void. The city is long gone now, there is nothing but darkness, nothing but void. Moments later I find myself back on the ground standing in the dust close to my car on El Burro Heights.

This example is a narratively coherent glitch, by this I mean it is one that is curiously sympathetic to *Grand Theft Auto V*'s narrative arc, and even in step with Rockstar Games' techniques for expanding the character of the game's protagonists (for example the drug induced psychedelic alien-killing skydiving level where the player descends from space into downtown LA). Yet despite this partial coherence there is no avoiding that this is a subversion of the gamespace and animated landscape, the game is behaving incoherently, the player falls through objects and is now placed in an inverted underground space. From this new vantage point the player is subject to Burke's aspects of the sublime, of darkness, obscurity, vastness, magnificence and suddenness (see Figures 15.1–15.3). Both *thematically*, through the single protagonist subject to the whim of the landscape, and the *allegoric*, through the falling into dark expanse, the dislocation and isolation of the protagonist, the glitched experience reconnects with the operatic sublime of Turner or Freidrich. Yet simultaneously to this aesthetic reconnection with the eighteenth-century sublime the glitched landscape also resonates with the technological sublime, in the visual spectacle of the inverted landscape, and in the foggy blankness beyond and underneath the gamespace we sense the power and presence of the algorithmic. For me the use of glitches, exploits or other acts of

Figure 15.1 The intended landscape (*Grand Theft Auto V*, Rockstar Games, 2013)

Figure 15.2 Glitched: swimming below the map (*Grand Theft Auto V*, Rockstar Games, 2013)

Figure 15.3 Glitched: the world inverted (*Grand Theft Auto V*, Rockstar Games, 2013)

remediation, rupture and puncture the logic and coherence of the gamespace and animated landscape. This substitutes designed coherence – Garbut's 'vistas and general sculptural composition, sense of place and history, and consistency' – with rupture and chaos, exposing the turbulent entropy within the algorithm.[17]

For me, the significance of videogame animated landscapes is not necessarily in what they present, whether the verisimilitude or spectacle of the representation, or indeed the rhetoric of individual mastery and ascendency as one begins to beat a hostile game environment, but instead in their capacity to challenge prevailing this rhetoric; to remediate, challenge and invert, and to speak of inscrutability and chaos rather than order and coherence. It is not what is designed and presented to the player that is significant, rather: we should pay attention to what exists beyond the animated landscape.

Notes

1   Alan Meades, 'Why We Glitch: Process, Meaning and Pleasure in the Discovery, Documentation, Sharing and Use of Videogame Exploits', *The Well Played* 2.2(2013): http://www.etc.cmu.edu/etcpress/content/volume-2-number-2-theories.

2   Edmund Burke, *A Philosophical Enquiry into the Sublime and Beautiful* (London: Penguin, 1998).

3 Jeremy Gilbert-Rolfe, *Beauty and the Contemporary Sublime* (New York: Allworth Press, 1999), 133.

4 Ibid., 133.

5 Ibid., 111.

6 Ibid., 135.

7 Ibid., 127–128.

8 Eugénie Shinkle, *Video Games and the Technological Sublime* (2013). Retrieved 2 May 2014, from http://www.tate.org.uk/: http://www.tate.org.uk/art/research -publications/the-sublime/eugenie-shinkle-video-games-and-the-technological -sublime-r1136830.

9 Ibid.

10 Ibid.

11 Chris Pallant, 'Now I Know I'm a Lowlife': Controlling Play in GTA: IV, Red Dead Redemption, and LA Noire,' in *Ctrl-Alt-Play: Essays on Control in Video Gaming*, ed. Matthew Wysocki (Jefferson, NC: McFarland, 2013).

12 Joseph Bernstein, 'Way Beyond Anything We've Done Before': Building the World of 'Grand Theft Auto V', (2013). Retrieved 6 May 2014, from BuzzFeed News: http:// www.buzzfeed.com/josephbernstein/way-beyond-anything-weve-done-before -building-the-world-of-g#qed6ya.

13 Ibid.

14 Ibid.

15 Michael Nitsche, 'Spatial Structuring, Cinematic Mediation, and Evocative Narrative Elements in the Design of an RT 3D VE: The Common Tales Project', *Digital Creativity* 15.1 (2004): 52–56.

16 Michael Nitsche, *Video Game Spaces: Image, Play, and Structure in 3D Worlds* (Cambridge, MA: MIT Press, 2008).

17 Bernstein, 'Way Beyond Anything We've Done Before'.

Contributors

Steven Allen is Senior Lecturer in Film and Media Studies at the University of Winchester, where he is programme director for the MA in Cultural Studies. He has published on representations of landscapes, cultural memory and the body, as well as producing a number of works on animation, including sound in Tex Avery's MGM cartoons (*Animation Journal*, 2009). His most recent research has focused on Australian cinema and includes 'The Undead Down Under' in *The Zombie Renaissance in Popular Culture* edited by Hubner, Leaning and Manning (Palgrave Macmillan, 2014). He is co-editor of *Framing Film: Cinema and the Visual Arts* (Intellect, 2012) and author of *Cinema, Pain and Pleasure: Consent and the Controlled Body* (Palgrave Macmillan, 2013).

Melanie Chan is a lecturer in Media and Film Studies at York St John University. Using a variety of theoretical frameworks that focus on simulation, hyper-reality and signification, her research focuses on the relationships between technology and embodiment in contemporary cultural forms. Melanie completed her PhD on the embodiment and virtual reality in 2007 at Leeds Metropolitan University (Now Leeds Beckett University). She has published several papers in the *Media Education Research Journal* and *International Journal of Baudrillard Studies*, as well as a book chapter in the edited collection *Twenty-First Century Gothic*. Dr Chan is currently working on a range of different research projects including a study of gamification and the mediated city.

Kiu-wai Chu is a PhD candidate and adjunct lecturer in Comparative Literature, University of Hong Kong. He received his previous degrees from SOAS, University of London and University of Cambridge. He was a visiting Fulbright scholar (2012–2013) in University of Idaho. He teaches courses in film theories and visual culture in University of Hong Kong and City University of Hong Kong. His research focuses on contemporary Chinese cinema and art, Ecocriticism and environmental thought in visual culture. His publications can be found in *Images of Lost and Othered Children in Contemporary Cinema* (2012), *World Film Locations* series (Beijing, Hong Kong, Shanghai, 2012–2013) and *Transnational Ecocinema* (2013).

Malcolm Cook is a lecturer at Middlesex University and Central Saint Martins, University of the Arts London. He was awarded a PhD at Birkbeck, University of London in 2013. His doctoral thesis *Animating perception: British cartoons from music hall to cinema, 1880–1928* addressed early British animated cartoons prior to the advent of sound cinema, with a particular focus on the relationship between the moving image and the graphic arts and other pre-cinematic entertainments, as well as the neurological processes involved in the perception of these forms. He has previously been awarded a BA in Film and Literature from the University of Warwick and an MA in History of Film and Visual Media from Birkbeck.

Malcolm has published a number of chapters and articles on animation, early cinema, and their relationship with prior forms. Most recently his chapter 'Performance times: The lightning cartoon and the emergence of animation' appeared in Frank Gray et al. *Performing New Media, 1890–1915* (London: John Libbey, 2014). The book *Adapting Science Fiction for Television*, co-authored with Dr Max Sexton, is forthcoming in 2015 with Rowman & Littlefield/Scarecrow.

Bryan Hawkins was inspired by Harvey Sklair art teacher, Quentin Crisp writer, artist's model and libertine, David Bowie resident singer Three Tuns, and by other London artists who attended Chelsea School of Art. He is now teaching at Canterbury Christ Church University with interests ranging across visual culture and including visual art, film and animation. He is active as an artist, filmmaker and curator and with a particular interest in landscape, magic and Romanticism in contemporary contexts.

Recent research has included curation of exhibition *Earth and Vision – Art and Archaeology* (Folkestone 2012), papers on David Jones artist and poet *Myth, Palimpsest and War* (Oxford 2014), film and paper on Michael Powell's 1944 film *A Canterbury Tale and Visionary Landscape* (Screen International Glasgow 2014). He is currently preparing work on John Ruskin, landscape, optics, discovery and invisibility and researching new and emerging relationships between drawing, photography and film.

María Lorenzo Hernández (1977), PhD in Fine Arts, is Animation Senior Lecturer at the Faculty of Fine Arts, Universitat Politècnica de València, Spain. Her main areas of interest are related to animation as an artistic language, and to the interchange between film, animation and literature. She is an awarded filmmaker, who has directed short animation films such as *Portrait of D* (2004), *The Carnivorous Flower* (2009), the collective project *The Cat Dances with Its Shadow* (2012) and more recently the adaptation to film of Robert Barlow's tale *The Night Ocean* (2015). She has delivered papers at several editions of the Society for Animation Studies annual conferences (in USA, UK and Greece), and in CONFIA (Portugal). She has published numerous essays on animation in *Animac Magazine, Animation Studies* and *Animation: An Interdisciplinary Journal*, and contributed regularly to *Animation Reporter* (India). From 2011 she is an editor of the annual journal *Con A de animación*, to promote animation studies among Spanish and South American scholars.

Artist, animator and curator, **Birgitta Hosea** is Course Director of MA Character Animation at Central Saint Martins, University of the Arts London. Interested in capturing the trace of movement, her work combines animation and digital video with live art and installation. In her practice-based PhD, completed at Central Saint Martins in 2012, she investigated animation as performance. She has exhibited widely in the UK and internationally, has been the recipient of numerous awards and artists residencies and her work is included in the Tate Britain archive. Most recently, she was artist-in-residence at Yarat Contemporary Art Space, Azerbaijan, and the School of Cinematic Arts, USC, Los Angeles. She curated *Seeafar* for Folkestone Triennial Fringe and Deptford X (UK), *Shadow Voices* for Yarat (Baku, Azerbaijan) and was part of the curatorial team for the UK Pavilion at the Shenzhen Architecture and Urbanism Biennale (China). Recent exhibitions include *Chatter*, Cinematic Arts Gallery (Los Angeles, USA); *Holographic Serendipity*, Kinetica Art Fair (London, UK); *Dans Ma Cellule une Silhouette*, Centre d'Art Contemporain, La Ferme du Buisson (Paris, France); *Out There in the Dark*, Mix 23 Queer Experimental Film Festival (New York, USA). Birgitta also writes for academic publications on animation, drawing, digital materiality, performance and liveness and keeps a blog at http://expandedanimation.myblog.arts.ac.uk. She likes to travel, but doesn't have a car and prefers to go by train (or bicycle).

Tom Klein is Associate Professor and the chair of Animation at Loyola Marymount University's School of Film and Television. His work on the avant-garde 'mini-films' of Shamus Culhane has been written about in *The New York Times*, leading to subsequent appearances on TV and radio, including the BBC,

Fox and CBC. His articles have appeared in such publications as *Animation, Griffithiana, Animation Journal* and *Animation Studies*, among others. He catalogued UCLA's Walter Lantz archive and also contributed to the Italian anthology, *What's Up, Tex? Il Cinema di Tex Avery*, published by Lindau. Klein served as the Director of Animation for Vivendi-Universal's educational software division, where he oversaw the creative development of the internationally best-selling *JumpStart* brand and its licensed products for Mac/PC, PlayStation and GameBoy. He was also a consultant for Universal Cartoon Studios during the productions of *Woody Woodpecker* (FoxKids) and *From the Earth to the Moon* (HBO). He is the game designer of the app *Pirate Ring* for iOS.

Alan Meades is Senior Lecturer in New Media Theory in the Department of Media, Art and Design at Canterbury Christ Church University, UK. He is a video games researcher, film-maker and artist, who makes use of videogame glitches as one of the ways of producing work. He has written extensively on the subject of counterplay and transgressive play, and holds a PhD from Brunel University exploring practices including glitching, hacking, illicit modding and grief-play. Alan's research utilizes ethnographic and netnographic methods to study a number of transgressive videogame communities. He also holds an MA in Electronic Arts from Middlesex University, a BA in Interactive Arts from Manchester Metropolitan University.

Mihaela Mihailova is a PhD candidate in the joint Film and Media Studies and Slavic Languages and Literatures program at Yale University. Her research interests include animation, Film and Media theory, early Soviet cinema, contemporary Eastern European cinema, video games and comics. She has published articles in *Animation: An Interdisciplinary Journal, Studies in Russian and Soviet Cinema, Post Script: Essays in Film and the Humanities* and *Kino Kultura*. Her piece 'Frame-Shot: Vertov's Ideologies of Animation' (co-written with John MacKay) is included in *Animating Film Theory* (ed. Karen Beckman). Her translation of Sergei Tretyakov's 'The Industry Production Screenplay' appears in *Cinema Journal* 51.4 (2012).

James Newton is Associate Lecturer in Film at the University of Kent. He is currently researching the relationship between anarchism and cinema. His research interests include political cinema, Horror, the Avant-Garde, Spaghetti Westerns and documentary. James is also an independent filmmaker whose work encompasses both narrative and experimental forms, and is the co-organizer of the Waves of Horror film festival. Twitter: @JamesEdNewton.

Chris Pallant is Senior Lecturer in Film Studies at Canterbury Christ Church University. His research focuses on animation and production studies. He is the author of *Demystifying Disney: A History of Disney Feature Animation* (Continuum, 2011) co-author of *Storyboarding: A Critical History* (Palgrave, forthcoming), and has also published in book chapter and journal form on a range of topics, including Disney animation, the 'cartoonism' of Quentin Tarantino's live-action films, performance capture technology, the animated landscape of New York City, and the work of Rockstar Games. Chris currently serves as Vice President for the Society for Animation Studies. Twitter: @cjpallant.

Fran Pheasant-Kelly is MA Course Leader, Reader in Film and Television Studies, and Co-Director of the Film, Media, Discourse and Culture Research Centre at the University of Wolverhampton, UK. Her research centres on fantasy, 9/11, abjection and space, which forms the basis for an edited collection *Spaces of the Cinematic Home: Behind the Screen Door* (Routledge, 2015) and two monographs, *Abject Spaces in American Cinema: Institutions, Identity and Psychoanalysis in Film* (Tauris, 2013) and *Fantasy Film Post 9/11* (Palgrave, 2013). Other recent publications include 'Between Knowingness and Innocence: Child Ciphers in *Marnie* and *The Birds*' in Debbie Olson (ed.) *Children in the Films of Alfred Hitchcock* (Palgrave, 2014); 'Reframing Gender and Visual Pleasure: New Signifying Practices in Contemporary Cinema' in Gilad Padva and Nurit Buchweitz (eds.) *Sensational Pleasures in Cinema, Literature and Visual Culture: The Phallic Eye* (Palgrave, 2014); 'Strange Spaces: Cult Topographies in Twin Peaks' in Marisa Hayes and Franck Boulegue (eds.) *Fan Phenomena – Twin Peaks* (Intellect, 2013); and 'Class, Loss, Space: Reframing *Secrets and Lies*', in Marc DiPaulo and Bryan Cardinale-Powell (eds.) *Devised and Directed by Mike Leigh* (Bloomsbury, 2013).

Dan Torre is a lecturer in animation production, history and theory at RMIT University in Melbourne, Australia. His current research interests include philosophy and animation, the animation process, documentary animation and Australian animation history.

Professor **Paul Wells** is Director of the Animation Academy, Loughborough University, UK, and Chair of the Association of British Animation Collections.

He has published widely in the field of Animation Studies, including his most recent book, *Animation, Sport and Culture* (Palgrave Macmillan). He is also an established writer and director for Film, TV, Radio and Theatre, his most recent work including a documentary, 'Whispers and Wererabbits: Claire Jennings' featuring Nick Park, 'Trios', six scripts on information sharing in public institutions, and the early drafts of a feature film. He is the editor of the Intellect journal *Animation Practice, Process and Production*, and is currently working on a collection of short stories.

Bibliography

Al-Khalili, Jim. *Paradox: The Nine Greatest Enigmas in Physics*. New York: Crown Publishing, 2012.

Allison, Lincoln. *The Changing Politics of Sport*. Manchester: Manchester University Press, 1993.

Álvarez Sarrat, Sara and María Lorenzo Hernández. 'How Computers Re-Animated Hand-Made Processes and Aesthetics for Artistic Animation'. *Animation Studies* 7, (2012). Accessed 10 May 2014. http://journal.animationstudies.org/sara-alvarez -sarrat-and-maria-lorenzo-hernandez-how-computers-re-animated-hand-made -processes-and-aesthetics-for-artistic-animation-2/.

Anastasi, William. 'Interview with Thomas McEvilley//2005'. In *Chance (Documents of Contemporary Art)*, edited by Margaret Iversen, 107–109. Cambridge: MIT Press, 2010.

Andrew, Dudley. *What Cinema Is!* Malden, MA: Wiley, 2010.

Ariely, Dan. *Predictably Irrational*. London: Harper Perennial, 2010.

Australian Bureau of Statistics. ' 2071.0 – Reflecting a Nation: Stories from the 2011 Census, 2012–2013'. 16 April 2013. Accessed 10 December 2014. http://www.abs.gov .au/ausstats/abs@.nsf/Lookup/2071.0main+features902012-2013#Endnote3.

Bal, Mieke. *A Mieke Bal Reader*. Chicago: University of Chicago Press, 2006.

Bale, John. *Landscapes of Modern Sport*. Leicester: Leicester University Press, 1994.

Barthes, Roland. *Camera Lucida: Reflections on Photography*. New York: Hill and Wang, 1981.

Batchen, Geoffrey. *Burning with Desire: The Conception of Photography*. Cambridge: MIT Press, 1999.

Bauman, Zygmunt. 'Liquid Arts'. *Theory, Culture & Society* 24.1 (2007): 117–126.

Bauman, Zygmunt. *Liquid Modernity*. Cambridge: Polity Press, 2013.

Baxter, Jennifer, Matthew Gray, and Alan Hayes. *Families in Regional, Rural and Remote Australia*. Melbourne: Australian Institute for Family Studies, 2011.

Bazin, Andre and Hugh Gray. *What Is Cinema?* Berkeley: University of California Press, 2004.

Beck, Ulrich. *Risk Society: Towards a New Modernity*. London: Sage, 1992.

Bekoff, Marc. *The Emotional Lives of Animals*. Novato: New World Library, 2007.

Bendazzi, Giannalberto. 'Quirino Cristiani, The Untold Story of Argentina's Pioneer Animator'. Translated by Charles Solomon. *Animation World Network*. Accessed 3 December 2014. http://www.awn.com/mag/issue1.4/articles/bendazzi1.4.html. Originally published in Graffiti by ASIFA-Hollywood, December 1984.

Bendazzi, Giannalberto. *Cartoons: One Hundred Years of Cinema Animation.* London: John Libbey Publishing, 2004.

Benjamin, Walter. *Charles Baudelaire a Lyric Poet in the Era of High Capitalism.* Translated by Harry Zohn. London: Verso, 1997.

Bernstein, Joseph. 'Way beyond Anything We've Done Before': Building the World of 'Grand Theft Auto V'. *BuzzFeed News,* 13 August 2013. Accessed 6 May 2014. http://www.buzzfeed.com/josephbernstein/way-beyond-anything-weve-done-before-building-the-world-of-g#qed6ya.

Beumers, Birgit. 'Folklore and New Russian Animation'. *KinoKultura* 43 (2014). Accessed 15 July 2014. http://www.kinokultura.com/2014/43-beumers.shtml.

Bigelow, Susan J. 'Technologies of Perception: Miyazaki in Theory and Practice'. *Animation* 4.1 (2009): 55–74.

Bill Desowitz. 'Selick Talks 'Coraline': The Electricity of Life'. *Animation World Network,* 6 February 2009. Accessed 3 December 2014. http://www.awn.com/articles/stop-motion/selick-talks-icoralinei-electricity-life.

Birtwistle, Andy. *Cinesonica, Sounding Film and Video.* Manchester: Manchester University Press, 2010.

Bishop, Kyle William. *American Zombie Gothic: The Rise and Fall (and Rise) of the Walking Dead in Popular Culture.* Jefferson, NC: McFarland, 2010.

Black, Andy. *The Dead Walk.* Hereford: Noir Publishing, 2000.

Blake, William. *1759–1827: The Poetic Works of William Blake.* Oxford: Oxford University Press, 1908.

Blinn, James, Julian Gomez, Nelson Max, and William Reeves. 'The Simulation of Natural Phenomena (Panel Session)'. *SIGGRAPH Computer Graphics* 17.3 (1983): 137–139.

BluBlu.org. Accessed 14 December 2014. http://blublu.org/sito/blog/?paged=101.

Bordwell, David and Kristin Thompson. *Film Art.* New York: McGraw Hill, 2010.

Boyd, David. 'Hari-Kuyo'. *The Japan Foundation.* Accessed 11 June 2014. http://www.jpf.org.au/onlinearticles/hitokuchimemo/issue7.html.

Bradbury, Keith. 'Australian and New Zealand Animation'. In *Animation in Asia and the Pacific,* edited by John A. Lent, 207–222. Eastleigh: John Libbey, 2001.

Bradley, Richard. *Ritual and Domestic Life in Prehistoric Europe.* London: Routledge, 2005.

Brand, Jo. 'Masstransiscope'. *Bill Brand* (2013). Accessed 14 December. http://www.bboptics.com/masstransiscope.html.

Brater, Enoch. *10 Ways of Thinking about Samuel Beckett.* London: Methuen Drama, 2011.

Brierton, Tom. *Stop Motion Armature Machining.* Jefferson, NC: McFarland, 2002.

Brierton, Tom. *Stop Motion Filming and Performance.* Jefferson, NC: McFarland, 2006.

Brown, Judy and Steve Cunningham. 'A History of ACM Siggraph'. *Communications of the ACM* 50.5 (2007): 54–61.

Buchan, Suzanne. 'Introduction'. In *Pervasive Animation,* edited by Suzanne Buchan, 1–21. New York: Routledge, 2013.

Buckland, Warren. 'Between Science Fact and Science Fiction: Spielberg's Digital Dinosaurs, Possible Worlds and the New Aesthetic Realism'. *Screen* 40.2 (1999): 177–192.

Bukatman, Scott. 'The Artificial Infinite: On Special Effects and the Sublime'. In *Post-War Cinema and Modernity: A Film Reader*, edited by John Orr and Olga Taxidou, 208–222. Edinburgh: Edinburgh University Press, 2000.

Burke, Edmund. *A Philosophical Enquiry into the Sublime and Beautiful*. London: Penguin, 1998.

Butler, David. *Fantasy Cinema: Impossible Worlds on Screen*. London: Wallflower Press, 2009.

Cahn, Iris. 'The Changing Landscape of Modernity: Early Film and America's "Great Picture" Tradition'. *Wide Angle* 18.3 (1996): 85–100.

Cameron, Allan. 'Zombie Media: Transmission, Reproduction, and the Digital Dead'. *Cinema Journal* 52.1 (2012): 66–89.

Caputo, Raffaele. 'The Animated Features of Yoram Gross'. In *Australian Film 1978–1992*, edited by Scott Murray, 352–354. Melbourne: Oxford University Press, 1993.

Carmichael, Deborah A. *The Landscape of Hollywood Westerns*. Utah: University of Utah Press, 2006.

Carpenter, Loren C. 'Computer Rendering of Fractal Curves and Surfaces'. *SIGGRAPH Computer Graphics* 14.3 (1980): 109.

Carpenter, Loren. 'The A-Buffer, an Antialiased Hidden Surface Method'. *SIGGRAPH Computer Graphics* 18.3 (1984): 103–108.

Carr, Valerie. 'An "Anonymous Actor"'. *The Australian Women's Weekly*, January 17, 1973.

Carson, Rachel. *Silent Spring*. Harmondsworth: Penguin, 1962.

Cartoon Brew. 'Meet "ParaNorman" Character Designer Heidi Smith'. Accessed 12 July 2014. http://www.cartoonbrew.com/feature-film/meet-paranorman-character-designer-heidi-smith-67775.html.

Cavallaro, Dani. *The Anime Art of Hayao Miyazaki*. Jefferson, NC: McFarland, 2006.

Child, Louise. *Tantric Buddhism and Altered States of Consciousness: Durkheim, Emotional Energy and Visions of the Consort*. Farnham: Ashgate Publishing, 2007.

Cholodenko, Alan. 'Still Photography?'. *International Journal of Baudrillard Studies* 5.1 (January 2008). Accessed 10 December 2014. http://www.ubishops.ca/baudrillardstudies/vol5_1/v5-1-article5-cholodenko.html.

Cilinska, Antra. 'Making Films in Latvia: Producers' Challenges'. *KinoKultura* 13 (2012). Accessed 15 July 2014. http://www.kinokultura.com/specials/13/cilinska.shtml.

Clark, Kenneth. *One Hundred Details from Pictures in the National Gallery*. London: National Gallery Company, 2008.

Clements, Jonathan. *Anime – A History*. London: Palgrave Macmillan and BFI, 2013.

Coleridge, Samuel Taylor. *Constancy to an Ideal Object*. Riverside, CA: H. Houghton and Company, 1826.

Committee on Science and Technology. *Computer Power for Film and Flight: Technical Memo No. 95*. First Session, 1983.

Confucius (Kongzi). *The Analects of Confucius.* Translated by Burton Watson. New York: Columbia Universty Press, 2007.

Connor, Steven. *A Philosophy of Sport.* London: Reaktion Books Ltd, 2011.

Cook, David A. *A History of Film Narrative.* New York: Norton, 1996.

Cook, Robert L. 'Shade Trees'. *SIGGRAPH Computer Graphics* 18.3 (1984): 223–231.

Cook, Robert L., Loren Carpenter, and Edwin Catmull. 'The Reyes Image Rendering Architecture'. *SIGGRAPH Computer Graphics* 21.4 (1987): 95–102.

Cousins, Mark. *The Study of Film.* London: Pavilion, 2011.

Crafton, Donald. *Shadow of a Mouse: Performance, Belief, and World-Making in Animation.* Berkeley: University of California Press, 2013.

Crary, Jonathan. *Techniques of the Observer: On Vision and Modernity in the Nineteenth Century.* Cambridge: MIT Press, 1990.

Cresswell, Tim. *On the Move: Mobility in the Western World.* New York: Routledge, 2006.

Crevits, Bram. 'The Roots of Vjing: A Historical Overview'. In *Vj: Audio-Visual Art + Vj Culture*, edited by Michael Faulkner, 14–19. London: Laurence King Publishing, 2006.

Cubitt, Sean. *EcoMedia.* Amsterdam: Rodopi Press, 2005.

Damasio, Antonio, R. *Descartes' Error: Emotion, Reason and the Human Brain.* London: Vintage, 2006.

Danto, Arthur C. *The Madonna of the Future Essays on a Pluralistic Art World.* London: University California Press, 2001.

Darley, Andrew. *Visual Digital Culture: Surface, Play and Spectacle.* London: Routledge, 2000.

DeFanti, Tom. 'Nicograph '82 Symposium'. *SIGGRAPH Computer Graphics* 17.2 (1983): 323–330.

Deleuze, Gilles. *Cinema I: The Movement Image.* Translated by Hugh Tomlinson and Barbara Habberjam. London: Continuum Books, 2012.

Deleuze, Gilles. *The Fold.* Minneapolis, MN: University of Minnesota Press, 1992.

Dentry, Terri. 'From Good Devils to Supermarket Musical Massacres: An Overview of Australian Animation'. *Metro Magazine* 157 (2008): 86–89.

Department for Transport. *National Travel Survey: 2012.* UK Government, 2013.

Deruma, Dita. 'Production Company AB'. *Film News from Latvia*, 2003.

Dimiševskis, Uldis and Simon Drewsen Holmberg. *Audiovisual Production in Latvia: A Nordic Context.* Riga: National Film Centre Latvia, 2007.

Dobson, Nichola. 'Innovation and Limitation'. *AnimationStudies 2.0.* 28 May 2013. Accessed 15 December 2014. http://blog.animationstudies.org/?p=266.

Dryje, František. 'The Force of Imagination'. Translated by Valerie Mason. In *Dark Alchemy: The Films of Jan Švankmajer*, edited by Peter Hames, 119–168. Trowbridge: Flicks Books, 1995.

Dubois, Bastien. *Madagascar carnet de tournage.* Clermont Ferrand: Reflets d'ailleurs, 2011.

Duncan, Jody. 'World War Z: Zombie Wars'. *CineFlex* 135 (2013): 13–31.

Dyer, Richard. 'Entertainment and Utopia'. In *Only Entertainmen*, edited by Richard Dyer, 19–35. London: Routledge, 2002. Originally published in *Movie* 24 (1977).

Dyson, Freeman. 'Characterizing Irregularity'. *Science* 200 (1978): 677–678.

Eisenstein, Sergei. *Eisenstein on Disney*, edited by Jay Leyda. Translated by Alan Upchurch. Calcutta: Seagull, 1986.

Elsaesser, Thomas and Kay Hoffman. *Cinema Futures: Cain, Abel or Cable? The Screen in the Digital Age*. Amsterdam: Amsterdam University Press, 1998.

Elsaesser, Thomas. 'The Mind-Game Film'. In *Puzzle Films: Complex Storytelling in Contemporary Cinema*, edited by Warren Buckland, 13–41. New York: John Wiley & Sons, 2009.

Emmer, Michele. 'Art, Math, and Cinema'. In *M. C. Escher's Legacy*, edited by Doris Schattschneider and Michele Emmer, 142–149. Berlin: Springer-Verlag, 2003.

Ezra, Elizabeth. *Georges Méliès: The Birth of the Auteur*. Manchester: Manchester University Press, 2000.

Fielding, Raymond. 'Hale's Tours: Ultra-Realism in the Pre-1910 Motion Picture'. *Cinema Journal* 10.1 (1970): 34–47.

Fish, Robert. *Cinematic Countrysides*. Manchester: Manchester University Press, 2007.

Foster, Hal. *The Return of the Real, The Avant-Garde at the End of the Century*. New York: MIT Press, 1996.

Fournier, Alain and Donald Fussell. 'On the Power of the Frame Buffer'. *ACM Trans. Graph.* 7.2 (1988): 103–128.

Fowkes, Katherine. *The Fantasy Film*. Malden: Wiley-Blackwell, 2010.

Fowler, Catherine and Gillian Helfield. *Representing the Rural: Space, Place and Identity in Films about the Land*. Detroit: Wayne State University Press, 2006.

Franke, Anselm. 'A Critique of Animation'. *e-flux Journal*. 2014. Accessed 15 December 2014. http://www.e-flux.com/journal/a-critique-of-animation/.

Freud, Sigmund. *Totem and Taboo and Other Works, The Standard Edition of the Complete Psychological Works of Sigmund Freud*, Vol. 13, translated by James Strachey. London: Vintage, 2001.

Furby, Jacqueline and Claire Hines. *Fantasy*. London: Routledge, 2012.

Furniss, Marueen. *Art in Motion: Animation Aesthetics*. Eastleigh: John Libbey, 2007.

Gibson, Ross. *South of the West: Postcolonialism and the Narrative Construction of Australia*. Bloomington: Indiana University Press, 1992.

Gibson, William. 'The Art of Fiction No. 211'. Interview by David Wallace-Wells. *The Paris Review* 197 (2011): 107–149.

Gilbert-Rolfe, Jeremy. *Beauty and the Contemporary Sublime*. New York: Allworth Press, 1999.

Gombrich, Ernst. *Art and Illusion a Study in the Psychology of Pictorial Representation*. Oxford: Oxford University Press, 2000.

Grant, John. *Masters of Animation*. London: B.T. Batsford, 2001.

Griffin, George. 'Concrete Animation'. *Animation: An Interdisciplinary Journal* 2.3 (2007): 259–274.

Grusin, R. *Culture, Technology, and the Creation of America's National Parks*. Cambridge: Cambridge University Press, 2004.

Gunning, Tom. 'An Aesthetic of Astonishment: Early Film and the (In)Credulous Spectator'. In *Viewing Positions*, edited by Linda Williams, 114–133. New Brunswick: Rutgers, 1995.

Gunning, Tom. 'Animating the Instant: The Secret Symmetry between Animation and Photography'. In *Animating Film Theory*, edited by Karen Beckman, 37–53. Durham and London: Duke University Press, 2014.

Gunning, Tom. 'Gollum and Golem: Special effects and the Technology of Artificial Bodies'. In *From Hobbits to Hollywood: Essays on Peter Jackson's Lord of the Rings*, edited by Ernest Mathijs and Murray Pomerance, 319–350. Amsterdam: Rodopi, 2006.

Gunning, Tom. 'Landscape and the Fantasy of Moving Pictures: Early Cinema's Phantom Rides'. In *Cinema and Landscape*, edited by Graeme Harper and Jonathan Rayner, 31–70. Bristol: Intellect, 2010.

Gunning, Tom. 'The Cinema of Attractions: Early Film, Its Spectator and the Avant-Garde'. In *Early Cinema: Space – Frame – Narrative*, edited by Thomas Elsaesser, 56–62. London: BFI, 1990.

Guo, Xi (Kuo Hsi). 'Kuo Hsi's The Significance of Landscapes (*Lin quan gao zhi ji: Shanshui Xun* 林泉高致集:山水訓)'. In *Early Chinese Texts on Painting*. Translated and edited by Susan Bush and Shih Hsio-yen, 150–154. Hong Kong: Hong Kong University Press, 2013.

Hall, Peter. *London 2000*. London: Faber, 1963.

Hall, Peter. *London 2001*. London: Unwin Hyman, 1989.

Hall, Stuart. 'Encoding/Decoding'. In *Culture, Media, Language*, edited by Stuart Hall, Dorothy Hobson, Andrew Lowe, and Paul Willis, 128–138. London: Hutchinson, 1980.

Hammond, Paul. *Marvelous Méliès*. London: Gordon Fraser, 1974.

Hao, Dazheng. 'Chinese Visual Representation: Painting and Cinema'. Translated by D. Wilkerson. In *Cinematic Landscapes: Observations on the Visual Arts and Cinema of China and Japan*, edited by Linda Ehrlich and David Desser, 45–62. Austin: University of Texas Press, 1994.

Harper, Graeme and Jonathan Rayner. *Cinema and Landscape*. Bristol: Intellect, 2010.

Harper, Graeme and Jonathan Rayner. *Film Landscapes: Cinema, Environment, and Visual Culture*. Newcastle: Cambridge Scholar's Press, 2013.

Harper, Graeme and Jonathan Rayner. 'Introduction – Cinema and Landscape'. In *Cinema and Landscape*, edited by Graeme Harper and Jonathan Rayner, 13–28. Bristol: Intellect, 2010.

Harris, Paul A. 'To See with the Mind and Think through the Eye: Deleuze, Folding Architecture, and Simon Rodia's Watts Towers'. In *Deleuze and Space*, edited by Ian Buchanan and Gregg Lambert. Edinburgh: Edinburgh University Press, 2005.

Hasegawa, Hiroyo. 'Scientist and Synthetic Thinker Kumagusu Minakata – Japan's First Ecologist'. *JFS Newsletter, Japanese Philosophers/Leaders for Sustainability* 3 (2012). Accessed 18 March 2014. http://www.japanfs.org/en/news/archives/news_id031657 .html.

Hayes, Christian. 'Phantom Rides'. *BFI Screen Online*. Accessed 7 July 2014. http://www .screenonline.org.uk/film/id/1193042/.

Haynes, Roslynn D. *Seeking the Centre: The Australian Desert in Literature, Art and Film*. Cambridge: Cambridge University Press, 1998.

Heidegger, Martin. 'The Question Concerning Technology'. In *Basic Writings: From Being and Time (1927) to the Task of Thinking (1964)*, edited by David Farrell Krell, 308–341. New York: Harper Collins, 1993.

Herguera, Isabel. 'Un experimento en el jardín de la ley'. *Animac Magazine '11. Escrits sobre animació* 10 (2011): 3–4.

Herring, Peter. *The Biology of the Deep Ocean*. Oxford: Oxford University Press, 2002.

Hickman, Robin, Iqbal Hamiduddin, Birgitta Hosea, Steve Roberts, Peter Hall, Peter Jones, and Colin Osborn. 'Animating the Future Seamless Public Transport Journey'. *Built Environment* 39.3 (2013): 369–84.

Hofstadter, Douglas R. 'Mystery, Classicism, Elegance: An Endless Chase After Magic'. In *M. C. Escher's Legacy*, edited by Doris Schattschneider and Michele Emmer, 24–51. Berlin: Springer-Verlag, 2003.

Hofstadter, Douglas R. *Gödel, Escher, Bach: An Eternal Golden Braid*. New York: Basic Books, 1979.

Hollander, Anne. *Moving Pictures*. New York: Alfred A. Knopf, 1989.

Homo Felix: The International Journal of Animated Film. Accessed 11 December 2014. http://homofelixjournal.com.

Hosea, Birgitta. 'Substitutive Bodies and Constructed Actors: A Practice-Based Investigation of Animation as Performance'. PhD diss., University of the Arts London, 2012.

Huhtamo, Erkki. *Illusions in Motion: A Media Archaeology of the Moving Panorama and Related Spectacles*. Cambridge: MIT Press, 2013.

Jensen, Casper Bruun and Anders Blok. 'Techno-Animism in Japan: Shinto Cosmograms, Actor-Network Theory, and the Enabling Powers of Non-Human Agencies'. *Theory, Culture, Society* 30.2 (2013): 84–115.

Jones, Stephen. *Coraline: A Visual Companion*. London: Titan, 2009.

Jullien, François. *In Praise of Blandness: Proceeding from Chinese Thought and Aesthetics*. Translated by Paula M. Varsano. New York: Zone Books, 2004.

Kahneman, Daniel. *Thinking Fast and Slow*. London: Farrar, Straus and Giroux, 2013.

King, Geoff. *Spectacular Narratives: Hollywood in the Age of the Blockbuster*. London: IB Tauris, 2000.

Kirby, Lynne. 'Male Hysteria and Early Cinema'. In *Male Trouble*, edited by Constance Penley and Sharon Willis, 67–86. Minneapolis: University of Minnesota Press, 1993.

Kirschner, Friedrich. 'Toward a Machinima Studio'. In *The Machinima Reader*, edited by Henry Lowood and Michael Nitsche, 53–73. Cambridge: MIT Press, 2011.

Kobori, Hiromi and Primarck, Richard B. 'Conservation for Satoyama the Traditional Landsape of Japan'. *Arnoldia* 62.4 (2003): 1–10.

Kozachik, Pete. '2 Worlds in 3 Dimensions'. *American Cinematographer* (February 2009). Accessed 3 December 2014. https://www.theasc.com/ac_magazine/February2009/Coraline/page4.php.

Kriger, Judith. *Animated Realism. A Behind-the-Scenes Look at the Animated Documentary Genre*. Oxford: Focal Press, 2012.

Lamarre, Thomas. *The Anime Machine: A Media Theory of Animation*. Minneapolis: University of Minnesota Press, 2009.

Lanier, Clinton, Scott Rader, and Aubrey Fowler. 'Anthropomorphism, Marketing Relationships, and Consumption Worth in the *Toy Story* Trilogy'. *Journal of Marketing Management* 29.1/2 (2013): 26–27.

Lash, John. *The Yin of Tai Chi*. London: Vega Books, 2002.

Latour, Bruno. 'War and Peace in an Age of Ecological Conflicts'. Paper presented at the Peter Wall Institute Vancouver, 23 September 2013.

'Latviiskaya animatsia nabiraet oboroty'. *Delfi*. 9 February 2006. Accessed 20 July 2014. http://www.delfi.lv/showtime/news/picsnsounds/pics/latvijskaya-animaciya -nabiraet-oboroty.d?id=13566717.

Lefebvre, Martin. 'Between Setting and Landscape in the Cinema'. In *Landscape and Film*, edited by Martin Lefebvre, 19–60. London: Routledge, 2006.

Lefebvre, Martin. *Landscape and Film*. London: Routledge, 2006.

Leotta, Alfio. *Touring the Screen: Tourism and New Zealand Film Geographies*. Bristol: Intellect, 2011.

Leschiov, Vladimir. 'Some Notes on Animation'. Interview by Kristīne Matīsa. *Film News from Latvia: Special Issue – Latvian Animation* (2009): 2–5.

Lin, Niantong. *Zhongguo dian ying mei xue* (中國電影美學). *Taibei: Yun chen wen hua shi ye gu fen you xian gong si*. Beijing: 1991.

Littleton, Scott C. *Understanding Shinto*. London: Duncan Baird Publishers, 2002.

Loiperdinger, Martin and Bernd Elzer. 'Lumiere's Arrival of the Train: Cinema's Founding Myth'. *The Moving Image* 4.1 (2004): 89–118.

Lorenzo Hernández, Encarnación. 'Madagascar: antropología y animación documental'. *Tinieblas en el corazón. Pensar la antropología* (2013). Accessed June 2014. http://anthropotopia.blogspot.com.es/2013/06/madagascar-antropologia-y-animacion.html/.

Lukinykh, Natalia. 'Inspired by the Oscar, Hardened by the Marketplace: On the Everydays and Holidays of Russian Animation'. *KinoKultura* 13 (2006). Accessed 15 July 2014. http://www.kinokultura.com/2006/13-lukinykh.shtml.

Lynn, Greg. *Animate Form*. New York: Princeton Architectural Press, 1999.

Macek, J. C. 'The Zombification Family Tree: Legacy of the Living Dead'. *PopMatters*. 14 June 2012. Accessed 29 August 2014. http://www.popmatters.com/column/159439 -legacy-of-the-living-dead/.

Mandelbrot, Benoit B. 'How Long Is the Coast of Britain? Statistical Self-Similarity and Fractional Dimension'. *Science* 156.3775 (1967): 636–638.

Mandelbrot, Benoit B. *Fractals: Form, Chance and Dimension*. San Francisco, CA: Freeman, 1977.

Mandelbrot, Benoit B. *The Fractal Geometry of Nature*. Oxford: Freeman, 1982.

Manovich, Lev. *The Language of New Media*. Cambridge: MIT Press, 2001.

Marinchevska, Nadezhda. *Bulgarsko Animatsionno Kino 1915–1995*. Sofia: Colibri, 2001.

Massey, Doreen. *For Space*. London: Sage Publications, 2005.

Mayumi, Kozo, Barry D. Soloman and Jason Chang. 'The Ecological and Consumption Themes of the Films of Hayao Miyazaki'. *Ecological Economics* 54 (2005): 1–7.

McCurry, Justin. 'Japan Remembers Minamata'. *The Lancet* 367 (2006): 99–100.

McDonald, Keiko. *Reading a Japanese Film – Cinema in Context*. Honolulu: University of Hawaii Press, 2006.

McFarlane, Brian. *Australian Cinema*. New York: Columbia University Press, 1988.

McLean, Thomas J. 'Mr. Selick's Other-Worldly Magic'. *Animation Magazine*, 10 March 2009. Accessed 9 December 2014. http://www.animationmagazine.net/features/mr -selicks-other-worldly-magic/.

Meades, Alan. 'Why We Glitch: Process, Meaning and Pleasure in the Discovery, Documentation, Sharing and Use of Videogame Exploits'. *Well Played* 2.2 (2012). Accessed 28 November 2014. http://www.etc.cmu.edu/etcpress/content/volume-2 -number-2-theories.

Mellon, Andrew. 'Before Industrial Light and Magic: The Independent Hollywood Special Effects Business, 1968–75'. *New Review of Film and Television* 7.2 (2009): 133–156.

Meyer, Rudolf. *The Wisdom of Fairy Tales*. Edinburgh: Floris, 1997.

Mihailova, Mihaela. 'The Mastery Machine: Digital Animation and Fantasies of Control'. *Animation: An Interdisciplinary Journal* 8.2 (2013): 131–148.

Miller, Tyrus. ' "Cut out from Last Year's Moldering Newspapers": Bruno Schulz and the Brothers Quay on the Street of Crocodiles'. In *Screening the City*, edited by Mark Shiel and Tony Fitzmaurice, 80–99. New York: Verso, 2003.

Minnaert, M. G. J. *Light and Color in the Outdoors*. Translated by Len Seymour. Berlin: Springer-Verlag, 1992.

Minnaert, M. G. J. *The Nature of Light and Colour in the Open Air*. Translated by H. M. Kremer-Priest and K. E. Brian Jay. New York: Dover Publications, 1954.

Miyazaki, Hayao. *The Art of Nausicaä of the Valley of the Wind – Watercolour Impressions*. San Francisco, CA: Viz Media, 2011.

Moritz, William. 'James Whitney'. In *Articulated Light: The Emergence of Abstract Film in America*, edited by Bruce Posner and Gerald O'Grady, Vol. 11. Boston, MA: Harvard Film Archive/Anthology Film Archives, 1995.

Moritz, William. 'Narrative Strategies for Resistance and Protest in Eastern European Animation'. In *A Reader in Animation Studies*, edited by Jayne Pilling, 38–47. Sydney: John Libbey, 1997.

Moritz, William. *Optical Poetry: The Life and Work of Oskar Fischinger*. Bloomington: Indiana University Press, 2004.

Mulvey, Laura. *Death 24× a Second: Stillness and the Moving Image*. London: Reaktion Books, 2006.

Murray, Robin and Joseph Neumann. *Ecology and Popular Film: Cinema on the Edge*. New York: New York University Press, 2009.

Nahid, Shahla. 'What Is the Future for Animated Films in Latvia?'. FIPRESCI. 15 February 2009. Accessed 12 December 2014. http://www.fipresci.org/festivals/archive/2006/riga/.

Napier, Susan. *Anime: From Akira to Howl's Moving Castle.* New York: Palgrave Macmillan, 2005.

Narine, Anil. *Eco-Trauma Cinema.* London: Routledge, 2014.

Nead, Lynda. 'Velocities of the Image C. 1900'. *Art History* 27.5 (2005): 745–769.

Neuberger, Joan. 'Strange Circus: Eisenstein's Sex Drawings'. *Studies in Russian & Soviet Cinema* 6.1 (2012): 5–52.

Newman, Kim. *Nightmare Movies: A Critical History of the Horror Film, 1968–88.* London: Bloomsbury, 1988.

Ni, Zhen. 'Classical Chinese Painting and Cinematographic Signification'. In *Cinematic Landscapes: Observations on the Visual Arts and Cinema of China and Japan*, edited by Linda Ehrlich and David Desser, 63–80. Austin: University of Texas Press. 1994.

Nitsche, Michael. 'Spatial Structuring, Cinematic Mediation, and Evocative Narrative Elements in the Design of an RT 3D VE: The Common Tales Project'. *Digital Creativity* 15.1 (2004): 52–56.

Nitsche, Michael. *Video Game Spaces: Image, Play, and Structure in 3D Worlds.* Cambridge: MIT Press, 2008.

Nye, Joseph. *Soft Power: The Means to Success in World Politics.* New York: PublicAffairs, 2004.

O'Connor, Kevin. *Culture and Customs of the Baltic States.* Westport, CT: Greenwood Press, 2006.

Oleksijczuk, Denise Blake. *The First Panoramas: Visions of British Imperialism.* Minneapolis: University of Minnesota Press, 2011.

O'Neill, Shevaun and Kathryn Wells. 'Animation in Australia'. 15 June 2012. Accessed 10 November 2014. http://australia.gov.au/about-australia/australian-story/animation-in-australia.

Osterfeld Li, Michelle. *Ambiguous Bodies – Reading the Grotesque in Japanese Setsuwa Tales.* Redwood City, CA: Stanford University Press, 2009.

Paik, Karen and Leslie Iwerks. *To Infinity and Beyond!: The Story of Pixar Animation Studios.* London: Virgin, 2007.

Pallant, Chris. '"Now I Know I'm a Lowlife": Controlling Play in *GTA: IV, Red Dead Redemption*, and *LA Noire*'. In *Ctrl-Alt-Play: Essays on Control in Video Gaming*, edited by Matthew Wysocki, 133–145. Jefferson, NC: McFarland, 2013.

Pallant, Chris. 'Disney-Formalism – Beyond Classic Disney'. *Animation: An Interdisciplinary Journal* 4.4 (2011): 341–352.

Pallant, Chris. 'The Animated Landscapes'. In *Film Landscapes: Cinema, Environment and Visual Culture*, edited by Graeme Harper and Jonathan Rayner, 187–202. Newcastle: Cambridge Scholars Publishing, 2013.

Parkes, Graham. 'Lao-Zhuang and Heidegger on Nature and Technology'. *Journal of Chinese Philosophy* 30.1 (2003): 19–38.

Peirce, Charles S. 'Logic as Semiotic the Theory of Signs'. In *Semiotics an Introductory Anthology*, edited by Robert. E. Innis, 1–24. Bloomington: Indiana University Press, 1985.

Perelman, Marc. *Barbaric Sport: A Global Plague*. London: Verso, 2012.

Pheasant-Kelly, Frances. *Fantasy Film Post 9/11*. London: Palgrave, 2013.

Pick, Anat and Guinevere Narraway. *Screening Nature: Cinema beyond the Human*. New York: Berghahn Books, 2013.

Pierce, Peter. *The Country of Lost Children: An Australian Anxiety*. Cambridge: Cambridge University Press, 1999.

Pierson, Michele. 'CGI Effects in Hollywood Science-Fiction Cinema 1989–95: The Wonder Years'. *Screen* 40.2 (1999): 158–176.

Pilger, Steve, *et al. 1001 Football Moments*. London: Carlton Books Ltd, 2007.

Pixar. 'The Pixar Timeline: 1979 to Present'. Accessed 15 November 2014. http://www.pixar.com/about/Our-Story.

Platts, Todd K. 'Locating Zombies in the Sociology of Popular Culture'. *Sociology Compass* 7.10 (2013): 547–560.

Porter, Thomas and Tom Duff. 'Compositing Digital Images'. *SIGGRAPH Computer Graphics* 18.3 (1984): 253–259.

Prescott, Nick. '"All We See and All We Seem…" – Australian Cinema and National Landscape'. Abstract for Understanding Cultural Landscapes Symposium, Flinders University, 11–15 July 2005. Accessed 30 July 2014. http://dspace.flinders.edu.au/xmlui/bitstream/handle/2328/1565/N_Prescott.pdf?sequence=1.

Price, David A. *The Pixar Touch: The Making of a Company*. New York: Alfred A. Knopf, 2008.

Price, Shinobu. 'Cartoons from Another Planet: Japanese Animation as Cross-Cultural Communication'. *The Journal of American Culture* 24.1–2 (2001): 153–169.

Priebe, Ken A. *The Art of Stop Motion Animation*. Boston, MA: Cengage, 2009.

Prince, Stephen. 'True Lies: Perceptual Realism, Digital Images, and Film Theory'. *Film Quarterly* 49.3 (1996): 27–37.

Purves, Barry. *Stop Motion: Passion, Process and Performance*. Oxford: Focal Press, 2008.

Purves, Barry. *Stop Motion*. Lausanne: AVA Publishing, 2010.

Queen, Ben. *The Art of Cars 2*. San Francisco, CA: Chronicle Books, Ltd, 2011.

Redovičs, Agris. *Ursus*. Riga: National Film Centre Latvia, 2011.

Reeves, William T. 'Particle Systems—A Technique for Modeling a Class of Fuzzy Objects'. *SIGGRAPH Computer Graphics* 17.3 (1983): 359–375.

Rescher, Nicholas. *Imagining Irreality: A Study of Unreal Possibilities*. Chicago: Open Court, 2003.

Ricouer, Paul. *From Text to Action: Essays in Hermeneutics II*. Translated by Kathleen Blamey and John B. Thompson. Evanston, IL: Northwestern University Press, 1991.

Rietuma, Dita. '"Firefly", Keeping on the Tradition of Bugs'. *Film News from Latvia*, 2003.

Rizvi, Samad. 'Silhouette Clues Us into 2011 Renderman Walking Teapot Design (Update: Design Revealed)'. 2 August 2011. Accessed 12 November 2014. http://pixartimes. com/2011/08/02/silhouette-clues-us-into-2011-renderman-walking-teapot-design/.

Robertson, Barbara. 'Pixar Goes Commercial in a New Market'. *Computer Graphics World* (June 1986): 61–70.

Robinson, Bruce H., Kim R. Reisenbichler, James C. Hunt, and Steven H. D. Haddock. 'Light Production by the Arm Tips of the Deep-Sea Cephalopod Vampyroteuthis Infernalis'. *Biological Bulletin* 205 (2003): 102–109.

Robinson, Chris. *Estonian Animation: Between Genius & Utter Illiteracy*. Eastleigh: John Libbey Publishing, 2006.

Robinson, Chris. *Unsung Heroes of Animation*. Eastleigh: John Libbey Publishing, 2005.

Roe, Annabelle Honness. *Animated Documentary*. Basingstoke: Palgrave Macmillan, 2013.

Roper, Jonathan. '*FernGully: The Last Rainforest* – Review'. In *Australian Film 1978–1992*, edited by Scott Murray, 339. Melbourne: Oxford University Press, 1993. Originally published in *Cinema Papers* 91 (January 1993).

Rosenberg, Harold. *The Tradition of the New*. New York: Da Capo Press, 1965.

Rubin, Michael. *Droidmaker: George Lucas and the Digital Revolution*. Gainesville, FL: Triad Publishing Company, 2006.

Ruskin, John. *The Elements of Drawing Three Letters to Beginners*. London: George Allen, 1904.

Russell, Jamie. *Book of the Dead: The Complete History of Zombie Cinema*. Godalming: FAB Press, 2005.

Russett, R. and C. Starr. *Experimental Animation: An Illustrated Anthology*. New York: Da Capo, 1988.

Rust, Stephen, Salma Monani, and Sean Cubitt. *Ecocinema Theory and Practice*. London: Routledge, 2012.

Seddon, George. 'The Landscapes of Australia'. *Studies in the History of Gardens & Designed Landscapes: An International Quarterly* 21.1 (2001): 1–10.

Sellers, Christian and Gary Smart. *The Complete History of the Return of the Living Dead*. London: Plexus, 2010.

Sharman, Alison. 'Commissioned Content'. Accessed 30 July 2014. http://www.sbs.com .au/shows/commissionedcontent.

Sharman, Leslie. '*FernGully: The Last Rainforest* – Review'. *Sight and Sound* 2.4 (1992): 53–54.

Shaw, Susannah. *Stop Motion: Craft Skills for Model Animation*. Oxford: Focal Press, 2008.

Shigemi, Inaga. 'Miyazaki Hayao's Epic Comic Series: Nausicaä in the Valley of the Wind: An Attempt at Interpretation'. *Japan Review* 11 (1999): 113–128.

Shinkle, Eugénie. 'Video Games and the Technological Sublime'. *Tate Papers* 14. 2010. Accessed 2 May 2014. http://www.tate.org.uk/art/research-publications/the-sublime/ eugenie-shinkle-video-games-and-the-technological-sublime-r1136830.

Sicart, Miguel. 'Defining Game Mechanics'. *Game Studies: The International Journal of Computer Game Research* 8.2. 2008. Accessed 16 December 2014. http://www .gamestudies.org/0802.

Siegel, Lewis N. 'Frozen on Ice: Rendering Frost and Ice on Frozen'. In *ACM SIGGRAPH 2014 Talks* 1–1. Vancouver: ACM, 2014.

Silbergeld, Jerome. 'Cinema and the Visual Arts of China'. *A Companion to Chinese Cinema*, edited by Yingjin Zhang, 400–416. Oxford: Blackwell, 2012.

Silbergeld, Jerome. *Chinese Painting Style: Media, Methods, and Principles of Form.* Seattle: University of Washington Press, 1982.

Sito, Tom. *Moving Innovation: A History of Computer Animation.* Cambridge: MIT Press, 2013.

Skapāns, Nils. 'Alone with Puppets'. Interview by Zane Balčus. *Wonderful Day.* Riga: National Film Centre Latvia, 2010.

Smith, Alvy Ray. 'Digital Filmmaking'. *Abacus* 1.1 (1983): 28–46.

Smith, Alvy Ray. 'Plants, Fractals, and Formal Languages'. *SIGGRAPH Computer Graphics* 18.3 (1984): 1–10.

Smith, Alvy Ray. 'Pt.Reyes'. Accessed 10 Decemeber 2014. http://alvyray.com/Art/ PtReyes.htm.

Smith, Michelle J. and Elizabeth Parsons. 'Animating Child Activism: Environmentalism and Class Politics in Ghibli's *Princess Mononoke* (1997) and Fox's *FernGully* (1992)'. *Continuum: Journal of Media & Cultural Studies* 26.1 (2012): 25–37.

Sobchack, Vivian. *Screening Space: The American Science Fiction* Film. New Brunswick, NJ: Rutgers University Press, 1987.

Solnit, Rebecca. *Motion Studies: Time, Space and Eadweard Muybridge.* London: Bloomsbury Books, 2004.

Staiger, Janet. *Perverse Spectators: The Practices of Film Reception.* New York: New York University Press, 2000.

Starosielski, Nicole. ' "Movements That Are drawn": A History of Environmental Animation from *The Lorax* to *FernGully* to *Avatar*'. *International Communication Gazette* 73.1–2 (2011): 145–163.

State Hermitage Museum. 'Restoration of Pyasetsky's Great Siberian Railway Panorama (1894–1899)'. *Hermitage News*, 2007. Accessed 12 November 2014. http://www .hermitagemuseum.org/html_En/11/2007/hm11_3_35.html.

Stewart, Garrett. *Between Film and Screen: Modernism's Photo Synthesis.* Chicago: University of Chicago Press, 1999.

Stitt, Alex 'Animation'. In *The Oxford Companion to Australian Film*, edited by Brian McFarlane, Geoff Mayer and Ina Bertrand, 13–14. Melbourne: Oxford University Press, 1999.

Stomakhin, Alexey, Craig Schroeder, Lawrence Chai, Joseph Teran, and Andrew Selle. 'A Material Point Method for Snow Simulation'. *ACM Transactions on Graphics* 32.4 (2013): 1–10.

Švankmajer, Jan. *Faust: The Script*. Trowbridge: Flicks Books, 1996.

Syer, John and Christopher Connelly. *Sporting Body, Sporting Mind*. London: Simon & Schuster, 1987.

Smith, Alvy Ray. 'The Road to Point Reyes'. *SIGGRAPH Computer Graphics* 17.3 (1983): Title Page.

Telotte, J.P. *Animating Space: From Mickey to WALL-E*. Lexington, KY: University Press of Kentucky, 2010.

'The Story of Thomas and Friends'. *Thomas & Friends*. Accessed 7 June 2014. http://www.thomasandfriends.com/en-gb/About/index.html.

Thompson, Kirsten Moana. 'Scale, Spectacle and Movement: The Massive Software and Digital Special Effects in *The Lord of the Rings*'. In *From Hobbits to Hollywood: Essays on Peter Jackson's Lord of the Rings*, edited by Ernest Mathijs and Murray Pomerance, 283–300. Amsterdam: Rodopi, 2006.

Thomson, David. *Moments That Made the Movies*. London: Thames & Hudson, 2013.

Torre, Dan. 'Cognitive Animation Theory: A Process-Based Reading of Animation and Human Cognition'. *Animation: An Interdisciplinary Journal* 9.1 (2014): 47–64.

Tu, Wei-ming. 'An "Anthropocosmic" Perspective on Creativity'. In *Dialogue of Philosophies, Religions and Civilizations in the Era of Globalization: Chinese Philosophical Studies, XXV*, edited by Zhao Dunhua, 143–153. Washington, DC: The Council for Research in Values and Philosophy, 2007.

Tu, Wei-ming. 'The Ecological Turn in New Confucian Humanism: Implications for China and the World'. *Daedalus* 130.4 (2001): 243–264.

Tucker, John A. 'Anime and Historical Inversion in Miyazaki Hayao's Princess Mononoke'. *Japan Studies Review* 7 (2003): 65–102.

Tufte, Edwards. *Visual Explanations: Images and Quantities, Evidence and Narrative*. Cheshire, CT: Graphics Press, 2005.

Turnock, Julie. 'The ILM Version: Recent Digital Effects and the Aesthetics of 1970s Cinematography'. *Film History* 24.2 (2012): 158–168.

Tylor, Edward B. *Primitive Culture: Researches into the Development of Mythology, Philosophy, Religion, Language, Art, and Custom*. London: John Murray, 1873.

Udden, James. 'Hou Hsiao-hsien and the Question of a Chinese Style'. *Asian Cinema*, 13.2 (2002): 54–75.

Uricchio, William. 'A "Proper Point of View": The Panorama and Some of Its Early Media Iterations'. *Early Popular Visual Culture* 9.3 (2011): 225–238.

Urry, John. *Mobilities*. Cambridge: Polity Press, 2010.

Ward, Paul. 'Animated Interactions: Animation Aesthetics and the World of the "Interactive" Documentary'. In *Animated 'Worlds'*, edited by Suzanne Buchan, 113–129. London: John Libbey, 2006.

Watts, Jonathan. 'Mercury Poisoning of Thousands Confirmed'. *The Guardian*, Tuesday 16, 2001. Accessed 8 May 2014. http://www.theguardian.com/world/2001/oct/16/japan.jonathanwatts.

Wells, Paul, Joanna Quinn, and Les Mills. *Drawing for Animation*. London: AVA Publishing, 2009.

Wells, Paul. 'Plasmatic Pitches, Temporal Tracks and Conceptual Courts: The Landscapes of Animated Sport'. In *Animated Landscapes: History, Form and Function*, edited by Chris Pallant, PP TBC. New York: Bloomsbury, 2015.

Wells, Paul. *Animation: Genre and Authorship*. London: Wallflower Press, 2002.

Wells, Paul. *Understanding Animation*. London: Routledge, 1998.

Whitehead, Alfred North. *Modes of Thought*. New York: The Free Press, 1968.

Whitehead, Alfred North. *Process and Reality* (Corrected Edition). New York: The Free Press, 1978.

Williams, Richard. *The Animator's Survival Kit: A Manual of Methods, Principles and Formulas for Classical, Computer, Games, Stop Motion and Internet Animators*. London: Faber, 2001.

Wilson, Keith, Aleka McAdams, Hubert Leo, and Maryann Simmons. 'Simulating Wind Effects on Cloth and Hair in Disney's Frozen'. In *ACM SIGGRAPH 2014 Talks*, 1–1. Vancouver: ACM, 2014.

Winter, Alfred Octavius. 'The Cinematograph'. In *The New Review*, Vol. XIV, edited by W. E. Henley, 507–513. London: Chatto & Windus, 1896.

Withnall, Adam. 'Crimea Just a Blip? Time Lapse Map Video Shows 1000 Years of Europe's History in Three Minutes'. *The Independent*. 19 March 2014. Accessed 16 December 2014. http://www.independent.co.uk/news/world/europe/crimea-just-a-blip-time-lapse-map-video-shows-1000-years-of-europes-history-in-three-minutes-9201414.html.

Wong, Wucius. *The Tao of Chinese Landscape Painting: Principles & Methods*. New York: Design Press. 1991.

Wood, Robin. *Hollywood from Vietnam to Reagan*. New York: Columbia University Press, 2003.

Wordsworth, William. *The Rainbow*. 1802.

World Zombie Day: Accessed 13 June 2014. http://worldzombieday.co.uk/.

Yoneyama, Shoko. ' "Life-World": Beyond Fukushima and Minamata'. *Asian Perspective* 4 (2013): 567–592.

Zhang, Huilin. *Ershi shiji Zhongguo Donghua Yishushi*. Shaanxi: Shaanxi Renmin Meisu Chubanshe. 2002.

Zhang, Songlin and Jianying Gong. *Shui chuangzao le 'Xiaokedou Zhao Mama': Te Wei he zhongguo donghua*/ 誰創造了"小蝌蚪找媽媽"：特偉和中國動畫. Shanghai: Shanghai Renmin Chubanshe. 2010.

Zong, Baihua. *Meixue Sanbu* (美學散步). Shanghai: Shanghai Renmin chubanshe, 2007.

Animation/Filmography/Other Media

$9.99. Israel/Australia. 2008 [Film].
2DTV. UK. 2001–2004 [TV series].
555 Kubrik. Germany. 2009 [Live Projection].
600th Anniversary of the Prague Clock Tower. Czech Republic. 2010 [Live Projection].
800th Anniversary of Santiago de Compostela Cathedral. Spain. 2012 [Live Projection].
A Close Shave. UK. 1995 [Film].
A Grand Day Out. UK. 1989 [Film].
A Kiss in the Tunnel. UK. 1899 [Film].
A Matter of Loaf and Death. UK. 2008 [Film].
A Town Called Panic. Belgium/Luxembourg/France. 2009 [Film].
Adventure Time. USA. 2010–present [TV series].
Adventures of Price Achmed, The. Germany. 1926 [Film].
Aladdin. USA. 1992 [Film].
Alien. UK/USA. 1979 [Film].
Ámár. Spain. 2010 [Film].
An Inconvenient Truth. USA. 2006 [Film].
Arrival of a Train. France. 1895 [Film].
Artist, The. France/Belgium/USA. 2011 [Film].
Avatar. USA/UK. 2009 [Film].
Avengers, The. USA. 2012 [Film].
Balance. Germany. 1989 [Film].
Bambi. USA. 1942 [Film].
Band Concert, The. USA. 1935 [Film].
Barque Sortant du Port/Boat Leaving the Port. France. 1895 [Film].
Baywatch. USA. 1989–2001 [TV series].
Belka i Strelka. Zvezdnye Sobaki/Space Dogs 3D. Russia. 2010 [Film].
Beyond Good & Evil. France. 2003 [Video Game].
Bezmiegs/Insomnia. Latvia. 2004 [Film].
Big Bang Big Boom. Argentina. 2010 [Street Art].
Blinky Bill. Australia. 1992 [Film].
Bottle. USA. 2010 [Film].
Boxtrolls, The. USA. 2014 [Film].
Call of Duty. USA. 2003–present [Video Game series].
Cameraman's Revenge, The. Russia. 1912 [Film].
Candy Crush. UK. 2012 [Video Game].

Canon. Canada. 1964 [Film].

Cars 2. USA. 2011 [Film].

Cars. USA. 2006 [Film].

Cartoon Train Journey. UK. c.1910–1920 [Film].

Cats and Dogs. USA/Australia. 2001 [Film].

Cave of Forgotten Dreams. Canada/USA/France/Germany/UK. 2010 [Film].

Chicken Run. UK/USA. 2000 [Film].

Chronicles of Narnia: The Lion, the Witch and the Wardrobe, The. USA/UK. 2005 [Film].

Citizen Kane. USA. 1941 [Film].

Combo. Italy. 2009 [Street Art].

Coraline. USA. 2009 [Film].

Corpse Bride. USA. 2005 [Film].

Countryman's First Sight of the Animated Pictures: A Farmer Viewing the Approaching Train on the Screen Takes to His Heels, The. UK. 1901 [Film].

Cowboy's Flute a.k.a. *Mu di, The.* China. 1963 [Film].

Dawn of the Dead. USA. 1978 [Film].

Day and Night. USA. 2010 [Film].

Day of Perpetual Night, The. China. 2012 [Video Installation].

Day of the Dead. USA. 1985 [Film].

De tre musketerer/The Three Musketeers. Denmark/Latvia/UK. 2006 [Film].

Dead Next Door, The. USA. 1989 [Film].

Dead Rising. Japan. 2006 [Video Game].

Deer's Bell. China. 1982 [Film].

Deputy Droopy. USA. 1955 [Film].

Destiny. USA. 2014 [Video Game].

Diary of the Dead. USA. 2007 [Film].

Dimensions of Dialogue. CZ. 1982 [Film].

Dnevnik (Diary). Yugoslavia. 1974 [Film].

Doktora D. Sala/Island of Doctor D. Latvia. 2005 [Film].

Dot and the Kangaroo. Australia. 1977 [Film].

Dragon Age: Inquisition. Canada/USA. 2014 [Video Game].

El Apóstol. Argentina. 1917 [Film].

Elder Scrolls V: Skyrim, The. USA. 2011 [Video Game].

European Journey 2030. UK. 2012. [Film].

Evil Dead, The. USA. 1981 [Film].

Eža Kažociņš/The Prickly. Latvia. 2004 [Film].

Fantasmagorie. France. 1908 [Film].

Fantastic Mr. Fox. USA. 2009 [Film].

Fantoche. Germany. 2007 [Street Art].

Far Cry. Germany/Canada. 2004–present [Video Game series].

Feeling of Mountain and Water a.k.a. *Shan shui qing.* China. 1988 [Film].

FernGully: The Last Rainforest. Australia/USA. 1992 [Film].

Flower. USA. 2009 [Video Game].

Frankenweenie. USA. 2012 [Film].

Frozen. USA. 2013 [Film].

Futureworld. USA. 1976 [Film].

Galaxy Quest. USA. 1999 [Film].

Get a Horse. USA. 2013 [Film].

*Ghost in the Shell/*攻殻機動隊. Japan. 1995 [Film].

Grand Theft Auto. UK/USA. 1997–Present [Video Game series].

Gravity. USA/UK. 2013 [Film].

Great Train Robbery, The. USA. 1903 [Film].

Green Zone. France/USA/Spain/UK. 2010 [Film].

Hand, The/Ruka. Czechoslovakia. 1965 [Film].

Happy Feet. Australia/USA. 2006 [Film].

Harry Potter and the Chamber of Secrets. USA/UK/Germany. 2002 [Film].

Harry Potter and the Goblet of Fire. USA/UK. 2005 [Film].

Harvie Krumpet. Australia. 2003 [Film].

Hell of the Living Dead. Italy. 1980 [Film].

Hobbit: The Desolation of Smaug, The. USA. 2013 [Film].

Howl's Moving Castle. Japan. 2005 [Film].

Hunger Games: Mockingjay – Part 1, The. USA. 2014 [Film].

I Walked with a Zombie. USA. 1943 [Film].

Impression Hainan. China. 2011–present [Stage Performance].

Impression Putuo. China. 2009–present [Stage Performance].

Inception. USA/UK. 2010 [Film].

Indiana Jones and the Kingdom of the Crystal Skull. USA. 2008 [Film].

Interstellar. USA/UK. 2014 [Film].

Invisible Picture Show. UK. 2012 [Interactive Film].

Ivor the Engine. UK. 1975 [TV series].

Jabberwocky. CZ. 1971 [Film].

James and the Giant Peach. UK/USA. 1996 [Film].

Jaws. USA. 1975 [Film].

Johnny Mnemonic. USA. 1995 [Film].

Journey. USA. 2012 [Video Game].

Jungle Book, The. USA. 1967 [Film].

Jurassic Park. USA. 1993 [Film].

Kill Bill. USA. 2004 [Film].

Kinostudija/Film Studio. Latvia. 1993 [Film].

Klucānija/Brickannia. Latvia. 2000 [Film].

Komēta/Comet. Latvia. 1997 [Film].

Kreise/Circles. Germany. 1933 [Film].

Kuģis/The Ship. Latvia. 2007 [Film].

LA Noire. USA. 2011 [Video Game].

Lady Vanishes, The. UK. 1938 [Film].

Land of the Dead. USA. 2005 [Film].

Lapis. USA. 1966 [Film].

Last of Us, The. USA. 2013 [Video Game].

Lawnmower Man. USA. 1992 [Film].

Left 4 Dead. USA. 2008 [Game].

Lego Movie. USA. 2014 [Film].

Leiutajateküla Lotte/Lotte from Gadgetville. Estonia/Latvia. 2006 [Film].

Letter A. USA. 2007 [Street Art].

Life of Pi. USA. 2012 [Film].

Lion King. USA. 1994 [Film].

Little Big Planet. UK. 2008–present [Video Game series].

Living Dead at Manchester Morgue, The. Spain/Italy. 1974 [Film].

Lone Ranger, The. USA. 1966–1969 [TV series].

Look Both Ways. Australia. 2005 [Film].

Looker. USA. 1981 [Film].

Lord of the Rings: The Fellowship of the Ring, The. USA/New Zealand. 2001 [Film].

Lord of the Rings: The Return of the King, The. USA/New Zealand. 2003 [Film].

Lord of the Rings: The Two Towers, The. USA/New Zealand. 2002 [Film].

Lullaby Land. USA. 1933 [Film].

Madagascar, carnet de voyage. Fiji/France. 2009 [Film].

Madame Tutli–Putli. Canada. 2007 [Film].

Magic Pudding, The. Australia. 2000 [Film].

Man with a Movie Camera. Soviet Union. 1929 [Film].

Mapping Projection of Christ the Redeemer. Brazil. 2010 [Live Projection].

Marco Polo Junior Versus the Red Dragon. Australia. 1972 [Film].

Mary and Max. Australia. 2008 [Film].

Mass Effect 2. USA. 2010 [Video Game].

Masstransiscope. USA. 1980 [Installation].

Matrix, The. USA. 1999 [Film].

Medĩbas/Hunting. Latvia. 2007 [Film].

Minecraft. Sweden. 2011 [Video Game].

A Tale of Momentum & Inertia. USA. 2014 [Film].

Monsters, Inc. USA. 2001 [Film].

Monument Valley. UK. 2014 [Video Game].

Morphing. Poland. 2009 [Street Art].

Music Land. USA. 1935 [Film].

Muto. Argentina. 2008 [Street Art].

Nausicaä of the Valley of the Wind. Japan. 1984 [Film].

Night of the Living Dead. USA. 1968 [Film].

Nightmare Before Christmas, The. USA. 1993 [Film].

Noah and Saskia. Australia/UK. 2004 [TV series].

Otesánek/Little Otik. Czech Republic/UK. 2000 [Film].

Pan's Labyrinth. Spain/Mexico. 2006 [Film].

Panoramic View of the Golden Gate. USA. 1902 [Film].

ParaNorman. USA. 2012 [Film].

Perfect Storm, The. USA. 2000 [Film].

Perspective Lyrique: An Interactive Architectural Mapping. France. 2010 [Live
    Projection].

Peter and the Wolf. UK/Poland/Norway/Mexico. 2006 [Film].

Peter the Puck. USA. 1973–1975 [TV series].

Pingu. UK/Switzerland. 1986–2006 [TV series].

Pirates of the Caribbean: At Worlds End. USA. 2007 [Film].

Pirates of the Caribbean: Dead Man's Chest. USA. 2006 [Film].

Pirates! In an Adventure with Scientists!, The. UK. 2012 [Film].

PixelJunk Eden. Japan. 2008 [Video Game].

Plague of the Zombies, The. UK. 1966 [Film].

Polar Explorer, The. USA. 2011 [Film].

Poltergeist. USA. 1982 [Film].

Pong. USA. 1972 [Video Game].

Portal. USA. 2007 [Video Game].

Postman Pat. UK. 1981–present [TV series].

Princess Mononoke. Japan. 1997 [Film].

Psycho. USA. 1960 [Film].

Railroad Smash-Up, The. USA. 1904 [Film].

Red Dead Redemption. USA. 2010 [Video Game].

Rescue on Fractalus! USA. 1984 [Video Game].

Resident Evil: Retribution. USA. 2012 [Film].

Resident Evil. Japan. 1996–2012 [Video Game series].

Return of the Living Dead, The. USA. 1985 [Film].

River of Wisdom: Animated Version of Along the Riverside Scene at Qingming Festival.
    China. 2010 [Animated Installation].

Rough Sea at Dover. UK. 1895 [Film].

Sand Castle, The. Canada. 1977 [Film].

Sasit spārnus!/Flap Your Wings! Latvia. 2008 [Film].

Serial Experiments Lain. Japan. 1998 [TV series].

Serious Games. USA. 2014 [Film installation].

Shadow of the Colossus. Japan. 2005. [Video Game].

Shrek. USA. 2001 [Film].

Side by Side. USA. 2012 [Film].

Sieviete/Woman. Latvia. 2002 [Film].

SimCity. USA. 1989–2013 [Video Game series].

Skatu meklētājs/View Finder. Latvia. 2010 [Film].

Skeleton Dance, The. USA. 1929 [Film].

Snezhnaya Koroleva/The Snow Queen. Russia. 2012 [Film].

Snow White and the Seven Dwarfs. USA. 1937 [Film].

Spārni un airi/Wings and Oars. Latvia. 2009 [Film].

Speculative Landscapes. UK. 2010 [Film].

Spirited Away. Japan. 2004 [Film].

Sports Cartoons. Canada. 1986 [Film].

Star Trek II: The Wrath of Khan. USA. 1982 [Film].

Star Wars. USA. 1977 [Film].

Sunrise. USA. 1927 [Film].

Surf at Monterey. USA. 1897 [Film].

Survival of the Dead. USA. 2009 [Film].

Tagebuch (Diary). Germany. 2000 [Film].

Teat Beat of Sex. USA/Italy. 2008 [Film series].

Tenebrae. Italy. 1982 [Film].

Tetris. USSR. 1984 [Video Game].

Texas Chain Saw Massacre, The. USA. 1974 [Film].

Theme Park. UK/USA. 1994 [Video Game].

This Could Be Me. Czech Republic. 1995 [Film].

Thomas the Tank Engine. UK. 1984–present [TV series].

Tomb Raider. UK. 1996–present [Video Game series].

Tommy Chat Chat Just E-Mailed Me. USA. 2006 [Film].

Tony Hawks. USA. 1999–present [Video Game series].

Tooned 50. UK. 2014 [Animated series].

Tooned. UK. 2012 [Animated series].

Total Recall. USA. 1990 [Film].

Total War. UK/USA. 2000–present [Video Game series].

Towering Inferno. USA. 1974 [Film].

Toy Story. USA. 1995 [Film].

Train Simulator 2014. UK. 2014 [Video Game].

Traion II (Train). UK. 2014 [Film].

Trashed. USA. 2012 [Film].

Trolley Troubles. USA. 1927 [Film].

Tron. USA. 1982 [Film].

Ursus. Latvia. 2011 [Film].

Velna Fudži/Devil's Fuji. Latvia. 2008 [Film].

Viagem a Cabo Verde. Portugal. 2010 [Film].

Virtuosity. USA. 1995 [Film].

Vol Libre. USA. 1980 [Film].

Waking Life. USA. 2001 [Film].

Walking. 2007 [Street Art].

WALL-E. USA. 2008 [Film].

Wallace & Gromit: The Curse of the Were-Rabbit. UK. 2005 [Film].

Waltz with Bashir. Israel/France/Germany/USA/Finland/Switzerland/Belgium/
  Australia. 2008 [Film].

War Game. UK. 2001 [Film].

We Are Rail Fans. UK. 2013 [Film].

Where Is Mama. China. 1960 [Film].

White Zombie. USA. 1932 [Film].

Wind in the Willows, The. UK. 1983–1989 [TV series].

Wizard of Oz, The. USA. 1939 [Film].

World War Z. USA. 2013 [Film].

Wrong Trousers, The. UK. 1993 [Film].

Young Sherlock Holmes. USA. 1985 [Film].

Index